FIJI ISLANDS
HANDBOOK

DIANA LASICH HARPER

FIJI ISLANDS
HANDBOOK
FOURTH EDITION

DAVID STANLEY

MOON
PUBLICATIONS INC.

FIJI ISLANDS HANDBOOK
FOURTH EDITION

Published by
Moon Publications, Inc.
P.O. Box 3040
Chico, California 95927-3040, USA

Printed by
Colorcraft Ltd., Hong Kong

ISBN: 1-56691-038-2

ISSN: 1082-4898

Editors: Charles Mohnike and Valerie Sellers Blanton
Copy Editor: Elizabeth Marie Kim
Production & Design: Karen McKinley
Cartographers: Bob Race and Brian Bardwell
Line Drawings: Louise Foote and Diana Lasich Harper
Index: Valerie Sellers Blanton

Front cover photo: An Island of the Mamanutha Group,
by Tom Servais

Fidschi-Handbuch. A German translation of this book is published by Verlag Gisela E. Walther,
Oppenheimerstr. 26, D-28307 Bremen, Germany.

Distributed in the U.S.A. by Publishers Group West
Printed in Hong Kong

Please send all comments,
corrections, additions,
amendments, and critiques to:

FIJI ISLANDS HANDBOOK
MOON PUBLICATIONS, INC.
P.O. BOX 3040
CHICO, CA 95927-3040, USA
e-mail: travel@moon.com

Printing History
1st edition — May 1985
Reprinted — July 1986
2nd edition — March 1990
Reprinted — January 1992
3rd edition — April 1993
Reprinted — October 1994
4th edition — February 1996

CONTENTS

MAPS

MAP SYMBOLS

──────── HIGHWAYS, ROADS, STREETS	▲ MOUNTAIN
─ ─ ─ ─ FOOT TRAILS	↗ WATERFALL
════════ BRIDGE	WATER
─ ─ ─ ─ FERRY (WHEN SHOWN OVER WATER)	REEF

O ■ SIGHTS, POINTS OF INTEREST
O TOWNS, CITIES
O VILLAGES
● ACCOMMODATIONS

CHARTS

ABBREVIATIONS

4WD—four-wheel drive
A$—Australian dollars
a/c—air conditioned
C—centigrade
C$—Canadian dollars
CDW—collision damage waiver
EEZ—Exclusive Economic Zone
E.U.—European Union
F$—Fiji dollars
G.P.O.—General Post Office
km—kilometer
kph—kilometers per hour
LDS—Latter-day Saints (Mormons)

LMS—London Missionary Society
mm—millimeters
MV—motor vessel
No.—number
NZ—New Zealand
NZ$—New Zealand dollars
pp—per person
P.W.D.—Public Works Department
SDA—Seventh-Day Adventist
tel.—telephone
U.S.—United States
US$—U.S. dollars
WW II—World War Two

SPELLING AND PRONUNCIATION

When 19th-century English missionaries created a written form of Fijian, they rendered "mb" as "b," "nd" as "d," "ng" as "g," "ngg" as "q," and "th" as "c." To relieve readers of the need to learn these complicated orthographic rules, all words and place-names in this book are rendered phonetically. However, we use historic spelling for the personal names of individuals, and in Fiji itself, historic spelling is used consistently on signboards and in printed texts. Thus you'll see "Nadi" for Nandi, "Sigatoka" for Singatoka, "Qamea" for Nggamea, and "Cicia" for Thithia. At the risk of upsetting purists, we feel it's important for travelers to pronounce the names properly rather than appear as ignorant tourists by saying Nadi and Sigatoka. Whichever spelling system is used, some confusion is inevitable, and a bit of attention is required at first. Turn to "Alternative Place-Names" just before the index for a list of the most common names with variable spellings.

ACKNOWLEDGMENTS

The nationalities of those listed below are identified by the following signs which follow their names: A (Austria), AUS (Australia), CDN (Canada), CH (Switzerland), D (Germany), DK (Denmark), F (France), FI (Fiji), GB (Great Britain), IL (Israel), J (Japan), N (Norway), NC (New Caledonia), NL (Netherlands), NZ (New Zealand), SI (Solomon Islands), and USA (United States).

The antique engravings by M.G.L. Domeny de Rienzi are from the classic three-volume work *Oceanie ou Cinquième Partie du Monde* (Paris: Firmin Didot Frères, 1836).

Special thanks to Tjalling Terpstra (NL) for help in updating Pacific air routes, to Jos Poelman (NL) of the Dutch STD Foundation (Box 9074, 3506 GB Utrecht), and Steven Vete (FI), editor of *Pacific AIDS Alert,* for information on AIDS, to Dianne Bain (FI) for information on Taveuni and yachting facilities around Fiji, to Philip R. Marshall (USA) for sundry travel tips, to Hanne Finholt (N) for a fascinating account of her travels through six Pacific countries, to Stacey M. King (AUS) for information on Rambi and the Banabans, to Udo Schwark (D) for arranging my latest research trip, to Asha Johnson (USA) for pulling the production process together, and to Ria de Vos (NL) for her continuing assistance, suggestions, and support.

Thanks too to the following readers who took the trouble to write us letters about their trips:

D.J. Adler (GB), Ian Anderson (USA), John and Mavis Dixon (GB), Juergen Eckstein (D), K.L. Eiden (USA), Bernard Fernandez (CDN), Bruce French (USA), Marcus F. Fuchs (USA), Shibolet Gilat (IL), Diane Goodwillie (CDN), Mary Graham (USA), Lorraine Guthrie (USA), Anne and Marcus Hackel (D), Adam Hall (GB), Bev and Frank Higgens (AUS), L. Himmelmann (D), Herbert Hans Hoppe (D), Anita Jackson (GB), Jon Jennings (GB), Jeffrey Jones (CDN), Prof. Dr. Ruprecht Keller (D), Marguerite Lake (AUS), Mike Long (AUS), Dieter Marmet (CH), Gerhard Martin (D), Jennewein Martin (A), Steve McCarthy (USA), Peter McQuarrie (FI), Claire Newton (GB), Susan and Charles Paclat (USA), Jeff Perk (USA), Jackie Plusch (USA), Gary Roberts (USA), Toru Sasaki (J), Maggie Smith (GB), Sarah Thompson-Copsly (GB), Thomas Uhlemann (DK), Brendan R. Whyte (NZ).

All their comments have been incorporated into the volume you're now holding. To have your own name included here next edition, write: David Stanley, c/o Moon Publications Inc., P.O. Box 3040, Chico, CA 95927, U.S.A.

Attention Hotel Keepers, Tour Operators, Divemasters:

The best way to keep your listing in *Fiji Islands Handbook* up to date is to send us current information about your business. If you don't agree with what we've written, please tell us why—there's never any charge or obligation for a listing. Thanks to the following island tourism workers and government officials who *did* write in:

Ron Blake (NZ), Ratu Kini Boko (FI), Gordon Burrow (NZ), Gavin Clarke (FI), D.B. Costello (FI), Simone Daulaca (FI), Wendy Dell (CDN), Ingrid Denk (FI), Michael Dennis (FI), Sylvia Dobry (FI), Carol Douglas (FI), Mrs. Akanisi Dreunimisimisi (FI), Gordon Edris (FI), Joanna Edwards (FI), Rick Elms (FI), Agatha Ferei (FI), Rena Forster (FI), Randy Gardner (USA), Ronna Goldstein (FI), Sally Johnson (FI), Loraini V. Jones (FI), Rehnuma Khan (FI), Stephen J. Kelly (AUS), Brij Lal (FI), Peni and Gail Lesuma (FI), Martin Livingston (FI), Hector Macdonald (FI), Max Macdonald (FI), Ms. J. Mamtora (FI), Jokapeci Maopa (FI), James F. McCann (FI), Brenda McCroskey (USA), Lee McLauchlan (FI), Lynette Mercer (FI), Robert Miller (FI), Joan and Tom Moody (FI), Anthony J. Morris (FI), Merle J. Murray (FI), Agnes Nateba (FI), Dr. Robert G. Neville (GB), Jill Palise (FI), Denis Pierce (AUS), Vijen Prasad (FI), Ross Pulvirenti (AUS), Bill William Reece (FI), David Robie (NZ), Jon Roseman (FI), Brian Rutherford (AUS), Jona Siva (FI), Virginia Smith (FI), Max Storck (FI), Margaret Thaggard (FI), Chris Thompson (FI), Niumaia Turaganicolo (FI), Piet van Zyl (F), Katrina Wards (NZ), Ric West (FI), Viti Whippy (FI), Jerry Wittert (USA), Roy F. Whitton (FI), Patrick Wong (FI), and Keith Zoing (FI).

While out researching my books I find it cheaper to pay my own way, and you can rest assured that nothing in this book is designed to repay freebies from hotels, restaurants, tour operators, or airlines. I prefer to arrive unexpected and uninvited and to experience things as they really are. On the road I seldom identify myself to anyone. The essential difference between this book and the myriad travel brochures free for the taking in airports and tourist offices around Fiji is that this book represents travelers and the brochures represent the travel industry. The companies and organizations included herein are there for information purposes only, and a mention in no way implies an endorsement.

IS THIS BOOK OUT OF DATE?

Travel writing is a little like trying to take a picture out the side of a bus: time frustrates the best of intentions. Things change fast—you'll understand how hard it is for us to keep up. A strong hurricane can blow away half the tourist facilities on an island overnight! So if something in this book doesn't sound quite right, please let us hear about it. Did anything lead you astray or inconvenience you? In retrospect, what sort of information would have made your trip easier?

Unlike many other travel writers, this author doesn't solicit "freebies" or announce who he is to one and all, and at times that makes it difficult to audit the expensive resorts. Thus we especially welcome comments from readers who stayed at upscale places, particularly when the facilities didn't match the rates. Legitimate complaints will most certainly influence future coverage in this book, and no hotel or restaurant is exempt from fair criticism.

When writing, please be as precise and accurate as you can. Write comments into your copy of *Fiji Islands Handbook* as you go along, then send us a summary when you get home. You can recycle travel brochures by sending them to us when you're done with them. If this book helped you, please help us make it even better. Address your letters to:

David Stanley
c/o Moon Publications Inc.
P.O. Box 3040
Chico, CA 95927, U.S.A.

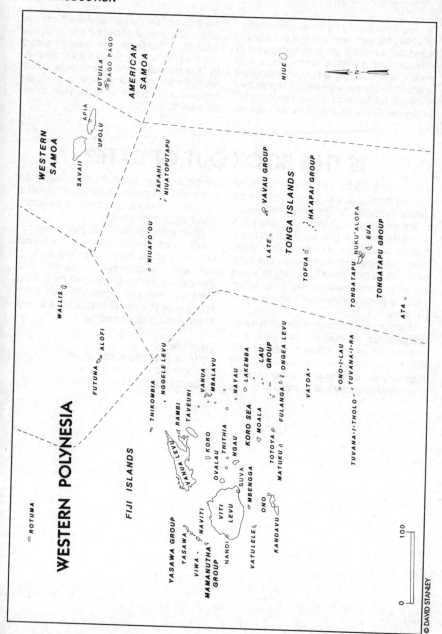

WESTERN POLYNESIA

FIJI ISLANDS

WESTERN SAMOA

AMERICAN SAMOA

TONGA ISLANDS

ROTUMA

WALLIS

FUTUNA ALOFI

NIUAFO'OU

TAFAHI
NIUATOPUTAPU

NIUE

SAVAII

APIA
UPOLU

TUTUILA
PAGO PAGO

N

VAVAU GROUP

LATE

HA'APAI GROUP

TOFUA

TONGATAPU NUKU'ALOFA
EUA

TONGATAPU GROUP

ATA

YASAWA GROUP
YASAWA

VIWA
NAVITI

MAMANUTHA
GROUP

NANDI

VITI
LEVU

VATULELE

ONO

KANDAVU

THIKOMBIA

VANUA LEVU

NGGELE LEVU

RAMBI
TAVEUNI

VANUA
MBALAVU

KORO

OVALAU

SUVA

MBENGGA

THITHIA

NGAU

NAYAU

KORO SEA

MOALA

LAKEMBA

LAU
GROUP

ONGEA LEVU

FULANGA

TOTOYA

MATUKU

VATOA

ONO-I-LAU

TUVANA-I-RA

TUVANA-I-THOLO

0   100

© DAVID STANLEY

SALVATORE CASA

INTRODUCTION

Once notorious as the "Cannibal Isles," Fiji is now the colorful crossroads of the Pacific. Of the 322 islands that make up the Fiji Group, over 100 are inhabited by a rich mixture of vibrant, exuberant Melanesians, East Indians, Polynesians, Micronesians, Chinese, and Europeans, each with a cuisine and culture of their own. Here Melanesia mixes with Polynesia, ancient India with the Pacific, and tradition with the modern world in a unique blend.

Fiji preserves an amazing variety of traditional customs and crafts such as kava or *yanggona* drinking, the presentation of the whale's tooth, firewalking, fish driving, turtle calling, tapa beating, and pottery making. Alongside this fascinating human history is a dramatic diversity of landforms and seascapes, all concentrated in a relatively small area. Fiji's sun-drenched beaches, blue lagoons, panoramic open hillsides, lush rainforests, and dazzling reefs are truly magnificent. Such things are duplicated on continents such as Africa, but over there you'd have to travel weeks or months to see what you can see in Fiji in days.

Fiji offers posh resorts, good food and accommodations, nightlife, historic sights, outer-island living, hiking, camping, surfing, snorkeling, scuba diving, and river-running, plus easy travel by small plane, interisland ferry, copra boat, outboard canoe, open-sided bus, and air-conditioned coach. One month would barely be enough scratch the surface of all there is to see and do.

Best of all, Fiji is a hassle-free country with uncrowded, inexpensive facilities available almost everywhere. There's something for everyone in Fiji and prices are affordable, with a wide range of accommodation and travel options. In a word, Fiji is a traveler's country *par excellence,* and whatever your budget, Fiji gives you good value for your money and plenty of ways to spend it. *Mbula,* welcome to Fiji, everyone's favorite South Pacific country.

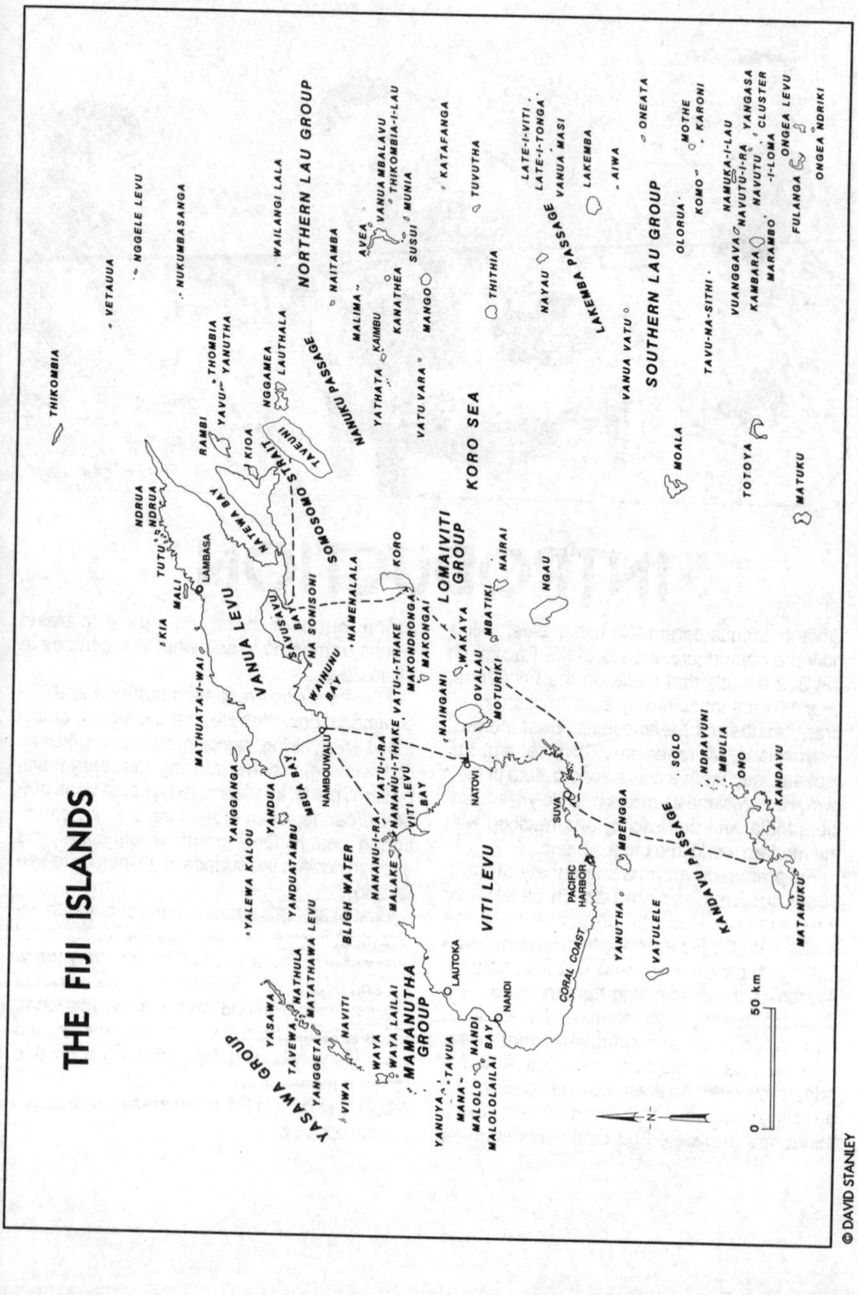
THE FIJI ISLANDS
YASAWA GROUP
YASAWA
TAVEWA
NATHULA
YANGGETA
MATATHAWA LEVU
NAVITI
VIWA
WAYA
WAYA LAILAI
MAMANUTHA GROUP
YANUYA
TAVUA
MANA
MALOLO
NANDI BAY
MALOLOLAILAI
NANDI
LAUTOKA
VITI LEVU
CORAL COAST
PACIFIC HARBOR
SUVA
NATOVI
VITI LEVU BAY
BLIGH WATER
YALEWA KALOU
YANDUATAMBU
YANDUA
YANGGANGA
MBUA BAY
NAMBOUWALU
NANANU-I-RA
VATU-I-RA
MALAKE
NANANU-I-THAKE
VATU-I-THAKE
MATHUATA-I-WAI
VANUA LEVU
KIA
MALI
LAMBASA
TUTU
NDRUA NDRUA
NATEWA BAY
WAINUNU BAY
SAVUSAVU BAY
NA SONISONI
NAMENALALA
SOMOSOMO STRAIT
TAVEUNI
KIOA
RAMBI
YAVU
THOMBIA
YANUTHA
NGGAMEA
LAUTHALA
THIKOMBIA
VETAUUA
NGGELE LEVU
NUKUMBASANGA
WAILANGI LALA
NORTHERN LAU GROUP
NAITAMBA
NANUKU PASSAGE
MALIMA
AVEA
VANUA MBALAVU
THIKOMBIA-I-LAU
MUNIA
SUSUI
KANATHEA
KAIMBU
YATHATA
VATU VARA
MANGO
KATAFANGA
TUVUTHA
THITHIA
NAYAU
LATE-I-VITI
LATE-I-TONGA
VANUA MASI
LAKEMBA
LAKEMBA PASSAGE
AIWA
ONEATA
KORO
KORO SEA
LOMAIVITI GROUP
MAKONDRONGA
MAKONGAI
WAKAYA
NAINGANI
OVALAU
MBATIKI
MOTURIKI
NAIRAI
NGAU
VANUA VATU
SOUTHERN LAU GROUP
MOALA
TOTOYA
MATUKU
TAVU-NA-SITHI
OLORUA
KOMO
MOTHE
KARONI
NAMUKA-I-LAU
VUANGGAVA
NAVUTU-I-RA
KAMBARA
NAVUTU
YANGASA CLUSTER
I-LOMA
MARAMBO
ONGEA LEVU
FULANGA
ONGEA NDRIKI
YANUTHA
VATULELE
MBENGGA
KANDAVU PASSAGE
SOLO
NDRAVUNI
MBULIA
ONO
KANDAVU
MATANUKU
N
0
50 km
© DAVID STANLEY

THE LAND

Fiji sits astride the main air route between North America and Australia, 5,100 km southwest of Hawaii and 3,150 km northeast of Sydney. Nandi is the hub of Pacific air routes, while Suva is a regional shipping center. The 180th meridian cuts through Fiji, but the international date line swings east so the entire group can share the same day. Together the Fiji Islands are scattered over 1,290,000 square km of the South Pacific Ocean.

The name Fiji is a Tongan corruption of the indigenous name "Viti." The Fiji Islands are arrayed in a horseshoe configuration with Viti Levu ("Great Fiji") and adjacent islands on the west, Vanua Levu ("Great Land") and Taveuni to the north, and the Lau Group on the east. This upside-down U-shaped archipelago encloses the Koro Sea, which is relatively shallow and sprinkled with the Lomaiviti, or central Fiji, group of islands.

If every single island were counted, the isles of the Fiji archipelago would number in the thousands. A mere 322 are judged large enough for human habitation, however, and of these only 106 are inhabited. That leaves 216 uninhabited islands, most of them prohibitively isolated or lacking fresh water.

Most of the Fiji Islands are volcanic, remnants of a sunken continent that stretched through Australia. This origin accounts for the mineral deposits on the main islands. None of Fiji's volcanoes are presently active, though there are a few small hot springs. The two largest islands, Viti Levu and Vanua Levu, together account for 87% of Fiji's 18,272 square km of land. Viti Levu has 50% of the land area and three-quarters of the people, while Vanua Levu, with 30% of the land, has 18% of the population. Viti Levu alone is bigger than all five archipelagos of Tahiti-Polynesia put together; in fact, Fiji has more land and people than all of Polynesia combined.

The 1,000-meter-high Nandrau Plateau in central Viti Levu is cradled between Tomanivi (1,323 meters) on the north and Monavatu (1,131 meters) on the south. On different sides of this elevated divide are the Tholo-East Plateau drained by the Rewa River, the Navosa

FIJI AT A GLANCE

ISLAND	AREA (square km)	HIGHEST POINT (m)	POPULATION (mid-1988 est.)	PERCENT FIJIAN*
Viti Levu	10,429	1,323	508,777	40.5
Vanua Levu	5,556	1,032	117,790	43.3
Taveuni	470	1,241	8,799	72.7
Kandavu	411	838	9,936	98.1
Ngau	140	747	3,054	99.4
Koro	104	522	3,654	98.5
Ovalau	101	626	6,660	88.3
Rambi	69	463	2,771	5.0
Lakemba	54	215	2,444	97.4
Rotuma	47	256	3,204	1.9
Mbengga	36	439	1,488	98.6
FIJI ISLANDS	18,272	1,323	758,275	49.7

* Viti Levu, Vanua Levu, and Taveuni have sizeable Fiji Indian populations, while Rambi is Micronesian and Rotuma is Polynesian.

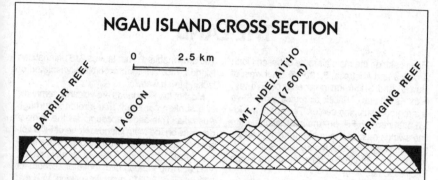

NGAU ISLAND CROSS SECTION

0   2.5 km

BARRIER REEF

LAGOON

MT. NDELAITHO (760 m)

FRINGING REEF

The difference between barrier and fringing reefs is illustrated in this southwest-northwest cross section of Ngau Island (see map on page 166). The vertical scale has been exaggerated. The barrier reef of Ngau's southwestern shore is separated from the main island's coast by a deep lagoon, while only a tidal flat lies between Ngau's northeastern coast and the edge of the fringing reef.

Plateau drained by the Mba, the Tholo-West Plateau drained by the Singatoka, and the Navua Plateau drained by the Navua. Some 29 well-defined peaks rise above Viti Levu's interior; most of the people live in the river valleys or along the coast.

The Nandi River slices across the Nausori Highlands, with the Mount Evans Range (1,195 meters) towering above Lautoka. Other highland areas of Viti Levu are cut by great rivers like the Singatoka, the Navua, the Rewa, and the Mba, navigable far inland by outboard canoe or kayak. Whitewater rafters shoot down the Navua and the Mba, while the lower Singatoka flows gently through Fiji's market garden "salad bowl." Fiji's largest river, the Rewa, pours into the Pacific through a wide delta just below Nausori. After a hurricane the Rewa becomes a dark torrent worth a special visit to Nausori just to see. Sharks have been known to enter both the Rewa and the Singatoka and swim far upstream.

Vanua Levu has a peculiar shape, with two long peninsulas pointing northeastward. A mountain range between Lambasa and Savusavu reaches 1,032 meters at Nasorolevu. Navotuvotu (842 meters), east of Mbua Bay, is Fiji's best example of a broad shield volcano, with lava flows built up in layers. The mountains are closer to the southeast coast, and a broad lowland belt runs along the northwest. Of the rivers only the Ndreketi, flowing west across northern Vanua Levu, is large; navigation on

the Lambasa is restricted to small boats. The interior of Vanua Levu is lower and drier than Viti Levu, yet scenically superb: the road from Lambasa to Savusavu is a visual feast.

Vanua Levu's bullet-shaped neighbor Taveuni soars to 1,241 meters, its rugged east coast battered by the southeast trades. Taveuni and Kandavu are known as the finest islands in Fiji for their scenic beauty and agricultural potential. Geologically, the uplifted limestone islands of the Lau Group have more in common with Tonga than with the rest of Fiji. Northwest of Viti Levu is the rugged limestone Yasawa Group.

Coasts and Reefs

Fringing reefs are common along most of the coastlines, and Fiji is outstanding for its many barrier reefs. The Great Sea Reef off the north coast of Vanua Levu is the fourth longest in the world, and the Astrolabe Reef north of Kandavu is one of the most colorful. Countless other unexplored barrier reefs are found off northern Viti Levu and elsewhere. The many cracks, crevices, walls, and caves along Fiji's reefs are guaranteed to delight the scuba diver.

The configuration of the Astrolabe Reef off Ono and Kandavu confirms Darwin's Theory of Atoll Formation. The famous formulator of the theory of evolution surmised that coral atolls form as high volcanic islands subside into lagoons. The original island's fringing reef grows into a barrier reef as the volcanic portion sinks.

When the last volcanic material finally disappears below sea level, the coral ring of the reef/atoll remains to indicate how big the island once was. Of course, this takes place over millions of years, but deep down below any coral atoll is the old volcanic core. Darwin's theory is well illustrated here, where Ono and the small volcanic islands to the north remain inside the Astrolabe Reef. Return in 25 million years and all you'll find will be the reef itself.

The Greenhouse Effect

The gravest danger facing the low-lying islands of Oceania is the greenhouse effect, a gradual warming of earth's environment due to fossil fuel combustion and the widespread clearing of forests. By the year 2030 the concentration of carbon dioxide in the atmosphere will have doubled from preindustrial levels. As infrared radiation from the sun is absorbed by the gas, the trapped heat melts mountain glaciers and the polar ice caps. In addition, seawater expands as it warms up and water levels could rise almost a meter by the year 2100, destroying shorelines created 5,000 years ago.

A 1982 study demonstrated that sea levels had already risen 12 cm in the previous century; in 1993 the United Nations Environment Program predicted a further rise of 20 cm by the year 2030 and 65 cm by the end of the next century. Not only will this reduce the growing area for food crops, but rising sea levels will mean saltwater intrusion into groundwater supplies—a horrifying prospect if accompanied by the droughts that have been predicted. Coastal erosion will force governments to spend millions of dollars on road repairs and coastline stabilization.

Increasing temperatures may already be contributing to the dramatic jump in the number of hurricanes in the South Pacific. For example, Fiji experienced only 12 tropical hurricanes from 1941 to 1980 but 10 from 1981 to 1989, and in the face of devastating hurricanes, insurance companies are withdrawing coverage from some areas. Widespread instances of coral bleaching and reefs being killed by rising sea temperatures have been confirmed. (Coral bleaching occurs when an organism's symbiotic algae are expelled in response to environmental stresses, such as changes in water temperature.) Reef destruction will reduce coastal fish stocks and impact tourism.

Unfortunately, those most responsible for the problem, the industrialized countries led by the United States, have strongly resisted taking any action to significantly cut greenhouse gas emissions. And as if that weren't bad enough, the hydrofluorocarbons (HFCs) presently being developed by corporate giants like Dupont to replace the ozone-destructive chlorofluorocarbons (CFCs) presently used in cooling systems are far more potent greenhouse gases than carbon dioxide. This is only one of many similar consumption-related problems, and it seems as if one section of humanity is hurtling down a suicidal slope, unable to resist the momentum, as the rest of our race watches the catastrophe approach in helpless horror. It will cost a lot to rewrite our collective ticket but there may not be any choice.

CORAL REEFS

Coral reefs cover some 200,000 square km worldwide, between 35° north and 32° south latitude. A reef is created by the accumulation of millions of tiny calcareous skeletons left by myriad generations of tiny coral polyps, some no bigger than a pinhead. Though the skeleton is usually white, the living polyps are of many different colors.

The polyps thrive in clear salty water where the temperature never drops below 18°C. They must also have a base not over 50 meters below the water's surface. The coral colony grows slowly upward on the consolidated skeletons of its ancestors until it reaches the low-tide mark, after which development extends outward on the edges of the reef. Sunlight is critical for coral growth. Colonies grow quickly on the ocean side due to clearer water and a greater abundance of food. A strong, healthy reef can grow four to five cm a year. Fresh or cloudy water inhibits coral growth, which is why villages and ports all across the Pacific are located at the reef-free mouths of rivers.

Polyps extract calcium carbonate from the water and deposit it in their skeletons. All reef-building corals also contain limy encrustations of microscopic algae within their cells. The algae, like all green plants, obtain their energy from the sun and contribute this energy to the growth of the reef's skeleton. As a result, corals behave (and

acropora

staghorn fire coral *(Millepora alcicornis)*

CORALS OF THE PACIFIC

table coral

mushroom coral
(Fungia fungites)

elkhorn fire coral
(Millepora platyphylla)

honeycomb coral *(Favia matthaii)*

brain coral *(Meandrina)*

DIANA LASICH HARPER

look) more like plants than animals, competing for sunlight just as terrestrial plants do. Many polyps are also carnivorous; with minute stinging tentacles they supplement their energy by capturing tiny planktonic animals and organic particles at night. A small piece of coral is a colony composed of large numbers of polyps.

Coral Types

Corals belong to a broad group of stinging creatures that includes polyps, soft corals, stony corals, sea anemones, sea fans, and jellyfish. Only those types with hard skeletons and a single hollow cavity within the body are considered true corals. Stony corals such as brain, table, staghorn, and mushroom corals have external skeletons and are important reef builders. Soft corals, black corals, and sea fans have internal skeletons. The fire corals are recognized by their smooth, velvety surface and yellowish brown color. The stinging toxins of this last group can easily penetrate human skin and cause swelling and painful burning that can last up to an hour. The many varieties of soft, colorful anemones gently waving in the current might seem inviting to touch, but beware: many are also poisonous.

The corals, like most other forms of life in the Pacific, colonized the ocean from the fertile seas of Southeast Asia. Thus the number of species declines as you move east. Over 600 species of coral make their home in the Pacific, compared to only 48 in the Caribbean. The diversity of coral colors and forms is endlessly amazing. This is our most unspoiled environment, a world of almost indescribable beauty.

Exploring a Reef

Until you've explored a good coral reef, you haven't experienced one of the greatest joys of nature. While you cannot walk through pristine forests due to the lack of paths, it's quite possible to swim over untouched reefs—the most densely populated living space on earth. Dive shops throughout the region rent or sell snorkeling gear, so do get into the clear, warm waters around you. Be careful, however, and know the dangers. Practice snorkeling in the shallow water; don't head into deep water until you're sure you've got the hang of it. Breathe easily; don't hyperventilate.

When snorkeling on a fringing reef, beware of deadly currents and undertows in channels that drain tidal flows. Observe the direction the water is flowing before you swim into it. If you feel yourself being dragged out to sea through a reef passage, try swimming across the current rather than against it. If you can't resist the pull at all, it may be better to let yourself be carried out. Wait till the current diminishes, then swim along the outer reef face until you find somewhere to come back in. Or use your energy to attract the attention of someone onshore.

Snorkeling on the outer edge or drop-off of a reef is thrilling for the variety of fish and corals, but attempt it only on a very calm day. Even then it's best to have someone stand onshore or on the edge of the reef (at low tide) to watch for occasional big waves, which can take you by surprise and smash you into the rocks. Also, beware of unperceived currents outside the reef—you may not get a second chance.

A far better idea is to limit your snorkeling to the protected inner reef and leave the open waters to the scuba diver. Commercial scuba operators know their waters and will be able to show you the most amazing things in perfect safety. If you wish to scuba dive you'll have to show your scuba certification card, and occasionally divers are also asked to show a medical report from their doctor indicating that they are in good physical condition. Serious divers will bring along their own mask, buoyancy compensator, and regulator. Many of the scuba operators listed in this book offer introductory "resort courses" for those who only want a taste of scuba diving, and full NAUI or PADI certification courses for those wishing to dive more than once or twice. The main constraint is financial: snorkeling is free, while scuba diving can get expensive.

Conservation

Coral reefs are one of the most fragile and complex ecosystems on earth, providing food and shelter for countless species of fish, crustaceans (shrimps, crabs, and lobsters), mollusks (shells), and other animals. The coral reefs of the South Pacific protect shorelines during storms, supply sand to maintain the islands, furnish food for the local population, form a living laboratory for science, and are major tourist attractions.

FIJI CLIMATE

LOCATION		JAN.	FEB.	MAR.	APRIL	MAY	JUNE
Nandi airport, Viti Levu	C	27.0	26.9	26.7	26.2	25.0	24.0
	mm	294	291	373	195	99	78
Yasawa Island	C	27.0	26.9	26.6	26.4	26.0	25.3
	mm	281	287	344	168	110	106
Mba, Viti Levu	C	27.2	27.1	26.9	26.5	25.3	24.1
	mm	322	409	387	203	101	67
Nandarivatu, Viti Levu	C	21.6	22.0	21.5	21.0	20.0	18.9
	mm	599	668	689	362	181	99
Rakiraki, Viti Levu	C	27.6	27.6	27.3	26.8	25.9	24.9
	mm	307	371	372	236	122	66
Suva, Viti Levu	C	26.8	26.9	26.8	26.1	24.8	23.9
	mm	314	299	386	343	280	177
Vunisea, Kandavu I.	C	26.4	26.8	26.1	25.4	24.2	23.2
	mm	239	225	313	256	208	102
Nambouwalu, Vanua Levu	C	26.9	27.1	26.7	26.3	25.5	24.7
	mm	328	354	352	275	198	130
Lambasa, Vanua Levu	C	26.8	26.8	26.6	26.2	25.3	24.4
	mm	449	457	465	236	97	86
Vunikondi, Vanua Levu	C	26.6	26.7	26.6	26.3	26.0	25.3
	mm	302	377	409	225	143	131
Rotuma Island	C	27.4	27.3	27.2	27.4	27.2	26.8
	mm	358	390	430	278	262	244
Matuku, Lau Group	C	26.8	27.0	26.8	26.3	25.1	24.1
	mm	231	230	265	192	151	116
Ono-i-Lau, Lau Group	C	26.3	26.5	26.4	25.7	24.3	23.4
	mm	201	199	266	196	144	109

Note: The top figure indicates the average monthly temperatures in degrees and tenths centigrade, while the monthly rainfall average in millimeters (mm) is given below. The last column gives the annual temperature and the total precipitation during the year. These figures have been averaged over a minimum

Without coral, the South Pacific would be immeasurably poorer.

Hard corals grow only about 10 to 25 mm a year, and it can take 7,000 to 10,000 years for a coral reef to form. Though corals look solid, they're easily broken; by standing on them, breaking off pieces, or carelessly dropping anchor you can destroy in a few minutes what took so long to form. Once a piece of coral breaks off it dies, and it may be years before the coral reestablishes itself and even longer before the broken piece is replaced. The "wound" may become infected by algae which can multiply and kill the entire coral colony. When this happens over a wide area the diversity of marinelife declines dramatically.

We recommend that you not remove seashells, coral, plantlife, or marine animals from the sea. In a small way, you are upsetting the delicate balance of nature, and coral is much

FIJI CLIMATE

JULY	AUG.	SEPT.	OCT.	NOV.	DEC.	ALL YEAR
23.3	23.8	24.5	25.2	25.9	26.6	25.4
51	62	88	73	137	181	1922
24.6	24.8	25.1	25.7	26.1	26.7	25.9
45	68	90	78	187	165	1929
23.3	23.8	24.7	25.5	26.1	26.1	25.6
46	65	72	91	126	228	2117
18.3	18.8	19.0	20.1	20.6	21.1	20.2
89	125	126	136	220	400	3694
24.2	24.6	25.1	25.9	26.6	27.1	26.2
47	68	74	83	140	221	2107
23.1	23.2	23.7	24.4	25.3	26.2	25.1
148	200	212	218	268	313	3158
22.4	22.6	23.1	23.9	24.7	26.1	24.6
112	121	122	126	151	177	2152
23.9	24.0	24.4	25.2	25.4	26.3	25.6
96	114	139	164	208	279	2637
23.8	24.2	24.7	25.4	25.9	26.4	25.6
38	60	77	96	210	263	2534
24.6	24.7	25.0	25.6	25.9	26.6	25.8
92	90	114	132	264	220	2499
26.4	26.5	26.7	26.8	27.0	27.2	27.0
207	230	277	283	327	331	3617
23.1	23.6	24.2	25.0	25.7	26.4	25.3
114	78	110	97	139	152	1875
22.4	22.4	22.7	23.6	24.5	25.3	24.4
90	94	106	114	128	145	1792

of 10 years, in most cases much longer. Altitude is a factor at Nandarivatu (835 meters); all the others are very near sea level. You will notice that temperatures don't vary too much year-round, but there is a pronounced dry season midyear. Note, too, that some areas of Fiji are far drier than others.

more beautiful underwater anyway! This is a particular problem along shorelines frequented by large numbers of tourists, who can completely strip a reef in very little time. The triton shell, for example, keeps in check the reef-destroying crown-of-thorns starfish. If you'd like a souvenir, content yourself with what you find on the beach (although even a seemingly empty shell may be inhabited by a hermit crab). Also think twice about purchasing jewelry or souvenirs made from coral or seashells. Genuine traditional handicrafts that incorporate shells are one thing, but by purchasing unmounted seashells or mass-produced coral curios you are contributing to the destruction of the marine environment.

The anchors and anchor chains of private yachts can do serious damage to coral reefs. Pronged anchors are more environmentally friendly than larger, heavier anchors, and plas-

SUVA'S CLIMATE

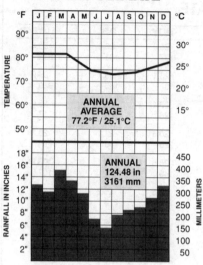

ANNUAL
AVERAGE
77.2°F / 25.1°C

ANNUAL
124.48 in
3161 mm

NANDI'S CLIMATE

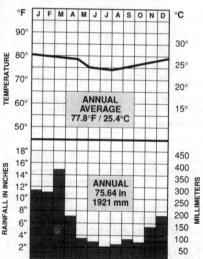

ANNUAL
AVERAGE
77.8°F / 25.4°C

ANNUAL
75.64 in
1921 mm

tic tubing over the end of the anchor chain helps minimize damage. If at all possible, anchor in sand. A longer anchor chain makes this easier and a good windlass is essential for larger boats. A recording depth sounder will help locate sandy areas when none are available in shallow water. If you don't have a depth sounder and can't see the bottom, lower the anchor until it just touches the bottom and feel the anchor line as the boat drifts. If it "grumbles" lift it up, drift a little, and try again. Later, if you notice your chain grumbling, motor over the anchor, lift it out of the coral, and move. Not only do sand and mud hold better, but your anchor will be less likely to become fouled. Try to arrive before 1500 to be able to see clearly where you're anchoring—Polaroid sunglasses make it easier to distinguish corals.

There's an urgent need for stricter regulation of the marine environment, and in some places coral reefs are already protected. Exhortations such as the one above have only limited impact—legislators must write stricter laws and impose fines. Resort developers can minimize damage to their valuable reefs by providing public mooring buoys so yachts don't have to drop anchor and pontoons so snorkelers aren't tempted to stand on coral. Licensing authorities can make such amenities mandatory whenever appropriate, and in extreme cases, especially endangered coral gardens should be declared off limits to private boats. As consumerism spreads, once-remote areas become subject to the problems of pollution and over-exploitation: the garbage is visibly piling up on many shores. As a visitor, don't hesitate to practice your conservationist attitudes, and leave a clean wake.

CLIMATE

Along the coast the weather is warm and pleasant, without great variations in temperature. The southeast trade winds sweep across Fiji from June to October, the ideal months to visit. In February and March the wind often comes directly out of the east. These winds dump 3,000 mm of annual rainfall on the humid southeast coasts of the big islands, increasing to 5,000 mm inland. The drier northwest coasts, in the lee, get only 1,500 to 2,000 mm.

The dry winter season (June to October) is not always dry at Suva, although much of the rain falls at night. Fiji's winter is cooler and less humid than summer, the best months for mountain trekking, and during the drier winter season the reef waters are clearest for the scuba diver. Yet even during the rainy summer months (December to April), bright sun often follows the rains, and the rain is only a slight inconvenience. Summer is hurricane season, with Fiji, Samoa, and Tonga receiving up to five tropical storms annually.

Over the past five years climatic changes have turned weather patterns upside down, so don't be surprised if you get prolonged periods of rain and wind during the official "dry season." Temperatures range from warm to hot year-round; however, the ever-present sea moderates the high humidity by bringing continual cooling breezes.

In Fiji you can obtain prerecorded weather information by dialing 301-642.

Currents and Winds

The Pacific Ocean has a greater impact on the world's climate than any other geographical feature on earth. By taking heat away from the equator toward the poles, it stretches the bounds of the area in which life can exist. Broad circular ocean currents flow from east to west across the tropical Pacific, clockwise in the North Pacific, counterclockwise in the South Pacific. North and south of the "horse latitudes" just outside the tropics the currents cool and swing east. The prevailing winds move the same way: the southeast trades south of the equator, the northeast trades north of the equator, and the low-pressure "doldrums" in between. Westerlies blow east above the cool currents north and south of the tropics. This natural air-conditioning system brings warm water to Australia and Japan, cooler water to Peru and California.

The climate of the high islands is closely related to these winds. As air is heated near the equator it rises and flows at high altitudes toward the poles. By the time it reaches about 30° south latitude it will have cooled enough to cause it to fall and flow back toward the equator near sea level. In the southern hemisphere the rotation of the earth deflects the winds to the left to become the southeast trades. When these cool moist trade winds hit a high island, they are warmed by the sun and forced up. Above 500 meters' elevation they begin to cool again and their moisture condenses into clouds. At night the winds do not capture much warmth and are more likely to discharge their moisture as rain. The windward slopes of the high islands catch the trades head-on and are usually wet, while those on the leeward side are dry.

carpilius maculatus

FLORA AND FAUNA

FLORA

The flora of Fiji originated in the Malaysian region; in the two regions ecological niches are filled by similar plants. There are over 3,000 species of plants in Fiji, a third of them endemic. Of the large islands, Taveuni is known for its rare climbing *tangimauthia* flower. The absence of leaf-eating animals in Fiji allowed the vegetation to develop largely without the protective spines and thorns found elsewhere, and one of the only poisonous plants is the *salato*, a tree with large, hairy leaves that inflict painful wounds when touched.

Patterns of rainfall are in large part responsible for the vegetation. Rainforests fill the valleys and damp windward slopes of the high islands, while brush and occasional thickets of bamboo and scrub grow in more exposed locations. Hillsides in the drier areas are covered with coarse grasses. Natural forests cover 40% of Fiji's total land area and about a quarter of this is classified as production forest suitable for logging. The towering *ndakua* tree, once carved into massive Fijian war canoes, has already disappeared from Viti Levu, and the last stands are now being logged on Vanua Levu.

Coconut groves fill the coastal plains. On the drier sides open savanna or *talasinga* of coarse grasses predominates where the original vegetation has been destroyed by slash-and-burn agriculture. Sugarcane is now cultivated in the lowlands here, and Caribbean pine has been planted in many dry hilly areas, giving them a Scandinavian appearance. The low islands of the Lau Group are restricted to a few hardy, drought-resistant species such as coconuts and pandanus.

Mangroves can occasionally be found in river deltas and along some high-island coastal lagoons. The cable roots of the saltwater-tolerant red mangrove anchor in the shallow upper layer of oxygenated mud, avoiding the layers of hydrogen sulfide below. The tree provides shade for tiny organisms dwelling in the tidal mudflats—a place for birds to nest and for fish or shellfish to feed and spawn. The mangroves also perform the same task as land-building coral colonies along the reefs. As sediments are trapped between the roots, the trees extend farther into the lagoon, creating a unique natural environment. The past decade has seen widespread destruction of the mangroves as land is reclaimed for agricultural use in northwest Viti Levu and around Lambasa.

Though only introduced to Fiji in the late 1860s, sugarcane probably originated in the South Pacific. On New Guinea the islanders have cultivated the plant for thousands of years, selecting vigorous varieties with the most colorful stems. The story goes that two Melanesian fishermen, To-Kabwana and To-Karavuvu, found a piece of sugarcane in their net one day. They threw it away, but after twice catching it again they decided to keep it and painted the stalk a bright color. Eventually the cane burst and a woman came forth. She cooked food for the men but hid herself at night. Finally she was captured and became the wife of one of the men. From their union sprang the whole human race.

FAUNA

Of the 70 species of land birds, 22 are endemic, including broadbills, cuckoos, doves, fantails, finches, flycatchers, fruitdoves, hawks, herons, honey eaters, kingfishers, lorikeets, parrots, pigeons, rails, silktails, and warblers. The Fijian

LOUISE FOOTE

pink-billed parrot finch

tree frog

names of some of these birds, such as the *kaka* (parrot) and *kikau* (giant honey eater), imitate their calls. Of the seabirds, boobies, frigate birds, petrels, and tropic birds are present. The best time to observe the forest birds is in the very early morning—they move around a lot less in the heat of the day.

More in evidence than the native birds is the Indian mynah, the bulbul, and the Malay turtledove. The hopping Indian mynah bird *(Acridotheres tristis)* was introduced at the turn of the century to control insects, which were damaging the citrus and coconut plantations. The mynahs multiplied profusely and have become major pests, inflicting great harm on the very trees they were brought in to protect. Worse still, many indigenous birds are forced out of their habitat by these noisy, aggressive birds with yellow beaks and feet. This and rapid deforestation by humans have made the South Pacific the region with the highest proportion of endangered endemic bird species on earth.

The only native mammals are the monkey-faced fruit bat or flying fox, the insect-eating bat, and the Polynesian gray rat. The Indian mongoose was introduced by planters in the 1880s to combat rats, which were damaging the plantations. Unfortunately, no one realized at the time that the mongoose hunts by day, whereas the rats are nocturnal; thus, the two seldom meet. Today, the mongoose is the scourge of chickens, native ground birds, and other animals, though Kandavu, Ngau, Ovalau, and Taveuni are mongoose-free (and thus the best islands for birdwatching).

In 1936 the giant toad was introduced from Hawaii to control beetles, slugs, and millipedes. When this food source is exhausted, they tend to eat each other. At night gardens and lawns may be full of them. The native land- and tree-dwelling frogs are noteworthy for the long suction discs on their fingers and toes. Because they live deep in the rainforests and feed at night, they're seldom seen. Some Fijian clans have totemic relationships with eels, prawns, turtles, and sharks, and are able to summon these creatures with special chants.

Reptiles

Four of the world's seven species of sea turtles nest in Fiji: the green, hawksbill, loggerhead, and leatherback. Nesting occurs between November and February, at night when there is a full moon and a high tide. The female struggles up the beach from which she originally hatched and lays as many as 100 eggs in a hole, which she digs and then covers with her hind flippers. Female turtles don't commence this activity until they are 20 years old, thus a drop in numbers today has irreversible consequences a generation later. It's estimated that breeding females already number in the hundreds or low thousands, and all species of these magnificent creatures (sometimes erroneously referred to as "tortoises") now face extinction. Turtles are often choked by floating plastic bags they mistake for food, or they drown in fishing nets. The turtles and their eggs are protected by law in Fiji (maximum penalty of six months in prison for killing a turtle), and importing any sea turtle product is now prohibited in most countries.

Geckos and skinks are small lizards often seen on the islands. The skink hunts insects by day; its tail breaks off if you catch it, but a new one quickly grows. The gecko is nocturnal and has no eyelids. Adhesive toe pads enable it to pass along vertical surfaces, and it changes

banded iguana

color to avoid detection. Unlike the skink, which avoids humans, the gecko often lives in people's homes where it eats insects attracted by electric lights. Its loud ticking call may be a territorial warning to other geckos.

One of the more unusual creatures found in Fiji and Tonga is the banded iguana, a lizard that lives in trees and can grow up to 70 cm long (two-thirds of which is tail). The iguanas are emerald green, and the male is easily distinguished from the female by his bluish-gray cross stripes. Banded iguanas change color to control their internal temperature, becoming darker when in the direct sun. Their nearest relatives are found in South America and Madagascar, and no lizards live farther east in the Pacific than these. In 1979 a new species, the crested iguana, was discovered on Yanduatambu, a small island off the west coast of Vanua Levu. How the iguanas could have reached the islands remains a mystery.

Two species of snakes inhabit Fiji: the very rare, poisonous *bolo loa,* and the harmless Pacific boa, which can grow up to two meters long. Venomous sea snakes are common on some coasts, but they're docile and easily handled. Fijians call the common banded black-and-white sea snake the *ndandakulathi.*

Marinelife

Fiji's richest store of life is found in the silent underwater world of the pelagic and lagoon fishes. Coral pinnacles on the lagoon floor provide a safe haven for angelfish, butterfly fish, damselfish, groupers, soldierfish, surgeonfish, triggerfish, trumpet fish, and countless more. These fish seldom venture more than a few meters away from the protective coral, but larger fish such as barracuda, jackfish, parrot fish, pike, stingrays, and small sharks range across lagoon waters which are seldom deeper than 30 meters. The external side of the reef is also home to many of the above, but the open ocean is reserved for bonito, mahimahi, swordfish, tuna, wrasses, and the larger sharks. Passes between ocean and lagoon can be crowded with fish in transit, offering a favorite hunting ground for predators.

In the open sea the food chain begins with phytoplankton, which flourish wherever ocean upswellings bring nutrients such as nitrates and phosphates to the surface. In the western Pacific this occurs near the equator, where massive currents draw water away toward Japan and Australia. Large schools of fast-moving tuna ply these waters feeding on smaller fish, which consume tiny phytoplankton drifting near the sunlit surface. The phytoplankton also exist in tropical lagoons where mangrove leaves, sea grasses, and other plant material are consumed by far more varied populations of reef fish, mollusks, and crustaceans.

Dolphins

While most people use the terms dolphin and porpoise interchangeably, a porpoise lacks the dolphin's beak (although many dolphins are also beakless). There are 62 species of dolphins, and only six species of porpoises. Dolphins leap from the water and many legends tell of them saving humans, especially children, from drowning (the most famous concerns Telemachus, son of Odysseus). Dolphins often try to race in front of ferries and large ships.

Because herds of dolphins in the Eastern Pacific tend to swim above schools of yellowfin tuna, tens of thousands a year drown in purse seine nets deliberately set around the marine mammals, crushing or suffocating them. In 1990, after a worldwide tuna boycott spearheaded by San Francisco's Earth Island Institute, H.J. Heinz (StarKist) and many other American tuna packers announced that they would only can tuna caught using dolphin-safe fishing methods. Unfortunately, some canneries in Italy, Japan, and other countries continue to accept tuna without reservations from dolphin-killing Mexican and South American vessels. If you care about marine mammals, look for the distinctive "dolphin-safe" label before buying any tuna at all. (No dolphins are killed by purse seiners in the South Pacific, and all fish canned in Fiji are caught using dolphin-safe methods.)

Sharks

The danger from sharks has been greatly exaggerated. Of some 300 different species, only 28 are known to have attacked humans. Most dangerous are the white, tiger, hammerhead, and blue sharks. Fortunately, all of these inhabit deep water far from the coasts. An average of only 50 shark attacks a year occur worldwide, so considering the number of people who swim in the sea, your chances of being involved are about one in a million. In Fiji shark attacks on snorkelers or scuba divers are extremely rare.

Sharks are not aggressive where food is abundant, but they can be very nasty far offshore. You're always safer if you keep your head underwater (with a mask and snorkel), and don't panic if you see a shark—you might attract it. Even if you do, they're usually only curious, so keep one eye on the shark and slowly back off. The swimming techniques of humans must seem very clumsy to fish, so it's not surprising if they want a closer look.

Sharks are attracted by shiny objects (a knife or jewelry), bright colors (especially yellow and red), urinating, spearfishing, blood, and splashing (divers should ease themselves into the water). Sharks normally stay outside the reef, but ask local advice. White beaches are safer than dark, and clear water safer than murky. Avoid swimming in places where sewage or edible wastes enter the water, or where fish have just been cleaned. You should also exercise care in places where local residents have been fishing with spears or even hook and line that day.

Never swim alone if you suspect the presence of sharks. If you see one, even a supposedly harmless nurse shark lying on the bottom, get out of the water calmly and quickly, and go elsewhere. Recent studies indicate that sharks, like most other creatures, have a "personal space" around them which they will defend. Thus an attack could be a shark's way of warning someone to keep his or her distance, since it's a fact that over half the victims of these incidents are not eaten, but merely wounded. Sharks are much less of a problem in the South Pacific than in colder waters because marine mammals (commonly hunted by sharks) are rare here, so you won't be mistaken for a seal or an otter.

Let common sense be your guide, not irrational fear or carelessness. Many scuba divers come actually *looking* for sharks, and local divemasters seem able to swim among them with impunity. If you're in the market for some shark action, most dive shops can provide it. Just be aware that getting into the water with feeding sharks always entails some danger, and the divemaster who admits this and lays down a few basic safety guidelines (such as keeping your hands clasped or arms folded) is probably a safer bet than the macho man who says he's been doing it for years without incident. Like all other wild animals, sharks deserve to be approached with respect.

Sea Urchins

Sea urchins (living pincushions) are common in tropical waters. The black variety is the most dangerous: their long, sharp quills can go right through a snorkeler's fins. Even the small ones, which you can easily pick up in your hand, can pinch you if you're careless. They're found on rocky shores and reefs, never on clear, sandy beaches where the surf rolls in.

Most sea urchins are not poisonous, though quill punctures are painful and can become infected if not treated. The pain is caused by an injected protein, which you can eliminate by holding the injured area in a pail of very hot water for about 15 minutes. This will coagulate the protein, eliminating the pain for good. If you can't heat water, soak the area in vinegar or urine for a quarter hour. Remove the quills if possible, but being made of calcium, they'll decompose in a couple of weeks anyway—not much of a consolation as you limp along in the meantime. In some places sea urchins are a favorite delicacy: the orange or yellow urchin gonads are delicious with lemon and salt.

Others

Although jellyfish, stonefish, crown-of-thorns starfish, cone shells, eels, and poisonous sea snakes are hazardous, injuries resulting from any of these are rare. Gently apply methylated spirit, alcohol, or urine (but not water, kerosene, or gasoline) to areas stung by jellyfish. Harmless sea cucumbers (bêche-de-mer) punctuate the lagoon shallows. Stonefish also rest on the bottom and are hard to see due to camouflaging; if you happen to step on one, its dorsal fins inject a painful poison, which burns like fire in the blood. It's worth knowing that the venom produced by most marine animals is destroyed by heat, so your first move should be to soak the injured part in very hot water for 30 minutes. (Also hold an opposite foot or hand in the same water to prevent scalding due to numbness.) Other authorities claim the best first aid is to squeeze blood from a sea cucumber scraped raw on coral directly onto the wound. If a hospital or clinic is nearby, go there immediately. Fortunately, stonefish are not common.

Never pick up a live cone shell; some varieties have a deadly stinger dart at the pointed end. The tiny blue-ring octopus is only five cm long but packs a poison that can kill a human. Eels hide in reef crevices by day; most are dangerous only if you inadvertently poke your hand or foot in at them. Of course, never tempt fate by approaching them (fun-loving divemasters sometimes feed the big ones by hand and stroke their backs).

HISTORY AND GOVERNMENT

HISTORY

The Pre-European Period

The first people to arrive in Fiji were of a broad-nosed, light-skinned Austronesian-speaking race, probably the Polynesians. They originated in insular Southeast Asia and gradually migrated east past the already occupied islands of Melanesia. Distinctive *Lapita* pottery, decorated in horizontal geometric bands and dated from 1290 B.C., has been found in the sand dunes near Singatoka, indicating they had reached here by 1500 B.C. or earlier. Much later, about 500 B.C., Melanesian people arrived, bringing with them their own distinct pottery traditions. From the fusion of these primordial peoples the Fijian race was born.

The hierarchical social structure of the early Fijians originated with the Polynesians. Status and descent passed through the male line, and power was embodied in the *turanga* (chief). The hereditary chiefs possessed the mana of an ancestral spirit or *vu*. This feudal aristocracy combined in confederations or *vanua* which extended their influence through war. Treachery and cannibalism were an intrinsic part of these struggles; women were taken as prizes or traded to form alliances. For defense, villages were fortified with ditches, or built along ridges or terraced hillsides.

The native aristocracy practiced customs that today seem barbarous and particularly cruel. The skull cap of a defeated enemy might be polished and used as a *yanggona* (kava) cup to humiliate the foe. Some chiefs even took delight in cooking and consuming bodily parts as their agonized victims looked on. Men were buried alive to hold up the posts of new houses, war canoes were launched over the living bodies of young girls, and the widows of chiefs were strangled to keep their husbands company in the spirit world. The farewells of some of these women are remembered today in dances and songs known as *meke*.

These feudal islanders were, on the other hand, guardians of one of the highest material cultures of the Pacific. They built great ocean-going double canoes *(ndrua)* up to 30 meters long, constructed and adorned large solid thatched houses *(mbures)*, performed marvelous song-dances called *meke*, made tapa, pottery, and sennit (coconut cordage), and skillfully plaited mats. For centuries the Tongans came to Fiji to obtain great logs from which to make canoes, and sandalwood for carving.

European Exploration

In 1643 Abel Tasman became the European discoverer of Fiji when he sighted Taveuni, although he didn't land. Tasman was searching for *terra australis incognita*, a great southern continent believed

FIJI ISLANDS CHRONOLOGY

1500 B.C. Polynesians reach Fiji

500 B.C. Melanesians reach Fiji

1643 Abel Tasman sights Taveuni

1774 Captain Cook visits southern Lau

1789 Bligh and crew paddle past Yasawas

1804 sandalwood discovered on Vanua Levu

1820 bêche-de-mer trade begins

1830 Tahitian missionaries in southern Lau

1835 Methodist missionaries arrive at Lakemba

1838 Dumont d'Urville visits Mbau

1840 American Exploring Expedition visits Fiji

1847 Tongan invasion of Lau led by Enele Ma'afu

1849 home of John Brown Williams burns

1851 first visit by hostile American gunboats

1854 Chief Cakobau accepts Christianity

1855 Cakobau puts down the Rewa revolt

1860 founding of the town of Levuka

1862 Britain refuses to annex Fiji

1867 American warship threatens to shell Levuka

1868 Polynesia Company granted the site of Suva

1871 Cakobau and Thurston form a government

1874 Fiji becomes a British colony

1875 measles epidemic kills a third of Fijians

1879 first indentured Indian laborers arrive

1881 first large sugar mill built at Nausori

1882 capital moved from Levuka to Suva

1904 first elected Legislative Council

1916 Indian immigration ends

1920 indenture system terminated

1939 Nandi Airport built

1940 Native Land Trust Board established

1942 Fijian troops sent to the Solomons

1966 internal self-government achieved

1970 Fiji's first constitution adopted

1970 Fiji becomes independent

1973 sugar industry nationalized

1977 governor-general overturns election results

1978 Fijian peacekeeping troops sent to Lebanon

1987 Labor defeats Alliance Party

1987 two military coups led by Lieutenant Colonel Rabuka

1987 Rabuka declares Fiji a republic

1987 Fiji expelled from British Commonwealth

1990 new constitution promulgated

1992 Rabuka elected under gerrymandered constitution

1994 Rabuka reelected with increased representation

to balance the continents of the north. He also hoped to find new markets and trade routes. Unlike earlier Spanish explorers, Tasman entered the Pacific from the west rather than the east. Apart from Fiji, he was the first European to see Tasmania, New Zealand, and Tonga. By sailing right around Australia from the Dutch East Indies he proved New Holland (Australia) was not attached to the elusive southern continent.

In 1774, Captain Cook anchored off Vatoa (which he named Turtle Island) in southern Lau. Like Tasman he failed to proceed farther or land, and it was left to Capt. William Bligh to give Europeans an accurate picture of Fiji for the first time. After the *Bounty* mutiny in May 1789, Bligh and his companions were chased by canoe-loads of Fijian warriors just north of the Yasawa Islands as they rowed through on their escape route to Timor. Some serious paddling, a timely squall, and a lucky gap in the Great Sea Reef saved the Englishmen from ending up as the main course at a cannibal feast. The section of sea where this happened is today known as Bligh Water. Bligh cut directly across the center of Fiji between the two main islands, and his careful observations made him the first real European explorer of Fiji, albeit an unwilling one. Bligh returned to Fiji in 1792, but once again he stayed aboard his ship.

Beachcombers and Chiefs

All of these early explorers stressed the perilous nature of Fiji's reefs. This, combined with tales told by the Tongans of cannibalism and warlike Fijian natives, caused most travelers to shun the area. Then in 1804 a survivor from the shipwrecked American schooner *Argo* brought word that sandalwood grew abundantly along the Mbua coast of Vanua Levu. This precipitated a rush of traders and beachcombers to the islands. A cargo of sandalwood bought from the islanders for $50 worth of trinkets could be sold to the Chinese at Canton for $20,000. By 1814 the forests had been stripped to provide joss sticks and incense, and the trade collapsed.

During this period Fiji was divided among warring chieftains. The first Europeans to actually mix with the Fijians were escaped convicts from Australia, who instructed the natives in the use of European muskets and were thus well received. White beachcombers such as the Swedish adventurer Charles Savage and the German Martin Bushart mediated between traders and Fijians and took sides in local conflicts. In one skirmish Savage

was separated from his fellows, captured, and eaten. With help from the likes of Savage, Naulivou, the cannibal chief of tiny Mbau Island just off eastern Viti Levu, and his brother Tanoa extended their influence over much of western Fiji.

In his book *Following the Equator*, Mark Twain had this to say about the beachcombers:

> *They lived worthless lives of sin and luxury, and died without honor—in most cases by violence. Only one of them had any ambition; he was an Irishman named Connor. He tried to raise a family of fifty children and scored forty-eight. He died lamenting his failure. It was a foolish sort of avarice. Many a father would have been rich enough with forty.*

From 1827 to 1850 European traders collected bêche-de-mer, a sea slug, which, when smoked and dried, also brought a good price in China. While the sandalwood traders only stayed long enough to take on a load, the bêche-de-mer collectors set up shore facilities where the slugs were processed. Many traders such as David Whippy followed the example of the beachcombers and took local wives, establishing the part-Fijian community of today. By monopolizing the bêche-de-mer trade and constantly warring, Chief Tanoa's son and successor, Ratu Seru Cakobau (pronounced Thakombau), became extremely powerful in the 1840s, proclaiming himself Tui Viti, or king of Fiji.

cannibal fork: It has been said that the Fijians were extremely hospitable to any strangers they did not wish to eat. Native voyagers wrecked on their shores, who arrived "with salt water in their eyes," were liable to be killed and eaten, since all shipwrecked persons were believed to have been cursed and abandoned by the gods. Many European sailors from wrecked vessels shared the same fate. Cannibalism was a universal practice and prisoners taken in war, or even women seized while fishing, were invariably eaten. Most of the early European accounts of Fiji emphasized this trait to the exclusion of almost anything else; at one time the island group was even referred to as the "Cannibal Isles." By eating the flesh of a conquered enemy, one incorporated their mana or psychic power. One chief on Viti Levu is said to have consumed 872 people, and to have made a pile of stones to record his achievement. The leaves of a certain vegetable (Solanum uporo) were wrapped around the human meat, and it was cooked in an earthen oven. Wooden forks such as the one pictured were employed at cannibal feasts by men who relied on their fingers for food, but used these because it was considered improper to touch cooked human flesh with the fingers or lips. Present-day Fijians do not appreciate tourists who make jokes about cannibalism.

The beginnings of organized trade brought a second wave of official explorers to Fiji. In 1838 Dumont d'Urville landed on Mbau Island and met Tanoa. The Frenchmen caused consternation and confusion by refusing to drink *yanggona* (kava), preferring their own wine. The American Exploring Expedition of 1840, led by Commodore Charles Wilkes, produced the first recognizable map of Fiji. When two Americans, including a nephew of Wilkes, were speared in a misunderstanding on a beach at Malolo Island, Wilkes ordered the offending fortified village stormed and 87 Fijians were killed. The survivors were made to water and provision Wilkes's ships as tribute. Captain H.M. Denham of the HMS *Herald* prepared accurate navigational charts of the island group in 1855-56, making regular commerce possible.

European and Tongan Penetration

As early as the 1830s an assortment of European and American beachcombers had formed a small settlement at Levuka on the east coast of Ovalau Island just northeast of Mbau, which whalers and traders used as a supply base. In 1846 John Brown Williams was appointed American commercial agent. On 4 July 1849 Williams's home on Nukulau Island near present-day Suva burned down. Though the conflagration was caused by the explosion of a cannon during Williams's own fervent celebration of his national holiday, he objected to the way Fijian onlookers carried off items they rescued from the flames. A shameless swindler, Williams had purchased Nukulau for only $30, yet he blamed the Tui Viti for his losses and sent Cakobau a $5001.38 bill. American claims for damages eventually rose to $44,000, and in 1851 and 1855 American gunboats called and ordered Cakobau to pay up. This threat hung over Cakobau's head for many years, the 19th-century equivalent of 20th-century Third World debt.

The early 1830s also saw the arrival from Tonga of the first missionaries. Though Tahitian pastors were sent by the London Missionary Society to Oneata in southern Lau as early as 1830, it was the Methodists based at Lakemba after 1835 who made the most lasting impression by rendering the Fijian language into writing. At first Christianity made little headway among these fierce, idolatrous people, and only after converting the powerful chiefs were the

missionaries successful. Methodist missionaries Cargill and Cross were appalled by what they saw during a visit to Mbau in 1838. A white missionary, Rev. Thomas Baker, was clubbed and eaten in central Viti Levu by the *kai tholo* (hill people) as late as 1867.

In 1847 Enele Ma'afu, a member of the Tongan royal family, arrived in Lau and began building a personal empire under the pretense of defending Christianity. In 1853 King George of Tonga made Ma'afu governor of all Tongans resident in Lau. Meanwhile, there was continuing resistance from the warlords of the Rewa River area to Cakobau's dominance. In addition the Europeans at Levuka suspected Cakobau of twice ordering their town set afire and were directing trade away from Mbau. With his power in decline, in 1854 Cakobau accepted Christianity in exchange for an alliance with King George, and in 1855, with the help of 2,000 Tongans led by King George himself, Cakobau was able to put down the Rewa revolt. In the process, however, Ma'afu became the dominant force in Lau, Taveuni, and Vanua Levu.

During the early 1860s, as Americans fought their Civil War, the world price of cotton soared, and large numbers of Europeans arrived in Fiji hoping to establish cotton plantations. In 1867 the USS *Tuscaroga* called at Levuka and threatened to bombard the town unless the still-outstanding American debt was paid. The next year an enterprising Australian firm, the Polynesia Company, paid off the Americans in exchange for a grant from Cakobau of 80,000 hectares of choice land, including the site of modern Suva. The British government later refused to recognize this grant, though they refunded the money paid to the Americans and accepted the claims of settlers who had purchased land from the company. Settlers soon numbered around 2,000 and Levuka boomed.

It was a lawless era and a need was felt for a central government. An attempt at national rule by a council of chiefs failed in 1867, then three regional governments were set up in Mbau (western), Lau (eastern), and Mbua (northern), but these were only partly successful. With cotton prices collapsing as the American South resumed production, a national administration under Cakobau and planter John Thurston was established at Levuka in 1871.

However, Cakobau was never strong enough to impose his authority over the whole country, so with growing disorder in western Fiji, infighting between Europeans and Fijian chiefs, and a lack of cooperation from Ma'afu's rival confederation of chiefs in eastern Fiji, Cakobau decided he should cede his kingdom to Great Britain. The British had refused an invitation to annex Fiji in 1862, but this time they accepted rather than risk seeing the group fall into the hands of another power, and on 10 October 1874 Fiji became a British colony. In 1877 the Western Pacific High Commission was set up to protect British interests in the surrounding unclaimed island groups as well. At first Levuka was the colony's capital, but in 1882 the government moved to a more spacious site at Suva.

The Making of a Nation

The first British governor, Sir Arthur Gordon, and his colonial secretary and successor, Sir John Thurston, created modern Fiji almost single-handedly. They realized that the easiest way to rule was indirectly, through the existing Fijian chiefs. To protect the communal lands on which the chieftain system was based, they ordered that native land could not be sold, only leased. Not wishing to disturb native society, Gordon and Thurston ruled that Fijians could not be required to work on European plantations. Meanwhile the blackbirding of Melanesian laborers from the Solomons and New Hebrides had been restricted by the Polynesian Islanders Protection Act of 1872.

By this time sugar had taken the place of cotton and there was a tremendous labor shortage on the plantations. Gordon, who had previously served in Trinidad and Mauritius, saw indentured Indian workers as a solution. The first arrived in 1879, and by 1916, when Indian immigration ended, there were 63,000 present. To come to Fiji the Indians had to sign a labor contract *(girmit)* in which they agreed to cut sugarcane for their masters for five years. During the next five years they were allowed to lease small plots of their own from the Fijians and plant cane or raise livestock. Over half the Indians decided to remain in Fiji as free settlers after their 10-year contracts expired, and today their descendants form about half the population, many of them still working small leased plots.

Though this combination of European capital, Fijian land, and Indian labor did help preserve traditional Fijian culture, it also kept the Fijians backward—envious onlookers passed over by European and (later) Indian prosperity. The separate administration and special rights for indigenous Fijians installed by the British over a century ago continue in force today. In early 1875 Cakobau and two of his sons returned from a visit to Australia infected with measles. Though they themselves survived, the resulting epidemic wiped out a third of the Fijian population. As a response to this and other public health problems the Fiji School of Medicine was founded in 1885. At the beginning of European colonization there were about 200,000 Fijians, approximately 114,748 in 1881, and just 84,000 by 1921.

CAINES JANNIF LTD., SUVA

Blackbirded Solomon Islanders, brought to work on European-owned plantations in Fiji, wait aboard ship off Levuka around the turn of the century. In 1910 the Melanesian labor trade was finally terminated by the British, but a few of the Solomon Islanders stayed on, and small communities of their descendants exist on Ovalau and near Suva.

(preceding page) preparing a *lovo* or underground oven at Korovou, central Viti Levu (David Stanley)
(this page top) A Fiji Indian family enjoys watermelon, Nandi. (John Penisten);
(this page bottom) handicraft seller, Nandi (Doug Hankin)

The Colonial Period

In 1912 a Gujerati lawyer, D.M. Manilal, arrived in Fiji from Mauritius to fight for Indian rights, just as his contemporary Mahatma Gandhi was doing in South Africa. Indentured Indians continued to arrive in Fiji until 1916, but the protests led to the termination of the indenture system throughout the empire in 1920 (Manilal was deported from Fiji after a strike that year).

Although Fiji was a political colony of Britain, it was always an economic colony of Australia: the big Australian trading companies Burns Philp and W.R. Carpenters dominated business. (The ubiquitous Morris Hedstrom is a subsidiary of Carpenters, though both are now owned by Malaysians.) Most of the Indians were brought to Fiji to work for the Australian-owned Colonial Sugar Refining Company, which controlled the sugar industry from 1881 right up until 1973, when it was purchased by the Fiji government for $14 million.

No representative government existed in Fiji until 1904, when a Legislative Council was formed with six elected Europeans and two Fijians nominated by the Great Council of Chiefs (Mbose Levu Vakaturanga), itself an instrument of colonial rule. In 1916 the governor appointed an Indian member to the council. A 1929 reform granted five seats to each of the three communities: three elected and two appointed Europeans and Indians, and five nominated Fijians. The council was only an advisory body and the governor remained in complete control. The Europeans generally sided with the Fijians against any demands for equality from the Indians—typical colonial divide and rule.

During WW I an indigenous resistance movement to this colonial exploitation emerged in the form of the Viti Kabani, or Fiji Company, led by Apolosi Ranawai, a commoner from western Viti Levu. The company began as a reaction to profiteering by Fijian chiefs and white traders who bought and sold village products, but it soon moved beyond economic matters to question the whole eastern-dominated chiefly system, which allowed the British to rule so easily. The chiefs reacted by having the movement branded seditious and Apolosi exiled.

Fijians were outstanding combat troops on the Allied side in the Solomon Islands campaign during WW II, and again in 1952-56 suppressing Malaya's national liberation struggle. So skilled were the Fijians at jungle warfare against the Japanese that it was never appropriate to list a Fijian as "missing in action"—the phrase used was "not yet arrived." Until 1952, Suva, the present Fijian capital, was headquarters for the entire British Imperial Administration in the South Pacific.

In 1963 the Legislative Council was expanded but still divided along racial lines; women and indigenous Fijians got the vote for the first time. Wishing to be rid of the British, whom they blamed for their second-class position, the Indians pushed for independence, but the Fijians had come to view the British as protectors and were somewhat reluctant. After much discussion, a constitution was finally adopted in 1970. Some legislature members were to be elected from a common roll (voting by all races), as the Indians desired, while other seats remained ethnic (voting in racial constituencies) to protect the Fijians. On 10 October 1970 Fiji became a fully independent nation and the first Fijian governor-general was appointed in 1973—none other than Ratu Sir George Cakobau, great-grandson of the chief who had ceded Fiji to Queen Victoria 99 years previously.

SINCE INDEPENDENCE

Political Development

During the 1940s Ratu Sir Lala Sukuna, paramount chief of Lau, played a key role in the creation of a separate administration for indigenous Fijians, with native land (83% of Fiji) under its jurisdiction. In 1954 he formed the Fijian Association to support the British governor against Indian demands for equal representation. In 1960 the National Federation Party (NFP) was formed to represent Indian cane farmers.

In 1966 the Alliance Party, a coalition of the Fijian Association, the General Electors' Association (representing Europeans, part-Fijians, and Chinese), and the Fiji Indian Alliance (a minority Indian group), won the legislative assembly elections. In 1970 Alliance Party leader Ratu Sir Kamisese Mara led Fiji into independence and in 1972 his party won Fiji's first post-independence elections. Ratu Mara served as prime minister almost continuously until the 1987 elections.

In 1975 Mr. Sakeasi Butadroka, a member of parliament previously expelled from the Al-

liance Party, presented a motion calling for all Indians to be repatriated to India at British expense. This was rejected but during the April 1977 elections Butadroka's Fijian Nationalist Party took enough votes away from the Alliance to allow the predominantly Indian NFP to obtain a majority in parliament. After a few days' hesitation, the governor-general reappointed Ratu Mara as prime minister, but his minority Alliance government was soon defeated. Meanwhile, Butadroka had been arrested for making racially inflammatory statements in violation of the Public Order Act, and in new elections in September 1977 the Alliance recovered its majority, due in part to a split of the NFP into Hindu and Muslim factions.

The formation of the Fiji Labor Party (FLP), headed by Dr. Timoci Bavadra, in July 1985 dramatically altered the political landscape. Fiji's previously nonpolitical trade unions had finally come behind a party that campaigned on bread-and-butter issues rather than race. Late in 1986 Labor and the NFP formed a coalition with the aim of defeating the Alliance in the next election. Dr. Bavadra, a former director of Primary and Preventive Health Services and president of the Fiji Public Service Association, was chosen as Coalition leader. In the 12 April 1987 elections the Coalition won 28 of 52 House of Representatives seats; 19 of the 28 elected Coalition members were Indians. What swung the election away from Alliance was not a change in Indian voting patterns but support for Labor from urban Fijians and part-Fijians, which cost Alliance four previously "safe" seats around Suva.

The Coalition had a broad base of public support, and all cabinet positions of vital Fijian interest (Lands, Fijian Affairs, Labor and Immigration, Education, Agriculture and Rural Development) went to indigenous Fijian legislators, though none of them was a traditional chief.

Coalition's progressive policies marked quite a switch from the conservatism of the Alliance—a new generation of political leadership dedicated to tackling the day-to-day problems of people of all races rather than perpetuating the privileges of the old chiefly oligarchy. Medical care was expanded, an Institute for Fijian Language and Culture was created, and Fijians were given greater access to Fiji Development Bank loans, which had previously been going mostly to foreign corporations.

The new government also announced that nuclear warships would be banned from a nonaligned Fiji. Foreign Minister Krishna Datt said he would join Vanuatu and New Zealand in pressing for a nuclear-free Pacific at the 24 May 1987 meeting of the South Pacific Forum. Alleged corruption in the previous administration was also to be investigated. Ratu Mara himself had allegedly accumulated a personal fortune of $4-6 million on his annual salary of $100,000. Given time the Coalition might have required the high chiefs to share the rental monies they received for leasing lands to Indians more fairly with ordinary Fijians. Most significant of all, the Coalition would have transformed Fiji from a plural society where only indigenous Melanesian Fijians were called Fijians into a truly multiracial society where all citizens would be Fijians.

The First Coup
After the election the extremist Fiji-for-Fijians Taukei (landowners) movement launched a destabilization campaign by throwing barricades across highways, organizing protest rallies and marches, and carrying out firebombings. On 24 April 1987 Senator Inoke Tabua and former Alliance cabinet minister Apisai Tora organized a march of 5,000 Fijians through Suva to protest "Indian domination" of the new government. Mr. Tora told a preparatory meeting for the demonstration that Fijians must "act now" to avoid ending up as "deprived as Australia's aborigines." (In fact, under the 1970 constitution the Coalition government would have had no way of changing Fiji's land laws without indigenous Fijian consent.) During the following weeks five gasoline bombs were thrown against government offices, though no one was injured. On 13 May 1987 Alliance Senator Jona Qio was arrested for arson.

At 1000 on Thursday 14 May 1987 Lt. Col. Sitiveni Rabuka (pronounced Rambuka), an ambitious officer whose career was stalled at number three in the Fiji army, and 10 heavily armed soldiers dressed in fatigues, their faces covered by gas masks, entered the House of Representatives in Suva. Rabuka ordered Dr. Bavadra and the Coalition members to follow a soldier out of the building, and when Dr. Bavadra hesitated the soldiers raised their guns. The legislators were loaded into army trucks and taken to Royal Fiji Military Forces headquarters. There was no bloodshed, though Rabuka later confirmed that his troops would have opened fire had there been any resistance. At a press conference five hours after the coup, Rabuka claimed he had acted to prevent violence and had no political ambitions of his own.

Most Pacific governments promptly denounced the region's first military coup. Governor-General Ratu Sir Penaia Ganilau attempted to reverse the situation by declaring a state of emergency and ordering the mutineers to return to their barracks. They refused to obey. The next day the *Fiji Sun* ran a black-bordered editorial that declared, "Democracy died in Fiji yesterday. What right has a third-ranking officer to attack the sacred institutions of Parliament? What right has he to presume he knows best how this country shall be governed? The answer is none." Soon after, Rabuka's troops descended on both daily papers and ordered publication suspended. Journalists were evicted from the buildings.

Later that day Rabuka named a 15-member Council of Ministers, chaired by himself, to govern Fiji, with former Alliance prime minister Ratu Mara as foreign minister. Significantly, Rabuka was the only military officer on the council; most of the others were members of Ratu Mara's defeated administration. Rabuka claimed he had acted to "safeguard the Fijian land issue and the Fijian way of life."

On 19 May Dr. Bavadra and the other kidnapped members of his government were released after the governor-general announced a deal negotiated with Rabuka to avoid the possibility of foreign intervention. Rabuka's Council of Ministers was replaced by a 19-member caretaker Advisory Council appointed by the Great Council of Chiefs, which would govern until new elections could take place. The council would be headed by Ratu Ganilau, with Rabuka in charge of Home Affairs and the security forces. Only two seats were offered to Dr. Bavadra's government and they were refused.

The Sunday before the coup Ratu Mara was seen playing golf with Rabuka at Pacific Harbor. At the time of the coup he was at the Fijian Hotel chairing a meeting of the Pacific Democratic Union, a U.S.-sponsored grouping of ultraright politicians from Australia, New Zealand, and elsewhere. Though Ratu Mara expressed "shock" at the coup, he accepted a position on Rabuka's Council of Ministers the next day, prompting New Zealand Prime Minister David Lange to accuse him of treachery under Fiji's constitution by acquiescing to military rule. Lange said Ratu Mara had pledged allegiance to the Queen but had brought about a rebellion in one of her countries. Ratu Ganilau was also strongly criticized for legitimizing a traitor by accepting Rabuka on his Advisory Council.

Behind the Coup

In 1982 American interest in the South Pacific picked up after the U.S. ambassador to Fiji, William Bodde, Jr., told a luncheon audience at the Kahala Hilton in Hawaii that the creation of a South Pacific nuclear-free zone would be "the most potentially disruptive development to U.S. relations with the region . . . I am convinced that the United States must do everything possible to counter this movement. It will not be an easy task, but it is one that we cannot afford to neglect." In 1983 Bodde's diplomacy resulted in the lifting of a ban on visits to Fiji by U.S. nuclear warships, and Fiji was soon rewarded by becoming the first South Pacific country to receive direct American aid. Substantial grants to the Fiji army for "weapons standardization" soon followed, and from 1984 to 1986 U.S. aid to Fiji tripled.

Immediately after the coup, rumors circulated throughout the South Pacific that the U.S. government was involved. On 16 June 1987 at a press conference at the National Press Club in Washington, D.C., Dr. Bavadra publicly accused the director of the South Pacific regional office of the U.S. Agency for International Development of channeling US$200,000 to right-winger Apisai Tora of the Taukei movement for destabilization purposes, something they both denied.

From 29 April to 1 May 1987 Gen. Vernon A. Walters, U.S. ambassador to the United Nations and a former CIA deputy director, visited Fiji. At a long meeting with Foreign Minister Datt, Walters tried to persuade the new government to give up its antinuclear stance. Walters told the Fiji press that the U.S. "has a duty to protect its South Pacific interests." Walters is believed to have been involved in previous coups in Iran (1953) and Brazil (1964), and during his stay in Fiji he also met with Rabuka and U.S. AID officials. During his 10-country Pacific trip Walters spread a bogus scare about Libyan subversion in the region, diverting attention from what was about to happen in Fiji.

On 22 October 1987 the U.S. Information Service in New Zealand revealed that the amphibious assault ship USS *Belleau Wood* was just west of Fiji immediately after the coup, supported by three C-130 Hercules transport planes, which staged through Nandi Airport 20-22 June. The same release mentioned four other C-130s at Nandi that month to support the gigantic hospital ship USNS *Mercy*, which was at Suva 23-27 June—an unprecedented level of U.S. military activity. By chance or design the U.S. would have been ready to intervene militarily within hours had anything gone wrong. Yet American involvement in the coup has never been conclusively proven and the full story may never be told. The events caught the Australian and New Zealand intelligence services totally by surprise, indicating that few knew of Rabuka's plans in advance.

Until the coup the most important mission of the Royal Fiji Defense Force was service in South Lebanon and the Sinai with peacekeeping operations. Half of the 2,600-member Fiji army was on rotating duty there, the Sinai force financed by the U.S., the troops in Lebanon by the United Nations. During WW II Fiji Indians refused to join the army unless they received the same pay as European recruits; indigenous Fijians had no such reservations and the force has been 95% Fijian ever since. Service in the strife-torn Middle East gave the Fiji military a unique preparation for its destabilizing role in Fiji itself.

The mass media presented the coup in simplistic terms as a racial conflict between Indians and Fijians, though commentators with a deeper knowledge of the nature of power in Fiji saw it quite differently. Anthony D. van Fossen of Griffith University, Queensland, Australia, summed it up this way in the *Bulletin of Concerned Asian Scholars* (Vol. 19, No. 4, 1987):

Although the first coup has been most often seen in terms of ethnic tensions between indigenous Fijians and Fijian Indians, it may be more accurately seen as the result of tensions between aristocratic indigenous Fijians and their commoner allies defending feudalism, on the one hand, and the cause of social democracy, small-scale capitalism, and multi-ethnic nationalism represented by middle-class indigenous Fijian commoners and Hindus on the other.

In their October 1987 issue, *Pacific Islands Monthly* published this comment by noted author Brij V. Lal of the Australian National University:

More than anything else, the coup was about power. The emergence in an incipient form of a class-minded multi-racial politics, symbolized by the Labor Party and made possible by the support of many urban Fijians, posed a grave threat to the politics of race and racial compartmentalization preached by the Alliance and thus had to be nipped in the bud. The ascent of Dr. Bavadra, a chief from the long-neglected western Viti Levu, to the highest office in the land posed an unprecedented challenge to the traditional dominance of eastern chiefs, especially from Lau and Thakaundrove.

The Second Coup

In July and August 1987 a committee set up by Governor-General Ganilau studied proposals for constitutional reform, and on 4 September talks began at Government House in Suva between Alliance and Coalition leaders under the chairmanship of Ratu Ganilau. With no hope of a consensus on a revised constitution the talks were aimed at preparing for new elections.

Then, on Friday, 26 September 1987, Rabuka struck again, just hours before the governor-general was to announce a Government of National Unity to rule Fiji until new elections could be held. The plan, arduously developed over four months and finally approved by veteran political leaders on all sides, would probably have resulted in Rabuka being sacked. Rabuka quickly threw out the 1970 constitution and pronounced himself "head of state." Some 300 prominent community leaders were arrested and Ratu Ganilau was confined to Government House. Newspapers were shut down, trade unions repressed, the judiciary suspended, the public service purged, the activities of political opponents restricted, a curfew imposed, and the first cases of torture reported.

At midnight on 7 October 1987 Rabuka declared Fiji a republic. Rabuka's new Council of Ministers included Taukei extremists Apisai Tora and Filipe Bole, Fijian Nationalist Party leader Sakeasi Butadroka, and other marginal figures. Rabuka appeared to have backing in the Great Council of Chiefs, which wanted a return to the style of customary rule threatened by the Indian presence and Western democracy. Regime ideologists trumpeted traditional culture and religious fundamentalism to justify their actions. Rabuka said he wanted Christianity adopted as Fiji's official religion and henceforth all trading (except at tourist hotels), sports, and public transport would be banned on Sunday. Rabuka even called for the conversion of Hindu and Muslim Indians to Christianity.

On 16 October Ratu Ganilau resigned as governor-general and two days later Fiji was expelled from the British Commonwealth (perhaps for good, as Commonwealth rules require a unanimous vote from other members for readmission). On 6 November Rabuka allowed the *Fiji Times* to resume publication after it pledged self-censorship, but the more independent *Fiji Sun* has never appeared again. Nobody accused the U.S. of having anything to do with Rabuka's second coup, and even Ratu Mara seemed annoyed that Rabuka had destroyed an opportunity to salvage the reputations of himself and Ratu Ganilau. Clearly Rabuka had become his own man.

The Republic of Fiji

Realizing that Taukei/military rule was a recipe for disaster, on 5 December 1987 Rabuka appointed Ratu Ganilau president and Ratu Mara prime minister of his new republic. The 21-member cabinet included 10 members of Rabuka's military regime, four of them army officers. Rabuka himself (now a self-styled brigadier) was once again Minister of Home Affairs. This interim government set itself a deadline of two years to frame a new constitution and return Fiji to freely elected representative government. By mid-1988 the army had been expanded into a highly disciplined 6,000-member force loyal to Brigadier Rabuka, who left no doubt he would intervene a third time if his agenda was not followed. The Great Council of Chiefs was to decide on Fiji's republican constitution.

The coups transformed the Fijian economy. In 1987 Fiji experienced 11% negative growth in the gross domestic product. To prevent a massive flight of capital the Fiji dollar was devalued 17.75% on 30 June 1987 and 15.25% on 7 October, and inflation, which had been under two percent before the coups, was up to 11.9% by the end of 1988. At the same time the public service (half the work force) had to accept a 25% wage cut as government spending was slashed. Food prices skyrocketed, causing serious problems for many families. At the end of 1987 the per capita average income was 11% *below* what it had been in 1980. Thousands of Indian professionals—accountants, administrators, dentists, doctors, lawyers, nurses, teachers—left for Australia, Canada, New Zealand, and the United States. In 1987 there were 18,359 emigrants, in 1988 another 10,360, crippling losses for a country with a total population of under 750,000. From January 1990 to June 1993 a further 16,118 Indians left.

On the other hand, the devaluations and wage-cutting measures, combined with the creation of a tax-free exporting sector and the encouragement of foreign investment, brought about a full economic recovery by 1990. At the expense of democracy, social justice, and racial harmony, Fiji embarked on the IMF/World Bank-style structural readjustment program which continues today. The imposition of a 10% value added tax (VAT) in 1992 has shifted the burden of taxation from rich to poor, standard IMF dogma. In effect, Rabuka and the old oligarchs have pushed Fiji squarely back into the Third World, and even the Fiji Visitors Bureau has had to scrap their former marketing slogan, "The Way the World Should Be."

Internal Security

On 31 May 1988 Australian customs officials at Sydney discovered a mysterious 12-metric tonne arms shipment bound for Lautoka, Fiji. In a container that had arrived from North Yemen were Czech-made weapons including AK-47 rifles, rocket launchers, antitank mines, and explosives. Evidently a second container had slipped into Fiji in April 1988, and by 8 June raids by security forces in western Fiji had netted over 100 rifles and other weapons, with 20 arrests.

For whom the arms were actually intended has never been precisely established, and the Fiji police were unable to establish any link to the Coalition. Right from the start Dr. Bavadra had consistently advocated nonviolence. Australian officials implicated Mohammed Rafiq Kahan, an ex-resident of Fiji with a long criminal background, as the one responsible for the shipment. Kahan, who fled Australia when the arms were uncovered, was apprehended in London, England. In March 1989 a London court considering his extradition to Fiji was told that the defendant had mentioned Alliance supporter Motibhai Patel, owner of the duty-free emporium at Nandi Airport, and Ratu Mara himself in connection with the arms shipment. Kahan was released on grounds that the case was political.

Kahan had been photographed wearing a military uniform in the Queen Elizabeth Barracks, Suva, just two months before the arms were discovered, and on the same visit to Fiji Kahan developed contacts with key Alliance ministers Apisai Tora, Taniela Veitata, and Ahmed Ali. The shipments appeared to have been either in preparation for a countercoup against Rabuka by disgruntled Alliance elements, or the pretext for a crackdown on the political opposition within Fiji by the security forces.

On 17 June 1988 the regime issued an 86-section Internal Security Decree giving the police and military unlimited powers to arrest and hold anyone up to two years without charge, to impose curfews, to shoot to kill within declared security areas, to search vehicles or premises without a warrant, to seize land and buildings, and to cancel passports. No inquests would be held into any killings under decree powers, and the penalty for possession of firearms or explosives was life imprisonment. The decree also made it illegal to publish anything "prejudicial to the national interest and security of Fiji." The decree was modeled on similar laws in Malaysia and Singapore, which have led to widespread human-rights violations. On 17 November 1988 the decree was suspended but not repealed.

On 22 June 1988 10 people were arrested in Suva, including the secretary of the Fiji Law Society, who had merely called a meeting to discuss the new security decree, and two lawyers who had defended persons charged with arms offenses. Despite a one-month amnesty to "surrender firearms" declared by Rabuka on 23 June, the arrests continued, with families fearing their relatives had "disappeared." Most were held incommunicado about a week, then released. Many reported being beaten in confinement.

The most notorious of the 22 June arrests was that of Som Prakash, a lecturer in English at the University of the South Pacific who wrote a critical review of Rabuka's biography. The review castigated the brigadier's "Messiah syndrome" and his intolerance of races and religions other than his own, and questioned Rabuka's claim that he had acted to prevent "bloodshed," suggesting that political considerations were paramount. Mr. Prakash was held in solitary confinement without legal advice or access to his family until 6 July, when he was released on the condition that he not speak to the news media. It was reported he had been beaten during his detention. Amnesty International called Mr. Prakash a "prisoner of conscience."

Meanwhile France stepped in with $8 million in military aid to Fiji, including 53 Renault vehicles for the army and a helicopter for Rabuka (the chopper was subsequently destroyed in an August 1994 crash). France hoped that by backing the military regime in Fiji it could divide the opponents of French nuclear testing in the South Pacific. As the U.S., Australia, New Zealand, and Britain maintained their freeze on military aid to Fiji, the regime turned to undemocratic governments in South Korea, Taiwan, and mainland China for military training and supplies.

Interim Government

In May 1989 the interim government eased Sunday restrictions on work, trading, and sports. This drew loud protests from Rev. Manasa Lasaro, fundamentalist general secretary of the Methodist Church of Fiji, who organized Sunday roadblocks in Lambasa, leading to the arrest and conviction of himself and 56 others for unlawful obstruction. On August 9 Rabuka flew to Lambasa by helicopter and arranged the release of Reverend Lasaro and the others on his own authority. On Sunday 15 October 1989 members of a Methodist youth group carried out firebombings against Hindu and Sikh temples and a Muslim mosque at Lautoka.

In November 1989 Dr. Bavadra died of spinal cancer at age 55, and 60,000 people attended his funeral at Viseisei, the largest in Fijian history. Foreign journalists were prevented from covering the funeral. The nominal head of the unelected interim government, Ratu Mara, considered Rabuka an unpredictable upstart and insisted that he choose between politics or military service. Thus in late 1989, the general and two army colonels were dropped from the cabinet, though Rabuka kept his post as army commander.

In May 1990 Fiji expelled the entire staff of the Indian Embassy in Suva in preparation for the launching of a new constitution approved by the Great Council of Chiefs in June and promulgated by President Ganilau on 25 July 1990. This constitution (still in force today) gives the chiefs the right to appoint the president and 24 of the 34 members of the Senate. In addition, one senator is appointed by the Rotuman Council and nine senators are appointed by the president to represent the other communities. The president has executive authority and appoints the prime minister from among the ethnic Fijian members of the House of Representatives. Cabinet ministers may be from either house.

Under the constitution the 70-member House of Representatives is elected directly, with voting racially segregated. Ethnic Fijians are granted 37 seats, 32 from 14 provincial constituencies and only five from five urban constituencies, despite the fact that 33% of indigenous Fijians live in towns and cities. The provincial Fijian constituencies are gerrymandered to ensure eastern dominance. For example, Mba with an ethnic Fijian population of 55,000 gets three Fijian seats, the same number as Lau with only 14,000 inhabitants. Fiji Indians (nearly half the population) get 27 seats based on 27 constituencies, while there is one Rotuman seat and five for other races (Chinese, part-Fijians, Europeans, etc.).

The constitution not only guarantees ethnic Fijians a majority in both houses, but explicitly reserves for them the posts of president, prime minister, and army chief. Christianity is the official religion and Rabuka's troops are granted amnesty for any crimes committed during the 1987 coups. Fijian customary laws have become the law of the land, and all decisions of the Native Lands Commission are final, with no further recourse to the courts. Continued military interference in civilian government is covered by the vague identification of the army as the final arbiter in determining "the security, defense, and well-being of Fiji and its peoples."

The Coalition promptly rejected this constitution as undemocratic and racist, and threatened to boycott elections held under it unless a referendum took place. They claimed the rigged voting system used race as a device to divide Fijians and perpetuate the power of the eastern elite. Urban and western Fijians, the very groups that challenged the status quo by voting Labor in 1987, are discriminated against, and Indians are relegated to the fringes of political life. Complicated registration requirements also deprive many rural Fijian commoners of the vote.

On 18 October 1990 a copy of the new constitution was burned during a nonviolent protest by a small group of academics and students. Six days later one of those involved, Dr. Anirudh Singh, a lecturer in physics at the University of the South Pacific, was abducted by five soldiers and taken to Tholo-i-Suva where he was tortured with lit cigarettes and had his hands broken by an iron bar during "interrogation." Later he was released. On 29 October three journalists of the *Daily Post* were arrested for publishing a story suggesting that there might be a second constitution burning, and on 31 October Dr. Singh and six other alleged constitution burners were arrested and charged with sedition. After a

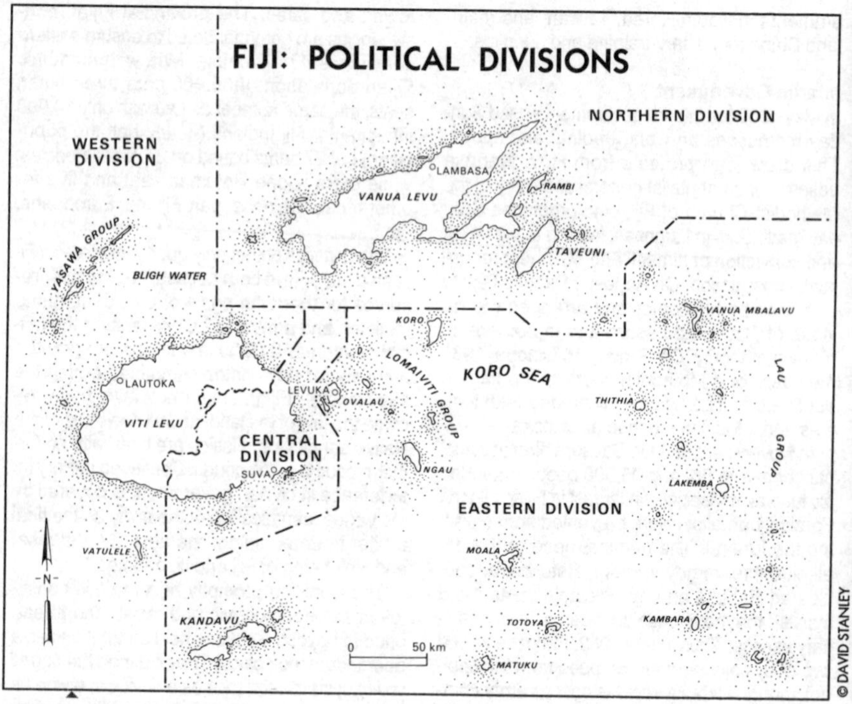

FIJI: POLITICAL DIVISIONS

NORTHERN DIVISION

WESTERN
DIVISION

LAMBASA

VANUA LEVU

RAMBI

YASAWA GROUP

BLIGH WATER

TAVEUNI

VANUA MBALAVU

KORO

LOMAIVITI GROUP

KORO SEA

LAU
GROUP

LAUTOKA

LEVUKA

OVALAU

THITHIA

VITI LEVU

CENTRAL
DIVISION

SUVA

NGAU

EASTERN DIVISION

LAKEMBA

N

VATULELE

MOALA

KANDAVU

0   50 km

TOTOYA

KAMBARA

MATUKU

© DAVID STANLEY

public outcry the soldiers who had tortured Dr. Singh were turned over to police by the army, given a brief trial, fined F$340 each, and set free. Incredibly, just a few months later, the Fiji Army picked one of the convicted torturers, Capt. Sotia Ponijiase, to head Fiji's contingent in a United Nations observer team sent to Kuwait. When the story came to light, Captain Ponijiase was sent packing back to Fiji by the U.N.

Not satisfied with control of the Senate, in early 1991 the Great Council of Chiefs decided to project their power into the lower house through the formation of the Songgosonggo ni Vakavulewa ni Taukei (SVT), meaning "Group of Decision Makers for the Indigenous People" but commonly called the Fijian Political Party. To avoid the embarrassment of a defeat for the chiefs and to allow more time for voter registration, the interim government postponed the elections several times. Meanwhile Fiji's multiethnic unions continued to rebuild their strength

by organizing garment workers and leading strikes in the mining and sugar industries.

In June 1991 Major-General Rabuka rejected an offer from Ratu Mara to join the cabinet as Minister of Home Affairs and co-deputy prime minister, since it would have meant giving up his military power base. Instead Rabuka attempted to widen his political appeal by making public statements in support of striking gold miners and cane farmers, and even threatening a third coup. By now Rabuka's ambition to become prime minister was obvious, and his new role as a populist rabble-rouser seemed designed to outflank both the Labor Party and the chiefs (Rabuka himself is a commoner). President Ganilau (Rabuka's paramount chief) quickly applied pressure, and in July the volatile general reversed himself and accepted the cabinet posts he had so recently refused. As a condition for reentering the government, Rabuka was forced to resign as army commander and the president's son, Major-Gen. Epeli Ganilau, was appointed his successor. With Rabuka out of the army everyone breathed a little easier, and the chiefs decided to co-opt a potential troublemaker by electing Rabuka president of the SVT.

Recent Elections

In July 1991 the NFP decided at its annual meeting that it would field candidates for the 27 Indian seats after all, to avoid their being won by "irresponsible persons." After a bitter internal debate the Fiji Labor Party (FLP), now led by Mahendra Chaudhry, also decided not to boycott the elections.

The long-awaited parliamentary elections took place in late May 1992 and the SVT captured 30 of the 37 indigenous Fijian seats, with another five going to Sakeasi Butadroka's Fijian Nationalist United Front (FNUF) and two to independents. The 27 Indian seats were split between the NFP with 14 and the FLP with 13. The five other races' seats went to the General Voters Party (GVP).

Just prior to the election, Ratu Mara (who had retired from party politics) was named vice-president of Fiji by the Great Council of Chiefs. An intense power struggle developed in the SVT between Ratu Mara's chosen successor, former finance minister Josevata Kamikamica, and ex-general Rabuka. Since the party lacked a clear majority in the 70-seat house, coalition partners had to be sought, and after much repositioning the pro-big business camp lined up behind Kamikamica, with NFP and GVP support. Rabuka had the backing of the FNUF, but most SVT members opposed a coalition with Butadroka's racial extremists, and in a remarkable turn of events populist Rabuka gained the support of the FLP by offering concessions to the trade unions and a promise to review the constitution and land leases. Thus Sitiveni Rabuka became prime minister thanks to the very party he had ousted from power at gunpoint exactly five years before!

The SVP formed a coalition with the GVP, and to consolidate his position, Rabuka called for a "government of national unity," but this concept failed to win approval by the powerful Great Council of Chiefs (which now holds a virtual power of veto on all matters of national interest). In November 1993 the Rabuka government was defeated in a parliamentary vote of no confidence over the budget, leading to fresh elections in February 1994. In these, Rabuka's SVT increased its representation to 31 seats, and both Kamikamica and Butadroka lost their parliamentary seats. Many Indians had felt betrayed by FLP backing of Rabuka's prime ministership in 1992, and FLP representation dropped to seven seats compared to 20 for the FLP.

Ratu Ganilau died of leukemia in December 1993, and Ratu Mara was sworn in as president in January. Meanwhile, Rabuka has tried to cultivate a pragmatic image to facilitate his international acceptance in the South Pacific. Yet the legacy of the coups continues to hang over Fiji. In early 1995 the government attempted to repeal the controversial Sunday Observance Decree imposed in 1988, but passage of the bill was blocked in the Senate after 12,000 Methodists marched through Suva in protest. Indian resentment over their second-class position continues and a lot is hanging on the constitutional review presently underway to restore business and social confidence.

GOVERNMENT

Aside from the national government described above, there's a well-developed system of local government. On the Fijian side, the basic unit is the village (koro) represented by a village herald (turanga-ni-koro) chosen by consensus. The villages are grouped into districts (tikina), the districts into 14 provinces (yasana), the provinces into four administrative divisions: central, eastern, northern, and western. The 14 provinces with the locations of their offices in parentheses are Kandavu (Vunisea), Lau (Lakemba), Lomaiviti (Levuka), Mathuata (Lambasa), Mba (Lautoka), Mbua (Nambouwalu), Naitasiri (Vunindawa), Namosi (Navua), Nandronga (Singatoka), Ra (Nanukuloa), Rewa (Nausori), Serua (Navua), Tailevu (Nausori), and Thakaundrove (Savusavu). The executive head of a provincial council is known as a roko tui, and each division except Eastern is headed by a commissioner assisted by a number of district officers. The Micronesians of Rambi govern themselves through a council of their own. City and town councils also function.

MINISTRY OF INFORMATION, GOVERNMENT OF FIJI

Taro, which grows marvelously well in the rich soils of Fiji's bush gardens, is one of the staples of the Pacific and ensures a steady supply of nourishing food for the villagers.

ECONOMY

Economic Development

Fiji has a diversified economy based on tourism, sugar production, garment manufacturing, gold mining, timber, commercial fishing, and coconut products. From WW II until 1987 a series of five-year plans guided public investment, resulting in the excellent modern infrastructure and advanced social services Fiji enjoys today. Devaluation of Fiji's currency immediately after the 1987 coups increased the country's competitiveness by giving exporters more Fiji dollars for their products. This lowered the real incomes of ordinary Fijians, but also led to a mini-economic boom which is now beginning to level out.

While eastern Viti Levu and the Lau Group dominate the country politically, western Viti Levu is Fiji's economic powerhouse, with sugar, tourism, timber, and gold mining all concentrated there. Almost all of Fiji's sugar is produced by small independent Indian farmers on contract to the government-owned Fiji Sugar Corporation, which took over from the Australian-owned Colonial Sugar Refining Company in 1973. Some 23,000 farmers cultivate cane on holdings averaging 4.5 hectares leased from indigenous Fijians. The corporation owns 644 km of 0.610-meter narrow-gauge railway, which it uses to carry the cane to the mills at Lautoka, Mba, Rakiraki, and Lambasa. Nearly half a million metric tonnes of sugar are exported annually to Britain, Malaysia, Japan, and other countries, providing employment for 40,000 people. A distillery at Lautoka produces rum and other liquors from the by-products of sugar. Over the next few years the viability of Fiji's sugar industry may be badly shaken as European Union import quotas are phased out (under the Lomé Convention, 163,000 metric tonnes of Fijian sugar are sold to the E.U. each year at fixed prices far above world market levels). If lease payments were concurrently increased, thousands of Fiji's cane growers would face bankruptcy.

Timber is increasingly important as tens of thousands of hectares planted in western Viti Levu and Vanua Levu by the Fiji Pine Commission and private landowners in the late 1970s reach maturity. Each year Fiji exports about F$26 million in sawed lumber and wood chips (the export of raw logs was banned in 1987). Yet Fiji's native forests are poorly protected from the greed of foreign logging companies and shortsighted local landowners, and each year large tracts of pristine rainforest are lost. Now that all of the lowland forests have been cleared, attention is turning to the highlands. The pine project has had the corollary benefit of reducing pressure on the natural forests to supply Fiji's timber needs.

Commercial fishing is booming, with a major tuna cannery at Levuka supplied in part by Fiji's own fleet of 17 longline vessels. The 15,000 metric tonnes of canned tuna produced each year comprise Fiji's fourth-largest export, shipped mostly to Britain and Canada (see "Ovalau Island" in the Lomaiviti Group chapter for more information). In addition, chilled yellowfin tuna is air freighted to Hawaii and Japan to serve the *sashimi* (raw fish) market.

Mining activity centers on gold at Vatukoula on northern Viti Levu, but extensive low-grade copper deposits exist at Namosi, 30 km northwest of Suva. In mid-1995 the Canadian company, Placer Pacific, announced it was putting development of the site on hold after a dispute with the Fiji government over taxation. If the US$1-billion Namosi mine ever goes ahead it will be one of the largest in the world, totally altering Fiji's economy and the country with it. Fiji now grows almost half its own rice needs and is trying to become self-sufficient. Much of the rice is grown around Nausori and Navua. Most of Fiji's copra is produced in Lau, Lomaiviti, Taveuni, and Vanua Levu, half by European or part-Fijian planters and the rest by indigenous Fijian villagers.

Yet, in spite of all this potential, unemployment is a major social problem as four times more young people leave school than there are jobs to take them. To stimulate industry, firms that export 95% of their production are granted 13-year tax holidays, the duty-free import of materials, and freedom to repatriate capital and profits. The garment industry is growing fast and already employs 11,000, with female workers earning an average of F$30 a week. At peak periods the factories operate three shifts, seven days a week. Women working in the industry have complained of being subjected to body searches and sexual harassment, with those who protest or organize collective action being fired and blacklisted. The clothing produced by the 200 foreign-owned and 12 locally owned companies in the sector is exported mostly to Australia and New Zealand, where partial duty- and quota-free entry is allowed under the South Pacific Regional Trade and Economic Cooperation Agreement (SPARTECA) for products with at least 50% local content, and many manufac-

HOW A SUGAR MILL WORKS

The sugarcane is fed through a shredder toward a row of huge rollers that squeeze out the juice. The crushed fiber (bagasse) is burned to fuel the mill or is processed into paper. Lime is then added to the juice and the mixture is heated. Impurities settle in the clarifier and mill mud is filtered out to be used as fertilizer. The clear juice goes through a series of evaporators, in which it is boiled into steam under partial vacuum to remove water and create a syrup. The syrup is boiled again under greater pressure in a vacuum pan, and raw sugar crystals form. The mix then enters a centrifuge, which spins off the remaining syrup (molasses—used for distilling or cattle feed). The moist crystals are sent on to a rotating drum, where they are tumble-dried using hot air. Raw sugar comes out in the end.

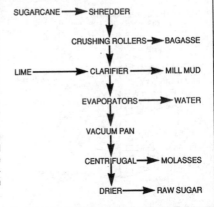

turers in those countries have moved their factories to Fiji to take advantage of the low labor costs. SPARTECA rules prevent local garment manufacturers from importing quality fabrics from outside the region, limiting them to the bottom end of the market.

Food processors and furniture and toy makers are also prominent in the tax-free exporting sector. Until recently it was believed that manufacturing would eventually overtake both sugar and tourism as the main source of income for the country, but current worldwide trade liberalization trends are cutting into Fiji's competitiveness. SPARTECA's local-content rule discourages local companies from cutting costs by introducing labor-saving technology, condemning them to obsolescence in the long term.

Aside from this cash economy, subsistence agriculture makes an important contribution to the life of indigenous Fijians in rural areas. About 40% of the work force has paid employment; the remainder is involved in subsistence agriculture, with manioc, taro, yams, sweet potato, and corn the principal subsistence crops. Kava gardens produce cash income.

Trade and Aid
Fiji is an important regional trading center. Although Fiji imports 50% more than it exports,

some of the imbalance is resold to tourists who pay in foreign exchange. In the Pacific islands, Fiji's trade deficit is exceeded only by that of the French colonies and it has grown much larger in recent years due to sharply increased imports of machinery and textiles by tax-free zone industry. Raw sugar accounts for nearly half of the nation's visible export earnings, followed by garments, unrefined gold, canned fish, wood chips, molasses, sawed timber, and ginger, in that order. Huge trade imbalances exist with Australia, Japan, and New Zealand.

Mineral fuels used to eat up much of Fiji's import budget, but this declined as the Monasavu Hydroelectric Project and other self-sufficiency measures came on-line a decade ago. Petroleum products, manufactured goods, food, textiles, and motor vehicles account for most of the import bill.

Fiji is the least dependent Pacific nation (excluding Nauru). In 1989 overseas aid totaled only A$75 per capita (as compared to A$1875 per capita in Tahiti-Polynesia); it accounts for just 11% of government expenditures. Development aid is well diversified among over a dozen donors; the largest amounts come from Australia, Japan, New Zealand, France, the Asian Development Bank, the European Union, Germany, and the United Kingdom, in that order,

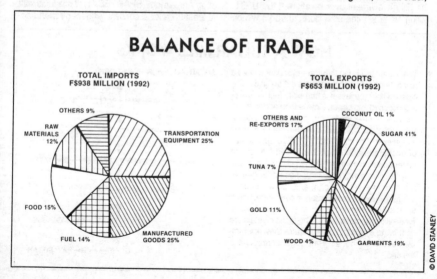

BALANCE OF TRADE

TOTAL IMPORTS F$938 MILLION (1992)

OTHERS 9%
RAW MATERIALS 12%
TRANSPORTATION EQUIPMENT 25%
FOOD 15%
FUEL 14%
MANUFACTURED GOODS 25%

TOTAL EXPORTS F$653 MILLION (1992)

OTHERS AND RE-EXPORTS 17%
COCONUT OIL 1%
SUGAR 41%
TUNA 7%
GOLD 11%
WOOD 4%
GARMENTS 19%

© DAVID STANLEY

with Australia alone contributing nearly half. North American aid to Fiji is negligible. Increasingly Fiji is looking to Asian countries such as Japan, China, Taiwan, South Korea, and Singapore for development assistance. Fiji is fortunate in its low level of foreign indebtedness, a result of cautious fiscal management during the 1980s, and government financing has largely come from domestic sources. In June 1995, however, Fiji's financial standing was severely shaken when it was announced that the National Bank of Fiji was holding F$100 million in bad debts, most of it resulting from politically motivated loans to indigenous Fijians and Rotumans. The subsequent run on deposits cost the bank another F$20 million, and the government was forced to step in to save the bank.

Law of the Sea
This treaty has changed the face of the Pacific. States traditionally exercised sovereignty over a three-mile belt of territorial sea along their shores; the high seas beyond these limits could be freely used by anyone. Then on 28 September 1945, Pres. Harry Truman declared U.S. sovereignty over the natural resources of the adjacent continental shelf. U.S. fishing boats soon became involved in an acrimonious dispute with several South American countries over their rich anchovy fishing grounds, and in 1952 Chile, Ecuador, and Peru declared a 200-nautical-mile Exclusive Economic Zone (EEZ) along their shores. In 1958 the United Nations convened a Conference on the Law of the Sea at Geneva, which accepted national control over shelves up to 200 meters deep. Agreement could not be reached on extended territorial sea limits.

National claims multiplied so much that in 1974 another U.N. conference was convened, leading to the signing of the Law of the Sea convention at Jamaica in 1982 by 159 states and other entities. This complex agreement—200 pages, nine annexes, and 320 articles—extended national control over 40% of the world's oceans. The territorial sea was increased to 12 nautical miles and the continental shelf was ambiguously defined as extending 200 nautical miles offshore. States were given full control over all resources, living or nonliving, within this belt. Fiji was the first country to ratify the convention, and by November 1994 a total of 60 countries had signed up, allowing the treaty to come into force for them.

Even before it became international law, many aspects of the Law of the Sea were accepted in practice. The EEZs mainly affect fisheries and seabed mineral exploitation; freedom of navigation within the zones is guaranteed. In 1976 the South Pacific Forum declared an EEZ for each member and decided to set up a fisheries agency soon after. The Law of the Sea increased immensely the territory of independent oceanic states, giving them real political weight for the first time. The land area of the 23 separate entities in Micronesia, Melanesia, and Polynesia (excluding Hawaii and New Zealand) total only 550,361 square km, while their EEZs total 29,878,000 square km! Fiji itself possesses only 18,272 square km of land but 1,290,000 square km of water. It's known that vast mineral deposits are scattered across this seabed, though the cost of extraction (estimated at US$1.5 billion) has prevented their exploitation to date.

Tourism
Tourism is the leading money-maker, earning over F$400 million a year—more than sugar and gold combined. In 1994 some 318,000 tourists visited Fiji—more than twice as many as visited Tahiti and 15 times as many as visited Tonga. Things appear in better perspective, however, when Fiji is compared to Hawaii, which is about the same size in surface area. Over-

packed Hawaii gets seven million tourists, 25 times as many as Fiji. Gross receipts figures from tourism are often misleading, as 58 cents on every dollar is repatriated overseas by foreign investors or used to pay for tourism-related imports. In real terms, sugar is far more profitable for Fiji. In 1994 paid employment in the hotel industry totaled 5,996 (3,556 males and 2,440 females) and an estimated 40,000 jobs in all sectors are related to tourism.

The main tourist resorts are centered along the Coral Coast of Viti Levu and in the Mamanutha Islands off Nandi/Lautoka. For years the Fiji government swore there would be no hotel development in the Yasawa and Lau groups, but several resorts now exist there. Japanese companies have investments in Fiji worth a half billion dollars, including the Sheraton and Regent hotels at Nandi. About 32% of Fiji's tourists come from Australia, 14% from New Zealand, 13% each from the U.S. and Japan, 11% from continental Europe, 6% from Britain, and 5% from Canada. The vast majority of visitors arrive in Fiji from Auckland, Sydney, Honolulu, and Los Angeles.

Most of the large resort hotels in Fiji are foreign-owned, and 80% of their purchases for food, beverages, linen, glassware, etc., are imported at concessional rates. The Fiji government has diverted large sums from its capital-improvements budget to provide infrastructure such as roads, airports, and other services to the resorts, yet the hotels can write off 55% of their capital expenditures against taxes over six-year periods. Management of the foreign-owned hotels is usually European, with Fiji Indians filling technical positions such as maintenance, cooking, accounting, etc., and indigenous Fijians working the high-profile positions such as receptionists, waiters, guides, and housekeepers.

Ecotourism

Recently "ecotourism" has become fashionable, and with increasing concern in Western countries over the damaging effects of the sun's rays, more and more people are looking for land-based activities as an alternative to lying on the beach. In Fiji the most widespread manifestation of ecotourism is the current scuba diving boom, and adventure tours by chartered yacht, ocean kayak, bicycle, or foot are increasing in number.

This presents both a danger and an opportunity. Income from visitors wishing to experience nature gives local residents and government an economic incentive to preserve the environment, although tourism can quickly degrade that environment through littering, the collection of coral and shells, and encouraging the development of roads, docks, and camps, in natural areas. Perhaps the strongest economic argument in favor of the creation of national parks and reserves in Fiji is the ability of such parks to attract visitors from industrialized countries while at the same time creating a framework for preserving nature. For in the final analysis it is government which must enact regulations that protect the environment—market forces usually do the opposite.

Too often what is called ecotourism is actually packaged consumer tourism with a green coating. A genuine ecotourism resort will be built of local materials using natural ventilation. This means no air-conditioning and only limited use of fans. The buildings should fit into the natural landscape and not restrict access to customary lands. Local fish and vegetables should be served at the expense of imported meats, and wastes minimized. The use of motorized transport should be kept to an absolute minimum. Cultural sensitivity is enhanced by local ownership, and bank loans should be avoided if at all possible, as debts create pressures to cater to ecoterrorism rather than ecotourism.

Through this handbook we've tried to encourage this type of people-oriented tourism which we feel is more directly beneficial to the islanders themselves. Whenever possible we've featured smaller, family-operated, locally owned businesses. By patronizing these you'll not only get to meet the inhabitants on a person-to-person basis, but also contribute to local development. Guesthouse tourism offers excellent employment opportunities for island women as proprietors, *and* it's exactly what most visitors want. Appropriate tourism requires little investment, there's less disruption, and full control remains with the people themselves. The luxury hotels are monotonously uniform around the world—the South Pacific's the place for something different.

THE PEOPLE

The Fijians

Fiji is a transitional zone between Polynesia and Melanesia. The Fijians bear a physical resemblance to the Melanesians, but like the Polynesians, the Fijians have hereditary chiefs, patrilineal descent, a love of elaborate ceremonies, and a fairly homogeneous language and culture. Fijians have interbred with Polynesians to the extent that their skin color is lighter than that of other Melanesians. In the interior and west of Viti Levu where the contact was less, the people tend to be somewhat darker than the easterners. Yet Fijians still have Melanesian frizzy hair, while most—but not all—Polynesians have straight hair.

The Fijians live in villages along the rivers or coast, with anywhere from 50 to 400 people led by a hereditary chief. To see a Fijian family living in an isolated house in a rural area is rare. *Matanggali* (clans) are grouped into *yavusa* of varying rank and function. Several *yavusa* form a *vanua,* a number of which make up a *matanitu.* Chiefs of the most important *vanua* are known as high chiefs. In western Viti Levu the units are smaller and here outstanding commoners could always achieve the prestige reserved for high chiefs in the east. Away from the three largest islands the population is almost totally Fijian. The traditional thatched

mbure is fast disappearing from Fiji as villagers rebuild in tin and panel (often following destructive cyclones). Grass is not as accessible as cement, takes more time to repair, and is less permanent.

Fijians work communal land individually, not as a group. Each Fijian is assigned a piece of native land. They grow most of their own food in village gardens, and only a few staples, such as tea, sugar, and flour, are imported from Suva and sold in local co-op stores. A visit to one of these stores will demonstrate just how little they import and how self-sufficient they are. Fishing, village maintenance work, and ceremonial presentations are done together. While village life provides a form of collective security, individuals are discouraged from rising above the group. Fijians who attempt to set up a business are often stifled by the demands of relatives and friends. The Fijian custom of claiming favors from members of one's own group is known as *kerekere.* This pattern makes it difficult for Fijians to compete with Indians, for whom life has always been a struggle.

The Indians

Most of the Indians now in Fiji are descended from indentured laborers recruited in Bengal

CAINES JANNIF LTD., SUVA

The descendants of late 19th-century arrivals, such as this characterful young woman, make up the majority of Fiji's population today. These indentured laborers faced many hardships and indignities, one of which stemmed from a British policy of allowing only 40 Indian women to be brought to the island for every 100 men.

and Bihar a century ago. In the first year of the system (1879) some 450 Indians arrived in Fiji to work in the cane fields. By 1883 the total had risen to 2,300 and in 1916, when the last indentured laborers arrived, 63,000 Indians were present in the colony. In 1920 the indenture system was finally terminated, the cane fields were divided into four-hectare plots, and the Indian workers became tenant farmers on land owned by Fijians. Indians continued to arrive until 1931, though many of these later arrivals were Gujerati or Sikh businesspeople.

In 1940 the Indian population stood at 98,000, still below the Fijian total of 105,000, but by the 1946 census Indians had outstripped Fijians 120,000 to 117,000—making Fijians a minority in their own home. In the wake of the coups the relative proportions changed when some 30,000 Indians emigrated to North America and Australia, and by early 1989 indigenous Fijians once again outnumbered Fiji Indians. At the end of 1992 of Fiji's estimated total population was 758,275, of which approximately 49.7% were Fijian while 45.3% were Indian (compared to 46%

Fijian and 48.7% Indian at the 1986 census). Compared to indigenous Fijian women, twice as many Fiji Indian women take contraceptives, thus their fertility rate is considerably lower.

Unlike the village-oriented Fijians, a majority of Indians are concentrated in the cane-growing areas and live in isolated farmhouses, small settlements, or towns. Many Indians also live in Suva, as do an increasing number of Fijians. Within the Fiji Indian community there are divisions of Hindu (80%) versus Muslim (20%), north Indian versus south Indian, and Gujerati versus the rest. The Sikhs and Gujeratis have always been somewhat of an elite as they immigrated freely to Fiji outside the indenture system.

The different groups have kept alive their ancient religious beliefs and rituals. Hindus tend to marry within their caste, although the restrictions on behavior, which characterize the caste system in India, have disappeared. Indian marriages are often arranged by the parents, while Fijians generally choose their own partners. Rural Indians still associate most closely with other members of their extended patrilineal family group, and Hindu and Muslim religious beliefs still restrict Indian women to a position subservient to men.

It's often said that Indians concentrate on accumulation while Fijians emphasize distribution. Yet Fiji's laws themselves encourage Indians to invest their savings in business by preventing them or anyone else from purchasing native communal land. High-profile Indian dominance of the retail sector has distorted the picture and the reality is that the per capita incomes of ordinary indigenous Fijians and Fiji Indians are not that different. Big business remains the domain of government and foreign investors. Fijians are not "poor" because they are exploited by Indians; the two groups simply amass their wealth in different ways. And if some Indians seem money-minded, it's largely because they have been forced into that role. In large measure, Fiji's excellent service and retail industries exist thanks to the thrift and efficiency of the Indians. When you consider their position in a land where most have lived four generations and where they form almost half the population, where the constitution precludes them from ever governing, and where all natural resources are in the hands of others, their industriousness and patience are admirable.

Land Rights

When Fiji became a British colony in 1874, the land was divided between white settlers who had bought plantations and the *taukei ni ngele,* the Fijian "owners of the soil." The government assumed title to the balance. Today the alienated (privately owned) plantation lands are known as "freehold" land—about 10% of the total. Another seven percent is Crown land and the remaining 83% is inalienable Fijian communal land, which can be leased (about 30% is) but may never be sold. Compare this 83% (much of it not arable) with only three percent Maori land in New Zealand and almost zero native Hawaiian land. Land ownership has provided the Fijians with a security that allows them to preserve their traditional culture, unlike most indigenous peoples in other countries.

Communal land is administered on behalf of some 6,600 clan groups *(matanggali)* by the Native Land Trust Board (Box 116, Suva; fax 679/303-164), a government agency established in 1940. The NLTB retains 25% of the lease money to cover administration, and a further 10% is paid directly to regional hereditary chiefs. In 1966 the Agricultural Landlords and Tenants Act increased the period for which native land can be leased from 10 to 30 years. The 30-year leases will begin coming up for renewal in 1997, and Fiji's 23,000 Indian sugarcane farmers are apprehensive about the new terms they'll receive. If rents are greatly increased or the leases terminated, Fiji's sugar industry could be badly damaged and an explosive social situation created.

At the First Constitutional Conference in 1965, Indian rights were promulgated, and the 1970 independence constitution asserted that everyone born in Fiji would be a citizen with equal rights. But land laws, right up to the present, have very much favored "Fiji for the Fijians." Fiji Indians have always accepted Fijian ownership of the land, provided they are granted satisfactory leases. Now that the leases seem endangered, many Indians fear they will be driven from the only land they've ever known. The stifling of land development may keep Fiji quaint for tourists, but it also condemns a large portion of the population of both races to backwardness and poverty.

Other Groups

The 5,000 Fiji-born Europeans or *Kai Viti* are descendants of Australians and New Zealanders who came to create cotton, sugar, or copra plantations in the 19th century. Many married Fijian women, and the 13,000 part-Fijians or *Kai Loma* of today are the result. There is almost no intermarriage between Fijians and Fiji Indians. Many other Europeans are present in Fiji on temporary contracts or as tourists.

Most of the 5,000 Chinese in Fiji are descended from free settlers who came to set up small businesses a century ago, although since

The three largest ethnic groups in Fiji are Indians, Fijians, and Polynesians.

DAVID STANLEY

1987 there has been an influx of about a thousand Chinese from mainland China who were originally admitted to operate market gardens but who have since moved into the towns. Fiji Chinese tend to intermarry freely with the other racial groups.

The people of Rotuma, a majority of whom now live in Suva, are Polynesians. On neighboring islands off Vanua Levu are the Micronesians of Rambi (from Kiribati) and the Polynesians of Kioa (from Tuvalu). The descendants of Solomon Islanders blackbirded during the 19th century still live in communities near Suva, Levuka, and Lambasa. The Tongans in Lau and other Pacific islanders who have immigrated to Fiji make this an ethnic crossroads of the Pacific.

Social Conditions
Some 98% of the country's population was born in Fiji. The partial breakdown in race relations after the Rabuka coups was a tragedy for Fiji, though racial antagonism has been exaggerated. Despite the rhetoric, the different ethnic groups have always gotten along well together, with remarkably little animosity. You may hear individuals make disparaging remarks about the other group, but it's highly unlikely you'll witness any local confrontations. Though there are few problems in everyday life, the attitude has changed since 1987. Most Fiji Indians seem to have resigned themselves to their second-class position in Fiji, and some of the brightest and best have left.

As important as race are the variations between rich and poor, or urban (39%) and rural (61%). The imposition in 1992 of a 10% value-added tax combined with reductions in income tax and import duties shifted the burden of taxation from the haves to the have nots, and about nine percent of the population lives in absolute poverty. Avenues for future economic growth are limited, and there's chronic unemployment. The population is growing at an annual rate of three percent (compared to 0.9% in the U.S.) and the subsistence economy has difficulty absorbing these numbers. The lack of work is reflected in an increasing crime rate.

Literacy is high at 87%. Although not compulsory, primary education is free and accessible to most children. Most schools are still racially segregated. Over 100 church-operated schools receive government subsidies. The Fiji Institute of Technology was founded at Suva in 1963, followed by the University of the South Pacific in 1968. The university serves the 12 Pacific countries that contribute to its costs. Medical services in Fiji are heavily subsidized. The main hospitals are at Lambasa, Lautoka, and Suva, though smaller hospitals, health centers, and nursing stations are scattered around the country. The most common infectious diseases are influenza, gonorrhea, and syphilis.

Women in Fiji
Traditionally native Fijian women were confined to the home, while the men would handle most matters outside the immediate family. The clearcut roles of the woman as homemaker and the man as defender and decision-maker gave stability to village life. Western education has caused many Fijian women to question their subordinate position, and the changing lifestyle has made the old relationship between the sexes outmoded. As paid employment expands and women are able to hold their jobs thanks to family planning, they demand equal treatment from society. Fijian women are more emancipated than their sisters in the other Melanesian countries, though men continue to dominate public life throughout the region. Tradition is often manipulated to deny women the right to express themselves publicly on community matters.

There are cultural barriers hindering women's access to education and employment, and the proportion of girls in school falls rapidly as the grade level increases. Female students are nudged into low-paying fields such as nursing or secretarial services; export-oriented garment factories exploit women workers with low wages and poor working conditions. Levels of domestic violence vary greatly, though it's far less accepted among indigenous Fijians than it is among Fiji Indians, and in Fiji's Mathuata Province women have a suicide rate seven times above the world average, with most of the victims Indians.

RELIGION

The main religious groups in Fiji are Hindus (290,000), Methodists (265,000), Catholics (70,000), Muslims (62,000), Assemblies of God (33,000), and Seventh-Day Adventists (20,000). Around 45% of the total population is Hindu or Muslim due to the large Indian population, and only two percent of Indians have converted to Christianity despite Methodist missionary efforts dating back to 1884. About 78% of indigenous Fijians are Methodist, 8.5% Catholic.

The ecumenical **Pacific Conference of Churches** (G.P.O. Box 208, Suva, Fiji Islands; tel. 679/311-277, fax 679/303-205) began in 1961 as an association of mainstream Protestant churches throughout the South Pacific but since 1976 many Catholic dioceses have been included as well. The publishing arm of the PCC, Lotu Pasifika Productions, produces many fascinating books on regional social issues. Both the Pacific Theological College (founded in 1966) and the Pacific Regional Seminary (opened in 1972) are in southern Suva, and the South Pacific is one of the few areas of the world with a large surplus of ministers of religion.

After the 1987 military coups extremist elements seized control of Fiji's Methodist Church and there have been allegations of thousands of dollars in German aid to the church being diverted for political purposes. Meanwhile an avalanche of well-financed American fundamentalist missionary groups has descended on Fiji and membership in the Assemblies of God and some other new Christian sects is growing quickly at the expense of the Methodists.

While the Methodist Church has long been localized, the new evangelical sects are dominated by foreign personnel, ideas, and money. The ultraconservative outlook of the new religious imperialists continues the tradition of allying Christianity with colonialism or neocolonialism. The fundamentalists tend to portray God as a white man and discourage self-sufficiency by telling the islanders to await their reward in heaven. They stress passages in the Bible calling for obedience to authority and resignation, thereby providing the ideological justification for the repression of dissent.

The Mormons

Mormonism dates back to 1827 when a 22-year-old upstate New Yorker named Joseph Smith claimed to have discovered inscribed gold plates in an Indian burial mound near his home. These he translated with help of a "seer stone" and in 1830 the resulting *Book of Mormon* was used to launch his Church of Jesus Christ of Latter-day Saints. After Smith's assassination in 1844, Brigham Young led a group of followers west to Salt Lake City, Utah, were the cult is headquartered today.

Smith's book purports to be a history of the native American Indians, who are portrayed as descendants of the 10 lost tribes of Israel that migrated to the Western Hemisphere around A.D. 600. According to the book, the skin color of these people turned red due to their abandonment of the faith, and to hasten the second coming of Christ, they must be reconverted. Like Thor Heyerdahl, Mormon ideologues believe native American Indians settled Polynesia, so the present church is willing to spend a lot of time and money spreading the word. The pairs of clean-cut young Mormon "elders" seen on the islands, each in shirt and tie, riding a bicycle or driving a minibus, are sent down from the States for two-year stays.

You don't have to travel far in the South Pacific to find the assembly-line Mormon chapels, schools, and sporting facilities, paid for by church members, who must contribute 10% of their incomes. The Mormon church spends over US$500 million a year on foreign missions and sends out almost 50,000 missionaries, more than any other American church by far. The Mormons are especially successful in countries which are too poor to provide public education for all. There's a strong link to Hawaii's Brigham Young University and many island students help pay for their schooling by representing their home country at the Mormon-owned Polynesian Cultural Center on Oahu.

In Fiji, Mormon missionary activity is a fairly recent phenomenon, as prior to a "revelation" in 1978 the church considered blacks spiritually inferior. Due to a change in government policies, the number of Mormon missionaries granted Fijian visas has increased tenfold since 1987, and 90% of the money used to support Mormon activities in Fiji comes from the church headquarters in Utah.

Other Religious Groups

More numerous than the Mormons are adherents of the **Seventh-Day Adventist Church,** a politically ultra-conservative group which grew out of the 19th-century American Baptist movement. The SDA Church teaches the imminent return of Christ, and Saturday (rather than Sunday) is observed as the Sabbath. SDAs regard the human body as the temple of the Holy Spirit, thus much attention is paid to health matters. Members are forbidden to partake of certain foods, alcohol, drugs, and tobacco, and the church expends considerable energy on the provision of medical and dental services. They're also active in education and local economic development.

The **Assemblies of God** (AOG) is a Pentecostal sect founded in Arkansas in 1914 and presently headquartered in Springfield, Missouri. Although the AOG carries out some relief work, it opposes social reform in the belief that only God can solve humanity's problems. In Fiji, followers of the sect increased in number twelvefold between 1966 and 1992. A large AOG Bible College operates in Suva, and from Fiji the group has spread to other Pacific countries. Disgraced American televangelists Jimmy Swaggart and Jim Bakker were both former AOG ministers.

The **Jehovah's Witnesses** originated in 19th-century America and since 1909 their headquarters has been in Brooklyn, from whence their worldwide operations are financed. Jehovah's Witnesses' teachings against military service and blood transfusions have often brought them into conflict with governments, and they in turn regard other churches, especially the Catholic Church, as instruments of the devil. Members must spread the word by canvassing their neighborhood door-to-door, or by standing on street corners offering copies of *The Watchtower*. This group focuses mostly on Christ's return, and since "the end of time" is fast approaching, it has little interest in relief work.

Another 40 new religious groups of various shades and hues are active in the South Pacific, far too many to include here. Anyone interested in the subject, however, should consult Manfred Ernst's trailblazing study, *Winds of Change*, which can be purchased at the office of Lotu Pasifika Productions, 4 Thurston St., Suva.

LANGUAGE

Fijian, a member of the Austronesian family of languages spoken from Easter Island to Madagascar, has more speakers than any other indigenous Pacific language. Fijian vowels are pronounced as in Latin or Spanish, while the consonants are similar to those of English. Syllables end in a vowel, and the next-to-last syllable is usually the one emphasized. Where two vowels appear together they are sounded separately. In 1835 two Methodist missionaries, David Cargill and William Cross, devised the form of written Fijian used in Fiji today. Since all consonants in Fijian are separated by vowels, they spelled *mb* as *b*, *nd* as *d*, *ng* as *g*, *ngg* as *q*, and *th* as *c*. (For convenience, this book employs phonetic spelling for place-names and words, but Fijian spelling for the names of individuals.)

Though Cargill and Cross worked at Lakemba in the Lau Group, the political importance of tiny Mbau Island just off Viti Levu caused the Mbauan dialect of Fijian to be selected as the "official" version of the language, and in 1850 a dictionary and grammar were published. When the Bible was translated into Mbauan that dialect's dominance was assured, and it is today's spoken and written Fijian. From 1920 to 1970 the use of Fijian was discouraged in favor of English, but since independence there has been a revival. In 1973 a project was set up to create a definitive monolingual Fijian dictionary, and in 1987 the shortlived Coalition government restructured this work to create the Fijian Institute of Culture under the Ministry of Fijian Affairs.

Hindustani or Hindi is the household tongue of most Fiji Indians. Fiji Hindi has diverged from that spoken in India with the adoption of many words from English and other Indian languages such as Urdu. Though a quarter of Fiji Indians are descended from immigrants from southern India where Tamil and Telegu are spoken, few use these languages today, even at home. Fiji Muslims speak Hindi out of practical considerations, though they might consider Urdu their mother tongue. In their spoken forms, Hindi and Urdu are very similar. English is the second official language in Fiji and is understood by almost everyone. All schools teach exclusively in English after the fourth grade. Fiji Indians and indigenous Fijians usually communicate with one another in English.

CUSTOMS

Fijians and Fiji Indians are very tradition-oriented people who have retained a surprising number of their own ancestral customs despite the flood of conflicting influences that have swept the Pacific over the past century. Rather than a melting pot where one group assimilated another, Fiji is a patchwork of varied traditions.

The obligations and responsibilities of Fijian village life include not only the erection and upkeep of certain buildings, but personal participation in the many ceremonies that give their lives meaning. Hindu Indians, on the other hand, practice firewalking and observe festivals such as Holi and Diwali, just as their forebears in India did for thousands of years.

Fijian Firewalking

In Fiji, both Fijians and Indians practice firewalking, with the difference being that the Fijians walk on heated stones instead of hot embers. Legends tell how the ability to walk on fire was first given to a warrior named Tui-na-vinggalita from Mbengga Island, just off the south coast of Viti Levu, who had spared the life of a spirit god he caught while fishing for eels. The freed spirit gave to Tui-na-vinggalita the gift of immunity to fire. Today his descendants act as *mbete* (high priests) of the rite of *vilavilairevo* (jumping into the oven). Only members of his tribe, the Sawau, perform the ceremony. The Tui Sawau lives at Ndakuimbengga village on Mbengga, but firewalking is now only performed at the resort hotels on Viti Levu.

Fijian firewalkers (men only) are not permitted to have contact with women or to eat any coconut for two weeks prior to a performance. In a circular pit about four meters across, hundreds of large stones are first heated by a wood fire until they're white-hot. If you throw a handkerchief on the stones, it will burst into flames. Much ceremony and chanting accompanies certain phases of the ritual, such as the moment when the wood is removed to leave just the red-hot embers. The men psych themselves up in a nearby hut, then emerge, enter the pit, and walk briskly once around it. Bundles of leaves and grass are then thrown on the stones and the men stand inside the steaming pit again to chant a final song. They seem to have complete immunity to pain and there's no trace of injury. The men appear to fortify themselves with the heat, to gain some psychic power from the ritual.

Indian Firewalking

By an extraordinary coincidence, Fiji Indians brought with them the ancient practice of reli-

Spikes piercing their cheeks, Fiji Indians walk over hot coals at a religious festival, to purify themselves or give thanks to Durga for assistance rendered.

gious firewalking. In southern India, firewalking occurs in the pre-monsoon season as a call to the goddess Kali (Durga) for rain. Fiji Indian firewalking is an act of purification, or fulfillment of a vow to thank the god for help in a difficult situation.

In Fiji there is firewalking in most Hindu temples once a year, at full moon sometime between May and September according to the Hindu calendar. The actual event takes place on a Sunday at 1600 on the Suva side of Viti Levu, and at 0400 on the Nandi/Lautoka side. In August there is firewalking at the Sangam Temple on Howell Road, Suva. During the 10 festival days preceding the walk, participants remain in isolation, eat only unspiced vegetarian food, and spiritually prepare themselves. There are prayers at the temple in the early morning and a group singing of religious stories at about 1900 from Monday through Thursday. The yellow-clad devotees, their faces painted bright yellow and red, often pierce their cheeks or other bodily parts with spikes as part of the purification rites. Their faith is so strong they feel no pain.

The event is extremely colorful; drumming and chanting accompany the visual spectacle. Visitors are welcome to observe the firewalking, but since the exact date varies from temple to temple according to the phases of the moon (among other factors), you just have to keep asking to find out where and when it will take place. To enter the temple you must remove your shoes and any leather clothing.

The *Yanggona* Ceremony

Yanggona (kava), a tranquilizing, nonalcoholic drink that numbs the tongue and lips, comes from the *waka* (dried root) of the pepper plant *(Macropiper methysticum)*. This ceremonial preparation is the most honored feature of the formal life of Fijians, Tongans, and Samoans. It is performed with the utmost gravity according to a sacramental ritual to mark births, marriages, deaths, official visits, the installation of a new chief, etc.

New mats are first spread on the floor, on which is placed a handcarved *tanoa* (wooden bowl) nearly a meter wide. A long fiber cord decorated with cowry shells leads from the bowl to the guests of honor. To step over this cord during the ceremony is forbidden. As many as 70 men take their places before the bowl. The officiants are adorned with tapa, fiber, and croton leaves, their torsos smeared with glistening coconut oil, their faces usually blackened.

The guests present a bundle of *waka* to the hosts, along with a short speech explaining their visit, a custom known as *sevusevu*. The *sevusevu* is received by the hosts and acknowledged with a short speech of acceptance. The *waka* are then scraped clean and pounded in a *tambili* (mortar). Formerly they were chewed. Nowadays the pulp is put in a cloth sack and mixed with water in the *tanoa*. In the chiefly ceremony the *yanggona* is kneaded and strained through *vau* (hibiscus) fibers.

Draped in croton leaves, the cupbearer offers a bowl of yanggona *to a visiting chief at a formal kava ceremony.*

MINISTRY OF INFORMATION, GOVERNMENT OF FIJI

The mixer displays the strength of the grog (kava) to the *mata ni vanua* (master of ceremonies) by pouring out a cupful into the *tanoa*. If the *mata ni vanua* considers the mix too strong, he calls for *wai* (water), then says *"lose"* ("mix"), and the mixer proceeds. Again he shows the consistency to the *mata ni vanua* by pouring out a cupful. If it appears right the *mata ni vanua* says *"lomba"* ("squeeze"). The mixer squeezes the remaining juice out of the pulp, puts it aside, and announces, *"Sa lose oti saka na yanggona, vaka turanga"* ("The kava is ready, my chief"). He runs both hands around the rim of the *tanoa* and claps three times.

The *mata ni vanua* then says *"talo"* ("serve"). The cupbearer squats in front of the *tanoa* with a *mbilo* (half coconut shell), which the mixer fills. The cupbearer then presents the first cup to the guest of honor, who claps once and drains it, and everyone claps three times. The second cup goes to the guests' *mata ni vanua,* who claps once and drinks. The man sitting next to the mixer says *"aa,"* and everyone answers *"matha"* ("empty"). The third cup is for the first local chief, who claps once before drinking, and everyone claps three times after. Then the *mata ni vanua* of the first local chief claps once and drinks, and everyone says *"matha."* The same occurs for the second local chief and his *mata ni vanua.*

After these six men have finished their cups, the mixer announces, *"Sa matha saka tu na yanggona, vaka turanga"* ("The bowl is empty, my chief"), and the *mata ni vanua* says *"thombo"* ("clap"). The mixer then runs both hands around the rim of the *tanoa* and claps three times. This terminates the full ceremony, but then a second bowl is prepared and everyone drinks. During the drinking of the first bowl complete silence must be maintained.

Social Kava Drinking

While the above describes one of several forms of the full *yanggona* ceremony, which is performed only for high chiefs, abbreviated versions are put on for tourists at the hotels. However, the village people have simplified grog sessions almost daily. Kava drinking is an important form of Fijian entertainment and a way of structuring friendships and community relations. Even in government offices a bowl of grog is kept for the staff to take as a refreshment at

yanggona breaks. Some say the Fijians have *yanggona* rather than blood in their veins. Excessive kava drinking over a long period can make the skin scaly and rough, a condition known as *kanikani.*

Visitors to villages are invariably invited to participate in informal kava ceremonies, in which case it's customary to present a bunch of kava roots to the group. Do this at the beginning, before anybody starts drinking, and make a short speech explaining the purpose of your visit (be it a desire to meet the people and learn about their way of life, an interest in seeing or doing something in particular on their island, or just a holiday from work). Don't hand the roots to anyone, just place them on the mat in the center of the circle. The bigger the bundle of roots, the bigger the smiles. (The roots are easily purchased at any town market for about F$7 a half kilo.) Kava doesn't grow well in dry, cane-growing areas or in the Yasawas, so carry a good supply with you when traveling there, as it can be hard to buy more.

Clap once when the cupbearer offers you the *mbilo,* then take it in both hands and say *"mbula"* just before the cup meets your lips. Clap three times after you drink. Remember, you're a participant, not an onlooking tourist, so don't take photos if the ceremony is rather formal. Even though you may not like the appearance or taste of the drink, do try to finish at least the first cup. Tip the cup to show you're done.

It's considered extremely bad manners to turn your back on a chief during a kava ceremony, to walk in front of the circle of people when entering or leaving, or to step over the long cord attached to the *tanoa*. At the other end of the cord is a white cowry, which symbolizes a link to ancestral spirits.

Presentation of the *Tambua*

The *tambua* is a tooth of the sperm whale. It was once presented when chiefs exchanged delegates at confederacy meetings and before conferences on peace or war. In recent times, the *tambua* is presented during chiefly *yanggona* ceremonies as a symbolic welcome for a respected visitor or guest or as a prelude to public business or modern-day official functions. On the village level, *tambuas* are still commonly presented to arrange marriages, to show sym-

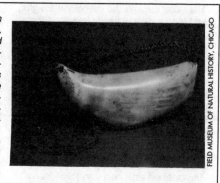

tambua: Yanggona *(or kava)* the Fijians share with the Polynesians, but the tambua, or whale's tooth, is significant only in Fiji. The tambuas *obtained from the sperm whale have always played an important part in Fijian ceremonies. During great festivals they were hung around the necks of warriors and chiefs in the 19th century; even today they are presented to distinguished guests and are exchanged at weddings, births, deaths, reconciliations, and also when personal or communal contracts or agreements are entered into. Tambuas, contrary to popular belief, have never been used as a currency and will not purchase goods or services. To be presented with a tambua is a great honor.*

FIELD MUSEUM OF NATURAL HISTORY, CHICAGO

pathy at funerals, to request favors, to settle disputes, or simply to show respect.

Old *tambuas* are highly polished from continuous handling. The larger the tooth, the greater its ceremonial value. *Tambuas* are prized cultural property and may not be exported from Fiji. Endangered species laws prohibit their entry into the United States, Australia, and many other countries.

Stingray Spearing and Fish Drives
Stingrays are lethal-looking creatures with caudal spines up to 18 cm long. To catch them, eight or nine punts are drawn up in a line about a kilometer long beside the reef. As soon as a stingray is sighted, a punt is paddled forward with great speed until close enough to hurl a spear.

Another time-honored sport and source of food is the fish drive. An entire village participates. Around the flat surface of a reef at rising tide, sometimes as many as 70 men and women group themselves in a circle a kilometer or more in circumference. All grip a ring of connected liana vines with leaves attached. While shouting, singing, and beating long poles on the seabed, the group slowly contracts the ring as the tide comes in. The shadow of the ring alone is enough to keep the fish within the circle. The fish are finally directed landward into a net or stone fish trap.

The Rising of the Mbalolo
Among all the Pacific island groups, this event takes place only in Samoa and Fiji. The *mbalo-*

lo (Eunice viridis) is a segmented worm of the Coelomate order, considered a culinary delicacy throughout these islands. It's about 45 cm long and lives deep in the fissures of coral reefs, rising to the surface only twice a year to propagate and then die. This natural almanac keeps both lunar and solar times, and has a fixed day of appearance—even if a hurricane is raging—one night in the third quarter of the moon in October, and the corresponding night in November. It has never failed to appear on time for over 100 years now and you can even check your calendar by it.

Because this thin, jointed worm appears with such mathematical certainty, Fijians are waiting in their boats to scoop the millions of writhing, reddish brown (male) and moss green (female) spawn from the water when they rise to the surface just before dawn. Within an hour after the rising the sacs burst, and the fertile milt spawns the next generation of *mbalolo*. This is one of the most bizarre curiosities in the natural history of the South Pacific, and the southeast coast of Ovalau is a good place to observe it.

CONDUCT AND CUSTOMS

Foreign travel is an exceptional experience enjoyed mostly by privileged Westerners. Too often, affluent visitors from developed countries try to transfer their lifestyles to tropical islands, thereby missing out on what is unique to the region. Travel can be a learning experience if approached openly and with a positive attitude, so read up on the local culture before you arrive and become aware of the social and environmental problems of the area. A wise traveler soon graduates from hearing and seeing to listening and observing. Speaking is good for the ego and listening is good for the soul.

The path is primed with packaged pleasures, but pierce the bubble of tourism and you'll encounter something far from the schedules and organized efficiency: time to learn how other people live. Walk gently, for human qualities are as fragile and responsive to abuse as the brilliant reefs. The Fijians are by nature soft-spoken and reserved. Often they won't show open disapproval if their social codes are broken, but don't underestimate them: they understand far more than you think. Consider that you're only one of thousands of visitors to their country, so don't expect to be treated better than anyone else. Respect is one of the most important things in life and humility is also greatly appreciated.

If you're alone you're lucky, for the single traveler is everyone's friend. Get away from other tourists and meet the people. There aren't many places on earth where you can still do this meaningfully, but Fiji is one. If you do meet people with similar interests, keep in touch by writing. This is no tourist's paradise, though,

and local residents are not exhibits or paid performers. They have just as many problems as you and if you see them as real people you're less likely to be viewed as a stereotypical tourist. You may have come to escape civilization, but keep in mind that you're just a guest.

Most important of all, try to see it their way. Take an interest in local customs, values, languages, challenges, and successes. If things work differently than they do back home, give thanks—that's why you've come. Reflect on what you've experienced and return home with a better understanding of how much we all have in common, outwardly different as we may seem. Do that and your trip won't have been wasted.

Fijian Customs
It's a Fijian custom to smile when you meet a stranger and say something like "Good morning," or at least "Hello." Of course, you needn't do this in the large towns, but you should almost everywhere else. If you meet someone you know, stop for a moment to exchange a few words.

Fijian villages are private property and it's important to get permission before entering one. Of course it's okay to continue along a road that

closing the ring during a Mbengga fish drive

MINISTRY OF INFORMATION, GOVERNMENT OF FIJI

DAVID STANLEY

Clad in a sulu, *the all-purpose garment of the Pacific, a Fijian poses before a traditional* mbure.

women with their legs to the side. Sitting with your legs stretched out in front is insulting. Fijian villagers consider it offensive to walk in front of a person seated on the floor (pass behind) or to fail to say *"Tulou"* ("Excuse me") as you go by. Don't stand up during a *sevusevu* to village elders. When you give a gift hold it out with both hands, not one hand. Never place your hand on another's head and don't sit in doorways.

There's no running or shouting when you arrive in a village, and they leave you alone if you wish. Fijian children are very well behaved, and all Fijians love children, so don't hesitate to bring your own. You'll never have to worry about finding a babysitter. Do you notice how Fijians rarely shout? Keep your voice down.

In a main tourist center such as Nandi or Suva, take care if a local invites you to visit his home as you may be seen mainly as a source of beer and other goods. Surprisingly friendly people at bars may expect you to buy them drinks. Alcohol is forbidden in many Fijian villages. Women should have few problems traveling around Fiji on their own, so long as they're prepared to cope with frequent offers of marriage. Littering is punished by a minimum F$40 fine and breaking bottles in public can earn six months in jail (unfortunately seldom enforced).

passes through a village, but do ask before leaving the road. It's good manners to take off your hat while walking through a village, where only the chief is permitted to wear a hat. Some villagers also object to sunglasses. Objects such as backpacks, handbags, and cameras are best carried in your hands rather than slung over your shoulders. Don't point at people in villages.

If you wish to surf off a village, picnic on their beach, or fish in their lagoon, you should also ask permission. You'll almost always be made most welcome and granted any favors you request if you present a *sevusevu* of kava roots to the village headman or chief (see "Staying in Villages" under "Accommodations" in the On the Road chapter for the correct way to present a *sevusevu*). If you approach the Fijians with respect you're sure to be so treated in return.

Take off your shoes before entering a *mbure* and stoop as you walk around inside. Clap three times when you join people already seated on mats on the floor. Men should sit cross-legged,

Dress

It's important to know that the dress code in Fiji is strict. Wearing short shorts, halter tops, and bathing costumes in public shows a lack of respect, and in the context of a Fijian village it's considered extremely offensive: a *sulu* wrapped around you solves this one. Men should always wear a shirt in town, and women should wear dresses that adequately cover their legs while seated. Nothing will mark you so quickly as a tourist nor make you more popular with street vendors than scanty dress. There *is* a place for it, of course: that's on the beach in front of a resort hotel. In a society where even bathing suits are considered extremely risqué for local women, public nudity is unthinkable, and topless sunbathing by women is also banned in Fiji.

Questions

The islanders are eager to please, so phrase your questions carefully. They'll answer yes or no according to what they think you want to hear—don't suggest the answer in your question. Test this by asking your informant to confirm something you know to be incorrect. Also don't ask negative questions, such as, "You're not going to Suva, are you?" Invariably the answer will be "Yes," meaning "Yes, I'm not going to Suva." It could also work like this: "Don't you have anything cheaper?" "Yes." "What do you have that is cheaper?" "Nothing." Yes, he doesn't have anything cheaper. If you want to be sure of something, ask several people the same question in different ways.

The surgeonfish gets its name from the knifelike spines just in front of its tail. Extreme care must be taken in handling the fish to avoid severe cuts.

M.G.L. DOMENY DE RIENZI

ON THE ROAD

Highlights

Fiji's many attractions are hard to shortlist but two outstanding natural features on the south side of Viti Levu are the Singatoka sand dunes and the Navua River with its cliff-hugging rapids. The three waterfalls at Mbouma Falls on the northeastern island of Taveuni are also magnificent. Fiji's finest bus rides take you through open rolling countryside from Lautoka to Rakiraki, or across the mountains of Vanua Levu from Savusavu to Lambasa. Without doubt, the most appealing town is the old capital Levuka. There are many candidates for best beach, reef, and outer island: all are tops. Two weeks is the absolute minimum amount of time required to get a feel for Fiji, and one month is much better.

SPORTS AND RECREATION

All of the high islands offer good, safe **hiking** possibilities and many remote villages are linked by well-used trails. The most important hikes described in this book are the two-day Singatoka River Trek down the Singatoka River from Nandarivatu and the Trans-Viti Levu Trek in central Viti Levu. Tholo-i-Suva Forest Park behind Suva is one of Fiji's most accessible hiking areas, but Levuka makes a better base with the trail to The Peak beginning right behind the town. A good cross-island trail to Lovoni is nearby. More challenging still is the all-day climb to Lake Tangimauthia on Taveuni. For some island hiking, walk right around Nananu-i-Ra in under a day. Kandavu also offers many hiking possibilities.

Exciting **whitewater rafting** on the Mba River is offered by the Roaring Thunder Company at Nandi. Less known are the rubber rafting possibilities on the upper Navua River. In central Viti Levu, villagers will pole you through the Waingga Gorge on a bamboo raft from Naitauvoli to Naivuthini villages.

Fiji has four important **surfing** camps. The more upmarket is Tavarua Island in the Mamanutha Group which receives mostly American surfers on packaged deals. You can also use speedboats from Seashell Cove Resort to surf the same breaks at less expense. Fiji's best budget surfing is available at the Club Masa Sports Resort near Singatoka. A new surfing camp called Frigate Surfriders has opened on Yanutha Island off southern Viti Levu. The best surfing season is generally July to September when the trade winds push the Antarctic swells north. During the hurricane season from January to March tropical storms can generate some spectacular waves.

Windsurfing is possible at a much wider range of locales and many upmarket hotels include equipment in their rates. Windsurfing is possible at most of the Mamanutha resorts, including Plantation Island, Musket Cove, Naitasi Resort, Castaway, Tokoriki, and Treasure Island. Other offshore resorts around Fiji offering windsurfing are Vatulele, Tomberua Island, Mbekana Island, Turtle Island, Naingani Island, and Nggamea Beach. For those on a budget, check out the windsurfing at Nandi's Club Fiji or Singatoka's Club Masa.

In the past, organized **ocean kayaking** expeditions have been offered among the Yasawa Islands, down the northeast coast of Taveuni, and in Vanua Levu's Natewa Bay. Those who only want to dabble can hire kayaks at Lautoka's Mbekana Island, Taveuni's Garden Island Resort, and Kandavu's Albert's Place, but it's much better to bring a folding kayak of your own if you're serious. See "Organized Tours" under "Getting There," which follows, for more information on kayaking.

Get in some **sailing** by taking one of the day cruises offered from Nandi by yacht. Fiji's two main bases for chartered yachts are Musket Cove Resort in the Mamanutha Group and Savusavu on Vanua Levu (turn to "Organized Tours" under "Getting There," following).

Golfers are well catered to in Fiji. The two most famous courses are the Ndenarau Golf Club, next to the Sheraton Hotel at Nandi, and the Pacific Harbor Country Club, one of the finest courses in the Pacific. Many tourist hotels have golf courses, including the Mocambo at Nandi; the Fijian Resort Hotel, Reef Resort, and

Naviti Beach Resort on the south side of Viti Levu; Kontiki Resort on Vanua Levu; and Taveuni Estates on Taveuni. More locally oriented are the city golf courses at Nandi Airport and in Suva, and the company-run courses near Rakiraki, Lautoka, and Lambasa sugar mills and at the Vatukuola gold mine, all built to serve former expatriate staffs. All are open to the public and only the Sheraton and Pacific Harbor courses could be considered expensive. Club and cart rentals are usually available and many of the courses have club houses with pleasant colonial-style bars.

The soccer season in Fiji is February to November, while rugby is played from April to September. Rugby is played only by Fijians, while soccer teams are both Fijian and Indian. Cricket is played from November to March, mostly in rural areas. Lawn bowling is also popular. Sports of any kind are forbidden on Sunday.

Scuba Diving

Diving is possible year-round in Fiji, with the marinelife most profuse from July to November. Fiji has been called "the soft coral capital of the world" and many fantastic dives are just 10 or 15 minutes away from the resorts by boat (whereas at Australia's Great Barrier Reef the speedboats often have to travel over 60 km to get to the dive sites). The worst underwater visibility conditions in Fiji are the equivalent of the very best off Florida. In the Gulf of Mexico you've about reached the limit if you can see for 15 meters; in Fiji visibility begins at 15 meters and increases to 45 meters in some places. Water temperatures vary from 24°C in June, July, and August to 30°C in December, January, and February.

Facilities for scuba diving exist at most of the resorts in the Mamanutha Group, along Viti Levu's Coral Coast, on Mbengga, Kandavu, Nananu-i-Ra, Leleuvia, at Nandi, Lautoka, Suva, and Savusavu, and on Taveuni and adjacent islands. Low-budget divers should turn to the Leleuvia, Kandavu, and Taveuni sections in this book and read. If you've never dived before, Fiji is an excellent place to learn, and the Nandi, Leleuvia, Kandavu, and Taveuni scuba operators offer certification courses from budget accommodations. Even if you aren't willing to put the necessary money and effort into scuba diving, you'd be foolish not to check out the many free snorkeling possibilities. Some dive shops take snorkelers out in their boats for a nominal rate.

Four liveaboard dive boats ply Fiji waters: the *Matangi Princess II,* a 26-meter cruise vessel operating around Taveuni, the 34-meter, eight-cabin *Nai'a* based at Suva, the five-stateroom *Mollie Dean II* also based at Suva, and the 18-meter cabin cruiser *Beqa Princess* based at Pacific Harbor. A seven-night stay on one of these vessels will run F$2775 pp (airfare extra), but the boat anchors right above the dive sites so no time is wasted commuting back and forth, all meals are included, and the diving is unlimited. Bookings can be made through any of the scuba wholesalers listed under "Getting There" below.

Jean-Michel Cousteau's **Ocean Search Project** offers all-inclusive two-week programs based at the Cousteau Fiji Islands Resort near Savusavu for serious scuba divers. For information contact Cousteau Productions (tel. 805/899-8899, fax 805/899-8898) in Santa Barbara, California.

ENTERTAINMENT

There are cinemas in towns such as Lambasa, Lautoka, Mba, Nandi, Nausori, Suva, and Tavua showing adventure and romance films for low admissions. These same four towns have local nightclubs where you can enjoy as much drinking and dancing as you like without spending an arm and a leg. When there's live music, a cover charge is collected.

A South Pacific institution widespread in Fiji is the old colonial clubs which offer inexpensive beer in safe, friendly surroundings. Such clubs are found in Nandi, Singatoka, Lautoka, Levuka, Lambasa, Savusavu, and Taveuni, and although they're all private clubs with Members Only signs on the door, foreign visitors are allowed entry (except at Suva). Occasionally the bartender will ask you to sign the guest book or tell you to request authorization from the club secretary.

Fiji's one unique spectacle is the **Fijian firewalking** performed several times a week at the large hotels along the southwest side of Viti Levu: Mocambo (Saturday), Sheraton (Thursday), Fijian Resort Hotel (Monday and Friday), Reef Resort (Friday), and Pacific Harbor (Tuesday and Saturday). A fixed admission price is charged but it's well worth going to at least once, if you have the chance. For more information on firewalking, see "Customs" in the main Introduction chapter. The same hotels which present firewalking usually stage a Fijian *meke* (described below) on an alternate night.

Fijian Dancing *(Meke)*
The term *meke* describes the combination of dance, song, and theater performed at feasts and on special occasions. Brandishing spears, their faces painted with charcoal, the men wear frangipani leis and skirts of shredded leaves. The war club dance reenacts heroic events of the past. Both men and women perform the *vakamalolo,* a sitting dance, while the *seasea* is danced by women flourishing fans. The *tralala,* in which visitors may be asked to join, is a simple two-step shuffle danced side-by-side (early missionaries forbade the Fijians from dancing face-to-face). As elsewhere in the Pacific the dances tell a story, though the music now is strongly influenced by Christian hymns and contemporary pop. Less sensual than Polynesian dancing, the rousing Fijian dancing evokes the country's violent past. Fijian *meke* are often part of a *mangiti* or feast performed at hotels. The Dance Theater of Fiji at Pacific Harbor is well regarded.

RICHARD GOODMAN

Grasping war clubs, Fijian men perform a meke.

PUBLIC HOLIDAYS AND FESTIVALS

Public holidays in Fiji include New Year's Day (1 January), National Youth Day (a Friday in early March), Good Friday and Easter Monday (March/April), Ratu Sukuna Day (a Monday around 29 May), Queen Elizabeth's Birthday (a Friday around 14 June), Constitution Day (a Saturday around 27 July), Prophet Mohammed's Birthday (anytime from August to December), Fiji Day (a Monday around 10 October), Diwali (October or November), and Christmas Days (25 and 26 December). Constitution Day commemorates promulgation of the racially weighted 1990 constitution.

Check with the Fiji Visitors Bureau to see if any festivals are scheduled during your visit. The best known are the Mbula Festival in Nandi (July), the Hibiscus Festival in Suva (August), and the Sugar Festival in Lautoka (September). Before Diwali, the Hindu festival of lights, Hindus clean their homes, then light lamps or candles to mark the arrival of spring. Fruit and sweets are offered to Lakshmi, goddess of wealth. Holi is an Indian spring festival in February or March.

ARTS AND CRAFTS

The traditional art of Fiji is closely related to that of Tonga. Fijian canoes, too, were patterned after the more advanced Polynesian type, although the Fijians were timid sailors. War clubs, food bowls, *tanoas* (kava bowls), eating utensils, clay pots, and tapa cloth *(masi)* are considered Fiji's finest artifacts.

There are two kinds of woodcarvings: the ones made from *vesi (Intsia bijuga)*—ironwood in English—or *nawanawa (Cordia subcordata)* wood are superior to those of the lighter, highly breakable *vau (Hibiscus tiliaceus)*. Though shells are sometimes used for polishing the finest artifacts, steel tools are employed for the most part these days. In times past it often took years to make a Fijian war club, as the carving was done in the living tree and left to grow into the desired shape. The best *tanoas* are carved in the Lau Group.

Though many crafts are alive and well, some Fijians have taken to carving "tikis" or mock New Guinea masks smeared with black shoe polish to look like ebony for sale to tourists. Also avoid objects made from turtle shell/leather, clam shell, or marine mammal ivory which are prohibited entry into many countries under endangered species acts. Failure to declare such

Fijian pottery making has changed very little since this 1845 Sherman and Smith engraving.

Fijian masi *(tapa)*

items to customs officers can lead to heavy fines. Also resist the temptation to purchase jewelry or other items made from seashells and coral, the collection of which damages the reefs. Souvenirs made from straw or seeds may be held for fumigation or confiscated upon arrival.

Pottery Making

Fijian pottery making is unique in that it is a Melanesian artform. The Polynesians forgot how to make pottery thousands of years ago. Today the main center for pottery making in Fiji is the Singatoka Valley on Viti Levu. Here, the women shape clay using a wooden paddle outside against a rounded stone held inside the future pot. The potter's wheel was unknown in the Pacific.

A saucerlike section forms the bottom; the sides are built up using slabs of clay, or coils and strips. These are welded and battered to shape. When the form is ready the pot is dried inside the house for a few days, then heated over an open fire for about an hour. Resin from the gum of the *dakua* (kauri) tree is rubbed on the outside while the pot is still hot. This adds a varnish that brings out the color of the clay and improves the pot's water-holding ability.

This pottery is extremely fragile, which accounts for the quantity of potsherds found on ancient village sites. Smaller, less breakable

pottery products such as ashtrays are now made for sale to visitors.

Weaving

Woven articles are among the most widespread handicrafts. Pandanus fiber is the most common, but coconut leaf and husk, vine tendril, banana stem, tree and shrub bark, and the stems and leaves of water weeds are all used. On some islands the fibers are passed through a fire, boiled, then bleached in the sun. Vegetable dyes of very lovely mellow tones are sometimes used, but gaudier store dyes are more prevalent. Shells are occasionally utilized to cut, curl, or make the fibers pliable.

Tapa Cloth

This is Fiji's most characteristic traditional product. Tapa is light, portable, and inexpensive, and a piece makes an excellent souvenir to brighten up a room back home. It's made by women on Vatulele Island off Viti Levu and on certain islands of the Lau Group.

To make tapa, the white inner bark of the tall, thin paper mulberry tree *(Broussonetia papyrifera)* is stripped and scraped with shells, rolled into a ball, and soaked in water. The sodden strips are then pounded with wooden mallets until four or five times their original length

(top left) Mbouma Falls, Taveuni, Fiji (Robert Leger); (top left) planting kava, Ovalau (Karl Partridge); (bottom) banana carrier, Mbengga Island (David Stanley)

(top) sunset, Suva Harbor (Peter McQuarrie)
(bottom) sugarcane delivery, Lambasa Sugar Mill, Vanua Levu (David Stanley)

and width. Next several pieces are placed one on top of the another, pressed and pounded, and joined together with a manioc juice paste, then left to dry in the sun. Sheets of tapa feel like felt when finished.

While Tongan tapa is decorated by holding a relief pattern under the tapa and overpainting the lines, Fijian tapa *(masi kesa)* is distinctive for its rhythmic geometric designs applied with stencils made from green pandanus and banana leaves. The stain is rubbed on in the same manner in which temple rubbings are made from a stone inscription.

The only colors used are red, from red clay, and a black pigment obtained by burning candlenuts. Both powders are mixed with boiled gums made from scraped roots. Sunlight deepens and sets the copper brown colors. Each island group had its characteristic colors and patterns, ranging from plantlike paintings to geometric designs. On some islands tapa is still used for bedding, for room dividers, and as ceremonial red carpets. Tablecloths, bedcovers, place mats, and wall hangings of tapa make handsome souvenirs.

SHOPPING

Shops in Fiji close at 1300 on Saturday, except in Nausori town where they stay open all day Saturday but only half a day on Wednesday. The 1987 military coups placed Fiji firmly in the South Pacific Bible Belt, which also encompasses Tonga, Western Samoa, and the Cook Islands, so most commercial business is suspended on Sunday (hotels excepted). Fiji Indians dominate the retail trade. If you're buying from an Indian merchant, always bargain hard and consider all sales final. Indigenous Fijians usually begin by asking a much lower price, in which case bargaining isn't so important.

Fiji's duty-free shops such as Prouds or Tappoo are not really duty-free, as all goods are subject to various fiscal duties plus the 10% value-added tax. Bargaining is the order of the day, but only in Suva is the selection really good. To be frank, Americans can usually buy the sort of Japanese electrical merchandise sold "duty-free" in Fiji cheaper in the States, where they'll get more recent models. If you do buy something, get an itemized receipt and international guarantee, and watch that they don't switch packages and unload a demo on you. Once purchased, items cannot be returned, so don't let yourself be talked into something. Camera film is cheap, however, and the selection good—stock up.

If you'd like to do some shopping in Fiji, locally made handicrafts such as tapa cloth,

Grog (kava) is mixed in a tanoa, *such as this fine example carved from a single block of* vesi *wood. It's said the Fijians have* yanggona *rather than blood in their veins.*

mats, kava bowls, war clubs, woodcarvings, etc., are a much better investment (see "Arts and Crafts," above). The four-pronged cannibal forks available everywhere make unique souvenirs. The Government Handicraft Center in Suva is a place to learn what's available, and if you're spending serious money for top-quality work, visit the Fiji Museum beforehand.

Try to purchase your souvenirs directly from the Fijian producers at street markets, etc. Just beware of aggressive Fijian "sword sellers" on the streets of Suva who sell fake handicrafts at high prices, high-pressure duty-free touts who may try to pull you into their shops, and self-appointed guides who offer to help you find the "best price." If you get the feeling you're being hustled, walk away.

ACCOMMODATIONS

With *Fiji Islands Handbook* in hand you're guaranteed a good, inexpensive place to stay on every island. Each and every hotel in the country is included herein, not just a selection. We do this consistently to give you a solid second reference in case your travel agent or someone else recommends a certain place. To allow you the widest possible choice, all categories are included, and throughout we've tried to point out which properties offer the best value for your money. If you think we're wrong or you were badly treated, be sure to send to the author of this book a written complaint. Equally important, please let us know when you agree with what's here or if you think a place deserves a better rave. Your letter will have an impact!

We don't solicit freebies from the hotel chains; our only income derives from the price you paid when you bought this book. So we don't mind telling you that, as usual, most of the luxury hotels are just not worth the exorbitant prices they charge. Many simply re-create Hawaii at four times the cost, offering far more luxury than you need. Even worse, they tend to isolate you in an Australian/American environment, away from the Fiji you came to experience. Most are worth visiting as sightseeing attractions, watering holes, or sources of entertainment, but unless you're a millionaire, sleep elsewhere.

One of the golden rules of independent travel is the more you spend, the less you experience. If you're on a budget, avoid prepaying hotel accommodations booked from home, as you can always do better locally upon arrival. If, however, you really do intend to spend most of your time at a specific first-class hotel, you'll benefit from bulk rates by taking a package tour instead of paying the higher "rack rate" the hotels

Campers, Kandavu Island. Where hotels don't exist, your tent is your home away from home.

DAVID STANLEY

charge individuals who just walk in off the street. Call Air New Zealand's toll-free number and ask them to mail you their *Hotpac* brochure, which lists deluxe hotel rooms in Fiji that can be booked on an individual basis at slightly reduced rates. Bear in mind, however, that on all the islands there are middle-level hotels that charge half what these top-end places ask, while providing adequate comfort.

When picking a hotel, bear in mind that although a thatched bungalow is cooler and infinitely more attractive than a concrete box, it's also more likely to have insect problems. If in doubt, check the window screens and carry mosquito coils and/or repellent. Hopefully there'll be a resident lizard or two to feed on the bugs.

A room with cooking facilities can save you a lot on restaurant meals, and some moderately priced establishments have weekly rates. If you have to choose a meal plan, take only breakfast and dinner (Modified American Plan or "half pension") and have fruit for lunch. As you check into your room, note the nearest fire exits. And don't automatically take the first room offered; if you're paying good money look at several, then choose.

Be aware that some of the low-budget places included in this book are a lot more basic than what is sometimes referred to as "budget" accommodations in the States. The standards of cleanliness in the common bathrooms may be lower than you expected, the furnishings "early attic," the beds uncomfortable, linens and towels skimpy, housekeeping nonexistent, and window screens lacking, but ask yourself, where in the U.S. are you going to find a room for a similar price? Luckily, good medium-priced accommodations are usually available for those of us unwilling to put up with spartan conditions, and we include all of them in this book too.

A 10% government tax is added to all accommodation prices. Some hotels include the tax in their quoted rates, while others don't. You can often tell whether tax is included by looking at the amount: if it's F$33 tax is probably included, whereas if it's F$30 it may not be. We've tried to include the tax in all prices quoted herein. When things are slow, specials are offered and some prices are negotiable. Occasionally you'll pay less than the prices quoted in this book.

Accommodation Categories

Fiji offers a wide variety of places to stay, from low-budget to world-class. Standard big-city international hotels are found in Nandi and Suva, while most of the huge upmarket beach resorts are on small islands in the Mamanutha Group off Nandi and along the Coral Coast on Viti Levu's south side.

In recent years smaller luxury resorts have multiplied on the outer islands, from the guest-accepting plantations near Savusavu and on Taveuni to isolated beach resorts on remote islands such as Turtle, Yasawa, Vatulele, Mbengga, Tomberua, Kandavu, Naingani, Wakaya, Nukumbati, Namenalala, Nggamea, Matangi, Lauthala, Kaimbu, and Vanua Mbalavu. Prices at these begin at several hundred dollars a day. A few such as Mbengga, Matana, and Matangi are marketed almost exclusively to scuba divers. If heading for any of these, pick up a bottle of duty-free liquor on the way as bar prices are high.

The **Mamanutha resorts** are secluded, with fan-cooled *mbure* accommodations, while at the **Coral Coast hotels** you often get an a/c room in a main building. The Coral Coast has more to offer in the way of land tours, shopping, and entertainment/eating options, while the offshore resorts are preferable if you want a rest or are into water sports. The Coral Coast beaches are only good at high tide. Most guests at the deluxe hotels in both areas are on package tours. For economy and flexibility, avoid prepaying hotel accommodations from home.

Low-budget accommodations are spread out, with concentrations in Nandi, Korolevu, Suva, Lautoka, Levuka, and Savusavu, and on Taveuni. Low-cost outer island beach resorts exist on Kandavu, Ono, Leleuvia, Naingani, Nananu-i-Ra, and Tavewa. Some Suva hotels lock their front doors at 1100, so ask first if you're planning a night on the town. A few of the cheapies double as whorehouses, making them cheap in both senses of the word. Some islands with air service from Suva, including Koro, Moala, Ngau, Rotuma, and Thithia, have no facilities whatsoever for visitors, so it really helps to know someone before heading that way.

Many hotels, both in cities and at the beach, offer **dormitory beds** as well as individual rooms. Most of the dorms are mixed. Women can sometimes request a women-only dorm when things are slow, but it's usually not guaranteed. Dormitory or "bunkroom" accommodations are excellent if you're traveling alone, and they're just the place to meet other travelers, although couples can usually get a double room for a price only slightly above two dorm beds. For the most part, the dormitories are safe and congenial for those who don't mind sacrificing their privacy to save money. Communal cooking facilities are usually provided.

Camping facilities (own tent) are found at Momi Bay south of Nandi, on Nukulau Island off Suva, and on Kandavu, Ono, Ovalau, and Taveuni islands. Elsewhere, get permission before pitching your tent as all land is owned by someone and land rights are sensitive issues in Fiji. Some freelance campers on beaches such as Natandola near Nandi have been robbed, so take care. Don't ask a Fijian friend for permission to camp beside his house in the village itself. Although he may feel obligated to grant the request of a guest, you'll be proclaiming to everyone that his home isn't completely to your liking. Of course, in places like Tavewa Island that receive visitors regularly this isn't a problem; elsewhere, if all you really want is to camp, make this clear from the start and get permission to do so on a beach or by a river, but *not* in the village. A *sevusevu* should always be presented in this case. Never camp directly under a coconut tree: falling coconuts are lethal.

Staying in Villages

A great way to meet the people and learn a little about their culture is to stay in a village for a few nights. A number of hiking tours now offer overnighting in remote villages, and it's also possible to arrange it for yourself. If you befriend someone from a remote island, ask them to write you a letter of introduction to their relatives back in the village. Mail a copy of it ahead with a polite letter introducing yourself, then start slowly heading that way.

In places off the beaten tourist track, you could just show up in a village and ask permission of the *turanga-ni-koro* (village herald) to spend the night. Rarely will you be refused. Similarly, both Fiji Indians and native Fijians will spontaneously invite you in. The Fijians' innate dignity and kindness should not be taken for granted, however.

All across the Pacific it's customary to reciprocate when someone gives you a gift—if not now, then sometime in the future. Visitors who accept gifts (such as meals and accommodations) from islanders and do not reciprocate are undermining traditional culture and causing resentment, often without realizing it. It's sometimes hard to know how to repay hospitality, but Fijian culture has a solution: the *sevusevu*. This can be money, but it's usually a 500-gram bundle of kava roots *(waka),* which can be easily purchased at any Fijian market for about F$7. *Sevusevus* are more often performed between families or couples about to be married, or at births or christenings, but the custom is certainly a perfect way for visitors to show their appreciation.

We recommend that travelers donate between F$10 and F$15 pp per night to village hosts (carry sufficient cash in small denominations). The *waka* is additional, and anyone traveling in remote areas of Fiji should pack some (take whole roots, not powdered kava). If you give the money up front together with the *waka* as a *sevusevu*, they'll know you're not a freeloader and you'll get better treatment, though in all cases it's absolutely essential to contribute something.

The *sevusevu* should be placed before (not handed to) the *turanga-ni-koro* or village chief so he can accept or refuse. If he accepts (by touching the package), your welcome is confirmed and you may spend the night in the village. It's also nice to give some money to the lady of the house upon departure, with your thanks. Just say it's your goodbye *sevusevu* and watch the smile. A Fijian may refuse the money, but he/she will not be offended by the offer if it is done properly.

In addition you could also take some gifts along, such as lengths of material, T-shirts, badges, pins, knitting needles, hats, acoustic guitar strings, school books, colored pens, toys, playing cards, fish hooks, line, or lures, or a big jar of instant coffee. Keep in mind, however, that Seventh-Day Adventists are forbidden to have coffee, cigarettes, or kava, so you might ask if there are any SDAs around in order to avoid embarrassment. Uncontroversial food items to donate include sugar, flour, rice, corned beef, matches, chewing gum, peanuts, and biscuits. One thing *not* to take is alcohol, which is always sure to offend somebody.

When choosing your traveling companions for a trip that involves staying in Fijian villages, make sure you agree on this before you set out. Otherwise you could end up subsidizing somebody else's trip, or worse, have to stand by and watch the Fijian villagers subsidize it. Never arrive in a village on a Sunday, and don't overstay your welcome.

A final note from Josje Hebbes of the Netherlands:

If people only meet Indians on the street or in tourist centers they will get a totally wrong idea of Indian culture. To appreciate their hospitality and friendliness one should also try to spend some time in rural Indian settlements. If you go on a day hike you might be invited for lunch. First they will serve you something sweet like juice or tea. That's their way. Make sure you don't leave Fiji with a mistaken impression of Fiji Indians!

Village Life
When you enter a Fijian village people will usually want to be helpful and will direct or accompany you to the person or place you seek. If you show genuine interest in something and ask to see how it is done, you will usually be treated with respect and asked if there is anything else you would like to know. Initially, Fijians may hesitate to welcome you into their homes because they fear you will not wish to sit on a mat and eat native foods with your fingers. Once you show them that this isn't true, you'll receive the full hospitality treatment.

Consider participating in the daily activities of the family, such as weaving, cooking, gardening, and fishing. Your hosts will probably try to dissuade you from "working," but if you persist you'll become accepted. Staying in a village is definitely not for everyone. Most houses contain no electricity, running water, toilet, furniture, etc., and only native food will be offered. Water and your left hand serve as toilet paper.

You should also expect to sacrifice most of your privacy, to stay up late drinking grog, and to sit in the house and socialize when you could be out exploring. On Sunday you'll have to stay put the whole day. The constant attention and lack of sanitary conditions may become tiresome, but it would be considered rude to attempt to be alone or refuse the food or grog. Staying in the villages of Fiji offers one of the most rewarding travel experiences in the South Pacific, and if everyone plays fair it will always be so.

The leatherback (Dermodhelys coriacea), *one of four species of sea turtles found in Fiji, is the only turtle that cannot retract its head or limbs. Its shell is a leathery skin rather than a horny plate. The seven lengthwise ridges on its back and five on its underside make it easily recognizable. Leatherbacks can grow up to 2.5 meters long and weigh up to a ton. In the Fiji Islands all leatherbacks and their eggs are fully protected year-round under the Fisheries Act.*

FOOD AND DRINK

Unlike some other South Pacific nations, Fiji has many good, inexpensive eateries. Chinese restaurants are everywhere. On the western side of Viti Levu, Indian restaurants sometimes use the name "lodge." Indian dishes are spicy, often curries with rice and *dhal* (lentil) soup. Mutton or goat curry are common Indian dishes, but orthodox Hindus don't eat beef and Muslims forgo pork. If you have the chance, try South Indian vegetarian dishes like *idly* (rice cake with soup) and *masala dosa* (filled rice pancake with sauce). Instead of bread Indians eat roti, a flat, tortilla-like pancake. If you have a delicate stomach you might avoid "exotic" meats like mutton and goat often served in Indian restaurants.

Real Fijian dishes such as baked fish *(ika)* in coconut cream *(lolo)* with cassava *(tavioka),* taro *(ndalo),* breadfruit *(uto),* and sweet potato *(kumala)* take a long time to prepare and must be served fresh, which makes it difficult to offer them in a restaurant. Try *nduruka,* a native vegetable tasting something like a cross between artichoke and asparagus. Taro leaves are used to make *palusami* (with coconut cream) and *rourou* (the local spinach). *Miti* is a sauce made of coconut cream, oranges, and chilies. "Bird meat" means chicken.

Kokonda is an appetizing dish made of diced raw fish marinated in coconut cream and lime juice. To prepare it, clean and skin the fish, then dice the fillet. Squeeze lemon or lime juice over it, and store in a cool place about 10 hours. When it's ready to serve, add chopped onions, garlic, green peppers, tomatoes, and coconut cream to taste. Local fishmongers know which species make the best raw fish, but know what you're doing before you join them—island stomachs are probably stronger than yours. It's sometimes safer to eat well-cooked food and to peel your own fruit.

A good opportunity to taste the local food and see traditional dancing is at a *lovo* or underground oven feast staged weekly at one of the large hotels around Nandi or on the Coral Coast for about F$40. These are usually accompanied by a Fijian *meke* or song and dance performance in which legends, love stories, and historical events are told in song and gesture. Alternatively, firewalking may be presented.

Many restaurants are closed on Sunday and a 10% tax is added to the bill. Fijians have their own pace and trying to make them do things more quickly is often counterproductive. Their charm and the friendly personal attention you receive more than make up for the occasionally slow service at restaurants.

Lobsters have become almost an endangered species on some islands due to the high prices they fetch on restaurant tables. Countless more are airfreighted to Hawaii. Before deciding to sacrifice one of these creatures for your dinner, consider that the world will be poorer for it.

The Hot Bread Kitchen chain of bakeries around Fiji serves delicious fresh fruit loaves, cheese and onion loaves, muffins, and other assorted breads. The Morris Hedstrom supermarket chain is about the cheapest, and many have milk bars with ice cream and sweets.

The famous Fiji Bitter beer is brewed by Australian-owned Carlton Brewery Ltd., with breweries in Suva and Lautoka. South Pacific Distilleries Ltd. in Lautoka produces brandy, gin, rum, vodka, and whisky under a variety of brand

slicing breadfruit

DAVID STANLEY

names. What could be better than a vodka and tonic in the midday heat or a rum and coke at sunset? Supermarkets in Fiji usually only sell beer and other alcohol weekdays 0800-1800, Saturday 0800-1300. Drinking alcoholic beverages on the street is prohibited.

Traditional Foods

The traditional diet of the Fijians consists of root crops and fruit, plus lagoon fish and the occasional pig. The vegetables include taro, yams, cassava (manioc), breadfruit, and sweet potatoes. The sweet potato *(kumala)* is something of an anomaly—it's the only Pacific food plant with a South American origin. How it got to the islands is not known, but it and tobacco seem to have been introduced into New Guinea about 1600, suggesting the possibility of an Hispanic connection.

Taro is an elephant-eared plant cultivated in freshwater swamps. Although yams are considered a prestige food, they're not as nutritious as breadfruit and taro. Yams can grow up to three meters long and weigh hundreds of kilos. Papaya (pawpaw) is nourishing: a third of a cup contains as much vitamin C as 18 apples. To ripen a green papaya overnight, puncture it a few times with a knife. Don't overeat papaya—unless you *need* an effective laxative.

The ancient Pacific islanders, who stopped making pottery over a millennium ago, developed an ingenious way of cooking in an underground earth oven *(lovo)*. First a stack of dry coconut husks is burned in a pit. Once the fire is going well, stones are heaped on top. When most of the husks have burnt away, the food is wrapped in banana leaves and placed on the hot stones, fish and meat below, vegetables above. A whole pig may be cleaned, then stuffed with banana leaves and hot stones. This cooks the beast from inside out as well as outside in, and the leaves create steam. The food is then covered with more leaves and stones, and in about two and a half hours everything will be cooked.

Breadfruit

The breadfruit *(uru)* is the plant most often associated with the South Pacific. The theme of a man turning himself into such a tree to save his family during famine often recurs in Polynesian legends. Ancient voyagers brought breadfruit shoots or seeds from Southeast Asia. When baked in an underground oven or roasted over flames, the now-seedless Polynesian variety resembles bread.

The breadfruit *(Artocarpus altilis),* a tall tree with broad green leaves, provides shade as well as food. A well-watered tree can produce as many as 1,000 pale green breadfruits a year. The starchy, easily digested fruit is rich in vitamin B. When consumed with a protein such as fish or meat it serves as an energy food. Robert Lee Eskridge described a breadfruit thus:

Its outer rind or skin, very hard, is covered with a golf-ball-like surface of small irregular pits or tiny hollows. An inner rind about a half-inch thick surrounds the fruit itself, which when baked tastes not unlike a doughy potato. Perhaps fresh bread, rolled up until it becomes a semifirm mass, best describes the breadfruit when cooked.

The Coconut Palm

Human life would not be possible on most of the Pacific's far-flung atolls without this all-purpose tree. It reaches maturity in eight years, then produces about 50 nuts a year for 60 years. Aside from the tree's esthetic value and usefulness in providing shade, the water of the green coconut provides a refreshing drink, and the white meat of the young nut is a delicious food. The harder meat of more mature nuts is grated and squeezed, giving rise to a coconut cream eaten alone or used in cooking. The oldest nuts are cracked open, and the hard meat is removed, then dried to be sold as copra. Copra is pressed to extract the oil, which in turn is made into candles, cosmetics, and soap. Millionaire's salad is made by shredding the growth cut from the heart of the tree. For each salad, a fully mature tree must be sacrificed.

The nut's hard inner shell can be used as a cup and makes excellent firewood. Rope, cordage, brushes, and heavy matting are pro-

DIANA LASICH HARPER

Every part of the coconut tree (Cocus nucifera) can be used. The husk provides cord, mats, brushes, and fuel; the leaves thatch, baskets, and fans; and the trunk building material. Food and oil from the nuts are the greatest prize. A healthy tree will produce 50 nuts a year for over 60 years.

duced from the coir fiber of the husk. The smoke from burning husks is a most effective mosquito repellent. The leaves of the coconut tree are used to thatch the roofs of the islanders' cottages or are woven into baskets, mats, and fans. The trunk provides timber for building and furniture. Actually, these are only the common uses: there are many others besides.

VISAS AND OFFICIALDOM

Everyone needs a passport valid at least three months beyond the date of entry. No visa is required of visitors from Western Europe, North America, or most Commonwealth countries for stays of 30 days or less, although everyone needs a ticket to leave. Tourists are forbidden to become involved in any sort of political activity, to engage in political studies, or to conduct research. The required vaccination against yellow fever or cholera only applies if you're arriving directly from an infected area, such as the Amazon jungles or the banks of the Ganges River.

Extensions of stay are given out two months at a time up to a maximum of four months free

of charge by the immigration offices in Suva and Lautoka, and at Nandi Airport. If you extend your stay somewhere else the police have to send your passport to Suva, and this process will take a week at least. You must apply before your current permit expires. After the first four months, you can get another two months to bring your total stay up to six months by paying a F$55 fee. Bring your passport, onward or return ticket, and proof of sufficient funds. After six months you must leave and aren't supposed to return until another six months have passed.

Fiji has three ports of entry for yachts: Suva, Lautoka, and Levuka. Calling at an outer island

DIPLOMATIC OFFICES

Permanent Mission to the United Nations, One U.N. Plaza, 26th Floor, New York, NY 10017, U.S.A. (fax 212/319-1896)

Embassy of Fiji, 2233 Wisconsin Ave. NW, Suite 240, Washington, DC 20007, U.S.A. (fax 202/337-1966)

Embassy of Fiji, Box E159, Queen Elizabeth Terrace, 9 Beagle St., Canberra, ACT 2600, Australia (fax 61-2/6295-3283)

Consulate-General of Fiji, Level 12, St. Martin's Tower, Box Q236, 31 Market St., Sydney, NSW 2000, Australia (fax 61-2/9267-1195)

Embassy of Fiji, 31 Pipitea St., Box 3940, Wellington, New Zealand (fax 64-4/499-1011)

Consulate-General of Fiji, Level 4, Federal House, 86 Federal St., Box 4238, Auckland, New Zealand (fax 64-9/377-3954)

Embassy of Fiji, Defense House, 4th Floor, Champion Parade, Box 6117, Port Moresby NCD, Papua New Guinea (fax 675/217-220)

Embassy of Fiji, 34 Hyde Park Gate, London SW7 5BN, England (fax 44-171/584-2838)

Embassy of Fiji, 66 avenue de Cortenberg, B.P. 7, 1040 Brussels, Belgium (fax 32-2/736-1458)

Embassy of Fiji, Noa Building, 10th Floor, 3-5, 2-Chome, Azabudai, Minato-Ku, Tokyo 106, Japan (fax 81-3/3587-2563)

Embassy of Fiji, Suite 2.03, 2nd Floor, Wisma Equity, 150 Jalan Ampang, 50450 Kuala Lumpur, Malaysia (fax 60-3/241-5636)

before clearing customs is prohibited. Levuka is by far the easiest place to check in or out, as all of the officials have offices right on the main wharf. To visit the outer islands, yachts require a letter of authorization from the Secretary of Fijian Affairs in Suva or the commissioner (at Lambasa, Lautoka, or Nausori) of the division they wish to visit.

Here's a list of Fiji's diplomatic offices around the world where you can inquire about the possibility of working in Fiji (special skills required) or just get information.

kalahimu

MONEY

The currency is the Fiji dollar, which is lower than the U.S. dollar in value (about US$1 = F$1.39). It's based on a basket of currencies, which means it doesn't fluctuate much. All prices quoted herein are in Fiji dollars unless otherwise stated. Each Monday the *Wall Street Journal* runs a "World Value of the Dollar" column which lists the current exchange rate of the Fiji dollar. For Australians and Canadians Fijian currency is easy to understand as it's almost one to one.

The first Fijian coins were minted in London in 1934, but Fiji continued to deal in British pounds, shillings, and pence until 1969 when dollars and cents were introduced (at the rate of two Fiji dollars to one pound). There are bills of F$1, F$2, F$5, F$10, F$20, and F$50, and despite Fiji's expulsion from the Commonwealth in 1987, the portrait of Queen Elizabeth still appears on them (and the Union Jack still forms part of the country's flag).

Banking hours are Monday to Thursday 0930-1500, Friday 0930-1600. Commercial banks operating in Fiji include the ANZ Bank, Indian-owned Bank of Baroda, Pakistani-owned Habib Bank, National Bank of Fiji, and Bank of Hawaii, and

Westpac Banking Corporation. Don't expect to change foreign currency outside the main towns. There are banks in all the towns, but it's usually not possible to change traveler's checks on remote outer islands; credit cards are strictly for the cities and resorts (the best cards to bring are American Express, Diners Club, MasterCard, and Visa), though most banks give cash advances. Take care changing at hotels, which often give a much lower rate than the banks.

The import of foreign currency is unrestricted, but only F$100 in Fijian banknotes may be exported. Avoid taking any Fijian banknotes out of the country at all, as Fijian dollars are difficult to change and heavily discounted outside Fiji. Change whatever you have left over into the currency of the next country on your itinerary or spend it on duty-free camera film.

The bulk of your travel funds should be in traveler's checks. American Express is probably the best kind to have, as they're represented by Tapa International in Suva (ANZ House, 4th Floor, 25 Victoria Parade; tel. 302-333, fax 302-048) and Nandi (Nandi Airport Concourse; tel. 722-325). If your American Express checks are lost or stolen, contact either of these. Thomas

Cook has an office of their own at 21 Thomson St., Suva (tel. 301-603, fax 300-304).

If you need money sent, have your banker make a telegraphic transfer to any Westpac Bank branch in Fiji. Many banks will hold a sealed envelope for you in their vault for a nominal fee—a good way to avoid carrying unneeded valuables with you all around Fiji. Don't show everyone how much money you have in your wallet, as this causes resentment and invites theft.

On 1 July 1992 Fiji introduced a 10% value added tax (VAT) which is usually (but not always) included in quoted prices. Among the few items exempt from the tax are unprocessed local foods and bus fares. Despite VAT, Fiji is perhaps the least expensive country in the South Pacific and inflation is low. Tipping isn't customary in Fiji, although some luxury resorts have a staff Christmas fund, to which contributions are welcome.

POST AND TELECOMMUNICATIONS

Post

Post offices are generally open weekdays 0800-1600 and they hold general delivery mail for two months. When collecting mail at general delivery, be sure to check for the initials of your first and second names, plus any initial that is similar. Have your correspondents print and underline your last name. Be aware that there are two post offices at Nandi which hold such mail, one in town, the other at the airport.

Fiji's postal workers are amazingly polite and efficient, and postage is inexpensive, so mail all of your postcards from here! Always use airmail when posting letters from Fiji. Airmail takes two weeks to reach North America and Europe, surface mail takes up to six months. Consider also using airmail for parcels, but if time isn't important, most surface parcels do arrive eventually and small packets weighing less that one kg benefit from an especially low tariff. The weight limit for overseas parcels is 10 kg. Express mail service (EMS) is more expensive but much faster and up to 20 kg may be sent (only available to Australia, Canada, France, Great Britain, New Zealand, U.S.A., Western Samoa, and Singapore). The only post offices accepting EMS mail are Lambasa, Lautoka, Mba, Nandi, Nandi Airport, and Suva.

When writing to individuals or businesses in Fiji, include the post office box number, as mail delivery is rare. If it's a remote island or small village you're writing to, the person's name will be sufficient. Include the words "Fiji Islands" in the address (otherwise the letter might go to Fuji, Japan) and underline Fiji (so it doesn't end up in Iceland). To send a picture postcard to an islander is a very nice way of saying thank you.

Telecommunications

Fiji has direct dialing via satellite and undersea cables, and most post offices have public telephones. Lift the receiver, wait for a dial tone, then deposit a coin and dial. Some coin telephones only accept new coins minted in 1990 or later. Card phones are much more convenient than coin phones and a telephone card is a very wise investment. The cards come in denominations of F$2, F$5, F$10, and F$20, and all post offices and many shops have them. In emergencies, dial 000. Domestic directory assistance is 011, international directory assistance 022, the domestic operator 010, the international operator 012. Domestic calls from public telephones are half price 1800-0600, and all day on Saturday, Sunday, and public holidays.

Fiji's international access code from public telephones is 05, so insert your card, dial 05, the country code, the area code, and the number. To call overseas collect (billed at the higher person-to-person rate), dial 031, the country code, the area code, and the number. If calling Fiji from abroad, dial your own international access code, Fiji's telephone code 679, and the local six-digit number listed in this book (there are no area codes in Fiji). If the line is inaudible, hang up immediately and try again.

A good way to place a long-distance call is to go to the FINTEL (Fiji International Telecommunications Ltd.) office on Victoria Parade, Suva, or to any post office. The basic charge for three minutes is F$5.28 to Australia or New Zealand, F$8.91 to North America, Europe, or Japan. All operator-assisted international calls have a three-minute minimum charge and ad-

$10 VAT INC.

Fijian History Series

Post & Telecom PHONECARD

ditional time is charged per minute, whereas international calls made using telephone cards have no minimum and the charges are broken down into flat six-second units (telephone cards with less than F$3 credit on them cannot be used for international calls). By using a telephone card you limit the amount the call can possibly cost and won't end up overspending should you forget to keep track of the time. International calls placed from hotel rooms are always much more expensive (ask the receptionist for the location of the nearest card phone).

In 1994 AT&T's "USADirect" service was introduced to Fiji, at tel. 004-890-100-1. This is about 40% more expensive than using a local telephone card for international calls as described above, and there are surcharges if you use a calling card or call collect. The advantage is that you're immediately connected to an AT&T operator or automated voice prompt, so it might be useful if you already have an AT&T calling card and don't mind paying extra for the convenience.

Fax

Faxes can be sent from the following main post offices: Lambasa, Lautoka, Mba, Nandi, Singatoka, and Suva. Outgoing faxes cost F$6.50 a page to regional countries, F$7.70 to other countries, both plus a F$3.30 handing fee. You can also receive faxes at these post offices for F$1.10 a page. One reader on a wide-ranging trip said he found it very effective to leave a list of his travel dates and an extra copy of this book with his family. Not only were they able to follow his travels around Fiji, but they had all the fax numbers needed to contact him.

If a fax you are trying to send to Fiji doesn't go through smoothly on the first or second try, wait and try again at another time of day. If it doesn't work then, stop trying as the fax machine at the other end may not be able to read your signal and your telephone company will levy a hefty minimum charge for each attempt. Call the international operator to ask what is going wrong.

TIME AND MEASUREMENTS

Time

The international date line generally follows 180° longitude and creates a difference of 24 hours in time between the two sides. It swings east at Tuvalu to avoid slicing Fiji in two. Everything in the Eastern Hemisphere west of the date line is a day later, everything in the Western Hemisphere east of the line is a day earlier (or behind). Air travelers lose a day when they fly west across the date line and gain it back when they return. Keep track of things by repeating to yourself, *If it's Sunday in Samoa, it's Monday on Malolo.*

In this book all clock times are rendered according to the 24-hour airline timetable system, i.e. 0100 is 1:00 a.m., 1300 is 1:00 p.m., 2330 is 11:30 p.m. The islanders operate on "coconut time"—the nut will fall when it is ripe. In the languid air of the South Seas, punctuality takes on a new meaning. Appointments are approximate and the service relaxed. Even the seasons are fuzzy: sometimes wetter, sometimes drier, but almost always hot. Slow down to the island pace and get in step with where you are. You may not get as much done, but you'll enjoy life a lot more. Daylight hours in the tropics run 0600-1800 with few seasonal variations and hardly any twilight. When the sun begins to do down, you have less than half an hour before darkness.

Measurements

The metric system is used in Fiji. Study the conversion table in the back of this handbook if you're not used to thinking metric. Most distances herein are quoted in kilometers and they become easy to comprehend when you know than one km is the distance a normal person walks in 10 minutes. A meter is slightly more than a yard and a liter is just over a quart.

Unless otherwise indicated, north is at the top of all maps in this handbook. When using official topographical maps you can determine the scale by taking the representative fraction (RF) and dividing by 100. This will give the number of meters represented by one cm. For example, a map with an RF of 1:10,000 would represent 100 meters for every centimeter on the map.

Electric Currents

If you're taking along a plug-in razor, radio, or other electrical appliance, be aware that Fiji uses 240 AC voltage, 50 cycles. Most appliances require a converter to change from one voltage to another. You'll also need an adapter to cope with three-prong sockets with the two on top at angles. Pick up both items before you leave home, as they're a nuisance to find in Fiji. Keep voltages in mind if you buy duty-free appliances: dual voltage (110-220 V) items are best.

Videos

Commercial travel videotapes make nice souvenirs, but always keep in mind that there are three incompatible video formats loose in the world: NTSC (used in North America), PAL (used in Britain, Germany, Japan, and Australia), and SECAM (used in France and Russia). Don't buy prerecorded tapes abroad unless they're of the system used in your country.

INFORMATION

MEDIA

The *Fiji Times* (G.P.O. Box 1167, Suva; tel. 304-111, fax 302-011), "the first newspaper published in the world today," was founded at Levuka in 1869 but is now owned by publishing mogul Rupert Murdoch's estate. The *Daily Post* (Box 7010, Valelevu, Nasinu; tel. 313-342, fax 340-455) is a government-owned morning newspaper with a local focus. The *Times* has a daily print run of 37,000, the *Post* about 10,000. Since 1987 the press in Fiji has had to walk a narrow line, and in late 1994 Fiji's Minister of Information called for 51% local ownership of the *Times* after mild criticism of his government appeared in the paper.

Two regional newsmagazines are published in Suva: *Pacific Islands Monthly* (tel. 304-111, fax 303-809), also part of the Murdoch empire; and *Islands Business Pacific* (tel. 303-108, fax 301-423), owned by several local European businesspeople. As well, there's a monthly Fijian business magazine called *The Review* (G.P.O. Box 12095, Suva; tel. 305-916, fax 305-256), owned by Fiji journalist Yashwant Gaunder. The *Review* has been threatened with suspension by the government due to its independent coverage. These magazines are well worth picking up during your trip, and a subscription will help you keep in touch. Turn to "Resources" at the end of this book for more Fiji-oriented publications.

The **Pacific Islands News Association** (46 Gordon St., Suva; fax 303-943) holds an annual conference of regional editors to discuss media issues. PINA is usually seen as representing management interests, while the **Pacific Journalists' Association** is comprised of working journalists. The regional news service **PacNews** (Box 116, Port Vila; tel. 678/26300, fax 678/26301) was founded in 1987 with the assistance of the Friedrich Ebert Stiftung of Germany. In 1990 PacNews was forced to evacuate its premises in Fiji due to official harassment.

THE **Fiji Times**

THE FIRST NEWSPAPER PUBLISHED IN THE WORLD TODAY

SATURDAY, JUNE 18, 1988   52 PAGES   30¢   119TH YEAR   NO. 145

TOURIST OFFICES

Fiji Visitors Bureau, G.P.O. Box 92, Suva, Fiji Islands (fax 679/300-970)

Fiji Visitors Bureau, Box 9217, Nandi Airport, Fiji Islands (fax 679/720-141)

Fiji Visitors Bureau, Suite 220, 5777 West Century Blvd., Los Angeles, CA 90045, U.S.A. (fax 310/670-2318)

Fiji Visitors Bureau, Level 12, St. Martin's Tower, 31 Market St., Sydney, NSW 2000, Australia (fax 61-2/9264-3060)

Fiji Visitors Bureau, Suite 204, 620 St. Kilda Rd., Melbourne 3000, Australia (fax 61-3/9510-3650)

Fiji Visitors Bureau, Box 1179, Auckland, New Zealand (fax 64-9/309-4720)

Fiji Visitors Bureau, NOA Building, 14th Floor, 3-5, 2-Chome, Azabudai, Minato-ku, Tokyo 106, Japan (fax 81-3/3587-2563)

Fiji Embassy, 34 Hyde Park Gate, London SW7 5DN, England (fax 44-171/584-2838)

Representation Plus, 375 Upper Richmond Rd. W, London SW14 7NX, England (fax 44-181/392-1318)

Interface Int. GmbH, Dirksenstrasse 40, 1020 Berlin, Germany (fax 49-302/381-7641)

The government-owned Fiji Broadcasting Commission (Box 334, Suva; tel. 314-333, fax 301-643) operates three public AM radio stations heard throughout the islands, Radio Fiji 1 in English and Fijian (BBC world news at 0800), Radio Fiji 2 in English and Hindi (local news in English at 0700 and 1900), and Radio Fiji 3 in English. They also run music-oriented FM 104. Privately owned Communications Fiji Ltd. (Private Mail Bag, Suva; tel. 314-766) operates two commercial FM stations, which broadcast around the clock, FM 96 in English and Fijian, and Radio Navtarang in Hindi. The latter two are not heard everywhere in the country.

Television broadcasting only began in Fiji in 1991, and at last report Fiji One was on the air weekdays 1700-2300, Saturday 1200-2400, Sunday 1200-2300. The Fiji government owns 65% of the company, and another 15% is owned by TV New Zealand which manages the station. A clause in Fiji TV's license forbids them from broadcasting "anything offensive to the Great Council of Chiefs." Local content is negligible and the steady stream of American sitcoms spreads alien cultural values in Fiji. News broadcasts on all of the government-owned radio stations are prepared by employees of the Ministry of Information, and government control of large segments of the media in Fiji is a matter of growing concern.

TOURIST INFORMATION

The government-funded Fiji Visitors Bureau (G.P.O. Box 92, Suva; fax 300-970) sends out free upon request general brochures and a list of hotels with current prices. In Fiji they have walk-in offices in Suva and at Nandi Airport. For a list of their overseas offices, see the "Diplomatic Offices" chart.

The Fiji Hotel Association (Private Mail Bag, G.P.O. Suva; fax 300-331) will mail you a brochure listing all upmarket hotels with specific prices, though low-budget accommodations are not included.

The free Fiji Magic magazine (Box 12511, Suva; tel. 313-944, fax 302-852) is very useful to get an idea of what's on during your visit. Also browse the local bookstores, Desai Bookshops, Zenon Book Shops, and the Singatoka Book Depot, with branches all over Fiji.

HEALTH

Fiji's climate is a healthy one and the main causes of death are noncommunicable diseases such as heart disease, diabetes, and cancer. There's no malaria here but a mosquito-transmitted disease known as dengue fever is endemic, so avoid getting bitten. The sea and air are clear and usually pollution-free. The humidity nourishes the skin and the local fruit is brimming with vitamins. If you take a few precautions, you'll never have a sick day. The information provided below is intended to make you knowledgeable, not fearful.

Health care is good, with an abundance of hospitals, health centers, and nursing stations scattered around the country. The largest hospitals are in Lambasa, Lautoka, Levuka, Mba, Savusavu, Singatoka, Suva, and Taveuni. Attention at these is inexpensive, but in the towns it's less time-consuming and much simpler to visit a private doctor. The facilities may not be up to American standards but the fee will be infinitely lower. American-made medications may be unobtainable in Fiji, so bring a supply of whatever you think you'll need. Antibiotics should only be used to treat serious wounds, and only after medical advice.

To call an ambulance dial 000. In case of scuba diving accidents, an operating dive recompression chamber (tel. 305-154) is available in Suva. The 24-hour recompression medical evacuation number is 362-172.

The sale of travel insurance is big business in the U.S., but the value of the policies themselves is often questionable. If your regular group health insurance also covers you while you're traveling abroad, it's probably enough. If you do opt for the security of travel insurance, insist on a policy that also covers theft or loss of luggage and emergency medical evacuations. If you'll be involved in any "dangerous activities," such as scuba diving or surfing, read the fine print to make sure your policy is valid.

Acclimatizing

Don't go from winter weather into the steaming tropics without a rest before and after. Minimize jet lag by setting your watch to local time at your destination as soon as you board the flight. Westbound flights into the South Pacific from North America or Europe are less jolting since you follow the sun and your body gets a few hours of extra sleep. On the way home you're moving against the sun and the hours of sleep your body loses cause jet lag. Airplane cabins have low humidity, so drink lots of juice or water instead of carbonated drinks and don't overeat in-flight. It's also best to forgo coffee, as it will only keep you awake, and alcohol helps dehydrate you. Scuba diving on departure day can give you a severe case of the bends.

If you start feeling seasick onboard ship, stare at the horizon, which is always steady, and stop thinking about it. Anti-motion-sickness pills are useful to have along.

Frequently the feeling of thirst is false and only due to mucous membrane dryness. Gargling or taking two or three gulps of warm water should be enough. Other means of keeping moisture in the body are a hot drink like tea or black coffee, or any kind of slightly salted or sour drink in small quantities. Salt in fresh lime juice is remarkably refreshing.

The tap water in Fiji is usually drinkable except just after a cyclone or during droughts, when care should be taken. If in doubt, boil it or use purification pills. Tap water that is uncomfortably hot to touch is usually safe. Allow it to cool in a clean container. If the tap water is contaminated, the local ice will be, too. Avoid brushing your teeth with water unfit to drink, and wash or peel fruit and vegetables if you can. Cooked food is less subject to contamination than raw.

Sunburn

Though you may think a tan will make you *look* healthier and more attractive, it's very damaging to the skin, which becomes dry, rigid, and prematurely old and wrinkled, especially on the face. And a burn from the sun greatly increases your risk of getting skin cancer. Begin with short exposures to the sun, perhaps half an hour at a time, followed by an equal period in the shade. Drink plenty of liquids to keep your pores open and avoid the sun from 1000 to 1400. Clouds and beach umbrellas will not protect you fully. Wear a T-shirt while snorkeling to protect your back. Sunbathing is the main cause of cataracts to the eyes, so wear sunglasses and a wide-brimmed hat and beware of reflected sunlight.

Use a sunscreen lotion containing PABA rather than oil (don't forget your nose, lips, forehead, neck, hands, and feet). Sunscreens protect you from ultraviolet rays (a leading cause of cancer), while oils magnify the sun's effect. A 15-factor sunscreen provides 93% protection (a more expensive 30-factor sunscreen is only slightly better at 97% protection). Apply the lotion *before* going to the beach to avoid being burned on the way, and reapply periodically to replace sunscreen washed away by perspiration. After sunbathing, take a tepid shower rather than a hot one, which would wash away your natural skin oils. Stay moist and use a vitamin E evening cream to preserve the youth of your skin. Calamine ointment soothes skin already burned, as does coconut oil. Pharmacists recommend Solarcaine to soothe burned skin. Rinsing off with a vinegar solution reduces peeling, and aspirin relieves some of the pain and irritation. Vitamin A and calcium counteract overdoses of vitamin D received from the sun. The fairer your skin, the more essential it is to take care.

As earth's ozone layer is deleted due to the commercial use of chlorofluorocarbons (CFCs) and other factors, the need to protect yourself from ultraviolet radiation becomes more urgent. In 1990 the U.S. Centers for Disease Control in Atlanta reported that deaths from skin cancer increased 26% between 1973 and 1985. Previously the cancers didn't develop until age 50 or 60, but now much younger people are affected.

Ailments

Cuts and scratches infect easily in the tropics and take a long time to heal. Prevent infection from coral cuts by immediately washing wounds with soap and fresh water, then rubbing in vinegar or alcohol (whiskey will do)—painful but effective. Use a good antiseptic, if you have one. Tahitians usually dab coral cuts with lime juice. All cuts turn septic quickly in the tropics, so try to keep them clean and covered.

For bites, burns, and cuts, an antiseptic such as Solarcaine speeds healing and helps pre-

vent infection. Pure aloe vera is good for sunburn, scratches, and even coral cuts. Bites by nono flies itch for days and can become infected. Not everyone is affected by insect bites in the same way. Some people are practically immune to insects, while traveling companions experiencing exactly the same conditions are soon covered with bites. You'll soon know which type you are.

Prickly heat, an intensely irritating rash, is caused by wearing heavy clothing that is inappropriate for the climate. When the glands are blocked and the sweat is unable to evaporate, the skin becomes soggy and small red blisters appear. Synthetic fabrics like nylon are especially bad in this regard. Take a cold shower, apply calamine lotion, dust with talcum powder, and take off those clothes! Until things improve, avoid alcohol, tea, coffee, and any physical activity that makes you sweat. If you're sweating profusely, increase your intake of salt slightly to avoid fatigue, but not without concurrently drinking more water.

Use antidiarrheal medications sparingly. Rather than take drugs to plug yourself up, drink plenty of unsweetened liquids like green coconut or fresh fruit juice to help flush yourself out. Egg yolk mixed with nutmeg helps diarrhea, or have a rice and tea day. Avoid dairy products. Most cases of diarrhea are self-limiting and require only simple replacement of fluids and salts lost in diarrheal stools. If the diarrhea is persistent or you experience high fever, drowsiness, or blood in the stool, stop traveling, rest, and consider attending a clinic. For constipation eat pineapple or any peeled fruit.

If you're sleeping in villages or with the locals you may pick up head or body lice. Pharmacists and general stores usually have a remedy that will eliminate the problem in minutes (pack a bottle with you if you're uptight). You'll know you're lousy when you start to scratch: pick out the little varmints and snap them between your thumbnails for fun. The locals pluck the creatures out of each other's hair one by one, a way of confirming friendships and showing affection. Intestinal parasites (worms) are also widespread. The hookworm bores its way through the soles of your feet, and if you go barefoot through gardens and plantations you're sure to pick up something.

AIDS

In 1981 scientists in the United States and France first recognized the Acquired Immune Deficiency Syndrome (AIDS) which was later discovered to be caused by a virus called the Human Immuno-deficiency Virus (HIV). HIV breaks down the body's immunity to infections leading to AIDS. The virus can lie hidden in the body for many years without producing any obvious symptoms or before developing into the AIDS disease.

HIV lives in white blood cells and is present in the sexual fluids of humans. It's difficult to catch and is spread mostly through sexual intercourse, by needle or syringe sharing among intravenous drug users, in blood transfusions, and during pregnancy and birth (if the mother is infected). Using another person's razor blade or having your body pierced or tattooed are also risky, but the HIV virus cannot be transmitted by shaking hands, kissing, cuddling, fondling, sneezing, cooking food, or sharing eating or drinking utensils. One cannot be infected by saliva, sweat, tears, urine, or feces; toilet seats, telephones, swimming pools, or mosquito bites do not cause AIDS. Ostracizing a known AIDS victim is not only immoral but absurd.

Most blood banks now screen their products for HIV, and you can protect yourself against dirty needles by only allowing an injection if you see the syringe taken out of a fresh unopened pack. The simplest safeguard during sex is the proper use of a condom. Unroll the condom onto the erect penis; while withdrawing after ejaculation, hold onto the condom as you come out. Never try to recycle a condom, and pack a supply with you as it's a nuisance trying to buy them locally.

HIV is spread more often through anal than vaginal sex because the lining of the rectum is much weaker than that of the vagina and ordinary condoms sometimes tear when used in anal sex. If you have anal sex, only use extra-strong condoms and special water-based lubricants since oil, Vaseline, and cream weaken the rubber. During oral sex you must make sure you don't get any semen or menstrual blood in your mouth. A woman runs 10 times the risk of contracting AIDS from a man than the other way around, and the threat is always greater when another sexually transmitted disease (STD) is present.

The very existence of AIDS calls for a basic change in human behavior. No vaccine or drug exists which can prevent or cure AIDS, and because the virus mutates frequently, no remedy may ever be totally effective. Other STDs such as syphilis, gonorrhea, chlamydia, hepatitis B, and herpes are far more common than AIDS and can lead to serious complications such as infertility, but at least they can usually be cured.

The euphoria of travel can make it easier to fall in love or have sex with a stranger, so travelers must be informed of these dangers. As a tourist you should always practice safe sex to prevent AIDS and other STDs. You never know who is infected or even if you yourself have become infected. It's important to bring the subject up *before* you start to make love. Make a joke out of it by pulling out a condom and asking your new partner, "Say, do you know what this is?" Or perhaps, "Your condom or mine?" Far from being unromantic or embarrassing, you'll both feel more relaxed with the subject off your minds and it's much better than worrying afterwards if you might have been infected. The golden rule is safe sex or no sex.

By mid-1994 an estimated 16 million people worldwide were HIV carriers, and hundreds of thousands had died of AIDS. Statistics released by the South Pacific Commission in February 1995 acknowledge 611 HIV infections and 220 cases of AIDS in the Pacific islands. Most affected were Tahiti-Polynesia (HIV 144, AIDS 43), New Caledonia (HIV 115, AIDS 37), Papua New Guinea (HIV 236, AIDS 87), and Guam (HIV 64, AIDS 24). In Fiji only 21 HIV infections and seven AIDS cases had been reported, but the real number could be 50 times higher, and other STDs such as syphilis, gonorrhea, and herpes have reached almost epidemic proportions in urban areas. Thus it's essential that everyone do their utmost to limit the spread of this killer disease.

An HIV infection can be detected through a blood test because the antibodies created by the body to fight off the virus can be seen under a microscope. It takes at least three weeks for the antibodies to be produced and in some cases as long as six months before they can be picked up during a screening test. If you think you may have run a risk, you should discuss the appropriateness of a test with your doctor. It's always better to know if you are infected so as to avoid infecting others, obtain early treatment of symptoms, and make realistic plans. If you know someone with AIDS you should give them all the support you can (there's no danger in such contact unless blood is present).

Toxic Fish

Over 400 species of tropical reef fish, including wrasses, snappers, groupers, barracudas, jacks, moray eels, surgeonfish, and shellfish, are known to cause seafood poisoning (ciguatera). There's no way to tell if a fish will cause ciguatera: a species can be poisonous on one side of the island, but not on the other.

Over a decade ago scientists on Tahiti determined that a one-celled dinoflagellate called *Gambierdiscus toxicus* was the cause. Normally these microalgae are found only in the ocean depths, but when a reef is disturbed by natural or human causes they can multiply dramatically in a lagoon. The dinoflagellates are consumed by tiny herbivorous fish and the toxin passes up through the food chain to larger fish where it becomes concentrated in the head and guts. The toxins have no effect on the fish that feed on them.

The symptoms (tingling, prickling, itching, nausea, vomiting, erratic heartbeat, joint and muscle pains) usually subside in a few days. Induce vomiting and take castor oil as a laxative if you're unlucky. Symptoms can recur for up to a year, and victims may become allergic to all seafoods. In the Marshall Islands, a drug called Mannitol has been effective in treating ciguatera, but as yet little is known about it. Avoid biointoxication by cleaning fish as soon as they're caught, discarding the head and organs, and taking special care with oversized fish. Whether the fish is consumed cooked or raw has no bearing on this problem. Local residents often know from experience which species may be eaten.

Other Diseases

Infectious hepatitis A (jaundice) is a liver ailment transmitted person to person or through unboiled water, uncooked vegetables, or other foods contaminated during handling. The risk of infection is highest for those who eat village food, so if you'll be spending much time in rural areas the hepatitus A vaccine or an immune globulin shot is recommended. You'll know you've got the hep when your eyeballs and urine turn yellow. Time and rest are the only cure. Viral hepatitis B is spread through sexual or blood contact.

There have been sporadic outbreaks of cholera in the Gilbert and Caroline islands (in Micronesia). Cholera is acquired via contaminated food or water, so avoid uncooked foods, peel your own fruit, and drink bottled drinks if you happen to arrive in an infected area. Typhoid fever is also caused by contaminated food or water, while tetanus (lockjaw) occurs when cuts or bites become infected. Horrible disfiguring diseases such as leprosy and elephantiasis are hard to catch, so it's unlikely you'll be visited by one of these nightmares of the flesh.

There's no malaria, but a mosquito-transmitted disease known as dengue fever is endemic in Fiji. Signs are headaches, sore throat, pain in the joints, fever, chills, nausea, and rash. The illness can last anywhere from five to 15 days; although you can relieve the symptoms somewhat, the only real cure is to stay in bed, drink lots of water, take aspirin for the headaches, and wait it out. It's painful, but dengue fever usually only kills infants. No vaccine exists, so just avoid getting bitten.

Vaccinations

Officially, most visitors are not required to get any vaccinations at all before coming to Fiji. Tetanus, diphtheria, typhoid fever, and polio shots are not required, but they're a good idea if you're going off the beaten track. Tetanus and diphtheria shots are given together, and a booster is required every 10 years. The typhoid fever shot is every three years, polio every five years.

The cholera vaccine is only 50% effective, valid just six months, and bad reactions are common, but get it if you know you're headed for an infected area (such as Micronesia). All passengers arriving in Fiji from Funafuti, Tarawa, or Majuro must show proof of a cholera vaccination. A yellow-fever vaccination is required if you've been in an infected area (such as the jungles of South America and Africa) within the six days prior to arrival. Since the vaccination is valid 10 years, get one if you're an inveterate globe-trotter.

Immune globulin (IG) isn't 100% effective against hepatitis A, but it does increase your general resistance to infections. IG prophylaxis must be repeated every five months. Hepatitis B vaccination involves three doses over a six-month period (duration of protection unknown) and is recommended mostly for people planning extended stays in the region.

WHAT TO TAKE

Packing

Assemble everything you simply must take and cannot live without—then cut the pile in half. If you're still left with more than will fit into a medium-sized suitcase or backpack, continue eliminating. You have to be tough on yourself and just limit what you take. Now put it all into your bag. If the total (bag and contents) weighs over 16 kg, you'll sacrifice much of your mobility. If you can keep it down to 10 kg, you're traveling *light.* Categorize, separate, and pack all your things into plastic bags or stuff sacks for convenience and protection from moisture. In addition to your principal bag, you'll want a day pack or flight bag. When checking in for flights, carry anything that cannot be replaced in your hand luggage.

Your Luggage

A soft medium-sized backpack with a lightweight internal frame is best. Big external-frame packs are fine for mountain climbing but get caught in airport conveyor belts and are very inconvenient on public transport. The best packs have a zippered compartment in back where you can tuck in the straps and hip belt before turning your pack over to an airline or bus. This type of pack has the flexibility of allowing you to simply walk when motorized transport is unavailable or unacceptable; with the straps zipped in it looks like a regular suitcase, should you wish to go upmarket for a while.

Make sure your pack carries the weight on your hips, has a cushion for spine support, and doesn't pull backwards. The pack should strap snugly to your body but also allow ventilation to your back. It should be made of a water-resistant material such as nylon and have a Fastex buckle.

Look for a pack with double, two-way zipper compartments and pockets you can lock with miniature padlocks. They might not *stop* a thief, but they will be a deterrent to the casual pilferer. A 60-cm length of lightweight chain and another padlock will allow you to fasten your pack to something. Keep valuables locked in your bag, out of sight, as even upmarket hotel rooms aren't 100% safe.

Camping Equipment and Clothing

A small nylon tent guarantees you a place to sleep every night, but it *must* be mosquito- and waterproof. Get one with a tent fly, then waterproof both tent and fly with a can of waterproofing spray. You'll seldom need a sleeping bag in the tropics, so that's one item you can easily cut. A Youth Hostel sleeping sheet is ideal—all YHA handbooks give instructions on how to make your own or buy one at your local hostel. You don't really need to carry a bulky foam pad, as the ground is seldom cold.

For clothes take loose-fitting cotton washables, light in color and weight. Synthetic fabrics are hot and sticky, and most of the things you wear at home are too heavy for the tropics—be prepared for the humidity. Dress is casual, with slacks and a sports shirt okay for men even at dinner parties. Local women often wear long colorful dresses in the evening, but shorts are okay in daytime. If in doubt, bring the minimum with you and buy tropical garb upon arrival. Stick to clothes you can rinse in your room sink.

The lavalava or *sulu* is a bright two-meter piece of cloth both men and women wrap about themselves as an all-purpose garment. Any islander can show you how to wear it. Missionaries taught the South Sea island women to drape their attributes in long, flowing gowns, called muumuus in Hawaii. In the South Pacific, the dress is better known as a Mother Hubbard for the muumuu-attired nursery rhyme character who "went to the cupboard to fetch her poor dog a bone."

Take comfortable shoes that have been broken in. Running shoes and rubber thongs (flip-flops) are very handy for day use but will bar you from nightspots with strict dress codes. Scuba divers' rubber booties are lightweight and perfect for both crossing rivers and reefwalking, though an old pair of sneakers may be just as good. Below we've provided a few checklists to help you assemble your gear. The listed items combined weigh well over 16 kg, so eliminate what doesn't suit you:

- pack with internal frame
- day pack or airline bag
- nylon tent and fly
- tent-patching tape
- mosquito net
- sleeping sheet
- sun hat or visor
- essential clothing only
- bathing suit
- sturdy walking shoes
- rubber thongs
- rubber booties
- mask and snorkel

Accessories

A clip-on book light with extra batteries allows campers to read at night. Serious scuba divers bring their own regulator, buoyancy compensator, and gauges, and perhaps a lightweight wetsuit for protection against coral. A mask and snorkel are essential equipment—you'll be missing half of Fiji's beauty without them.

Also take along postcards of your hometown and snapshots of your house, family, workplace, etc; islanders love to see these. Always keep a promise to mail the islanders photos you take of them. Think of some small souvenir of your country (such as a lapel pin bearing a kangaroo or maple leaf, or Kennedy half dollars), which you can take along as gifts. Miniature compasses sold in camping stores also make good gifts.

Neutral gray eyeglasses protect your eyes from the sun and give the least color distortion. Take an extra pair (if you have them). Keep the laundry soap inside a couple of layers of plastic bags. To cook at campsites you'll often need a small stove: trying to keep rainforest wood burning will drive you to tears from smoke and frustration. Camping fuel cannot be carried on commercial airliners, however, so choose a stove that uses a common fuel like kerosene or gasoline.

- camera and 10 rolls of film
- compass
- pocket flashlight
- extra batteries
- candlepocket alarm calculator
- pocket watch
- extra pair of glasses

- sunglasses
- padlock and lightweight chain
- collapsible umbrella
- string for a clothesline
- powdered laundry soap
- universal sink plug
- minitowel
- silicon glue
- sewing kit
- miniscissors
- nail clippers
- fishing line for sewing gear
- plastic cup and plate
- can and bottle opener
- corkscrew
- penknife
- spoon
- water bottle
- matches
- tea bags

Toiletries and Medical Kit

Since everyone has his/her own medical requirements and since brand names vary from country to country, there's no point going into detail here. Note, however, that even the basics (such as aspirin) are unavailable on some outer islands, so be prepared. Bring medicated powder for prickly heat rash. Charcoal tablets are useful for diarrhea and poisoning (they absorb the irritants). Bring an adequate supply of any personal medications, plus your prescriptions (in generic terminology).

High humidity causes curly hair to swell and bush, straight hair to droop. If it's curly have it cut short or keep it long in a ponytail or bun. A good cut is essential with straight hair. Water-based makeup is best, as the heat and humidity cause oil glands to work overtime. High-quality locally made shampoo, body oils, and insect repellent are sold on all the islands, and the bottles are conveniently smaller than those sold in Western countries. See "Health," above, for more ideas.

- wax earplugs
- soap in plastic container
- soft toothbrush
- toothpaste
- roll-on deodorant

- shampoo
- comb and brush
- skin creams
- makeup
- tampons or napkins
- white toilet paper
- vitamin/mineral supplement
- Cutter's insect repellent
- PABA sunscreen
- Chap Stick
- a motion-sickness remedy
- contraceptives
- iodine
- water-purification pills
- delousing powder
- a diarrhea remedy
- Tiger Balm
- a cold remedy
- Alka-Seltzer
- aspirin
- antihistamine
- antifungal
- Calmitol ointment
- antibiotic ointment
- painkiller
- antiseptic cream
- disinfectant
- simple dressings
- adhesive bandages (like Band-Aids)
- prescription medicines

Money and Documents

All post offices have passport applications. If you lose your passport you should report the matter to the local police at once, obtain a certificate or receipt, then proceed to your consulate (if any!) for a replacement. If you have your birth certificate with you it facilitates things considerably. By official agreement, Canadian citizens can turn to any of the numerous Australian diplomatic offices throughout the region for assistance.

Traveler's checks in U.S. dollars are recommended, and in the South Pacific, American Express is the most efficient company when it comes to providing refunds for lost checks. Bring along a small supply of US$1 and US$5 bills to use if you don't manage to change money immediately upon arrival or if you run out of local currency and can't get to a bank.

If you have a car at home, bring along the insurance receipt so you don't have to pay insurance every time you rent a car. Ask your agent about this.

Carry your valuables in a money belt worn around your waist or neck under your clothing; most camping stores have these. Make several photocopies of the information page of your passport, personal identification, driver's license, scuba certification card, credit cards, airline tickets, receipts for purchase of traveler's checks, etc.—you should be able to get them all on one page. A brief medical history with your blood type, allergies, chronic or special health problems, eyeglass and medical prescriptions, etc., might also come in handy. Put these inside plastic bags to protect them from moisture, then carry the lists in different places, and leave one at home.

- passport
- vaccination certificates
- airline tickets
- scuba certification card
- driver's license
- traveler's checks
- some U.S. cash
- photocopies of documents
- money belt
- address book
- notebook
- envelopes
- extra ballpoints

FILM AND PHOTOGRAPHY

Look at the ads in photographic magazines for the best deals on mail-order cameras and film, or buy at a discount shop in any large city. Run a roll of film through your camera to be sure it's in good working order; clean the lens with lens-cleaning tissue and check the batteries. Remove the batteries from your camera when storing it at home for long periods. Register valuable cameras or electronic equipment with customs before you leave home so there won't be any argument over where you bought the items when you return, or at least carry the original bill of sale.

The type of camera you choose could depend on the way you travel. If you'll be staying mostly in one place, a heavy single-lens reflex (SLR) camera with spare lenses and other equipment won't trouble you. If you'll be moving around a lot for a considerable length of time, a 35-mm automatic compact camera may be better. The compacts are mostly useful for close-up shots; landscapes will seem spread out and far away. A wide-angle lens gives excellent depth of field, but hold the camera upright to avoid converging verticals. A polarizing filter prevents reflections from glass windows.

Although film is cheap and readily available in Fiji, you never know if it's been spoiled by an airport X-ray on the way there. In the U.S. film can be purchased at big discounts through mail-order companies, which advertise in photography magazines. Choose 36-exposure film over 24-exposure to save on the number of rolls you have to carry. Whenever purchasing film in Fiji take care to check the expiration date.

Films are rated by their speed and sensitivity to light, using ISO numbers from 25 to 1600. The higher the number, the greater the film's sensitivity to light. Slower films with lower ISOs (like 100-200) produce sharp images in bright sunlight. Faster films with higher ISOs (like 400) stop action and work well in low-light situations, such as in dark rainforests or at sunset. If you have a manual SLR you can avoid overexposure at midday by reducing the exposure half a stop, but *do* overexpose when photographing dark-skinned Melanesians. From 1000 to 1600 the light is often too bright to take good photos, and panoramas usually come out best early or late in the day.

Wayne J. Andrews of Eastman Kodak offers the following suggestions for enhanced photography. Keep your photos simple with one main subject and an uncomplicated background. Get as close to your subjects as you can and lower or raise the camera to their level. Include people in the foreground of scenic shots to add interest and perspective. Outdoors a flash can fill in unflattering facial shadows caused by high sun or backlit conditions. Most of all, be creative. Look for interesting details and compose the photo before you push the trigger. Instead of taking a head-on photo of a group of people, step to one side and ask them to face you. The angle improves the photo. Photograph subjects coming toward you rather than passing by. Ask permission before photographing people. If you're asked for money (rare) you can always walk away—give your subjects the same choice. There is probably no country in the world where the photographer will have as interesting and willing subjects as in Fiji.

When packing, protect your camera against vibration. Checked baggage is scanned by powerful airport X-ray monitors, so carry both camera and film aboard the plane in a clear plastic bag and ask security for a visual inspection. Some airports will refuse to do this, however. Otherwise, use a lead-laminated pouch. The old high-dose X-ray units are the worst, but even low-dose inspection units can ruin fast film (400 ASA and above). Beware of the cumulative effect of X-ray machines.

Keep your camera in a plastic bag during rain and while traveling in motorized canoes, etc. In the tropics the humidity can cause film to stick to itself; silica-gel crystals in the bag will protect film from humidity and mold growth. Protect camera and film from direct sunlight and load the film in the shade. When loading, check that the takeup spool revolves. Never leave camera or film in a hot place like a car floor, glove compartment, or trunk.

GETTING THERE

LOUISE FOOTE

Fiji's geographic position makes it the hub of transport for the entire South Pacific, and Nandi Airport is the region's most important international airport, with long-haul services to points all around the Pacific Rim. Eight international airlines fly into Nandi: Air Calédonie International, Air Marshall Islands, Air Nauru, Air New Zealand, Air Pacific, Air Vanuatu, Qantas Airways, and Solomon Airlines. Air Marshall Islands, Air Nauru, and Air Pacific also use Suva's Nausori Airport, a regional distribution center with flights to many of the nearby Polynesian countries to the east.

Fiji's national airline, **Air Pacific,** was founded as Fiji Airways in 1951 by Harold Gatty, a famous Australian aviator who had set a record in 1931 by flying around the world in eight days with American Willy Post. In 1972 the airline was reorganized as a regional carrier and the name changed to Air Pacific. Thanks to careful management, the Nandi-based company has made a profit every year since 1985. The carrier arrives at Nandi from Apia, Auckland, Brisbane, Christchurch, Honiara, Los Angeles, Melbourne, Osaka, Port Vila, Sydney, Tokyo, and Tongatapu, and at Suva from Apia, Auckland, and Tongatapu. Flying with Air Pacific means you enjoy the friendly flavor of Fiji from the moment you leave the ground.

Air Pacific flies nonstop from Los Angeles to Fiji and Air New Zealand arrives direct from Honolulu, Los Angeles, Papeete, and Rarotonga. Unfortunately Canadian Airlines International passengers originating in Toronto and Vancouver must change planes in Honolulu. Europeans must transfer at Los Angeles. It's a five-and-a-half-hour flight from California to Hawaii, then another six and a half hours from Hawaii to Fiji. The nonstop flights from Los Angeles take only 11 hours and you also save all

the time Air New Zealand spends on the ground in Hawaii.

From Australia, you can fly to Nandi on Air Pacific and Qantas, both of which arrive from Brisbane, Melbourne, and Sydney. From New Zealand, both Air New Zealand and Air Pacific fly to Nandi, but Air Pacific also flies from Christchurch to Nandi and Auckland to Suva. From Japan, both Air New Zealand and Air Pacific arrive from Tokyo, and Air New Zealand also arrives from Nagoya and Air Pacific from Osaka.

Other regional carriers landing at Nandi include Air Calédonie International (from Nouméa and Wallis), Air Marshall Islands (from Funafuti, Majuro, and Tarawa), Air Nauru (from Nauru and Tarawa), Air Vanuatu (from Port Vila), and Solomon Airlines (from Honiara and Port Vila).

Airlines offering direct flights to Suva include Air Marshall Islands (from Funafuti, Majuro, and Tarawa), Air Nauru (from Nauru and Tarawa), and Air Pacific (from Apia, Auckland, and Tongatapu). A F$15 turnover tax is charged on all international air tickets purchased in Fiji.

AIR SERVICES

From North America

Air New Zealand, Air Pacific, and Qantas are the carriers serving Fiji out of Los Angeles. Unfortunately there are no direct flights from Canada to Fiji and all passengers must change planes at Honolulu or Los Angeles, although there are immediate connections from **Canadian Airlines International** flights.

Excursion fares to Fiji often have restrictions and some have an advance-purchase deadline, so it's best to begin shopping early. The month of outbound travel from the U.S. determines which seasonal fare you pay and inquiring far in advance could allow you to reschedule your vacation slightly to take advantage of a noticeably lower fare. Most carriers from the U.S. to Fiji have their **low season** from April to August, **shoulder season** from September to mid-November and in

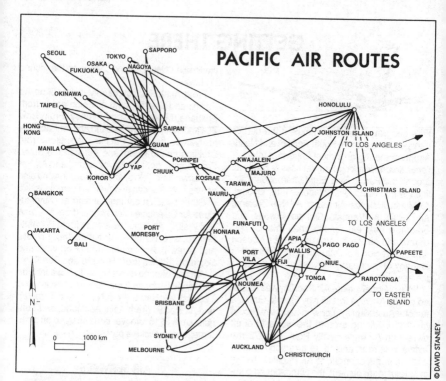

PACIFIC AIR ROUTES

© DAVID STANLEY

March, and **high season** from mid-November to February. The airlines have made April to mid-November, the best months in Fiji, their off-season because that's winter in Australia and New Zealand. If you're only going to Fiji and can make it at that time, it certainly works to your advantage.

In the 1950s **Air New Zealand** pioneered its "Coral Route" across the South Pacific using Solent flying boats. Return "Coral Experience" tickets from Los Angeles to Fiji are US$998/1098/1298 low/shoulder/high if you leave on Monday, Tuesday, and Wednesday, US$60 more if you begin your trip toward the end of the week. If you only want to stay one month and buy your ticket 21 days in advance, a "Coral Direct" ticket is US$100 cheaper, but no date changes are allowed and there's a 50% cancellation fee.

Special "add-on" fares to Los Angeles are available from cities right across the U.S. and Canada. One problem with Air New Zealand is its schedules, which are built around Auckland and California: they'll probably drop you off in the middle of the night in Fiji. Rather than be forced to watch their insipid *Blue Pacific* videos and read their dull *Pacific Way* inflight magazine, bring along some reading material as Air New Zealand seldom supplies any.

In July 1994 Fiji's **Air Pacific** launched a weekly nonstop Boeing 747 service from Los Angeles to Nandi. They offer very competitive fares, so check. Air Pacific's U.S. office is at 6151 West Century Blvd., Suite 524, Los Angeles, CA 90045, U.S.A. (tel. 310/417-2236, fax 310/337-1380).

Circle-Pacific Fares

Thanks to agreements between the carriers mentioned above and Asian or American companies, you can get a Circle-Pacific fare, which combines Fiji with Jakarta, Singapore, Bangkok, Hong Kong, Manila, Taipei, Tokyo, and many other cities. These tickets must be purchased 21 days in advance, but they're valid up to six months and only the initial flight out of North America has to be booked 21 days ahead. The rest of the ticket can be left open-dated.

Air New Zealand has the most to offer in the South Pacific, but the different carriers offer differing routes in Asia, so ask your travel agent to explain the alternatives to you. The Circle-Pacific fares are excellent value if you have enough time for a wide-ranging trip. Also ask about round-the-world tickets via Fiji.

From Australia

From Brisbane, Melbourne, and Sydney there are nonstop flights to Nandi on **Air Pacific. Qantas** also flies to Nandi. Advance Purchase Excursion (APEX) and Circle-Pacific fares are available in Australia, and the airlines sometimes offer specials during the off months, so see a travel agent. For information on slightly reduced fares available from STA Travel, see "Student Fares," below.

From New Zealand

Unrestricted low air fares to Fiji are surprisingly hard to come by in New Zealand. Some tickets have advance purchase requirements, so start shopping well ahead. Ask around at a number of different travel agencies for special unadvertised or under-the-counter fares.

Air New Zealand offers reduced excursion fares from Auckland to Fiji with a minimum stay of seven days and a maximum stay of 60 days. These fares typically cost NZ$831-996 roundtrip to Fiji depending on the season, and it's possible to change flight dates. It's actually cheaper to buy a package tour to Fiji with airfare, accommodations, and transfers all included, but these are usually limited to seven nights on one island and you're stuck in a boring touristic environment.

From Europe

Since no European carriers reach Fiji, you may have to use a gateway city such as Sydney, Auckland, Honolulu, or Los Angeles. Air New Zealand offers nonstop flights London-Los Angeles three times a week, Frankfurt-Los Angeles twice a week, with connections in L.A. to their Coral Route.

Air New Zealand reservations numbers around Europe are: tel. 32-3/202-1355 (Belgium), tel. 33/0590-7712 (France), tel. 49-1/3081-7778 (Germany), tel. 39/1678-76126 (Italy), tel. 41/0800-2527 (Luxemburg), tel. 31-060/221016 (Netherlands), tel. 34-900/993241 (Spain), tel. 020-910-150 (Sweden), tel. 41/155-7778 (Switzerland), and tel. 44-181/741-2299 (United Kingdom). Call them up and ask about their Coral Route fares.

Important Note

Airfares, rules, and regulations tend to fluctuate a lot, so some of the above may have changed. This is only a guide; we've included precise fares to give you a rough idea of costs. Your travel agent will know best what's available at the time you're ready to travel, but if you're not satisfied with his/her advice, keep shopping around. The biggest step is deciding to go—once you're over that the rest is easy!

AIR TICKETS

Your plane ticket will be your biggest single expense, so spend some time considering the possibilities. Start by calling the airlines directly at their toll-free 800 numbers to get current information on fares. In the U.S., the ones to call are Air New Zealand (tel. 800/262-1234), Air Pacific (tel. 800/227-4500), and Qantas Airways (tel. 800/227-4500), all with flights to the South Pacific. Sometimes Canada and the various parts of the U.S. have different toll-free numbers, so if the number given above doesn't work, dial 800 information at 800/555-1212 (all 800 numbers are free). In Canada, Air New Zealand's toll-free number is 800/663-5494.

Call all of these carriers and say you want the *lowest possible fare*. Ask about fare seasons and restrictions. If you're not happy with the answers you get, call the number later and try again. Many different agents take calls on these lines, and some are more knowledgeable than others. The numbers are busy during business hours, so call at night or on the weekend. *Be persistent.*

Cheaper Flights

Check the Sunday travel section in a newspaper like the *San Francisco Examiner* or the *Toronto Star,* or a major entertainment weekly. They often carry ads for bucket shops, agencies that deal in bulk and sell seats for less than airline offices will. Many airlines have more seats than they can market through normal channels, so they sell their unused long-haul capacity on this gray market at discounts of 40-50% off the official IATA tariffs.

Globetrotters regularly pick up such tickets at well-known centers around the world (Amsterdam, Athens, Bangkok, Hong Kong, London, Penang, San Francisco, and Singapore are only a few—unfortunately none are in the South Pacific itself). Rates are competitive, so check a few agencies before deciding. In Thailand, for example, **J. Travel & Trading** (21/33 Soi Ngam Dupli, Near Malaysia Hotel, Rama 4 Rd., Bangkok 10120; fax 66-2/287-1468) offers Singapore-Auckland-Nandi-Rarotonga-Papeete-Los Angeles for US$965. Despite their occasionally shady appearance, most bucket shops are perfectly legitimate, and your ticket will probably be issued by the airline itself. Most discounted tickets look and are exactly the same as regular full-fare tickets but they're usually nonrefundable.

Travel Agents

Use your local travel agent, but be aware that any agent worth his/her commission will probably want to sell you a package tour, and it's a fact that some vacation packages actually cost less than regular roundtrip airfare! If they'll let you extend your stay to give you some time to yourself this could be a good deal, especially with the hotel thrown in for "free." But check the restrictions.

Pick your agent carefully, as many are pitifully ignorant about the South Pacific. Many don't want to hear about discounts, cheap flights, or alternative routes. With alarming frequency, they give wrong or misleading information in an offhand manner. Ask an airline to suggest a travel agent. They won't *recommend* any, but they will give you the names of a few in your area that specialize in Pacific travel. Agencies belonging to the American Society of Travel Agents (ASTA), the Alliance of Canadian Travel Associations (ACTA), or the Association of British Travel Agents must conform to a strict code of ethics. A travel agent's commission is paid by the airline, so you've got nothing to lose.

Even if you decide to take advantage of the convenience of an agent, do call the airlines yourself beforehand so you'll know if you're getting a good deal. Airline tickets are often refundable only at the place of purchase, so ask about this before you invest in a ticket you may not use. There can be tremendous variations in what different passengers on the same flight have paid for their tickets. Allow yourself time to shop around; a few hours spent on the phone, asking questions, could save you hundreds of dollars.

Agents in the U.S.

A wholesaler specializing in Fiji is **Fiji Travel** (3790 Dunn Dr., Suite A, Los Angeles, CA 90034, U.S.A.; tel. 800/500-FIJI, fax 310/202-8233). Ask for Vijen Prasad, who offers excellent airfares to Fiji.

Discover Wholesale Travel (2192 Dupont Dr., Suite 105, Irvine, CA 92715, U.S.A.; tel. 800/576-7770 in California, tel. 800/759-7330 elsewhere in the U.S., fax 714/833-1176) is one of the few large tour operators willing to sell discounted air tickets alone directly to the public. President Mary Anne Cook claims everyone on her staff has 10 years of experience selling the South Pacific and "most importantly, we all love the area!"

Similar tickets are sold through travel agents in the U.S. by the **Adventure Center** (1311 - 63rd St., Suite 200, Emeryville, CA 94608, U.S.A.; tel. 800/227-8747). They don't accept direct consumer sales, however, so ask your travel agent to check with them. One agent who can help you is Rob Jenneve of **Island Adventures** (574 Mills Way, Goleta, CA 93117, U.S.A.; tel. 800/289-4957, fax 805/685-0960).

Agents in Canada

One of the most knowledgeable Canadian travel agents for South Pacific tickets is the **Adventure Centre** (25 Bellair St., Toronto, Ontario M5R 3L3; tel. 800/267-3347) with offices in Calgary, Edmonton, Toronto, and Vancouver.

Also try **Travel Cuts** with offices throughout Canada (check the phone book). Their Toronto office (tel. 416/979-2406) has a special South Pacific department.

Goway Travel (Suite 300, 3284 Yonge St., Toronto, Ontario M4N 3M7, Canada; tel. 800/387-8850) sells adventure tour packages to Fiji.

Agent in Australia

Rosie The Travel Service (Level 5, Suite 505, 9 Bronte Rd., Bondi Junction, Sydney, NSW 2022, Australia; tel. 61-2/9389-3666, fax 61-2/9369-1129) specializes in travel to Fiji.

Agents in Europe

The British specialist in South Pacific itineraries is **Trailfinders** (42-50 Earls Court Rd., Kensington, London W8 6FT, England; tel. 44-171/938-3366), in business since 1970. They offer a variety of discounted round-the-world tickets through Fiji which are often much cheaper than the published fares. All rates are seasonal and depend on the airlines actually giving them deals, plus exchange rates play a part. Call or write for a free copy of their magazine, *Trailfinder,* which appears in April, July, and December. Also check the ads in *Time Out* for other such companies.

In Holland **Pacific Island Travel** (Dam 3, 1012 JS Amsterdam, the Netherlands; tel. 31-20/626-1325, fax 31-20/623-0008) sells most of the tickets and tours mentioned in this section. Manager Rob Kusters is quite knowledgeable about the Pacific. **Barron & De Keijzer Travel** (Herengracht 340, 1016 CG Amsterdam, the Netherlands; tel. 31-20/625-8600, fax 31-20/622-7559) sells Air New Zealand's Coral Route with travel via London. Also in Amsterdam, **Reisbureau Amber** (Da Costastraat 77, 1053 ZG Amsterdam, the Netherlands; tel. 31-20/685-1155) is one of the best places in Europe to pick up books on Fiji.

In Switzerland try **Globetrotter Travel Service** (Rennweg 35, CH-8023 Zürich, Switzerland; tel. 41-1/211-7780, fax 41-1/211-2035), with offices in Baden, Basel, Bern, Luzern, St. Gallen, Winterthur, and Zürich. Their quarterly newsletter, *Ticket-Info,* lists hundreds of cheap flights, including many through Fiji.

Bucket shops in Germany sell a "Pacific Airpass" on Air New Zealand from Frankfurt to the South Pacific for around DM 2500 low season, DM 3000 high season. You may stop at a choice of any six of Tahiti, Rarotonga, Fiji, Auckland, Tonga, Apia, and Honolulu, and the ticket is valid six months. All flights must be booked prior to leaving Europe and there's a US$50 charge to change the dates once the ticket has been issued. One agency selling such tickets is **Walther-Weltreisen** (Hirschberger Strasse 30, D-53119 Bonn, Germany; tel. 49-228/661-239, fax 49-228/661-181).

Agents in Fiji

If you want the security of advance reservations but aren't interested in joining a regular package tour, two established companies specialize in prebooking Blue Lagoon cruises, first-class hotel rooms, airport transfers, sightseeing tours, rental cars, etc. Their prices are competitive with what you'd pay on the spot, and they're sometimes cheaper.

The Nandi Airport office of **Rosie The Travel Service** (Box 9268, Nandi Airport; tel. 722-935, fax 722-607) can arrange hotels, transfers, cruises, bus tours, etc., for you upon arrival in Fiji. Be aware, however, that if your flight arrives at Nandi in the middle of the night, their airport office only opens at 0800. Rosie's bus tours from Nandi and all the Coral Coast hotels are cheaper than those of other companies because lunch and admissions aren't included (lunch is included on all the cruises). For information on hiking tours offered by **Adventure Fiji,** a division of Rosie The Travel Service, see "Organized Tours," below. This locally owned business has provided efficient, personalized service since 1974.

Another large wholesaler handling Fiji bookings is **A.T.S. Pacific** with offices in the U.S. (Suite 325, 2381 Rosecrans Ave., El Segundo, CA 90245, U.S.A.; tel. 310/643-0044), Aus-

STA TRAVEL OFFICES

Here's a partial list of STA Travel offices and affiliates around the world:

STA Travel, 297 Newbury St., Boston, MA 02115, U.S.A. (tel. 617/266-6014)

STA Travel, 7202 Melrose Ave., Los Angeles, CA 90046, U.S.A. (tel. 213/934-8722)

STA Travel, 10 Downing St. (6th Ave. and Bleecker), New York, NY 10014, U.S.A. (tel. 212/477-7166, fax 212/477-7348)

STA Travel, 3730 Walnut St., Philadelphia, PA 19104, U.S.A. (tel. 215/382-2928)

STA Travel, 51 Grant Ave., San Francisco, CA 94108, U.S.A. (tel. 415/391-8407)

STA Travel, 120 Broadway #108, Santa Monica, CA 90401, U.S.A. (tel. 310/394-5126, fax 310/394-8640)

STA Travel, 2401 Pennsylvania Ave. #G, Washington, DC 20037, U.S.A. (tel. 202/887-0912)

STA Travel, 222 Faraday St., Carlton, Melbourne 3053, Australia (tel. 61-3/9349-2411, fax 61-3/9347-8070)

STA Travel, 1st Floor, 732 Harris St., Ultimo, Sydney, NSW 2007, Australia (tel. 61-2/9212-1255, fax 61-2/9281-4183)

STA Travel, 10 High St., Auckland, New Zealand (tel. 09/366-6673, fax 64-9/309-9723)

STA Travel, #02-17 Orchard Parade Hotel, 1 Tanglin Rd., Singapore 1024 (tel. 65/734-5681, fax 65/737-2591)

STA Travel, Wall Street Tower, Suite 1405, 33 Surawong Rd., Bangrak, Bangkok 10500, Thailand (tel. 66-2/233-2582)

SRID Reisen, Bockenheimer Landstrasse 133, D-60325 Frankfurt, Germany (tel. 49-69/703-035, fax 49-69/777-014)

STA Travel, Priory House, 6 Wright's Lane, London W8 6TA, England (tel. 44-171/937-9962)

tralia (3rd Floor, 40 Miller St., North Sydney, NSW 2060, Australia; tel. 61-2/9957-3811, fax 61-2/9957-1385), and New Zealand (48 Emily Place, 10th Floor Jetset Center, Auckland 1, New Zealand; tel. 64-9/379-7105, fax 64-9/309-3239). The A.T.S. Pacific representative in Fiji is United Touring Company with an office (Box 9172, Nandi Airport; tel. 722-811, fax 790-389) in the arrival concourse at Nandi Airport open around the clock. A.T.S. Pacific can put together any itinerary you may wish, but you must work through your regular travel agent as they don't deal directly with the public.

STUDENT FARES

If you're a student, recent graduate, or teacher, you can sometimes benefit from lower student fares by booking through a student travel office. There are two rival organizations of this kind: Council Travel Services, with offices in college towns across the U.S. and a sister organization in Canada known as Travel Cuts; and STA Travel (Student Travel Australia), formerly called the Student Travel Network in the United States. Both organizations require you to pay a nominal fee for an official student card, and to get the cheapest fares you have to prove you're really a student. Slightly higher fares on the same routes are available to nonstudents, so they're always worth checking out.

STA Travel has been flying students across the Pacific for years. They offer special airfares for students and young people under 26 years with minimal restrictions. A one-year return ticket Los Angeles-Honolulu-Fiji-Rarotonga-Los Angeles will cost US$1380/1471/1654 low/shoulder/high. One-way tickets run about half the roundtrip price and cheaper fares are available for shorter stays. Call their toll-free number, (800) 777-0112 for the latest information.

Slightly different student fares are available from **Council Travel Services**, a division of the nonprofit Council on International Educational Exchange (CIEE). Both they and **Travel Cuts** in Canada are much stricter about making sure

COUNCIL TRAVEL OFFICES

Here are a few Council Travel offices:

2000 Guadalupe St., Austin, TX 78705, U.S.A. (tel. 512/472-4931)

2486 Channing Way, Berkeley, CA 94704, U.S.A. (tel. 510/848-8604)

729 Boylston St., Suite 201, Boston, MA 02116, U.S.A. (tel. 617/266-1926)

1153 N. Dearborn St., 2nd Floor, Chicago, IL 60610, U.S.A. (tel. 312/951-0585)

1138 13th St., Boulder, CO 80302, U.S.A. (tel. 303/447-8101)

1093 Broxton Ave., Suite 220, Los Angeles, CA 90024, U.S.A. (tel. 310/208-3551)

One Datran Center, Suite 320, 9100 South Dadeland Blvd., Miami, FL 33156, U.S.A. (tel. 305/670-9261)

205 East 42nd St., New York, NY 10017-5706, U.S.A. (tel. 212/661-1450)

715 S.W. Morrison, Suite 600, Portland, OR 97205, U.S.A. (tel. 503/228-1900)

953 Garnet Ave., San Diego, CA 92109, U.S.A. (tel. 619/270-6401)

919 Irving St., Suite 102, San Francisco, CA 94122, U.S.A. (tel. 415/566-6222, fax 415/566-6730)

1314 N.E. 43rd St., Suite 210, Seattle, WA 98105, U.S.A. (tel. 206/632-2448)

Travel Cuts, 187 College St., Toronto, Ontario M5T 1P7, Canada (tel. 416/979-2406, fax 416/979-8167)

110D Killiney Rd., Tah Wah Building, Singapore 0923 (tel. 65/7387-066)

108/12-13 Kosan Rd., Banglumpoo, Bangkok 10200, Thailand (tel. 66-2/282-7705)

Sanno Grand Building, Room 102, 14-2 Nagata-cho 2-chome, Chiyoda-ku, Tokyo 100, Japan (tel. 81-3/3581-5517)

18 Graf Adolph Strasse, D-40212 Düsseldorf 1, Germany (tel. 49-211/329-088, fax 49-211/327-469)

22 rue des Pyramides, 75001 Paris, France (tel. 33-1/4455-5565)

28A Poland St., near Oxford Circus, London W1V 3DB, England (tel. 44-171/437-7767)

you're a "real" student: you must first obtain the widely recognized International Student Identity Card (US$16) to get a ticket at the student rate. Some fares are limited to students and youths under 26 years of age, but part-time students and teachers also qualify. Seasonal pricing applies, so plan ahead. Get hold of a copy of their free *Student Travel Catalog,* which, although mostly oriented toward travel to Europe, contains useful information for students. Circle-Pacific and round-the-world routings are also available from Council Travel Services and there are special connecting flights to Los Angeles from other U.S. points.

REGIONAL CARRIERS

In 1995 the Association of South Pacific Airlines introduced a "Visit South Pacific Pass" to coincide with "Visit South Pacific Year." This allowed travelers to include the services of eight regional carriers in a single ticket at US$150, US$200, or US$300 per leg. The initial two-leg air pass had to be purchased in conjunction with an international ticket into the region, but additional legs up to eight maximum could be purchased after arrival. Only the first sector had to be booked ahead. The pass was so successful that at last report the Association was planning to extend it beyond 1995. If this happens, it will continue to be a great way of getting around the South Pacific. Ask Air New Zealand or Air Pacific if it's still available.

Air Pacific

Air Pacific has two different "triangle fares," good ways to get around and experience the region's variety of cultures: Fiji-Apia-Tonga-Fiji (F$667) and Fiji-Nouméa-Port Vila-Fiji (F$785), plus F$15 tax if purchased in Fiji. Both are valid for one year and can be purchased at any travel agency in Fiji or direct from the airline. Usually they're only good for journeys commencing in Fiji. Flight dates can be changed at no charge. When booking these circular tickets, be aware that it's much better to go Fiji-Apia-Tonga-Fiji than vice versa, because the flights between Apia and Tonga leave Apia in the late morning but return from Tonga to Apia late at night. In addition, the flights between Apia and Fiji are often fully booked while it's easy to get on between Tonga and Fiji. Also obtainable locally are Air Pacific's special 28-day roundtrip excursion fares from Fiji to Apia (F$659), Tonga (F$569), Port Vila (F$560), and Honiara (F$1015).

A "Pacific Air Pass" allows 30 days of travel (on Air Pacific flights only) from Fiji to Apia, Tonga, and Port Vila (US$449). This pass can only be purchased from Qantas Airways offices in North America and Europe; or from Mr. Karl Philipp, Guiollett Strasse 30, D-60325 Frankfurt/Main, Germany (tel. 49-69/172260; fax 69/729314); or from Air Pacific's U.S. office, 6151 West Century Blvd., Suite 524, Los Angeles, CA 90045 (tel. 800/227-4500, fax 310/337-1380). The in-flight service on Air Pacific is good.

Solomon Airlines

Solomon Airlines offers a 30-day "Discovery Pacific Pass," which includes two international flights for US$399, three flights for US$499, or four flights for US$599. To include Australia or New Zealand is US$100 extra. A typical three-coupon routing is Nandi-Port Vila-Honiara-Nandi. All flights must be booked in advance and there's a US$50 fee to make changes.

These tickets must be purchased prior to arrival in the South Pacific, in North America through Air Promotions Systems, 5757 West Century Blvd., Suite 660, Los Angeles, CA 90045-6407, U.S.A. (tel. 310/670-7302; fax 310/338-0708), and in Europe through Mr. Karl Philipp, Guiollett Strasse 30, D-60325 Frankfurt/Main, Germany (tel. 49-69/172260; fax 49-69/729314).

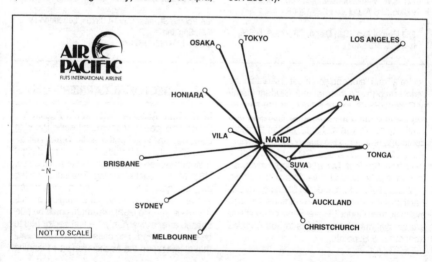

Air Nauru

Air Nauru (Level 49, 80 Collins St., Melbourne, Victoria 3000, Australia; tel. 61-3/9653-5602; fax 61-3/9654-7376), flag carrier of the tiny phosphate-rich Republic of Nauru, links the North and South Pacific. Most Air Nauru fares are calculated point to point via Nauru, so to work out a routing combine any two of these one-way economy fares out of Nauru itself: Auckland (A$503), Guam (A$339), Honiara (A$183), Manila (A$546), Melbourne (A$486), Nandi (A$271), Pohnpei (A$289), Suva (A$282), Sydney (A$432), Tarawa (A$144). Although the exchange rate is currently about US$1 = A$1.33, if you buy your ticket in a U.S. dollar area you'll probably be charged the same figure, but in U.S. currency rather than Australian! All the above services operate at least once a week.

In the past Air Nauru has had a reputation for canceling flights on a moment's notice and bumping confirmed passengers to make room for local VIPs, but they fly modern Boeing 737-400 aircraft and have a good safety record. In recent years Air Nauru's prices have increased 50% as their routes contracted, so they're no longer the big bargain they once were.

In the South Pacific, Air Nauru has offices at Suite 502, 17 Castlereagh St., Sydney, Australia (tel. 61-2/9221-8622, fax 61-2/9221-7032); Sheraton Mall, 105 Symonds St., Auckland, New Zealand (tel. 64-9/379-8113, fax 64-9/379-3763); and Ratu Sakuna House, Macarthur St., Suva, Fiji Islands (tel. 679/312-377). Their general sales agent in the U.S. is Air Nauru, 1221 Kapiolani Blvd., PH60, Honolulu, HI 96814, U.S.A. (tel. 808/591-2163, fax 808/593-8433). You can call them toll-free from Canada and the U.S. at 800/998-6287.

PROBLEMS

When planning your trip allow a minimum two-hour stopover between connecting flights at U.S. airports, although with airport delays on the increase even this may not be enough. In Fiji allow at least a day between flights. In some airports flights are not called over the public address system, so keep your eyes open. Whenever traveling, always have a paperback or two, some toiletries, and a change of underwear in your hand luggage.

If your flight is canceled due to a mechanical problem with the aircraft, the airline will cover your hotel bill and meals. If they reschedule the flight on short notice for reasons of their own or if you're bumped off an overbooked flight, they should also pay. They may not feel obligated to pay, however, if the delay is due to weather conditions, a strike by another company, national emergencies, etc., although the best airlines still pick up the tab in these cases. Just don't expect much from local, "third-level" airlines on domestic routes inside Fiji where such difficulties are routine.

It's an established practice among airlines to provide light refreshments to passengers delayed two hours after the scheduled departure time and a meal after four hours. Don't expect to get this on an outer island, but politely request it if you're at a gateway airport. If you are unexpectedly forced to spend the night somewhere, the airline may give you a form offering to telephone a friend or relative to inform them of the delay. Don't trust them to do this, however. Call your party yourself if you want to be sure they get the message. (Air New Zealand is notorious for not conveying messages of this kind.)

Overbooking

To compensate for no-shows, most airlines overbook their flights. To avoid being bumped, ask for your seat assignment when booking, check in early, and go to the departure area well before flight time. Of course, if you *are* bumped by a reputable airline at a major airport you'll be regaled with free meals and lodging and sometimes even free flight vouchers (don't expect anything like this from a domestic Fijian carrier).

Whenever you break your journey for more than 72 hours, always reconfirm your onward reservations and check your seat assignment at the same time. Get the name of the person who takes your reconfirmation so they cannot later deny it. Failure to reconfirm could result in the cancellation of your complete remaining itinerary. This could also happen if you miss a flight for any reason. If you want special vegetarian or kosher food in-flight, request it when buying your ticket, booking, and reconfirming.

When you try to reconfirm your Air New Zealand flight the agent will probably tell you that this formality is no longer required. Theoretically this may be true, but unless you request your *seat assignment* in advance, either at an Air New Zealand office or over the phone, you could be "bumped" from a full flight, reservation or no reservation. Air New Zealand's ticket cover bears this surprising message:

. . . no guarantee of a seat is indicated by the terms "reservation," "booking," "O.K." status, or the times associated therewith.

They do admit in the same notice that confirmed passengers denied seats may be eligible for compensation, so if you're not in a hurry, a night or two at an upmarket hotel with all meals courtesy of Air New Zealand may be no hardship. Your best bet if you don't want to get "bumped" is to request seat assignments for your entire itinerary before you leave home, or at least at the first Air New Zealand office you pass during your travels. Any good travel agent selling tickets on Air New Zealand should know enough to automatically request your seat assignments as they make your bookings. Check Air New Zealand's reconfirmation policy at one of their offices, as it could change.

Baggage

International airlines allow economy-class passengers either 20 kg of baggage or two pieces not over 32 kg each (ask which applies to you). Under the piece system, neither bag must have a combined length, width, and height of over 158 cm (62 inches) and the two pieces together must not exceed 272 cm (107 inches). On most long-haul tickets to/from North America or Europe, the piece system applies to all sectors, but check this with the airline. The frequent flier programs of some major airlines allow participants to carry up to 10 kg of excess baggage free of charge. Small commuter carriers often restrict you to as little as 10 kg, so it's better to pack according to the lowest common denominator.

Bicycles, folding kayaks, and surfboards can usually be checked as baggage (sometimes for an additional US$50-100 charge), but Windsurfers may have to be shipped airfreight. If you do travel with a Windsurfer, be sure to call it a surfboard at check-in.

Tag your bag with name, address, and phone number inside and out. Stow anything that could conceivably be considered a weapon (scissors, penknife, toy gun, Mace, etc.) in your checked luggage. Incidentally, it can be considered a criminal offense to make jokes about bombings or hijackings in airports or aboard aircraft.

One reason for lost baggage is that some people fail to remove used baggage tags after they claim their luggage. Get into the habit of tearing off old baggage tags, unless you want your luggage to travel in the opposite direction! As you're checking in, look to see if the three-letter city codes on your baggage tag receipt and boarding pass are the same. If you're headed to Nandi the tag should read NAN (Suva is SUV).

If your baggage is damaged or doesn't arrive at your destination, inform the airline officials *immediately* and have them fill out a written report, otherwise future claims for compensation will be compromised. Airlines usually reimburse out-of-pocket expenses if your baggage is lost or delayed over 24 hours. The amount varies from US$25 to US$50. Your chances of getting it are better if you're polite but firm. Keep receipts for any money you're forced to spend to replace missing articles.

Claims for lost luggage can take weeks to process. Keep in touch with the airline to show your concern and hang onto your baggage tag until the matter is resolved. If you feel you did not receive the attention you deserved, write the airline an objective letter outlining the case. Get the names of the employees you're dealing with so you can mention them in the letter. Of course, don't expect any pocket money or compensation on a remote outer island. Report the loss, then wait till you get back to the airline's main office. Whatever happens, avoid getting angry. The people you're dealing with don't want the problem any more than you do.

BY BOAT

Even as much Pacific shipping was being sunk during WW II, airstrips were springing up on all the main islands. This hastened the inevitable replacement of the old steamships with modern aircraft, and it's now extremely rare to arrive in Fiji by boat (private yachts excepted). Most islands export similar products and there's little interregional trade; large container ships headed for Australia, New Zealand, and Japan don't usually accept passengers.

Those bitten by nostalgia for the slower prewar ways may like to know that a couple of passenger-carrying freighters do still call at the islands, though their fares are much higher than those charged by the airlines. A specialized agency booking such passages is **TravLtips** (Box 188, Flushing, NY 11358, U.S.A.; tel. 800/872-8584 in the U.S. and 800/548-7823 in Canada). They can place you aboard a British-registered **Banks Line** container ship on its way around the world from England via the Panama Canal, Papeete, Apia, Suva, Lautoka, Nouméa, Port Vila, Honiara, and Papua New Guinea. A round-the-world ticket for the four-month journey is US$12,125, but segments are sold if space is available 30 days before sailing. Similarly, TravLtips books German-registered **Columbus Line** vessels, which make 45-day roundtrips between Los Angeles and Australia via Suva (US$4500 roundtrip double occupancy). One-way segments (when available) are half price. These ships can accommodate only about a dozen passengers, so inquire well in advance. Also ask about passenger accommodation on cargo vessels of the **Blue Star Line** which call at Suva and Nouméa between the U.S. and New Zealand.

ORGANIZED TOURS

Packaged Holidays

While this book is written for independent travelers rather than packaged tourists, reduced group airfares and hotel rates make some tours worth considering. For two people with limited time and a desire to stay at a first-class hotel, this may be the cheapest way to go. The "wholesalers" who put these packages together get their rooms at rates far lower than individuals pay. Special-interest tours are very popular among sportspeople who want to be sure they'll get to participate in the various activities they enjoy. The main drawback to the tours is that you're on a fixed itinerary among other tourists, out of touch with local life. Singles pay a healthy supplement. Some of the companies mentioned below do not accept consumer inquiries and require you to work through a travel agent.

Fiji Holidays (3790 Dunn Dr., Suite A, Los Angeles, CA 90034, U.S.A.; tel. 800/500-FIJI, fax 310/202-8233) can reserve rooms at almost any hotel in Fiji, has packages to all the top island resorts, and books Blue Lagoon or Captain Cook cruises. **Sunmakers** (Box 9170, Seattle, WA 98109, U.S.A.) also books customized itineraries in Fiji. **Islands in the Sun** (Box 550, El Segundo, CA 90245, U.S.A.; tel. 800/828-6877 in the U.S., 800/667-4648 in Canada, fax 310/536-6266) has a useful brochure describing many package tours to Fiji.

Qantas Holidays (141 Walker St., North Sydney, NSW 2060, Australia; tel. 800/427-399) offers a variety of standard package tours to Fiji. In Europe these trips can be booked through **Jetabout Holidays** (Sovereign House, 361 King St., Hammersmith, London W6 9NJ, England; tel. 44-181/748-8676, fax 44-181/748-7236).

Swingaway Holidays (Level 5, 22 York St., Sydney, NSW 2000, Australia; tel. 61-2/9237-0300, fax 61-2/9262-6024) runs package tours to Fiji and books Blue Lagoon Cruises. **Hideaway Holidays** (994 Victoria Rd., West Ryde, NSW 2114, Australia; tel. 61-2/9807-4222, fax 61-2/9808-2260) specializes in off-the-beaten-track packages to Fiji and can organize complicated itineraries.

From New Zealand **ASPAC Vacations Ltd.** (Box 4330, Auckland; tel. 64-9/623-0259, fax 64-9/623-0257) has the same sort of package tours and cruises as Swingaway. ASPAC can book services in remote areas upon request.

Tours for Children

About the only packages to the South Pacific especially designed for families traveling with children are the "Rascals in Paradise" programs offered by **Adventure Express** (650 5th St.,

Suite 505, San Francisco, CA 94107, U.S.A.; tel. 800/U-RASCAL, fax 415/442-0289). Special "family week" group tours to Fiji's Vatulele Island Resort are operated between July and September. The US$7180 price is based on two adults with one or two children aged 2-11, and international airfares and transfers to Vatulele are additional. Less expensive independent one-week family trips are available year-round to places like Plantation Island, Fiji (US$1005 per adult with two kids under 16 free, airfare additional). A single parent with child would have to pay two adult fares. Adventure Express also books regular scuba diving tours and upmarket hotel rooms throughout the Pacific.

Scuba Tours

Fiji is one of the world's prime scuba locales, and most islands have good facilities for divers. Although it's not difficult to do it on your own, if you have limited time and want to get in as much diving as possible, you should consider joining an organized scuba tour. To stay in business, dive travel specialists are forced to charge prices similar to what you'd pay if you just walked in off the street, and the convenience of having all your arrangements made for you by a company able to pull weight with island suppliers is often worth it. Request the brochures of the companies listed below, and before booking, find out exactly where you'll be staying and ask if daily transfers and meals are provided. Of course, diver certification is mandatory.

Tropical Adventures Travel (111 2nd Ave. N, Seattle, WA 98109, U.S.A.; tel. 800/247-3483, fax 206/441-5431) specializes in diving off Vanua Levu and Taveuni with packages to all the main resorts. Tropical's president, Bob Goddess, claims he's always accessible by phone. Over 6,000 divers a year book through this company, which has been in business since 1973.

Founded in 1966, **See & Sea Travel Service** (50 Francisco St., Suite 205, San Francisco, CA 94133, U.S.A.; tel. 800/DIV-XPRT, fax 415/434-3409) is *the* authority on live-aboard dive experiences. This is a bit more expensive than land-based diving, but you're offered up to five dives each day and a total experience. See & Sea represents the selected cream of Pacific dive boats, such as the *Nai'a* in Fiji (US$1980 a week). All meals are included, but

feeding fish

BOB HALSTEAD

airfare is extra. See & Sea's president is the noted underwater photographer and author, Carl Roessler.

The Fiji specialist is **Aqua-Trek** (110 Sutter St., Suite 811, San Francisco, CA 94104, U.S.A.; tel. 800/541-4334). **Sea Safaris** (3770 Highland Ave., Suite 102, Manhattan Beach, CA 90266, U.S.A.; tel. 800/821-6670, fax 310/545-1672) has complete dive packages at about a dozen different resorts in Fiji (but we've heard unfavorable comments about this company).

Poseidon Ventures Tours (359 San Miguel Dr., Newport Beach, CA 92660, U.S.A.; tel. 800/854-9334; or 505 North Belt, Suite 675, Houston, TX 77060, U.S.A.; tel. 713/820-3483) offers seven-night diving tours to Fiji beginning at US$1775 including five days of two-tank diving, airfare from Los Angeles, double-occupancy hotel accommodations, meals, taxes, and transfers.

New Zealanders requiring information about scuba diving facilities in and around the Pacific should call Ed Meili of **The Diving Network** (Box 38-023, Howick, Auckland, New Zealand; tel. 64-9/367-5066). Ed has first-hand knowledge of diving facilities in the islands and can provide valuable tips.

Dive 'N Fishing Travel (15E Vega Place, Mairangi Bay, Auckland 10, New Zealand; tel. 64-9/479-2210, fax 64-9/479-2214) offers a wide range of scuba tours to Fiji at competitive rates.

Alternatively, you can make your own arrangements directly with island dive shops. Information about these operators is included under the heading "Sports and Recreation" in the respective chapters of this book.

Tours for Naturalists

Perhaps the most rewarding way to visit the South Seas is with **Earthwatch** (Box 403, Watertown, MA 02272, U.S.A.; tel. 800/776-0188, fax 617/926-8532), a nonprofit organization founded in 1971 to serve as a bridge between the public and the scientific community. The programs vary from year to year, but in the past they've sent teams to examine the coral reefs or study the rainforests of Fiji. These are not study tours but opportunities for amateurs to help out with serious work, kind of like a short-term scientific Peace Corps. As a research volunteer, a team member's share of project costs is tax-deductible in the U.S. and some other countries. For more information contact Earthwatch at the address above; or 453-457 Elizabeth St., 1st Floor, Melbourne, Victoria 3000, Australia (tel. 61-3/9600-9100, fax 61-3/9600-9066); or Belsyre Court, 57 Woodstock Rd., Oxford OX2 6HU, England (tel. 44-1865/311-600, fax 44-865/311-383), or Technova Inc., 13th Floor, Fukoku Building, 2-2 Uchisaiwai-Cho, 2-Chome, Chiyoda-Ku, Tokyo 100, Japan (tel. 81-3/3508-2280, fax 81-3/3508-7578).

Kayak Tours

Among the most exciting tours to Fiji are the 10- to 16-day kayaking expeditions offered from April to November by **Southern Sea Ventures** (51 Fishermans Dr., Emerald Beach, NSW 2456, Australia; tel. 61-2/6656-1907, fax 61-2/6656-2109). Their groups of 10 persons maximum paddle stable two-person sea kayaks through the sheltered tropical waters of the Yasawa chain. Accommodations are tents on the beach, and participants must be in reasonable physical shape, as three or four hours a day are spent on the water. The price varies US$1073-1850 and doesn't include airfare. In April 1992 Southern Sea Ventures launched

10-day kayak trips to remote Santa Isabel in the Solomon Islands. In the U.S. book through **Journeys** (1536 N.W. 23rd Ave., Portland, OR 97210-2618, U.S.A.; tel. 503/226-7200, fax 503/226-4940), in New Zealand through **Suntravel** (Box 12-424, Auckland; tel. 64-9/525-3074, fax 64-9/525-3065).

Mountain Travel/Sobek Expeditions (6420 Fairmount Ave., El Cerrito, CA 94530, U.S.A.; tel. 800/227-2384, fax 510/525-7710) runs a 16-day combination hiking/sea kayaking tour to Fiji four times a year at US$1850 plus airfare. Participants spend four days trekking through central Viti Levu, then eight days kayaking the Yasawas.

Fiji By Kayak (Box 43, Savusavu, Fiji; tel. 679/850-372, fax 679/850-344) offers kayak/camping tours in Vanua Levu's Natewa Bay monthly from July to October at US$945 for six nights, plus 10% Fijian tax (US$50 single supplement). Groups are restricted to eight participants and the staff of four does all the chores. The first and last nights are spent at Kontiki Resort and transfers to/from Savusavu Airport are included. Bookings can be made through Adventure Express (650 5th St., Suite 505, San Francisco, CA 94107, U.S.A.; tel. 800/443-0799, fax 415/442-0289). Kayaking tours of this kind are highly recommended for the adventurous, active traveler.

Of course, it would be much cheaper to bring your own, and most airlines accept folding kayaks as checked baggage at no charge. Companies like **Long Beach Water Sports** (730 E. 4th St., Long Beach, CA 90802, U.S.A.; tel. 310/432-0187, fax 310/436-6812) sell inflatable one- or two-person sea kayaks for around US$1800, fully equipped. If you're new to the game, try one of the LBWS four-hour introductory sea kayaking classes (US$55) every Saturday. All-day intermediate classes (US$70) are held monthly—a must for L.A. residents. They also rent kayaks by the day or week. Write for a free copy of their newsletter, *Paddle Strokes*.

Hiking Tours

From May to October **Adventure Fiji,** a division of Rosie The Travel Service (Box 9268, Nandi Airport, Fiji Islands; tel. 679/722-755, fax 679/722-607), runs adventuresome five-night hiking trips in the upper Wainimbuka River area of central Viti Levu south of Rakiraki. Horses carry trekkers' backpacks, so the trips are feasible for almost anyone in good condition. The F$570 pp price includes transport to the trailhead, food and accommodations at a few of the 11 Fijian villages along the way, guides, and a bamboo raft ride on the Wainimbuka River. Trekkers only hike about five hours a day, allowing lots of time to get to know the village people. These tours begin from Nandi every Monday. In Australia bookings can be made through Rosie The Travel Service (Level 5, Suite 505, 9 Bronte Rd., Bondi Junction, Sydney, NSW 2022; tel. 61-2/9389-3666, fax 61-2/9369-1129), in North America through **Goway Travel** (3284 Yonge St., Suite 300, Toronto, Ontario M4N 3M7, Canada; tel. 800/387-8850). Highly recommended.

Surfing Tours

The largest operator of surfing tours to Fiji is **The Surf Travel Company** (Box 446, Cronulla, NSW 2230, Australia; tel. 61-2/9527-4722, fax 61-2/9527-4522), with packages to Frigates Pass and Seashell Cove. Their groups are never bigger than 12. In New Zealand book through Mark Thompson (7 Danbury Dr., Torbay, Auckland; tel./fax 09-473-8388), in the U.S. through Fiji Holidays (3790 Dunn Dr., Suite A, Los Angeles, CA 90034, U.S.A.; tel. 800/500-FIJI, fax 310/202-8233).

Yacht Charters

If you were planning on spending a substantial amount to stay at a luxury resort, consider chartering a yacht instead! Divided up among the members of your party, the per-person charter price will be about the same, but you'll experience much more of Fiji's beauty on a boat than you would staying in a hotel room. Yacht charters are available either "bareboat" (for those with the skill to sail on their own) or "crewed" (in which case charterers pay a daily fee for a skipper plus his/her provisions). On a "flotilla" charter a group of bareboats follow an experienced lead yacht.

Moorings Rainbow Yacht Charters offers bareboat yacht charters among the Mamanutha and Yasawa islands from their base at Musket Cove Resort on Malololailai Island in the Ma-

manutha Group. Prices begin at F$510 a day for a Rainbow 350 yacht and increase to F$1015 for a Beneteau 51. Due to the risks involved in navigating Fiji's poorly marked reefs, all charter boats are required by law to carry a Fijian guide (included in the basic charter price), and they check you out to make sure you're really capable of handling their vessels. Additional extras include F$156 daily for an optional skipper, F$94 daily for an optional cook, F$47 pp a day for provisioning, F$28 daily security insurance, and F$78-125 for a starter kit. Alcohol is not included and all charges are subject to 10% tax. As will be seen, chartering isn't for the budget-minded traveler, though small groups planning on staying at a luxury resort may find prices comparable and the experience more rewarding. For more information contact The Moorings (4th Floor, 19345 U.S. 19 North, Clearwater, FL 34624, U.S.A.; tel. 800/535-7289), Moorings Rainbow Yacht Charters (Box 8327, Symonds St., Auckland, New Zealand; tel. 64-9/377-4840, fax 64-9/377-4820), or Adventure Holidays (Postfach 920113, 90266 Nürnberg, Germany; fax 49-911/979-9588).

Perhaps the finest charter yacht available at Fiji is the 14-meter ketch *Seax of Legra,* based at Taveuni (Box 89, Waiyevo, Taveuni; tel./fax 679/880-141). The charge is F$930 daily for two persons, F$985 for three, F$1035 for four, all-inclusive. Warwick and Dianne Bain who live next to Lisi's Campground on Taveuni will be your distinguished hosts on an unforgettable cruise. Larger groups could consider the 27-meter ketch *Tau* at the Raffles Tradewinds Hotel, Suva, which charges F$13,600 a week for up to six persons, meals included. For full information on these and other boats available in Fiji waters, write the **Fiji Yacht Charter Association** (Box 3084, Lami, Fiji Islands; tel. 361-256, fax 880-141).

A few private brokers arranging bareboat or crewed yacht charters are **Ocean Voyages Inc.** (1709 Bridgeway, Sausalito, CA 94965, U.S.A.; tel. 415/332-4681, fax 415/332-7460), **Sun Yacht Charters** (Box 737, Camden, ME 04843, U.S.A.; tel. 800/772-3500, fax 207/236-3972), **Charter World Pty. Ltd.** (579 Hampton St., Hampton, Melbourne 3188, Australia; tel. 61-3/9521-0033, fax 61-3/9521-0081), **Sail Connections Ltd.** (Freepost 4545, Box 3234,

Auckland, New Zealand; tel. 64-9/358-0556, fax 64-9/358-4341), and **Yachting Partners International** (28/29 Richmond Place, Brighton, BN2 2NA, East Sussex, England; tel. 44-1273/571722, fax 44-1273/571720). As they don't own their own boats (as the Moorings does), they'll be more inclined to fit you to the particular boat that suits your individual needs.

Mini-Cruise Ships
Blue Lagoon Cruises Ltd. (Box 130, Lautoka; tel. 661-622, fax 664-098) has been offering upmarket minicruises from Lautoka to the Yasawa Islands since its founding in 1950 by Capt. Trevor Withers. The three-night "original" trips (from F$605) leave daily, while the six-night "club" cruise (from F$1350) is weekly. Prices are per person, double or triple occupancy, and include meals (excluding alcohol), entertainment, and shore excursions. On the three-night cruises they use older three-deck, 40-passenger vessels, while larger four-deck, 60-passenger mini-cruise ships are used on the six-night (and some of the three-night) voyages. In July 1996 a new 72-passenger, US$8-million luxury cruiser is to begin operating trips to more remote island groups. The meals are often beach barbecue affairs, with Fijian dancing. You'll have plenty of opportunities to snorkel in the calm, crystal-clear waters (bring your own gear).

Though expensive, these trips have a good reputation. Departures are daily but reservations are essential, as they're usually booked solid months ahead—they're that popular.

Captain Cook Cruises (Box 23, Nandi; tel. 701-823, fax 702-045), on Narewa Road near the bridge into Nandi town, also offers luxury three-day cruises to the southern Yasawa Islands aboard the 38-meter MV *Duchess of the Isles,* departing Nandi Tuesday and Friday. The 31 double-occupancy staterooms cost F$695 pp on the upper deck (with TV), or F$590 pp on the lower deck (without TV).

In addition, Captain Cook operates three-day cruises to the southern Yasawas on the square-rigged brigantine *Ra Marama.* These depart Nandi every Monday morning and cost F$378 pp. You sleep in large tents at night, the food is good with lots of fresh vegetables and salads, and the staff is friendly and well organized. The snorkeling is glorious and scuba diving off Waya Island is possible at F$130 extra for three tanks. Your biggest disappointment will probably be that they have the diesel engine on all the time, and they don't bother trying to use the sails (logical—they haven't got a clue how to sail). Still, the *Na Marama* is a fine vessel built of teak planks at Singapore in 1957 for a former governor-general of Fiji. These trips can be booked through most travel agents; readers who've gone report having a great time.

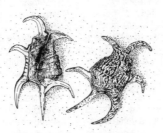

the spider conch (Lambris chiragra)

GETTING AROUND

BY AIR

While most international flights are focused on Nandi, Fiji's domestic air service radiates from Suva. **Air Fiji** (Box 1259, Suva; tel. 314-666, fax 300-771) flies their fast Brazilian-made Bandeirantes and sturdy Canadian-made Twin Otters from Nausori Airport four times a week to Kandavu (F$52) and twice a week to Lakemba (F$98). More common destinations such as Lambasa (F$73), Levuka (F$33), Nandi (F$63), Savusavu (F$68), and Taveuni (F$87) are served several times daily (all fares one-way).

Air Fiji's **Air Fiji Holiday Pass** allows you to fly from Suva to Kandavu, Levuka, Nandi, Savusavu, and Taveuni and back anytime within 30 days for F$253 (or US$150 if sold abroad). You can also use it to go Savusavu-Taveuni. If you were to fly Nandi-Suva-Kandavu-Suva-Taveuni-Savusavu-Suva-Levuka-Suva-Nandi on regular tickets you'd pay a total of F$496, so the pass does offer savings if you love flying and want to see a lot in one month. Some services are infrequent and heavily booked, so you should reserve all sectors when the ticket is issued and be prepared to show your passport every time you use the pass. This pass is sold at Air Fiji offices in Nandi and Suva, or by travel agents worldwide. If you're sure you want this pass, order it from your travel agent well ahead as some sectors could be full by the time you reach Fiji.

Sunflower Airlines (Box 9452, Nandi Airport; tel. 723-016, fax 790-085) bases much of its domestic network in Nandi, with daily flights to Lambasa (F$96), Savusavu (F$96), Suva (F$60), and Taveuni (F$116). Kandavu (F$66) and Vatulele (F$62) are served from Nandi four times a week. Sunflower's seven-day roundtrip excursion fare between Nandi and Lambasa is F$140. From Suva, Sunflower has flights to Lambasa (twice daily, F$72), Moala (three weekly, F$77), Nandi (twice daily, F$60), Ngau (three weekly, F$42), Koro (three weekly, F$60), and Rotuma (twice weekly, F$250). From Taveuni, they go to Savusavu (daily, F$45) and Lam-

basa (three weekly, F$45). Flying in their 10-seat Britten Norman Islanders and Twin Otters is sort of fun.

Fiji's third domestic carrier, **Vanua Air** (Box 2523, Government Buildings, Suva; tel. 381-226, fax 386-460), flies from Suva to Lambasa twice daily (F$66), to Lakemba twice weekly (F$98), to Moala twice weekly (F$73), to Rotuma twice weekly (F$250), to Savusavu twice daily (F$67), to Taveuni twice daily (F$87), to Thithia twice weekly (F$95), and to Vanua Mbalavu twice weekly (F$98). Unlike Sunflower Airlines, however, Vanua Air also flies between the different islands themselves: Thithia to/from Vanua Mbalavu twice weekly (F$22), Lakemba to/from Moala twice weekly (F$39), and Savusavu to/from Taveuni twice daily (F$42). When traffic warrants, they schedule flights from Suva to Koro (F$52), Ngau (F$44), and Rambi (F$94). It should be noted that Vanua Air is mainly an air charter operator and their schedules are far more "flexible" than those of the other two carriers mentioned above.

The busy little resort island of Malololailai gets eight flights a day by Sunflower Airlines (F$28) and five by **Island Air** (Office Suite 30, The Concourse, Nandi Airport, Nandi; tel. 722-077). Sunflower's day excursion from Nandi to Malololailai is F$58 roundtrip, lunch included. **Turtle Airways Ltd.** (Private Mail Bag, Nandi Airport, Nandi; tel. 722-988) flies their five Cessna floatplanes three times a day from Nandi to Castaway and Mana islands (F$90 one-way, F$180 roundtrip).

All flights are during daylight hours. Always reconfirm your return flight immediately upon arrival at an outer island, as the reservation lists are sometimes not sent out from Suva. Failure to do this could mean you will be "bumped" without compensation. Student discounts are for local students only and there are no standby fares. Children aged 12 and under pay 50%, infants two and under carried in arms 10%. All of the local airlines allow 15 kg of baggage only (overweight costs one percent of the full one-way fare per kg with a F$5 minimum).

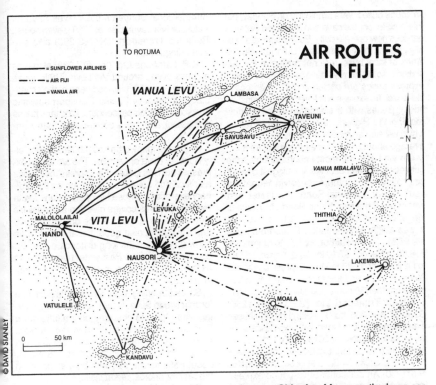

AIR ROUTES IN FIJI

— = SUNFLOWER AIRLINES
— ·· — = AIR FIJI
— · — = VANUA AIR

TO ROTUMA

VANUA LEVU

LAMBASA

TAVEUNI

SAVUSAVU

VANUA MBALAVU

LEVUKA

THITHIA

MALOLOLAILAI

VITI LEVU

NANDI

NAUSORI

LAKEMBA

VATULELE

MOALA

0   50 km

KANDAVU

— N —

© DAVID STANLEY

BY BOAT

Since most shipping operates out of Suva, passenger services by sea both within Fiji and to neighboring countries are listed in the Suva chapter, under "Transportation."

The largest company is **Patterson Brothers Shipping,** set up by Levuka copra planter Reg Patterson and his brother just after WW I. Patterson's four Japanese-built ferries are the barge *Yaumbula,* which shuttles between Natuvu and Taveuni; the 40-meter car ferries *Jubilee* and *Princess Ashika,* usually used on the Mbure-sala-Natovi-Nambouwalu-Ellington Wharf run; and the large car ferry *Ovalau,* which sails Suva-Ngau-Koro-Savusavu-Taveuni weekly. Delays due to the mechanical failures of Patterson's aging fleet are routine.

Consort Shipping Line runs the large car ferry *Spirit of Free Enterprise* from Suva to Koro, Savusavu, and Taveuni once or twice a week.

In August 1995 **Beachcomber Cruises** (Box 364, Lautoka; tel. 661-500, fax 664-496) launched a direct service from Lautoka to Savusavu and Natovi on the 60-passenger, 18-meter high-speed catamaran *Ndrondrolangi* ("Rainbow"). Turn to the Lautoka, Savusavu, and Suva sections for details.

BY BUS

Scheduled bus service is available all over Fiji, and fares are low. If you're from the States you'll be amazed how accessible, inexpensive, and convenient the bus service is. Local people are always happy to supply information about buses and to help you catch one. Right after the Rabuka coups buses were prohibited on Sunday, but this is no longer the case and most long-distance services now operate daily. Bus stations are usually adjacent to local markets. Unfortunately the times of local buses are not posted at the bus stations, so you always have to ask (the times of express buses *are* posted and it's often possible to pick up express bus timetables at tourist offices). Buses with a signboard in the window reading Via Highway are local "stage" buses which will stop anywhere along their route. Fares average about F$1.50 for each hour of travel.

On Viti Levu, the most important routes are between Suva and Lautoka, the biggest cities. If you follow the southern route via Singatoka you'll be on Queens Road, the faster and smoother of the two. Kings Road via Tavua is longer and can be rough and dusty, but you get to see a little of the interior. Fares from Suva are F$2 to Pacific Harbor, F$4.70 to Singatoka, F$6.80 to Nandi, F$7.10 to Nandi Airport, F$7.80 to Lautoka, and F$9 to Mba. Express buses are 20 cents extra and to reserve a seat on a bus costs another 50 cents (usually unnecessary).

Pacific Transport Ltd. (G.P.O. Box 1266, Suva; tel. 304-366, fax 303-668) has nine buses a day along Queens Road, with expresses leaving Suva for Lautoka at 0645, 0930, 1210, 1500, and 1730 (five hours). Eastbound, the expresses leave Lautoka for Suva at 0630, 0700, 1210, and 1730. An additional Suva-bound express leaves Nandi at 0900. These buses stop at Navua, Pacific Harbor, Singatoka (coffee break), Nandi, and Nandi Airport only. The 1500 bus continues on to Mba. If you want off at a Coral Coast resort or some other smaller place, you must take one of the five local "stage" buses, which take six and a half hours to reach Lautoka via Queens Road.

Sunbeam Transport Ltd. (tel. 382-122) services the northern Kings Road from Suva to Lautoka five times a day, with expresses leaving Suva at 0645, 1330, and 1715 (six hours). From Lautoka, they depart at 0630, 1215, and 1630. A Sunbeam express bus along Kings Road is a comfortable way to see Viti Levu's picturesque back side. These expresses only stop at Nausori, Korovou, Vaikela (Rakiraki), Tavua, and Mba. If you want off anywhere else you must take one of the two local buses, which take nine fun-filled hours to reach Lautoka via Kings Road.

Another local Sunbeam bus leaves Suva for Vatukoula via Tavua daily at 0730 (seven hours). **Reliance Transport** (tel. 382-296) also services Kings Road.

K.P. Latchans Ltd. (tel. 477-268) also runs express buses around Viti Levu. Their buses often run about 30 minutes ahead of the scheduled Sunbeam or Pacific Transport services and scoop all their passengers. Latchans buses are newer and more comfortable than Sunbeam's.

There are many other local buses, especially closer to Suva or Lautoka. The a/c tourist expresses such as UTC's "Fiji Express" cost twice as much and are not as much fun as the ordinary expresses, whose big open windows with roll-down canvas covers give you a panoramic view of Viti Levu. Bus service on Vanua Levu and Taveuni is also good. Local buses often show up late, but the long-distance buses are usually right on time. Passenger trucks serving as "carriers" charge set rates to and from interior villages.

Shared "running" taxis also shuttle back and forth between Suva, Nandi, and Lautoka, leaving when full and charging only a little more than the bus. Look for them in the markets around the bus stations. It's possible to hire a complete taxi from Nandi Airport to Suva for about F$50 for the car, with brief stops along the way for photos, resort visits, etc.

Often the drivers of private or company cars and vans try to earn a little money on the side by stopping to offer lifts to persons waiting for buses beside the highway. They ask the same as you'd pay on the bus but are much faster and will probably drop you off exactly where you want to go. If you're hitching, be aware that truck drivers who give you a lift may also expect the equivalent of bus fare; locals pay this without question.

TAXIS

Fijian taxis are plentiful and among the cheapest in the South Pacific, usable even by low-budget travelers. This could soon change, however, due to a government decision to force taxi drivers to take cars over 10 years old out of service. There's also a move to force Fiji Indians out of the taxi business by issuing new permits only to ethnic Fijians.

Many taxis have meters but it's usually easier to ask the driver for a flat rate before you get in. If the first price you're quoted is too high you can often bargain (although bargaining is much more accepted by Fiji Indian than by ethnic Fijian drivers). A short ride across city can cost F$1-2, a longer trip into a nearby suburb about F$3. Taxis returning to their stand after a trip will pick up passengers at bus stops and charge the regular bus fare (ask if it's the "returning fare"). Taxis are sometimes hard to find in Suva after dark or on Sunday, though this is less of a problem in Nandi/Lautoka.

Don't tip your driver; tips are neither expected nor necessary. And don't invite your driver for a drink or become overly familiar with him as he may abuse your trust. If you're a woman taking a cab alone in the Nandi area, don't let your driver think there is any "hope" for him, or you could have problems (videos often portray Western women as promiscuous, which leads to mistaken expectations).

CAR RENTALS

Rental cars are expensive in Fiji, due in part to high import duties on cars, and a 10% government tax is added, so with public transportation as good as it is here, you should think twice before renting a car. By law, third-party public liability insurance is compulsory for rental vehicles and is included in the basic rate, but collision damage waiver (CDW) insurance is about F$16 per day extra. Even with CDW, you're often still responsible for a "nonwaivable excess" which can be as high as the first F$1500 in damage to the car! Many cars are on the road have no insurance, so you could end up paying even if you're not responsible for the accident.

Your home driver's license is recognized for your first six months in Fiji and driving is on the left (as in Britain and Japan). Seat belts must be worn in the front seat and the police are empowered to give roadside breath-analyzer tests. The police around Viti Levu occasionally employ hand-held radar. Speed limits are 50 kph in towns, 80 kph on the highway. Pedestrians have the right of way at crosswalks.

Unpaved roads can be very slippery, especially on inclines, and gravel roads throw up stones. Beware of poorly marked speed humps on roads through villages and narrow bridges, and take care with local motorists, who sometimes stop in the middle of the road, pass on blind curves, and drive at high speeds. Driving can be an especially risky business at night. Many of the roads are atrocious (check the spare tire), although Queens Road, which passes the Coral Coast resorts, is now completely paved from Lautoka to Suva, and there isn't a lot of traffic.

If you plan to use a rental car to explore rough country roads in Viti Levu's mountainous interior, think twice before announcing your plans to the agency, as they may suddenly decline your business. The rental contracts all contain clauses stating that the insurance coverage is not valid under such conditions. Some companies offer 4WD Suzukis made just for mountain roads. Tank up on Saturday, as many gas stations are closed on Sunday. If you run out of gas in a rural area, small village stores sometimes sell fuel from drums.

All of the international car rental chains are represented in Fiji, including Avis, Budget, Hertz, National, and Thrifty. Local companies like Beta Rent-A-Car, Central Rent-A-Car, Dove Rent-A-Car, Khan's Rental Cars, Letz Rent-A-Car, Nandroga Car Hire, Roxy Rentals, Satellite Rentals, Sharmas Rental Cars, Sheik's Rent-A-Car, Skyline Car Rental, and UTC Rent-A-Car are often cheaper, but check around as prices and service vary. The international companies rent only new cars, while the less expensive local companies may offer secondhand vehicles. If in doubt, check the vehicle carefully before driving off. Budget, Central, and National won't rent to persons under age 25, while Avis, Hertz, and Thrifty will, so long as you're over 21.

A dozen companies have offices in the concourse at Nandi Airport and three are also at Nausori Airport. Agencies with town offices in Suva include Avis on Scott Street (tel. 313-833); Budget, 123 Forster Rd., Walu Bay (tel. 315-899); Central, 293 Victoria Parade (tel. 311-908); Dove, Harifam Center, Greig Street (tel. 311-755); and Hertz, 56 Grantham Rd., Raiwannga (tel. 370-518). In Lautoka there's Budget on Marine Drive (tel. 666-166) and Central at

73 Vitongo Parade (tel. 664-511). Avis and Thrifty also have desks in many resort hotels on Viti Levu. On Vanua Levu, Avis, Budget, and Thrifty are at Savusavu, and Budget is also at Lambasa.

Both unlimited-kilometer and per-kilometer rates are available. **Thrifty Car Rental** (tel. 722-755) offers good unlimited-kilometer prices (from F$85 daily, F$510 weekly), which include CDW (F$600 nonwaivable) and tax, but there's a 150-km limit on one-day rentals. Prices at Avis start at F$88 a day (plus F$16.50 CDW), at Hertz F$85 (plus F$17 CDW plus 10% tax). **Sharmas Rental Cars** (tel. 701-055) at Nandi Airport and near the ANZ Bank in Nandi town advertises unlimited-kilometer rates of F$222 a week or F$700 a month (10% tax and F$10 a day insurance extra). On a per-kilometer basis, rates at Sharmas begin at F$14 a day, plus 14 cents a kilometer, plus F$10 CDW, plus tax. **Khan's Rental Cars** (tel. 701-009) in Nandi is also good at F$15 daily plus 17 cents a kilometer and F$10 CDW (F$1500 nonwaivable).

On a per-kilometer basis, you'll only want to use the car in the local area, as a drive around Viti Levu is 486 km. If you want the cheapest economy subcompact, reserve ahead. Beware of companies like Central, which list extremely low prices in their brochure, only mentioning in very small type at the bottom that these are the "off-season" rates (period not specified). Others, such as Budget and National, also advertise low prices with the qualification in tiny type below that these apply only to rentals of three days or more. Most companies charge a F$30 delivery fee if you don't return the vehicle to the office where you rented it.

BY SAILING YACHT

Getting Aboard

Hitch rides into the Pacific on yachts from California, New Zealand, and Australia, or around the yachting triangle Papeete-Suva-Honolulu. At home, scrutinize the classified listings of yachts seeking crews, yachts to be delivered, etc., in magazines like *Yachting, Cruising World, Sail,* and *Latitude 38.* You can even advertise yourself for about US$25 (plan to have the ad appear three months before the beginning of the season). Check the bulletin boards at yacht clubs. The **Seven Seas Cruising Association** (1525 South Andrews Ave., Suite 217, Fort Lauderdale, FL 33316, U.S.A.; tel. 305/463-2431, fax 305/463-7183) is in touch with yachties all around the Pacific, and the classified section "Crew Exchange" in their monthly *Commodores' Bulletin* (US$53 a year) contains ads from captains in search of crew.

Cruising yachts are recognizable by their foreign flags, wind-vane steering gear, sturdy appearance, and laundry hung out to dry. Put up notices on yacht club and marine bulletin boards, and meet people in bars. When a boat is hauled out, you can find work scraping and repainting the bottom, varnishing, and doing minor repairs. It's much easier, however, to crew on yachts already in the islands. Suva, Lautoka, and Malololailai are good places to look for a boat.

If you've never crewed before, it's better to try for a short passage the first time. Once at sea on the way to the South Pacific, there's no way they'll turn around to take a seasick crew member back to Hawaii. Good captains evaluate crew on personality and attitude more than on experience, so don't lie. Be honest and open when interviewing with a skipper—a deception will soon become apparent. It's also good to know what a captain's *really* like before you commit yourself to an isolated month with her/him. To determine what might happen should the electronic gadgetry break down, find out if there's a sextant aboard and whether he/she knows how to use it. A run-down-looking boat may often be mechanically unsound too. Once you're on a boat and part of the yachtie community, things are easy. (P.S. from veteran yachtie Peter Moree: "We do need more ladies out here—adventurous types naturally.")

Time of Year

The weather and seasons play a deciding role in any South Pacific trip by sailboat and you'll have to pull out of many beautiful places, or be unable to stop there, because of bad weather. The best season for rides in the South Pacific is May to October; sometimes you'll even have to turn one down. Around August or September start looking for a ride from the South Pacific to Hawaii or New Zealand.

Be aware of the hurricane season: November to March in the South Pacific, July to December in the northwest Pacific (near Guam), and June to October in the area between Mexico and Hawaii. Few yachts will be cruising these areas at these times. A few yachts spend the winter at Pago Pago and Vava'u (the main "hurricane holes"), but most South Pacific cruisers will have left for hurricane-free New Zealand by October.

Also, know which way the winds are blowing; the prevailing trade winds in the tropics are from the northeast north of the equator, from the southeast south of the equator. North of the Tropic of Cancer and south of the Tropic of Capricorn the winds are out of the west. Due to the action of prevailing southeast trade winds boat trips are smoother from east to west than west to east throughout the South Pacific, so that's the way to go.

Yachting Routes

The South Pacific is good for sailing; there's not too much traffic and no piracy like you'd find in the Mediterranean or in Indonesian waters. The common yachting route across the Pacific utilizes the northeast and southeast trades: from California to Tahiti via the Marquesas or Hawaii, then Rarotonga, Vava'u, Suva, and New Zealand. Some yachts continue west from Fiji to Port Vila. In the other direction, you'll sail on the westerlies from New Zealand to a point south of the Australs, then north on the trades to Tahiti.

Some 300 yachts leave the U.S. West Coast for Tahiti every year, almost always crewed by couples or men only. Most stay in the South Seas about a year before returning to North America, while a few continue around the world. About 60-80 cross the Indian Ocean every year (look for rides from Sydney in May, Cairns or Darwin June to August, Bali August to October, Singapore October to December); around 700 yachts sail from Europe to the Caribbean (from Gibraltar and Gran Canaria October to December).

Cruising yachts average about 150 km a day, so it takes about a month to get from the U.S. west coast to Hawaii, then another month from Hawaii to Papeete. To enjoy the best weather conditions many yachts clear the Panama Canal or depart California in February to arrive in the Marquesas in March. Many yachts stay on for the *Heiva i Tahiti* festival, which ends on 14 July, at which time they sail west to Vava'u or Suva, where you'll find them in July and August. In mid-September the yachting season culminates with a race by about 40 boats from Fiji's Malololailai Island to Port Vila (it's very easy to hitch a ride at this time). By late October the bulk of the yachting community is sailing south via New Caledonia to New Zealand or Australia to spend the southern summer there. In April or May on alternate years (1995, 1997, etc.) there's a yacht race from Auckland and Sydney to Suva, timed to coincide with the cruisers' return after the hurricane season.

A law enacted in New Zealand in February 1995 requires foreign yachts departing New Zealand to obtain a "Certificate of Inspection" from the New Zealand Yachting Federation prior to customs clearance. Before heading into a situation where thousands of dollars might have to be spent upgrading safety standards on their boats, yachties should query others who have left New Zealand recently about the impact of this law.

Life Aboard

To crew on a yacht you must be willing to wash and iron clothes, cook, steer, keep watch at night, and help with engine work. Other jobs might include changing and resetting sails, cleaning the boat, scraping the bottom, pulling up the anchor, climbing the main mast to watch for reefs, etc. Do more than is expected of you. A safety harness must be worn in rough weather. As a guest in someone else's home you'll want to wash your dishes promptly after use and put them, and all other gear, back where you found them. Tampons must not be thrown in the toilet bowl. Smoking is usually prohibited as a safety hazard.

You'll be a lot more useful if you know how to use a sextant—the U.S. Coast Guard Auxiliary holds periodic courses in its use. Also learn how to tie knots like the clove hitch, rolling hitch, sheet bend, double sheet bend, reef knot, square knot, figure eight, and bowline. Check your local library for books on sailing or write away for the comprehensive free catalog of nautical books available from International Marine/TAB Books, Blue Ridge Summit, PA 17294-0840, U.S.A.

Anybody who wants to get on well under sail must be flexible and tolerant, both physically and emotionally. Expense-sharing crew members pay US$50 a week or more per person. After 30 days you'll be happy to hit land for a freshwater shower. Give adequate notice when you're ready to leave the boat, but *do* disembark when your journey's up. Boat people have few enough opportunities for privacy as it is. If you've had a good trip, ask the captain to write you a letter of recommendation; it'll help you hitch another ride.

Food for Thought

When you consider the big investment, depreciation, cost of maintenance, operating expenses, and considerable risk (most cruising yachts are not insured), travel by sailing yacht is quite a luxury. The huge cost can be surmised from charter fees (US$400 a day and up for a 10-meter yacht). International law makes a clear distinction between passengers and crew. Crew members paying only for their own food, cooking gas, and part of the diesel are very different from charterers who do nothing and pay full costs. The crew is there to help operate the boat, adding safety, but like passengers, they're very much under the control of the captain. Crew has no say in where the yacht will go.

The skipper is personally responsible for crew coming into foreign ports: he's entitled to hold their passports and to see that they have onward tickets and sufficient funds for further traveling. Otherwise the skipper might have to pay their hotel bills and even return airfares to the crew's country of origin. Crew may be asked to pay a share of third-party liability insurance. Possession of dope can result in seizure of the yacht. Because of such considerations, skippers often hesitate to accept crew. Crew members should keep in mind that at no cost to themselves they can learn a bit of sailing and see places nearly inaccessible by other means.

AIRPORTS

Nandi International Airport

Nandi Airport (NAN) is between Lautoka and Nandi, 22 km south of the former and eight km north of the latter. There are frequent buses to these towns until around 2200. To catch a bus to Nandi (45 cents), cross the highway; buses to Lautoka (90 cents) stop on the airport side of the road. A few express buses drop passengers right outside the international departures hall. A taxi from the airport should be F$6 to downtown Nandi, F$20 to Lautoka.

Most hotels around Nandi have their rates listed on a board inside the customs area, so peruse the list while you're waiting for your baggage. The Fiji Visitors Bureau office (fax 720-141) is to the left as you come out of customs. They open for all international arrivals and can advise you on accommodations. Pick up brochures, hotel lists, and the free tourist magazines.

There's a 24-hour ANZ Bank (F$2 commission) in the commercial arcade near the Visitors Bureau and another bank in the departure lounge. Many travel agencies, car rental companies, and airline offices are also located in the arrivals arcade. The rent-a-car companies you'll find here are Avis, Budget, Central, Hertz, Khan's, Letz, National, Roxy, Sharmas, and Thrifty.

The post office is across the road from the terminal (ask). The luggage storage service near the snack bar in the departure terminal charges F$1 per bag per day. Most hotels around Nandi will also store luggage. The airport never closes. NAN's 24-hour flight arrival and departure information number is 722-076.

Duty-free shops are found in both the departure lounge and the arrivals area near the baggage pickup. Prices in the duty-free shop for arriving passengers are higher than those in the much larger shop in the departure lounge. You can use leftover Fijian currency to stock up on cheap film and cigarettes just before you leave (film prices here are the lowest in the South Pacific).

A departure tax of F$20 is payable on all international flights, but transit passengers connecting within 12 hours and children under the age of 16 are exempt (no airport tax on domestic flights). Have a look at the museum exhibits near the departure gates upstairs as you're waiting for your flight. There's zero tolerance for drugs in Fiji and a three-dog sniffer unit checks all baggage passing through NAN.

Nausori Airport

Nausori Airport (SUV) is on the plain of the Rewa River delta, 23 km northeast of downtown Suva. After Hurricane Kina in January 1993 the whole terminal was flooded by Rewa water for several days. There's no special airport bus and a taxi direct to/from Suva will run about F$17. You can save money by taking a taxi from the airport only as far as Nausori (four km, F$4), then a local bus to Suva from there (19 km, 80 cents, with services every 10 minutes daily until 2100). Airport-bound, catch a local bus from Suva to Nausori, then a taxi to the airport (only F$2 in this direction). It's also possible to catch a local bus to Nausori from the highway opposite the airport about every 15 minutes (35 cents).

Avis, Budget, and Hertz all have car rental offices in the terminal, and a lunch counter provides light snacks. You're not allowed to sleep overnight at this airport. The departure tax is F$20 on all international flights, but no tax is levied on domestic flights. The inevitable duty-free shop is on the premises.

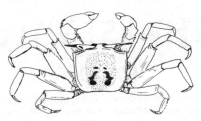

racing crab (Octypode ceratophthalma)

SALVATORE CASA

SOUTHWEST VITI LEVU

NANDI

Nandi (population 16,000), on the dry side of Fiji's largest island, offers a multitude of places to stay for incoming visitors landing at Nandi International Airport. A small airstrip existed at Nandi even before WW II, and after Pearl Harbor the Royal New Zealand Air Force began converting it into a fighter strip. Before long the U.S. military was there, building a major air base with paved runways for bombers and transport aircraft serving Australia and New Zealand. In the early 1960s, Nandi Airport was expanded to accommodate jet aircraft, and today the largest jumbo jets can land here. This activity has made Nandi what it is today.

All around Nandi are cane fields worked by the predominantly Indian population. There aren't many sandy, palm-fringed beaches on the western side of Viti Levu—for that you have to go to the nearby Mamanutha Group where a string of sun-drenched "Robinson Crusoe" resorts soak up vacationers in search of a place to relax. The long gray mainland beaches near Nandi face shallow murky waters devoid of snor-keling possibilities but fine for windsurfing and water-skiing. Fiji's tropical rainforests are on the other side of Viti Levu.

Nandi town has a kilometer of concrete duty-free tourist shops with high-pressure sales staffs peddling mass-produced souvenirs. Yet there's also a surprisingly colorful market (best on Saturday morning). It's a rather touristy town, so if you're not that exhausted after your transpacific flight you'd do better to head for Lautoka (see the separate Lautoka chapter later in this book). All of the hotels around Nandi tend to experience quite a bit of air-craft/traffic/disco noise, while those at Lautoka are out of range.

Sights

Nandi's only substantial sight is the **Sri Siva Sub-ramaniya Swami Temple** at the south entrance to town, erected by local Hindus in 1994 after the lease on their former temple property expired. This colorful South Indian-style temple, built by craftspeople flown in from India itself, is the largest and finest of its kind in the South Pacific.

Sports and Recreation

Aqua-Trek (Box 10215, Nandi Airport; tel. 702-413, fax 702-412), located at 465 Queens Road, opposite the Mobil station in Nandi town, arranges scuba diving at Mana Island and elsewhere. **Tropical Divers** (Box 9063, Nandi; tel. 750-777) in the beach hut at the Sheraton offers overpriced scuba diving at F$95 one tank, F$135 two tanks, or F$585 for a PADI certification course.

Much less expensive diving is offered by **Inner Space Adventures** (Box 9535, Nandi Airport; tel./fax 723-883), between the Horizon and Travellers beach resorts at Wailoaloa Beach. They go out daily at 0900, charging F$44/77/99 for one/two/three tanks, equipment and pickup anywhere around Nandi included. Snorkelers are welcome to tag along at F$25 pp, gear included. The four-day open-water PADI certification course costs F$299.

The **Roaring Thunder Company** (Box 545, Nandi; tel. 780-029, fax 790-094) offers white-water rubber rafting on the Mba River (F$70).

Sri Siva Subramaniya Swami Temple, Nandi

M. E. DE VOS

The trips are designed for those aged 15-45, although physically fit older persons can join by signing a liability disclaimer. Bookings can be made at Cardo's Restaurant in Nandi town, which is owned by the same company. The degree of excitement will depend on how much rain they've been getting in the mountains, and during droughts the ride will be rather placid. Even then, it's a very scenic trip.

Thirty-minute jet boat rides around the mouth of the Nandi River are offered by **Shotover Jet** (Box 1932, Nandi; tel. 750-400, fax 750-666) about every half hour from the Ndenarau Island Marina (adults F$55, children under 16 years F$24). It's fairly certain the birds and fish of this mangrove area are less thrilled by these energy-guzzling, high-impact craft than the tourists seated therein. The raft trips mentioned above are better value and more environmentally friendly.

The 18-hole, par-71 **Nandi Airport Golf Club** (Box 9015, Nandi; tel. 722-148), between the airport runways and the sea at Wailoaloa Beach, is said to be the toughest course in Fiji. Green fees are F$13.50 plus F$12 for a half set of clubs. There's a bar and pool table in the clubhouse.

Other golf courses are available at the Mocambo and Sheraton hotels. The 18-hole, par-72 course at the Japanese-owned **Ndenarau Golf & Racquet Club** (Box 9081, Nandi Airport; tel. 750-477, fax 750-484) opposite the Sheraton was designed by Eiichi Motohashi. The course features bunkers shaped like a marlin, crab, starfish, and octopus, and water shots across all four par-three holes (the average golfer loses four balls per round). Green fees are F$77 and cart hire is mandatory. Ask about their special "nine, wine & dine" deal on Friday and Saturday afternoons: tee time for the nine holes is at 1500, followed by the barbecue and wine at 1830 (F$35). Ten tennis courts are available. Higher prices may apply for those not staying at the Sheraton or Regent, so call ahead for information.

During the February-to-November sports season, see rugby or soccer on Saturday afternoon at the A.D. Patel Stadium, near the bus station.

ACCOMMODATIONS

Budget Accommodations in Town

Most of the hotels offer free transport from the airport, which is lucky because there aren't any

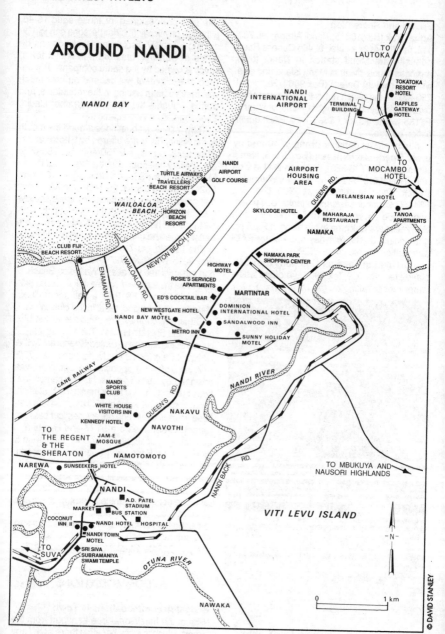

AROUND NANDI

NANDI BAY

TO LAUTOKA

NANDI INTERNATIONAL AIRPORT

TERMINAL BUILDING

TOKATOKA RESORT HOTEL

RAFFLES GATEWAY HOTEL

TO MOCAMBO HOTEL

AIRPORT HOUSING AREA

QUEENS RD.

MELANESIAN HOTEL

NANDI AIRPORT GOLF COURSE

TURTLE AIRWAYS

TRAVELLERS BEACH RESORT

WAILOALOA BEACH

HORIZON BEACH RESORT

SKYLODGE HOTEL

MAHARAJA RESTAURANT

TANOA APARTMENTS

NAMAKA

CLUB FIJI BEACH RESORT

NEWTON BEACH RD.

WAILOALOA RD.

ENAMANU RD.

Namaka Park SHOPPING CENTER

HIGHWAY MOTEL

ROSIE'S SERVICED APARTMENTS

ED'S COCKTAIL BAR

NEW WESTGATE HOTEL

NANDI BAY MOTEL

METRO INN

MARTINTAR

DOMINION INTERNATIONAL HOTEL

SANDALWOOD INN

SUNNY HOLIDAY MOTEL

CANE RAILWAY

NANDI SPORTS CLUB

WHITE HOUSE VISITORS INN

KENNEDY HOTEL

JAM-E MOSQUE

QUEEN'S RD.

NAKAVU

NAVOTHI

NANDI RIVER

TO THE REGENT & THE SHERATON

NAMOTOMOTO

NAREWA

SUNSEEKERS HOTEL

NANDI

A.D. PATEL STADIUM

MARKET

BUS STATION

COCONUT INN II

NANDI HOTEL

HOSPITAL

NANDI TOWN MOTEL

SRI SIVA SUBRAMANIYA SWAMI TEMPLE

TO SUVA

OTUNA RIVER

NAWAKA

NANDI BACK RD.

TO MBUKUYA AND NAUSORI HIGHLANDS

VITI LEVU ISLAND

-N-

0   1 km

© DAVID STANLEY

budget places within walking distance of the airport itself. As you leave customs you'll be besieged by a group of men representing the hotels. If you know which one you want, call out the name; if a driver from that hotel is there, you'll get a free ride. If not, the Fiji Visitors Bureau (tel. 722-433, fax 720-141) to the left will help you telephone them for a small fee. Don't be put off by the hotel drivers at the airport, but do question them about the rates and facilities before you let them drive you to their place.

There are three choices in the downtown area, two with confusingly similar names but under separate managements. The seedy **Nandi Town Motel** (Box 1326, Nandi; tel. 700-600, fax 701-541), occupying the top floor of an office building opposite the BP service station in the center of Nandi, is a bit of a dive and the only attraction here is price: F$20/22 single/double with fan, F$23/28 with a/c, both with private bath. The five-bed dormitory is just F$6 pp and basic rooms with shared bath are F$11/15. Breakfast is supposed to be included in all rates but don't be surprised if they try to charge extra. Definitely ask to see the room before accepting, expect dirty sheets, and, if you're a woman, don't tolerate any nonsense from the male motel staff. The adjacent Rupeni's Nightclub sends out a steady disco beat well into the morning. The travel agency below the motel arranges transport to Nananu-i-Ra Island for F$26 pp.

Around the corner on Koroivolu Street is the two-story, 36-room **Nandi Hotel** (Box 91, Nandi; tel. 700-000, fax 700-280). Rooms with private bath here begin at F$22/28 single/double with fan, F$33/39 with a/c, or F$11 pp in an eight-bed dorm. The neat courtyard with a swimming pool out back makes this a pleasant, convenient place to stay. Nice people too. Some rooms are also subjected to nightclub noise, though, so ask for a room in the block farthest away from Rupeni's.

The two-story **Coconut Inn II** (Box 2756, Nandi; tel. 701-011, fax 701-169) is down the side street opposite the Nandi Handicraft Market, a block from the Nandi Hotel and the Nandi Town Motel. The 22 a/c rooms with private bath upstairs begin at F$30/35 single/double, and downstairs is a F$10 dorm. Until recently this was the dodgy Fong Hing Hotel, but things have changed and prostitutes are no longer admit-

ted. The restaurant downstairs still serves good Chinese food, however.

On Narewa Road at the north edge of Nandi town is **Sunseekers Hotel** (Box 100, Nandi; tel. 700-400, fax 702-047). The 20 rooms here are F$25 single or double with fan, F$35 single or double with a/c, F$6 dorm (extra charge if you want a sheet, F$1 surcharge for one night, airport transfers F$3). There's a tiny pool (dry) out back. Despite the prominent Youth Hostel signs outside, there's no YHA discount. Unfortunately this poorly managed hotel has fallen on hard times and can no longer be recommended.

Much better is the two-story **White House Visitors Inn** (Box 2150, Nandi; tel./fax 700-022), 40 Kennedy Ave., up Ray Prasad Road just off Queens Road, a 10-minute walk north of central Nandi. The 12 fan-equipped rooms are F$20 double with shared bath, F$25/30 single/double with private bath, or F$8 pp in the dorm. Rooms with a/c cost F$5 extra. The beds are comfortable and a weight-watchers' toast-and-coffee breakfast is included in the price. You can cook your own meals in the communal kitchen, and there's a grocery store across the street. This new hotel is a fairly peaceful place to stay, with a small swimming pool, video lounge, and free airport pickup. Baggage storage is F$1 per day. Though you'll hear a bit of traffic and animal noise, you won't be bothered by disco music. It's very popular and might be full.

Half a block up Kennedy Avenue from the White House is the three-story **Kennedy Hotel** (Box 9045, Nandi Airport; tel. 702-360, fax 702-218), the highest-priced hotel in this category. At F$44/50 single/double with bath, tax included, the 16 a/c rooms are a reasonable value. Deluxe two-bedroom apartments with cooking facilities are F$99. They've converted a few less appealing rooms near the reception area into three-bed dorms at F$10 pp. All rooms at the Kennedy have a/c, TV, fridge, and coffee-making facilities. Another big plus are the spacious gardenlike grounds with a large swimming pool, and there's a restaurant/bar on the premises.

Budget Airport Hotels
The listings below are arranged from the airport into town. The low-budget hotel closest to the terminal is the **Kon Tiki Private Hotel** (tel.

722-836), set in cane fields a 15-minute walk in from the main highway, past the Mocambo Hotel. The 16 rooms go for F$17/22 single/double with private bath and fan, F$7 pp dormitory. Some hard drinking goes on at the bar, so don't accept a room near it. Kon Tiki is all by itself down a side road, so you're dependent on the hotel restaurant for food. Considering the many other budget accommodations around Nandi, Kon Tiki doesn't have much going for it. They do arrange daily transfers to Nananu-i-Ra Island at F$22 each way.

The **Melanesian Hotel** (Box 9242, Nandi Airport; tel. 722-438, fax 720-425) has 16 rooms beginning at F$26/31 single/double, F$9 extra for a/c. A mixed five-bed dorm (F$8 pp) is also available. The rooms are okay and the Melanesian looks fine, though it's got a reputation for occasional carousing, as suggested by the name of the hotel restaurant, the "Jolly Jumpbuck!"

More basic is the **Highway Motel** (Box 9236, Nandi; tel. 723-761), a single-story block with rooms at F$20/25 single/double, all with private facilities. Rooms with a/c are F$5 more. The Highway offers shared cooking facilities for F$3 extra and luggage storage. You can bargain for a discount when things are slow, but it's a rather grungy place to stay.

A newer place to stay is the **Valentino Hotel** (Box 9609, Nandi Airport; tel. 720-640), behind Ed's Cocktail Bar, with nine fan-cooled rooms with bath at F$20/25 single/double. Their restaurant specializes in seafood and Italian food.

The two-story **Sandalwood Inn** (John and Ana Birch, Box 9454, Nandi Airport; tel. 722-044, fax 790-103), on Ragg Street beside the Dominion International Hotel, is F$22/28/34 single/double/triple for one of the five rooms with shared bath in the old wing, or F$29/35 single/double for one of the 20 rooms with fridges and private baths in the new wing (a/c rooms F$42/48). The cheaper rooms may all be full and the a/c rooms aren't worth it. The atmosphere is pleasant and the layout attractive with pool, bar, and a restaurant serving authentic Fijian dishes. The food and drinks are a little overpriced.

Close by and less expensive is the 14-room **Sunny Holiday Motel** (Box 1326, Nandi Airport; tel. 722-158, fax 701-541), located at 67 Northern Press Rd. behind Hamacho Japanese Restaurant. It's F$11/16 single/double with shared bath, F$20/22 with private bath, or F$5 dorm (five beds). Self-contained apartments with cooking facilities are F$28/33. Show your Youth Hostel card for a 10% discount. Inveterate campers may like to know that this is about the only place around Nandi where you're allowed to unroll your tent (F$3 pp). There's a pool table, TV room, bar, and luggage storage. It's all a little run-down, but friendly, uncrowded, and fine for those on the lowest of budgets. They book the daily shuttle to Nananu-i-Ra Island (F$26 one-way).

A few hundred meters down Wailoaloa Beach Road off the main highway, in the opposite direction from the Sunny Holiday, is the **Nandi Bay Motel** (Private Mail Bag, Nandi; tel. 723-599, fax 720-092), a two-story concrete edifice enclosing a small swimming pool. The 25 rooms are F$21/28 single/double with fan, F$7 extra for private bath, F$15 extra for private bath and a/c. An apartment with cooking facilities is F$49. There's also a F$8 dorm with a 10% discount on dormitory beds to YHA cardholders. Washing machines are available, plus a congenial bar, inexpensive restaurant, and luggage room. This uninteresting place is always full of bored tourists reading Lonely Planet as they hang around waiting for their flights out of Fiji. The airport flight path passes right above Nandi Bay and the roar of jets on the adjacent runway can be jarring. Don't agree to take any scuba lessons in the motel swimming pool unless you're prepared for a steady stream of wisecracks from the jerks lounging by the pool. We've heard that the scuba instruction arranged by this hotel isn't up to scratch.

Budget Beach Hotels

There are four inexpensive places to stay on Wailoaloa Beach, also known as Newtown Beach, on the opposite side of the airport runway from the main highway. The first three are adjacent to the seaplane base and golf club, a three-km hike from the Nandi Bay Motel, so ask for their free shuttle buses at the airport or take a taxi (F$6). The Wailoaloa Newtown bus from Nandi market also passes nearby three times a day. These places are probably your best bet on the weekend, and sporting types can play a round of golf on the public course or go jogging along the beach (the swimming in the knee-deep water isn't great). The main base of Inner Space Adventures is here, with scuba diving and horseback riding on offer.

The cheapest of the lot is the **Horizon Beach Resort** (Box 1401, Nandi; tel. 722-832, fax 720-662), a large wooden two-story house just across a field from the beach. The 14 rooms with shared bath are F$18/26 single/double with fan, F$29/34 with a/c. Horizon's 10-bed dormitory is F$5 pp. No cooking facilities are provided but there's a restaurant/bar.

A hundred meters inland from the Horizon is the two-story **Newtown Beach Motel** (Box 787, Nandi; tel. 723-332, fax 720-087). The seven clean rooms with fan are F$19/25/30 single/double/triple. There's no cooking, but a huge dinner is offered for F$7.

A hundred meters along the beach from the Horizon is **Travellers Beach Resort** (Box 700, Nandi; tel. 723-322, fax 720-026). The 20 rooms with private bath are F$25/30 single/double with fan, F$5 extra for a/c; dorm is F$10 pp. The restaurant/bar and pool make this a self-contained resort. It's good value and often full, so call ahead.

Also on Wailoaloa Beach, about one km southwest of the three places mentioned above, is **Club Fiji Beach Resort** (Box 9619, Nandi Airport; tel. 702-189, fax 720-350). The 22 attractive thatched bungalows with veranda, private bath, solar hot water, and fridge cost F$55 double (garden) or F$65 (beachfront). One bungalow has been converted into a four-bunk, eight-person dormitory at F$11 pp. Club Fiji's staff does its best to keep the accommodations and grounds spotless. The units have only tea- and coffee-making facilities (no cooking), but the restaurant serves authentic Fijian food and a variety of dishes, which are good when the cook resists the urge to put sugar in everything. The continental breakfast is F$5. Special evening events include the *lovo* on Wednesday, the *meke* and Italian buffet on Saturday, and the beach barbecue on Sunday. Horseback riding (F$10), sailing, water-skiing (F$15), and windsurfing (free) are also available. At low tide the beach resembles a tidal flat, but there's a small clean swimming pool and the location is lovely—the equivalent of the Sheraton at a fifth the price and without the stuffy upmarket at-

mosphere. Club Fiji is highly recommended as your best choice in this price range. Call ahead as they're often full and book well ahead if you're sure it's where you want to stay.

Medium-Priced Airport Hotels

Back at the airport, let's work our way into Nandi again looking at the medium-priced properties. The two-story, colonial-style **Raffles Gateway Hotel** (Box 9891, Nandi Airport; tel. 722-444, fax 720-620) is just across the highway from the terminal, within easy walking distance. Its 93 a/c rooms begin at F$90/100/110 single/double/triple. Happy hour in the Flight Deck Bar is 1800-1900 (half-price drinks)—worth checking out if you're stuck at the airport waiting for a flight.

The **Tokatoka Resort Hotel** (Box 9305, Nandi Airport; tel. 790-222, fax 790-400), right next to the Raffles Gateway, caters to families by offering 70 villas with cooking facilities and video for F$127 double and up. A small supermarket and a large swimming pool with water slide are on the premises.

Four km from the airport is the **Skylodge Hotel** (Box 9222, Nandi Airport; tel. 722-200, fax 720-212), which was constructed in the early 1960s as Nandi Airport was being expanded to take jet aircraft. Airline crews on layovers originally stayed here and business travelers still make up 50% of the clientele. The 53 a/c units begin at F$100 single or double; children under 16 are free, provided the bed configurations aren't changed. It's better to pay F$25 more and get a room with cooking facilities in one of the four-unit clusters well-spaced among the greenery, rather than a smaller room in the main building or near the busy highway. The six family units cost F$500 a week. If you're catching a flight in the middle of the night there's a half-price "day use" rate valid until 2300. Pitch-and-putt golf, half-size tennis facilities, and a swimming pool are on the premises. Airport transfers are free.

Rosie's Serviced Apartments (Box 9268, Nandi Airport; tel. 722-755, fax 722-607) near Ed's Cocktail Bar offers studio apartments accommodating four at F$55, one-bedrooms for up to five at F$88, and two-bedrooms for up to seven at F$99. All eight units have cooking facilities and private balcony. Rosie The Travel

Service at the airport arranges special car/apartment packages here (minimum stay four nights). Rosie's is fine for families and small groups looking for comfortable accommodations near the airport for a night or two, but you wouldn't want to spend your whole holiday in a busy commercial area like this.

The **Dominion International Hotel** (Box 9178, Nandi Airport; tel. 722-255, fax 720-187), an appealing three-story building facing a pool, is halfway between the airport and town. The Dominion was built in 1973, but they've done their best to keep the place up. The 85 a/c rooms with bright bedspreads and curtains are good value at F$89/94/99 single/double/triple. Their 50% "day rate" allows you to keep your room until 1800 only. There's a Rosie The Travel Service desk in this hotel and a barber shop/beauty salon.

The two-story **New Westgate Hotel** (Box 10097, Nandi Airport; tel. 720-044, fax 720-071), next to the Dominion International, is affiliated with the Best Western chain. The 62 rooms begin at F$65 single or double with fan, or F$85/95 single/double with a/c. A swimming pool, restaurant, business center, and "adult" disco are on the premises.

The **Metro Inn** (Box 9043, Nandi Airport; tel. 790-088, fax 720-522), between the New Westgate Hotel and Hamacho Japanese Restaurant, consists of two-story blocks surrounding a swimming pool with a nice grassy area on which to sunbathe. The 60 a/c rooms with fridge are F$50/55 single/double. Cooking facilities are not provided, but there's a restaurant/bar on the premises. It's a good medium-priced choice if you only need a place for the night.

Upmarket Airport Hotels

Three upmarket places off Votualevu Road, a 15-minute walk inland from the airport (take a taxi), cater mostly to people on brief prepaid stopovers in Fiji. The first is **Tanoa Apartments** (Box 9203, Nandi Airport; tel. 721-144, fax 721-193), on a hilltop overlooking the surrounding countryside, two km from the airport. The 23 self-catering apartments begin at F$140 (weekly and monthly rates available).

A few hundred meters inland from Tanoa Apartments is the Malaysian-owned **Fiji Mocambo Hotel** (Box 9195, Nandi Airport; tel. 722-

000, fax 720-324), a sprawling two-story hotel which is probably the best in its category. The 128 a/c rooms with patio or balcony begin at F$155 single or double. Secretarial services can be arranged for businesspeople, and there's a par-27, nine-hole executive golf course on the adjacent slope (green fees F$10, clubs F$8). Their much-touted restaurant is said to be overrated, so ask another guest about it before sitting down to a pricey meal. Alternatively, stick to the salads. Lots of in-house entertainment is laid on, including *mekes* four nights a week. A live band plays in the Vale ni Marau Lounge Thursday, Friday, and Saturday 2100-0100.

Across the street from the Mocambo is the two-story **Tanoa International Hotel** (Box 9203, Nandi Airport; tel. 720-277, fax 720-191), formerly the Nandi Travelodge Hotel and now owned by local businessman Yanktesh Permal Reddy. The 114 a/c rooms are F$160 single or double, F$190 suite, and children under 16 may stay free. They also have a half-price day-use rate, which gives you a room from noon until midnight if you're leaving in the middle of the night (airport transfers free), and the coffee shop here is open 24 hours a day. A swimming pool, fitness center, and floodlit tennis courts are on the premises.

Grande Luxe Beach Hotels

Nandi's two big transnational hotels, The Regent and the Sheraton, are on Ndenarau Beach opposite Yakuilau Island, seven km west of the bridge on the north side of Nandi town and a 15-minute drive from the airport. These are Nandi's only upmarket hotels right on the beach, though the gray sands here can't compare with those of the Mamanutha Islands. The murky waters lapping Sheraton and Regent shores are okay for swimming, and two pontoons are anchored in deeper water, but there'd be no point in snorkeling here. Windsurfing, water-skiing, and sailboating are more practicable activities.

Sidestepping the Waikiki syndrome, neither hotel is taller than the surrounding palms, though the manicured affluence has a dull Hawaiian neighbor-island feel. The Regent opened in 1975 and its vegetation is lush and dense compared to that surrounding the newer Sheraton. In mid-1988 a Japanese company bought control of both The Regent and the Sheraton, and in 1993 a F$15-million championship golf course opened on the site of a former mangrove swamp adjacent to the Sheraton. Two-thirds of the hotel staffs and all of the taxi drivers based here belong to the landowning clan.

Almost all the tourists staying at these places are on a package tour and they pay only a fraction of the rack rates quoted below. Both hotels are rather isolated, and restaurant-hopping possibilities are restricted to the pricey hotel restaurants, so you should take the meal package if you intend to spend most of your time here. Also bring insect repellent unless you yourself want to be on the menu!

The Regent of Fiji (Box 9081, Nandi Airport; tel. 750-000, fax 750-259) is arguably Fiji's finest (and most pretentious) hotel. The 285 spacious a/c rooms in this sprawling series of two-story clusters between the golf course and the beach begin at F$253 single or double. Facilities include an impressive lobby with shops to one side, a thatched pool bar you can swim right up to, and 10 floodlit tennis courts. Yachties anchored offshore are not welcome at this hotel.

The Regent's neighbor, the **Sheraton-Fiji Resort** (Box 9761, Nandi Airport; tel. 750-777, fax 750-818), has 300 a/c rooms which begin at F$295 single or double including a buffet breakfast. This $60-million two-story hotel complex opened in 1987, complete with a 16-shop arcade and an 800-seat ballroom.

There's no bus service to either the Sheraton or The Regent. A taxi to/from Nandi town should be around F$6, though cabs parked in front of the hotels may expect much more. Avis Rent A Car has a desk in each of the hotels. If your travel agent didn't book you into one of these enclaves, don't bother taking the trouble to visit.

FOOD

Several excellent places to eat are opposite the Mobil service station on Queens Road at the north end of Nandi town. For Cantonese and European food try the upstairs dining room at **Poon's Restaurant** (tel. 700-896; closed Sunday), which is recommended for its filling meals at reasonable prices, pleasant atmosphere, and friendly service. **Mama's Pizza Inn** (tel. 700-

221), just up the road from Poon's, serves pizzas big enough for two or three people for F$8-20. **Cardo's Chargrill Restaurant** (tel. 702-704), a few doors away from Mama's, specializes in steaks costing anywhere from F$13-20 depending on size and type. It's popular among the local expat community who drop in around 1800 for happy hour drinks.

The new **Gelato Restaurant**, next to the ANZ Bank on the main street, offers a filling six-course Indian lunch 1000-1400 for F$3.50. Only pure vegetarian food is served here, and you'll like the clean, attractive decor. It's a bit cheaper than the famous Hari Krishna Vegetarian Restaurant in Suva, and the ice cream is also excellent.

The **Curry Restaurant** (closed Sunday) on Clay Street has a wide range of inexpensive Indian dishes (though they close at 1800). **Bombay Lodge** on Queens Road near the Nandi Town Motel looks basic but they serve good curries at the right price.

The **Kababish Restaurant** (tel. 723-430), next to the Shell service station opposite the Dominion International Hotel, features upmarket Indian and Pakistani cuisine. They claim to offer authentic India Indian dishes different from Fiji Indian food, and you pay tourist-level prices to try it.

The **Maharaja Restaurant** (tel. 722-962; closed Sunday), out near the Skylodge Hotel, is popular with flight crews who come for the good Indian curries. It's expensive but good. The **Namaka Inn** (tel. 722-276), near the Melanesian Hotel a bit closer to the airport, serves large portions of quality food.

ENTERTAINMENT

There are three movie houses in Nandi: Westend Twin Cinema on Ashram Road, Karishma Cinema next to the Coconut Inn on Vunavau Street, and Novelty Cinema (formerly Lotus Cinema), upstairs from a mall next to the Nandi Town Council, not far from the post office. All show an unusual mix of Hollywood and Indian films.

Rupeni's Night Club, formerly the Bamboo Palace, next to the Nandi Hotel, has a live band 2100-0100 on Thursday, Friday, and Saturday nights. Locals call it "the zoo."

handicraft seller

DOUG HANKIN

The **Nandi Farmers Club** (tel. 700-415), just up Ashram Road from the Mobil station, is a good local drinking place.

Entertainment possibilities out on the hotel strip toward the airport include **Ed's Cocktail Bar** (tel. 720-373), a little north of the Dominion International Hotel, and **Jessica's Disco** in the New Westgate Hotel (tel. 720-044; Thursday, Friday, and Saturday 2100-0100).

Cultural Shows for Visitors

The **Sheraton** (tel. 750-777) has a free *meke* Tuesday and Saturday at 2100. Thursday at 1900 Fijian firewalking comes with the *meke* and a F$11 fee is charged. The *meke* and *mangiti* (feast) at **The Regent** (tel. 750-000) happen Monday and Friday at 1830 (F$44).

At the **Fiji Mocambo Hotel** (tel. 722-828) there's Fijian firewalking Saturday at 1830 (F$13.50), followed by a *lovo* feast and *meke* (F$27.50). The **Dominion International Hotel** (tel. 722-255) stages a *meke* on Thursday night and Polynesian dancing on Saturday night when the house is full (call to ask).

Shopping

The **Nandi Handicraft Market** opposite the Nandi Hotel just off Queens Road is worth a look. Before going there, have a look around **Jack's Handicrafts** (tel. 700-744) on the main street to get an idea of what is available and how much things cost. Beware the friendly handshake in Nandi, for you may find yourself buying something you neither care for nor desire.

If you have an interest in world literature, you can buy classical works of Indian literature and books on yoga at very reasonable prices at the **Ramakrishna Mission** (Box 716, Nandi; tel. 702-786), across the street from the Farmers Club. It's open weekdays 0900-1300/1500-1700, Saturday 0900-1300.

SERVICES

Money

The **Westpac Bank** opposite the Nandi Handicraft Market and the **ANZ Bank** near Morris Hedstrom change traveler's checks without commission. Both are open Monday to Thursday 0930-1500, Friday 0930-1600.

Tapa International (tel. 722-325) in the concourse at Nandi Airport is the American Express representative. If you buy traveler's checks from them using a personal check and your American Express card, you'll have to actually pick up the checks at the ANZ Bank in Nandi town, so go early.

Post

There are two large post offices, one next to the market in central Nandi, and another between the cargo warehouses directly across the park in front of the arrivals hall at Nandi Airport. Check both if you're expecting general delivery mail; open weekdays 0800-1600.

Health

The public health clinic is up the street from the Nandi Hotel, but you'll save time by visiting Dr. Ram Raju, 36 Clay St. (tel. 701-375).

There are public toilets on the corner of Nandi Market closest to the post office.

TRANSPORTATION

Turtle Airways (Box 717, Nandi; tel. 722-988), next to the golf course at Wailoaloa Beach, runs a seaplane shuttle to the offshore resorts at F$90 one-way, F$180 roundtrip (baggage limited to one 15-kg suitcase plus one carry-on). Combined catamaran/seaplane trips to the resorts are F$116 roundtrip. Scenic flights with Turtle are F$49 pp for 10 minutes, F$100 for 30 minutes (minimum of three persons). See "By Air" under "Getting Around" in the On the Road chapter for information on regular flights to Malololailai Island and other parts of Fiji.

If you're headed for the offshore resorts on Malololailai, Malolo, Castaway, or Mana islands, the 300-passenger catamaran *Island Express* of **South Sea Cruises** (Box 718, Nandi; tel. 722-988, fax 720-346) departs Nandi's Ndenarau Marina twice daily at 0900 and 1330 (F$40 one-way, F$72 roundtrip). Interisland hops are F$20 each. A four-hour, four-island, nonstop roundtrip cruise on this 25-meter boat provides a fair glimpse of the lovely Mamanutha Group for F$35, or pay F$69 for a day-trip to Mana Island, including lunch and nonmotorized activities. Be prepared to wade on and off the boat. Bookings with free twice-daily hotel transfers can be made through Rosie The Travel Service.

Pacific Transport (tel. 701-386) has express buses to Suva via Queens Road daily at 0720, 0750, 0900, 1300, and 1820 (four hours, F$6.80). The 0900 bus is the most convenient, as it begins its run at Nandi (the others all arrive from Lautoka). Four other "stage" buses also operate daily to Suva (five hours). Nandi's bus station adjoining the market is an active place.

You can bargain for fares with the collective taxis cruising the highway from the airport into Nandi. They'll usually take what you'd pay on a bus, but ask first. Collective taxis take five passengers nonstop from Nandi to Suva in three hours for F$10 pp.

For information on car rentals, turn to "Getting Around" in the On the Road chapter.

Tours

Many day cruises and bus tours that operate in the Nandi area are listed in the free tourist magazine *Fiji Magic*. Reservations can be made through hotel reception desks or at Rosie The Travel Service, with several offices around Nandi. Bus transfers to/from your hotel are included in the price, though some trips are arbitrarily canceled when not enough people sign up. The actual vessels used to operate the cruises vary, and the trips described below are only an indication of the sort of thing to expect.

South Sea Cruises (tel. 722-988, fax 720-346) operates day-trips to Plantation Resort on the two-masted schooner *Seaspray* (F$59 including lunch). The sunset cruise on the *Seaspray* is F$32 pp. The same company has day cruises to Castaway Island Resort on the 22-meter ketch *Ariadne*.

Captain Cook Cruises (tel. 701-823) runs day cruises to Plantation Island Resort on Thursday, Friday, and Sunday aboard the 34-meter brigantine *Ra Marama* for F$54 including a picnic lunch. Sunset cruises on the same vessel are every Wednesday afternoon.

Every Tuesday and Friday the 30-meter schooner *Whale's Tale,* built at Suva's Whippy Shipyard in 1985, does a one-day cruise to Malamala Island, or "Daydream Island" as they call it. The cost is F$69 pp, including a beach buffet lunch, snorkeling, sailing, and hotel transfers. Book through **Daydream Cruises** (Box 9777, Nandi Airport; tel. 723-375, fax 790-441) or Rosie The Travel Service. The **Oceanic Schooner Co.** (Box 9626, Nandi Airport; tel. 723-590, fax 720-134) runs more upscale cruises on the *Whale's Tale,* which also include champagne breakfast, gourmet lunch served aboard, open bar, sunset cocktails, and limited participation for F$150 pp.

Mediterranean Villas (tel. 664-011, fax 661-773) offers day-trips (F$50 pp) to "Mediterranean Island," a typical Mamanutha speck of sand also known as Tivoa Island, 10 km west of Lautoka. The clean, clear water (except when it rains), abundant fish, and beautiful coral make this an excellent place to snorkel or scuba dive. Ask about camping possibilities here. Avoid the day cruise to "Aqualand" as the snorkeling is only fair, and there are very few support staff on the island.

Young travelers will enjoy a day cruise to **Beachcomber Island** (tel. 661-500), Fiji's unofficial Club Med for the under 35 set. Operating daily, the F$58 pp fare includes bus transfers from Nandi hotels, the return boat ride via Lautoka, and a buffet lunch. Large families especially should consider Beachcomber because after two full adult fares are paid, the first child under 16 is half price and additional children are quarter price. Infants under two are free.

Rosie The Travel Service (tel. 722-935), at Nandi Airport and opposite the Nandi Handicraft Market in town, offers the cheapest "road tours" because lunch and some admissions aren't included. Their day-trips to Suva (F$59) involve too much time on the bus, so instead go for the Singatoka Valley/Tavuni Hill Fort (F$52) or Emperor Gold Mine (F$39) full-day tours. If you're looking for a good morning tour around Nandi, sign up for the four-hour Vunda Lookout/Viseisei Village/Garden of the Sleeping Giant tour which costs F$29 pp, plus F$10 admission to the garden; other than Viseisei, these places are not accessible on public transport. These trips only operate Monday to Saturday, but on Sunday Rosie offers a half-day drive to the Vunda Lookout and Lautoka for F$36 pp. Also ask about their full-day hiking tours to the Nausori Highlands (daily except Sunday, F$55), the easiest way to see this beautiful area.

The **Tourist Information Center** (Box 251, Nandi; tel. 700-243, fax 702-746), with offices in central Nandi (daily 0800-1700, Sunday until 1500) and opposite the Dominion International Hotel, is actually a commercial travel agency run by Victory Tours. Also known as "Fiji Island Adventurers," they offer a variety of 4WD and trekking excursions into the Nausori Highlands, and book low-budget beach resorts on Mana, Malolo, Waya, Leleuvia, and Kandavu islands. Their prices are often lower than those charged by the more upmarket tour companies mentioned above, but we suggest you approach this agency with caution as you only get what you pay for. **PVV Tours** (tel. 701-310) at the Nandi Town Motel is similar (their specialty is Nananui-Ra bookings and transfers).

Peni's Waterfall Tours (Box 474, Nandi; tel. 701-355), in the Westpoint Arcade off Queens Road in central Nandi, promises three to five nights of "real Fijian life" at Mbukuya, a mountain village in the Nausori Highlands, for F$160 pp. We've received varying reports about these trips, which seem to be a mixture of good and bad. Reader Andy Bray of Hampshire, England, sent us this:

Peni's tour is very much what you make of it. We got three good meals a day, transportation, a wild pig hunt, eel fishing, a waterfall trip, visits to neighboring villages, and various river and jungle treks. If you're content to settle into the typically slow Fijian pace and be satisfied with maybe one good activity a day, you'll enjoy it. If you're used to hot running water, electricity, and constant activity, it's not for you. I found it helped to gently badger the hosts so they wouldn't forget we had activities in mind.

Similar hiking trips offered by Adventure Fiji, a division of Rosie The Travel Service, are more expensive but the quality is superior (see "Organized Tours" under "Getting There" in the On the Road chapter).

SOUTH OF NANDI

Sonaisali Island Resort

Opened in June 1991, this upmarket resort (Box 2544, Nandi; tel. 720-411, fax 720-392), down Nathombi Road from Queens Road, is on a long, low island in Momi Bay, just 300 meters off the coast of Viti Levu. The 32 a/c rooms in the main two-story building are F$190 single or double, and there are six thatched two-bedroom *mbures* at F$260 (no cooking facilities). The meal plan is F$48 pp and guests are expected to dress up for dinner in the restaurant. The resort features a full-service marina, a swimming pool with swim-up bar, tennis courts, a children's program, and water sports, but the snorkeling off their beach is poor. A shuttle boat provides free access to the island 24 hours a day.

Momi Bay

On a hilltop overlooking Momi Bay 28 km from Nandi are two **British six-inch guns,** one named Queen Victoria (1900), the other Edward VIII (1901). Both were recycled from the Boer War and set up here in 1941 by the New Zealand army to defend the southern approach to Nandi Bay. Take a bus along the old highway to Momi, then walk three km west. The Nambilla village bus runs directly there from Nandi four times a day. The site is closed on Sunday.

Seashell Cove

Seashell Cove Resort (Box 9530, Nandi Airport; tel. 720-100, fax 720-294), on Momi Bay, 37 km southwest of Nandi, sells itself as a surfing/diving destination. They have 12 duplex *mbures* with fans and cooking facilities at F$77 single or double, and clean rooms with shared bath in the lodge at F$35 single or double. Larger units are available for families, and baby-sitters are provided. The big 25-bed dormitory above the bar is divided into five-bed compartments for F$13 pp. Otherwise, pitch your own tent for F$7 per tent. Cooking facilities are not provided for campers, lodge, or dormitory guests, although a special "backpacker's dinner" is offered at F$5.50 and the buffet continental breakfast is F$4.50; a full meal plan costs F$17.50. A *meke* (F$16) occurs Wednesday, a Fijian feast (F$15) Friday. Seashell's coffee shop is open until midnight, with a pool table and table tennis. There's a small store at the entrance to the resort. Baggage storage is available free of charge.

The beach here isn't exciting, but the amenities and activities include a swimming pool, day-trips to Natandola Beach (F$28 including lunch), tennis (F$2 an hour), water-skiing, and volleyball (free). At F$20 pp, Seashell has two boats to shuttle surfers out to the reliable left at Namotu Island breakers or long right at Wilkes Passage; the famous Cloudbreak lefthander at Navula Reef is between here and the resort. In 1995 the well-organized scuba diving operation was upgraded with new equipment and a new boat; the cost is now F$77 for two tanks and F$330 for a PADI certification course. Seashell divers experience lots of fish/shark action at Navula Lighthouse, and there's great drift diving at Canyons.

Airport transfers are F$8 pp—call to find out about their free pickup from Nandi town at 1100. A public bus direct to Seashell Cove leaves Nandi bus station Monday through Saturday at 0845 and 1315 (from Seashell to Nandi it goes at 0630, 0830, and 1215), and there's a good onward connection from the resort by public bus to Singatoka weekdays at 0845 and 1315. From Singatoka, buses to Seashell Cove leave at 0645, 0930, 1045, 1145, 1230, 1530, and 1710 (these times could change). From the letters we get, opinions about Seashell are mixed.

Natandola Beach

The long, white, unspoiled sandy beach here has become popular for surfing and camping. You can camp on the beach, but campers and sunbathers should be aware that theft by locals is a daily occurrence and the police make no effort to stop it. It might be better to stay at Sanasana village by the river at the far south end of the beach. There's a store on the hill just before your final descent to Natandola. In 1995 the upmarket **Natandola Beach Club** (tel./fax 721-000) opened with 10 deluxe units and an Olympic-length swimming pool. Additional details were unavailable at press time.

Get there on the bus to Sangasanga village, which leaves Singatoka at 0900, 1300, 1500, and 1745. You have to walk the last three km to the beach. Otherwise get off at the Maro School stop on the main highway and hitch 10 km to the beach. The sugar train passes close to Natandola, bringing day-trippers from the Coral Coast.

THE MAMANUTHA GROUP

The Mamanutha Group is a paradise of eye-popping reefs and sand-fringed isles shared by traditional Fijian villages and jet-set resorts. The white coral beaches and super snorkeling grounds attract visitors aplenty; boats and planes arrive constantly, bringing folks in from nearby Nandi or Lautoka. These islands are in the lee of big Viti Levu, which means you'll get about as much sun here as anywhere in Fiji. Some of the South Pacific's best skin diving, surfing, game fishing, and yachting await you, and many nautical activities are included in the basic rates. Dive spots include the Pinnacles, Sunflower Reef, Wilkes Passage, and Land of the Giants. As yet only a few have noticed the potential for ocean kayaking in this area. Unpack your folding kayak on the beach a short taxi ride from the airport, and you'll be in for some real adventure. The Mamanuthas are fine for a little time in the sun, though it's mostly a tourist scene irrelevant to the rest of Fiji.

Malololailai Island

Malololailai or "Little Malolo," 22 km west of Nandi, is the first of the Mamanutha Group. It's a fair-sized island eight km around (a nice walk). In 1860 an American sailor named Louis Armstrong bought Malololailai from the Fijians for one musket; in 1966 Dick Smith purchased it for many muskets. You can still be alone at the

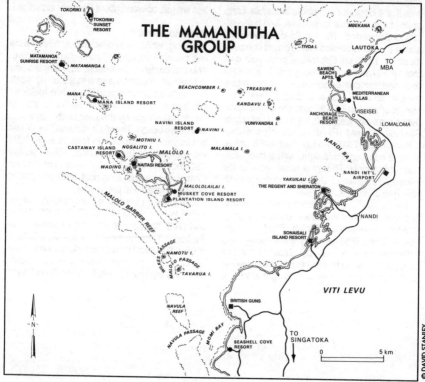

beaches on the far side of the island, but with two growing resorts, projects for a golf course and marina, and lots more time-share condominiums in the pipeline it's in danger of becoming overdeveloped. An airstrip across the island's waist separates its two resorts; inland are rounded, grassy hills.

Plantation Island Resort (Box 9176, Nandi Airport; tel. 722-333, fax 720-163), on the southwest side of Malololailai, is one of the largest of the resorts off Nandi. The 110 rooms (beginning at F$160 single or double) are divided between 40 a/c hotel rooms in a two-story building and 70 individual *mbures*. Add F$49 pp for breakfast and dinner, as no cooking facilities are provided. Snorkeling gear, rowboats, and windsurfing are free, but boat trips cost extra. Coral viewing on Plantation's 30-passenger "yellow submarine" is F$33.

Also on Malololailai Island is **Musket Cove Resort** (Private Mail Bag NAPO352, Nandi Airport; tel. 662-215, fax 662-633), which opened as Dick's Place way back in 1977. The 24 fully-equipped *mbures* and six two-bedroom villas are F$250 single or double, or F$345 for six adults. Unlike Plantation, at Musket Cove the units have small kitchenettes where you can cook, and a well-stocked grocery store selling fresh fruit and vegetables is on the premises. There's also a bar and restaurant by the pool, with a F$71 meal package available. Entertainment is provided at the Thursday night pig roast.

Activities at Musket Cove such as snorkeling, windsurfing, water-skiing, line fishing, and boat trips are free for guests. Scuba diving with Musket Cove Divers costs F$55/88 one/two tanks, or F$390 for the four-day PADI certification course, which begins every Monday. Certified divers can also rent tanks and other gear and organize their own beach diving for much less.

Malololailai is a favorite stopover for cruising yachts. Membership in the **Musket Cove Yacht Club** (F$1 for skippers, F$5 pp for crew) gets you water and clean showers. The marked anchorage is protected and 15 meters deep, with good holding. Fuel and groceries are sold ashore. Several charter yachts are also based here, and **Rainbow Moorings Yacht Charters** (tel./fax 666-710) runs a sailing school at Musket Cove with two-day courses at F$200 pp (maxi-

mum of four persons). Shorter one-day "cruise 'n learn" sailing (F$135) is also available.

In mid-September there's a yacht regatta at Musket Cove, culminating in a 965-km yacht race from Fiji to Port Vila. Among the unique rules: the first yacht to arrive at Vila is disqualified unless it can be proven that blatant cheating occurred. The "race" is timed for the boats' annual departure east, prior to the onset of the hurricane season. It costs F$100 per boat to enter the regatta and for that you get feasts, parties, prizes, groceries, and exemption from harbor fees at Port Vila. If you're on a boat in Fiji at this time, Musket Cove is *the* place to be, and if you're trying to hitch a ride as crew you can't go wrong. There are even stories of people being *paid* to serve as crew for the race! Most evenings at 1700 there's also a "cocktail hour race" with four rum-punch-primed boats racing for prizes.

Malololailai's grass-and-gravel airstrip is the busiest one in the Mamanutha Group and serves as a distribution point for the other resorts. You can fly to Malololailai from Nandi Airport (F$28 one-way, F$44 same day return) eight times a day on Sunflower Airlines and five times a day on Island Air. Otherwise take the twice-daily 25-meter catamaran *Island Express* from Nandi's Ndenarau Marina for F$31 one-way, F$62 roundtrip; call 722-988 for free pickup.

Malolo Island

At low tide you can wade from Malololailai to nearby Malolo Island, largest of the Mamanutha Group, which has two Fijian villages. One of them is known to tourists as "shell village" for what the locals offer for sale. Camping is possible in the villages at F$8 pp; dormitory accommodations are available for F$12 pp, plus another F$10 pp for all meals. The **Tourist Information Center** (tel. 700-243) in central Nandi takes bookings, and a stay here can be combined with a sojourn at the backpackers' places on Mana Island. A boat between Malolo and Mana costs F$15 pp.

The **Naitasi Resort** (Box 10044, Nandi Airport; tel. 720-178, fax 720-197), at Malolo's western tip, offers 28 one-bedroom bungalows with fan at F$275 for up to three adults, and nine two-bedroom family villas at F$385 for up to six. The units are privately owned by 10 individuals, and each is decorated differently. The Island Store sells basic groceries that allow you to make use of the cooking facilities provided, but you should also bring a few things with you. The Terrace Restaurant does its best to serve local produce, such as five types of edible seaweeds and six different salads. The *lovo* and *meke* is on Saturday night.

Naitasi Resort has a freshwater swimming pool, and nonmotorized water sports are free; scuba diving with Mamanutha Divers costs extra. Instructors here will teach you how to windsurf, and this is the only resort offering ocean kayaking and horseback riding on a regular basis. Self-guided trail brochures are available to those who would like to discover Malolo's unique plant- and birdlife, so it's a good choice for hikers. Get there on the twice-daily *Island Express* tourist boat from the Ndenarau Marina, Nandi, for F$36 one-way, F$62 roundtrip. The Turtle Airways seaplane from Nandi is F$90 one-way, and there are also speedboats from Malololailai. No daytrippers are allowed at the resort. Due to pressure from the resort owners, campers wishing to stay at one of the villages on Malolo may have difficulty using the *Island Express,* in which case it might be better to arrive via Malololailai (call the numbers provided above to check).

Tavarua Island

Tavarua Island Resort (Box 1419, Nandi; tel. 723-513, fax 720-395), just south of Malololailai, operates as a surfing base camp. Guests are accommodated in 12 beach *mbures* at F$210/360 single/double a day, including meals, boat transfers from the landing, and most activities (three-night minimum stay). A small reduction is available from December to February, and children under 16 pay F$78 each, so long as they sleep in the same *mbure* as their parents and don't surf. Couples get preference. There are both lefts and rights in Malolo Passage at Tavarua, although the emphasis is usually on the lefts. When the swell is high enough you'll have some of the best surfing anywhere. On the off days you can get in some deep-sea fishing, windsurfing, snorkeling, or scuba diving (extra charge).

Bookings must be made through **Tavarua Tours** (Box 60159, Santa Barbara, CA 93160, U.S.A.; tel. 805/686-4551, fax 805/683-6696). They're usually sold out, especially in June, July, and August. You can always try calling upon arrival, and they'll probably take you if vacancies have materialized. If not, or if you simply can't afford those prices, stay at Seashell Cove Resort south of Nandi and charter one of their boats out to Wilkes Passage or nearby Namotu Island. Registered guests are transferred out to Tavarua from Seashell Cove.

Castaway Island

Castaway Island Resort (Private Mail Bag, Nandi Airport; tel. 661-233, fax 665-753), on 174-hectare Nggalito Island just west of Malolo and 15 km from Nandi, was erected in 1966 as Fiji's first outer-island resort. The 66 thatched *mbures* sleep four—F$310 and up including breakfast. No cooking facilities. Among the free water sports are sailing, windsurfing, canoeing, tennis, and snorkeling, but scuba diving and game fishing are extra. There's the daily catamaran from Nandi's Ndenarau Marina (F$36 one-way, F$60 roundtrip), and Turtle Airways has three seaplane flights a day from Nandi for F$90. Many Australian holidaymakers return to Castaway year after year; families with small children are welcome.

Mana Island

Mana Island, 32 km west of Lautoka, is best known for the **Mana Island Resort** (Box 610, Lautoka; tel. 661-455, fax 661-562). This is by far the biggest of the resorts off Nandi, with 32 hotel rooms and 128 tin-roofed bungalows clustered between the island's grassy rounded hilltops, white sandy beaches, and crystal-clear waters. Standard bungalows begin at F$260 single or double, F$300 triple, while deluxe beachfront bungalows and hotel rooms are around F$100 more, breakfast included. Cooking facilities are not provided, so you'll have to patronize either the Mamanutha Restaurant, the Bulamakau Steak House, or the North Beach Barbecue Buffet (breakfast and dinner plan F$62 pp). Mana Island Resort should be your choice if you like the excitement of large crowds and a wide range of organized activities. Live entertainment is presented nightly except Sunday, and three nights a week there's a Fijian or Polynesian floor show.

The room rates include all nonmotorized water sports, although the 45-minute semisubmersible rides (F$29 pp), water-skiing, paraflying, water scooters, game fishing, and scuba diving are all extra. The **Aqua-Trek** base here is one of only two five-star PADI scuba diving centers in Fiji (the other is Suva's Scubahire), and it offers a great variety of dive courses, beginning with a four-day open-water certification course (F$572). Boat dives cost F$66 for one tank or F$363 for a six-dive package. The Mana Main Reef is famous for its drop-offs with visibility never less than 25 meters, and you'll see turtles, fish of all descriptions, and the occasional crayfish. Divemaster Apisi Bati specializes in underwater shark feeding at a dive site called "Supermarket," a 30-minute boat ride away.

The *Island Express* catamaran from Ndenarau Marina, Nandi, calls at Mana Island Resort twice a day (F$70 roundtrip). In 1995 an airstrip opened on Mana, and Sunflower Airlines now has six flights a day from Nandi.

There are lots of lovely beaches all around Mana, most of them empty because the tourists seldom stray far from their resort. This works to your advantage because on the other side of the island is a place known as **Mana Island Backpackers** where you can sleep in an eight-bed dormitory for F$17 pp, plus another F$11 pp for three buffet-style meals; cooking for yourself is also possible. Activities include deep-sea fishing trips (F$33 an hour), four-island boat excursions (F$25), and a *lovo* picnic on a small island (F$25—free for guests staying a week). Those staying two weeks get an extra night free and several complimentary trips. There's a great view from the highest point on Mana, a 15-minute hike away. Bookings can be made by calling 667-520 on Mana, at which time transfers from Nandi on the *Tui Mana* (one hour, F$50 roundtrip) will be arranged.

In the Fijian village a couple of hundred meters from Backpackers is **Ratu Kini Boko's Hostel** (Box 5818, Lautoka; tel. 667-520), also known as "Mama's Place." Here you can rent a pleasant thatched *mbure* at F$77 double, or stay in a dormitory at F$28 pp, both including three filling meals. It's cleaner and nicer than Backpackers for about the same price, and Ratu Kini and his wife Veronica prepare very good

meals, which you take with the family. Sometimes it gets a little crowded.

Ratu Kini is an interesting character. He's the chief of 20 islands in the Mamanutha Group, but he made the mistake of leasing part of Mana Island to an Australian company which sublet their property to the Japanese investors who now run Mana Island Resort, and of course the resort people would like nothing better than to oust the backpackers and Fijian villagers from the island. Ratu Kini claims his main purpose in running the hostel is "to show the world the way Fijians live and to teach visitors about Fijian customs and culture."

For information on the current situation, call the hostel or their Lautoka office (tel. 663-724), or ask at **Margaret Travel Service** (Box 9831, Nandi Airport; tel. 721-988, fax 721-992). In light of the above, it's obvious that people staying at Backpackers or Ratu Kini's aren't welcome at Mana Island Resort, and these problems even extend to the use of the *Island Express* to get to Mana. (The resort management warns their upscale clientele not to visit the Fijian village after dark because "hippies" are staying there!) It's all a bit of an adventure, and the chance to enjoy Mana's stunning beauty at a fraction of the price tourists at the Japanese resort are paying makes it worth the intrigue.

Matamanoa Island
Matamanoa Sunrise Resort (Box 9729, Nandi Airport; tel. 660-511, fax 720-679), to the northwest of Mana Island, has four a/c rooms for F$170 single or double, or F$297 for one of the 20 fan-cooled *mbures* sleeping four. Meals are F$99 extra for all three (no cooking facilities). Matamanoa's rugged volcanic core gives it a certain character, and as if the tiny island's fine white beach and blue lagoon weren't enough, there's also a swimming pool and lighted tennis court. It's more expensive to reach because the launch transfers from Mana to Matamanoa (F$30 pp each way) are in addition to the catamaran from Nandi.

Tokoriki Island
Tokoriki Sunset Resort (Box 9729, Nandi Airport; tel. 661-999, fax 665-295), 27 km due west of Lautoka, is the farthest offshore resort from Nandi. There are 20 fan-cooled *mbures* at

F$250 for four adults and two children (no cooking facilities). The resort faces west on a kilometer-long beach and water sports such as reef fishing, windsurfing, and Hobie Cats are free (water-skiing, scuba diving, and sport fishing available at additional charge). At the center of the island is a 94-meter-high hill offering good views of the Yasawa and Mamanutha groups. Tokoriki is under the same management as Matamanoa, and as on Matamanoa, you must take the catamaran to Mana, then a launch to Tokoriki (F$33 pp each way). The regular launch to Matamanoa and Tokoriki leaves Mana daily at 1100.

Vomo Island

Standing alone midway between Lautoka and Waya Island (see the "Yasawa Islands" map), 91-hectare Vomo has since 1993 been the site of the **Sheraton Vomo Island Resort** (Box 9761, Nandi Airport; tel. 667-955, fax 667-997). The 30 a/c villas run F$700 single or double, F$987 triple, breakfast included. Other meals are additional (no cooking facilities). Add F$585 per couple for return helicopter transfers from Nandi Airport and you've got the most expensive resort in the Mamanutha Group.

Navini Island

Navini Island Resort (Box 9445, Nandi Airport; tel. 662-188, fax 665-566) is the smallest of Mamanutha resorts, a tiny coral isle with only seven thatched *mbures*. Rates vary from F$255 double for a fan-cooled beachfront unit to F$375 for the honeymoon *mbure* with spa and enclosed courtyard. Discounts are available for stays over a week. The meal package is F$57 pp a day (no cooking facilities). Everyone gets to know one another by eating at a long table (private dining is also possible). Complimentary morning boat trips are offered, as are snorkeling gear, Windsurfers, and kayaks. Car/boat transfers from Nandi via Vunda Point (one hour, F$96 roundtrip for adults, F$48 for children under 13) are arranged anytime upon request.

Beachcomber Island

Beachcomber Island (Box 364, Lautoka; tel. 661-500, fax 664-496), 18 km west of Lautoka, is Club Med at a fraction of the price. The resort caters mostly to young Australians, and it's a good place to meet travelers of the opposite sex. You'll like the informal atmosphere and late-night parties; there's a sand-floor bar, dancing, and floor shows four nights a week. The island is so small you can stroll around it in 10 minutes, but there's a white sandy beach and buildings nestled among coconut trees and tropical vegetation. A beautiful coral reef extends far out on all sides and scuba diving is available with Subsurface Fiji (F$65 for one tank). A full range of sporting activities is available at an additional charge (parasailing F$45, windsurfing F$20, water-skiing F$26, Jet Skis F$32 for 15 minutes).

Accommodations include all meals served buffet style. Most people opt for the big, open mixed dormitory where the 40 double-decker bunks cost F$69 each a night, but you can also get one of 18 thatched *mbures* with ceiling fan and private facilities for F$182/242/302 single/double/triple. A good compromise for the budget-conscious traveler is one of the 14 lodge rooms with shared bath at F$146/189 single/double (fridge and fan provided). Former water problems have been solved by laying pipes from the mainland and installing solar water heating.

Of course, there's also the F$58 roundtrip boat ride from Lautoka to consider, but that includes lunch on arrival day. You can make a day-trip to Beachcomber for the same price if you only want a few hours in the sun. There's a free shuttle bus from all Lautoka/Nandi hotels to the wharf; the connecting boat leaves daily at 1000. Beachcomber has been doing it right since the 1960s, and the biggest drawback is its very popularity, which makes it crowded and busy. Reserve well ahead at their Lautoka or Nandi Airport offices, or at any travel agency.

Treasure Island Resort

Beachcomber's neighbor, **Treasure Island** (Box 2210, Lautoka; tel. 661-599, fax 663-577), caters to couples and families less interested in an intense singles' social scene. Instead of helping yourself at a buffet and eating at a long communal picnic table, you'll eat regular meals in Treasure's restaurant (meal plan F$60 pp daily). Cooking facilities are not provided. The 68 units, each with three single beds (F$240 single or double), are contained in 34 functional duplex bungalows packed into the greenery behind the island's white sands. Some nautical activities such as windsurfing, sailing, canoes, and spy board, which cost extra on Beachcomber, are free on Treasure Island. Guests arrive on the Beachcomber Island shuttle boat from Lauto-

ka (which leaves daily at 1000 and 1400, F$58 roundtrip), but unlike Beachcomber, Treasure doesn't get any day-trippers. There's no wharf here, so be prepared to wade ashore. Formerly owned by the same company, Beachcomber and Treasure have been under separate managements since 1991.

THE CORAL COAST

Scuba Diving
Sea Sports Ltd. (Box 688, Singatoka; tel. 500-225, fax 520-239) offers scuba diving from their dive shops at The Fijian, Hideaway, and Warwick hotels. Their free red-and-blue minibus picks up clients at all the other Coral Coast resorts just after 0700 (just after 0900 on Sunday). The charge is F$52 for one tank, F$90 for two tanks (both on the same morning), plus tax. Sea Sports runs NAUI open-water certification courses (F$422), and night dives are possible. Most dive sites are within 15 minutes of the resort jetties, so you don't waste much time commuting.

Getting Around
An easy way to get between the Coral Coast resorts and Nandi/Suva is on the a/c **Fiji Express** shuttle bus run by United Touring Company (tel. 722-811). The bus leaves the Travelodge and Courtesy Inn hotels in Suva (F$25) at 0800 and calls at Pacific Harbor Hotel (F$22), Warwick Hotel (F$17), Naviti Resort, Hideaway, Tambua Sands, Reef Resort (F$16), The Fijian Hotel (F$14), Sheraton Resort (F$5), and The Regent, arriving at Nandi Airport at 1230 (quoted fares are to the airport). It leaves Nandi Airport at 1330 and returns along the same route, reaching Suva at 1800. Bookings can be made at the UTC office in the airport arrival concourse or at hotel tour desks.

Also ask about the a/c **Queen's Deluxe Coach,** which runs in the opposite direction, leaving The Fijian Hotel for Suva at 0910, the Warwick Hotel and Naviti Resort at 1030, and the Pacific Harbor Hotel at 1115. The return trip departs the Suva Travelodge around 1600.

Many less expensive non-a/c buses pass on the highway, but make sure you're waiting somewhere they'll stop. Pacific Transport's

"stage" or "highway" buses between Lautoka/Nandi and Suva will stop at any of the Coral Coast resorts, but the express buses call only at Singatoka, Pacific Harbor, and Navua. If you're on an express, get a ticket to Singatoka and look for a local bus or taxi from there.

Yanutha Island
Shangri-La's Fijian Resort Hotel, commonly referred to as The Fijian (Private Mail Bag NAPO353, Nandi Airport; tel. 520-155, fax 500-402), occupies all 40 hectares of Yanutha Island, not to be confused with another Yanutha Island just west of Mbengga. This Yanutha Island is connected to the main island by a causeway 10 km west of Singatoka and 61 km southeast of Nandi Airport. Opened in 1967, the 436-room complex of three-story Hawaiian-style buildings was Fiji's first large resort and is still Fiji's biggest hotel, catering to a predominantly Japanese clientele. In 1995 the entire complex was renovated by its Malaysian owners. The a/c rooms begin at F$275 single or double, F$320 triple, or F$703 for a deluxe beach *mbure.* There's no charge for two children 15 or under sharing their parents' room. The Fijian offers a nine-hole golf course (par 31), five tennis courts, four restaurants and five bars, two swimming pools, and a white sandy beach. Weekly events include a *meke* on Tuesday and Friday (and sometimes Thursday), and firewalking on Monday and Friday nights. Scuba diving is arranged by Sea Sports Limited. Avis Rent A Car has a desk in The Fijian.

A local attraction is the Fijian Princess, a restored narrow-gauge railway originally built to haul sugarcane but that now runs 16-km daytrips to Natandola Beach daily at 1000. The train station is on the highway opposite the access road to The Fijian Hotel, and the ride costs

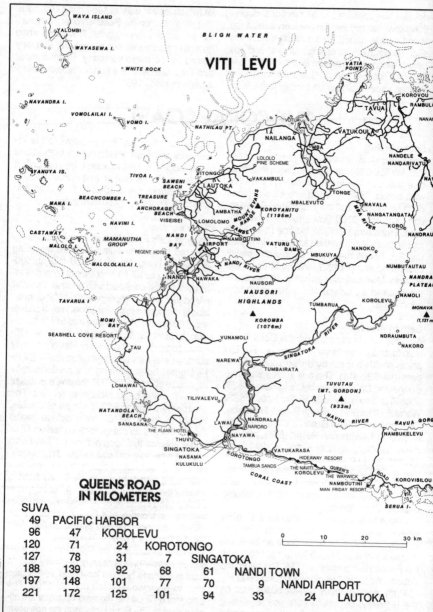

WAYA ISLAND
YALOMBI
WAYASEWA I.
BLIGH WATER
WHITE ROCK
VATIA POINT
VITI LEVU
KOROVOU
RAMBUL
NAVANDRA I.
VOMOLAILAI I.
VOMO I.
NATHILAU PT.
VOTU
TAVUA
NANAN
VATUKOULA
NAILANGA
CMBA
NANDELE
NANDARIVATU
LOLOLO
PINE SCHEME
TIVOA I.
SAWENI
BEACH
VITONGO
VAKAMBULI
NAVALA
YANUYA IS.
LAUTOKA
TONGE
MBALEVUTO
NANGATANGATA
BEACHCOMBER I.
TREASURE
I.
ANCHORAGE
BEACH
AMBATHA
LOMOLOMO
MOUNT EVANS
RANGE
KOROYANITU
(1195m)
SAMBETO R.
KORO
NANDRAU
MANA I.
NAVINI I.
VISEISEI
NNAMBOUTINI
VATURU
DAM
CASTAWAY
I.
MAMANUTHA
GROUP
NANDI
BAY
AIRPORT
MBUKUYA
NANOKO
NUMBUTAUTAU
MALOLO
REGENT HOTEL
MALOLOLAILAI I.
NANDI
NAWAKA
NANDI RIVER
NAUSORI
NANDRA
PLATEA
NAMOLI
KOROLEVU
TAVARUA I.
MOMI
BAY
NAUSORI
HIGHLANDS
TUMBARUA
MONAVA
(1,131 m.
SEASHELL COVE RESORT
KOROMBA
(1076m)
NDRAUMBUTA
NAKORO
TAU
VUNAMOLI
SINGATOKA
RIVER
NAREWA
TUMBAIRATA
NAVUA RIVER
LOMAWAI
TILIVALEVU
TUVUTAU
(MT. GORDON)
(933m)
NAVUA GORG
NATANDOLA
BEACH
SANASANA
THE FIJIAN HOTEL
THUVU
LAWAI
NANDRALA
NARORO
NAMBUKELEVU
NANAYAWA
SINGATOKA
NASAMA
KULUKULU
KOROTONGO
VATUKARASA
HIDEAWAY RESORT
TAMBUA SANDS
THE NAVITI
KOROLEVU
QUEEN'S
THE WARWICK
CORAL COAST
NAMBOUTINI
MAN FRIDAY RESORT
ROAD
KOROVISILOU
SERUA I.

QUEENS ROAD
IN KILOMETERS

SUVA							
49	PACIFIC HARBOR						
96	47	KOROLEVU					
120	71	24	KOROTONGO				
127	78	31	7	SINGATOKA			
188	139	92	68	61	NANDI TOWN		
197	148	101	77	70	9	NANDI AIRPORT	
221	172	125	101	94	33	24	LAUTOKA

0   10   20   30 km

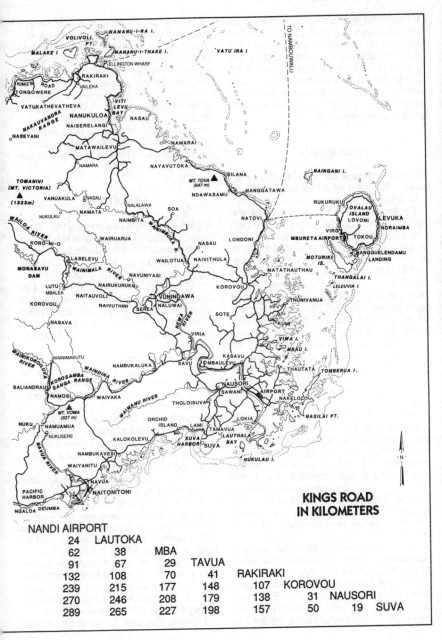

KINGS ROAD
IN KILOMETERS

NANDI AIRPORT							
24	LAUTOKA						
62	38	MBA					
91	67	29	TAVUA				
132	108	70	41	RAKIRAKI			
239	215	177	148	107	KOROVOU		
270	246	208	179	138	31	NAUSORI	
289	265	227	198	157	50	19	SUVA

F$55 pp including a barbecue lunch if you book here. Otherwise pay F$59 pp including bus transfers from any Coral Coast hotel or F$69 from Nandi-area hotels. For information call the **Coral Coast Railway Co.** (Box 571, Singatoka; tel. 520-599). Across the road from the train station is the **Ka Levu Center,** a mock-Fijian village dispensing instant Fijian culture to tourists for F$10 pp admission.

KULUKULU

Fiji's best **surfing beach** is at Kulukulu, five km south of Singatoka, where the Singatoka River breaks through Viti Levu's fringing reef. The surf is primarily a rivermouth point break with numerous beachbreaks down the beach. It's one of the only places for beachbreak surfing on Viti Levu, and unlike most other surfing locales around Fiji, no boat is required here. The **windsurfing** in this area is fantastic, as you can either sail "flat water" across the rivermouth or do "wave jumping" in the sea (all-sand bottom and big rollers with high wind). The surfing is good all the time, but if you want to combine it with windsurfing, it's best to surf in the morning and windsurf in afternoon when the wind comes up. Be prepared, however, as these waters are treacherous for novices. You can also bodysurf here. There's a nice place nearby where you can swim in the river and avoid the currents in the sea.

Incredible 20-meter-high **sand dunes** separate the cane fields from the two-km-long beach, and giant sea turtles come ashore here now and then to lay their eggs. Winds sometimes uncover human bones from old burials, and potsherds lie scattered along the seashore—these fragments have been carbon dated at up to 3,000 years old. It's a fascinating, evocative place, now protected as a national park. Please show some sensitivity in the way you approach this unique environment.

American surfer Marcus Oliver has opened a base camp behind the dunes called **Club Masa Sports Resort** (Box 710, Singatoka; no telephone), also known as "Sand Dunes Lodge." So far there's a 10-bed dormitory (F$11 pp), double rooms (F$15 pp), and fenced camping area (F$6). There's no electricity, but the lay-

out is attractive. No cooking facilities are provided, but the three-meal plan is worth taking at F$5.50 (otherwise you go hungry). Have a beer on their pleasant open porch. Boogie boards are for hire at F$5 a day. It's a nice place to hang out—friendly people.

There are buses from Singatoka to Kulukulu village seven times a day on Wednesday and Saturday, five times on other weekdays, but none on Sunday and holidays. Taxi fare to Club Masa should be around F$4, and later you may only have to pay 50 cents for a seat in an empty taxi returning to Singatoka.

SINGATOKA

Singatoka is the main center for the Coral Coast tourist district and the headquarters of Nandronga/Navosa Province. The town's setting is made picturesque by the long single-lane highway bridge crossing the Singatoka River here, and it's pleasant to stroll around. You'll find the ubiquitous duty-free shops and a colorful local market (best on Wednesday and Saturday) with a large handicraft section. **Jack's Handicrafts** (tel. 500-810) on the main street is also worth a look.

Strangely, the traditional handmade **Fijian pottery** for which Singatoka is famous is not available here. Find it by asking in Nayawa (where the clay originates), Yavulo, and Nasama villages near Singatoka. Better yet, take the two-hour **Bounty Cruise** (tel. 500-669) up the river from Singatoka to Nakambuta and Lawai villages, where the pottery is displayed for sale. Cruises leave daily except Sunday at 1000, 1200, and 1430 (F$16).

Upriver from Singatoka is a wide valley known as Fiji's "salad bowl" for its rich market gardens by Fiji's second-largest river. Vegetables are grown in farms on the west side of the valley, while the lands on the east bank are planted with sugarcane. Small trucks use the good dirt road up the west side of the river to take the produce to market, while a network of narrow-gauge railways collects the cane from the east side. You can drive right up the valley in a normal car. The locals believe that Dakuwangga, shark god of the Fijians, dwells in the river.

Also near Singatoka, five km up the left (east)

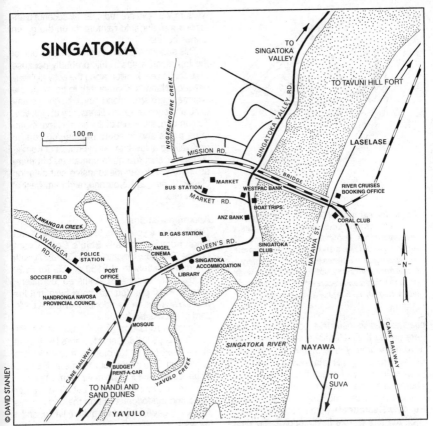

SINGATOKA

0   100 m

NGGERENGGERE CREEK

TO SINGATOKA VALLEY

TO TAVUNI HILL FORT

LASELASE

MISSION RD.

SINGATOKA VALLEY RD.

BRIDGE

RIVER CRUISES BOOKING OFFICE

Market

Bus Station

Market Rd.

Westpac Bank

Boat Trips

ANZ Bank

Coral Club

LAWANGGA CREEK

LAWANGGA RD.

Police Station

B.P. Gas Station

Angel Cinema

Queen's Rd.

Singatoka Club

Nayawa St.

Soccer Field

Post Office

Singatoka Accommodation

Library

Nandronga Navosa Provincial Council

Mosque

CANE RAILWAY

SINGATOKA RIVER

NAYAWA

- N -

Budget Rent-A-Car

Yavulo Creek

TO NANDI AND SAND DUNES

TO SUVA

CANE RAILWAY

YAVULO

© DAVID STANLEY

bank of the river from the one-way bridge, is the **Tavuni Hill Fort** on a bluff at Naroro village. The fort was established by the 19th-century Tongan chief Maile Latemai and destroyed by native troops under British control in 1876. An interpretive center and walkways have been established, and F$6 admission is collected. There's a good view of the river and surrounding countryside from here. Those without transport could take a taxi from Singatoka to the reception area (about F$5), then walk back to town in an hour or so.

Practicalities
The **Singatoka Club** (Box 38, Singatoka; tel. 500-026) has four pleasant fan-cooled rooms with private bath at F$22/33 single/double. It's a good untouristy place to stay, and the bar here is perfect for a beer or a game of pool (three tables). The bar is open Monday to Saturday 1000-2200. In contrast to drinks, meals at the Club are expensive.

The basic **Singatoka Accommodations** (Box 35, Singatoka; tel. 500-833), opposite the BP service station on Queens Road, has nine rooms at F$20/25 single/double, and a six-bed dorm at F$10 pp. Bargaining should quickly lower these prices, and camping on the back lawn is possible. Check the lock on your door. Singatoka Accommodations should be considered only a place to crash. The **Oriental Pacific Restaurant** (tel. 520-275) in front of the

LOUISE FOOTE

The original explorers of Oceania, the Polynesians, left distinctive lapita pottery, decorated in horizontal bands, scattered across the Pacific. Around 500 B.C. the art was lost and no more pottery was made in Polynesia. Melanesian pottery stems from a different tradition. This antique water pot was shaped and decorated by hand, as are those made in the Singatoka Valley today.

bus station dispenses fast food to bus passengers during their 15-minute stop here. If you have more time, you're better off seeking out **Eddie Hin Ching's Restaurant** (tel. 500-376), upstairs in a row of shops behind the market. There's also the darker and more expensive **Rattan Restaurant** (tel. 500-818) and unmarked **Reddy's Restaurant,** both by the market.

Of the four **banks** in Singatoka, the Westpac is the most convenient since they have a separate overseas section upstairs and you don't have to join the long queue of local customers.

Pacific Transport (tel. 500-088) express buses leave Singatoka for Suva at 0845, 0910, 1025, 1425, and 1945 (3.5 hours, F$4.70), for Nandi Airport at 0935, 1220, 1500, 1800, and 2020 (1.5 hours, F$2.75).

KOROTONGO

The south side of Viti Levu along the Queens Road east of Singatoka is known as the Coral Coast. East of Korotongo the sugar fields of western Viti Levu are replaced by coconut plantations merging into rainforests on the green slopes behind.

This shoreline is heavily promoted as one of the top resort areas in Fiji, probably because of its convenient location along the busy highway between Nandi and Suva, but to be frank, the beaches here are second rate, with good swimming and snorkeling conditions only at high tide. To compensate, most of the hotels have swimming pools and in some places you can go reefwalking at low tide. All the hotels at Korolevu farther east are quite upmarket, but there are nearly a dozen inexpensive self-catering places to stay at Korotongo, eight km east of Singatoka.

Accommodations
The first place you come to as you enter Korotongo from Singatoka is **Shiu's Coral Coast Lodge** (Box 389, Singatoka; tel. 500-237), with five rooms with bath at F$30 double (or F$20 double after bargaining). A shared "dormitory" room is F$10 pp. You can cook here, but the whole place has an abandoned feel to it. A backyard overlooks the bay.

Korotongo Lodge (Box 37, Singatoka; tel. 500-755, fax 520-182), next to Tom's Restaurant at the west end of Korotongo, a few minutes away from Shiu's, has four rooms at F$22/25 single/double or F$11 pp in the dorm. You can use the communal kitchen, but it's all rather basic and the lodge is not on the beach. This place has been around for quite a while, and it shows.

The **Crow's Nest Motor Lodge** (Box 270, Singatoka; tel. 500-513, fax 520-354), 500 meters east of Korotongo Lodge, offers 18 split-level duplex bungalows with cooking facilities at F$82/110 single/double. Reduced rates of F$55 single or double are possible if you just stroll in without reservations at a time when things are slow. The **Crow's Nest Dormitory** at the bottom of the hill is F$11 pp for the 10 beds. The nautical touches in the excellent moderately priced restaurant behind the swimming pool spill over into the rooms, and good views over the lagoon are obtained from the Crow's Nest's elevated perch.

The **Vakaviti Motel** (Box 5, Singatoka; tel. 500-526, fax 520-319), next to the Crow's Nest, has six self-catering units at F$50/55 single/double and a six-bed dorm at F$13 pp. A five-bed family cabin is F$66 double, plus F$6 per additional person. They have a swimming pool, and the manager's half dozen dogs greet newcomers enthusiastically. It's often full.

The **Casablanca Hotel** (Box 86, Singatoka; tel. 520-600) next door is a two-story building on a hillside on the inland side of Queens Road. Its eight a/c rooms with cooking facilities and arched balconies begin at F$80 single or double. This place has gone through several changes of ownership in recent years as it tries to find its market niche.

A new upmarket place to stay is **Bedarra House** (Box 1213, Singatoka; tel. 500-476, fax 520-116), with only four rooms at F$125 double including breakfast and dinner. This spacious two-story hotel prides itself on the personalized service, and it's a mystery how they can afford to keep such a large staff for only a dozen guests maximum. There isn't even a reception area: you check in at the bar. A swimming pool, video room, and upstairs lounge round out the facilities of this unusual hotel.

Just a few hundred meters east near the Reef Resort is **Waratah Lodge** (Box 86, Singatoka; tel. 500-278, fax 520-219), with five very nice self-catering units—good value at F$33/44 single/double. The swimming pool and charming management add to the allure. Recommended.

The **Reef Resort** (Box 173, Singatoka; tel. 500-044, fax 520-074), about a kilometer east of the Crow's Nest, is a three-story building facing right onto a white sandy beach. The 72 a/c rooms are F$140 for up to three persons, family suites F$160; most nonmotorized recreational activities are free. The hotel tennis courts, nine-hole par-31 golf course, and horses are available to both guests and nonguests at reasonable rates. Even if you're not staying there, check out the firewalking (F$12) on Friday and the Fijian dancing (F$3) on Wednesday and Saturday nights. Meals in the hotel restaurant are prepared to please the mostly Australian clientele, and the all-you-can-eat buffet (F$16) is excellent value. Thrifty Car Rental and Sea Sports Ltd. have desks here. For a large hotel it's fairly pleasant.

Sandy Point Beach Cottages (Box 23, Singatoka; tel. 500-125, fax 520-147) shares the same beach with the adjacent Reef Resort. Three fan-cooled double units with full cooking facilities are offered at F$55 single, F$72 double or triple, and a five-bed cottage is F$127. Set in spacious grounds right by the sea, Sandy Point has its own freshwater swimming pool. It's a good choice for families or small groups, but it's often full so you must reserve well ahead.

A bit east again is **Tumbakula Beach Resort** (Box 2, Singatoka; tel. 500-097, fax 340-236). The 27 pleasant A-frame bungalows with fan, cooking facilities, and private bath, each capable of sleeping three or more, are F$48 in the garden or F$58 facing the beach. Their "Beach Club" consists of eight rooms, each with three or four beds at F$11 a bed. A communal kitchen is available, plus a swimming pool, game room, nightly videos, minimarket, and Tuesday *lovo* (F$15). The snorkeling here is good, there's surfing and scuba diving nearby, and bus excursions are available. What more do you want? Basically, Tumbakula is a quiet, do-your-own-thing kind of place for people who don't need lots of organized activities. Seated on your terrace watching the sky turn orange and purple behind the black silhouettes of the palms along the beach, a bucket of cold Fiji Bitter stubbies close at hand, you'd swear this was paradise! It's one of the most popular backpacker resorts in Fiji and well worth a couple of nights.

All of the hotels mentioned above to the west of the Reef Resort are on the inland side of the highway; in contrast, the Reef, Sandy Beach, and Tumbakula are right on the beach.

Food

Opposite the Reef Resort is a small grocery store and two paltry restaurants, one with pizza and the other Chinese. These cater mostly to hungry tourists staying at the Reef who don't have access to cooking facilities. Unless all you want is to fill your stomach, it's better to walk 800 meters west to the more atmospheric **Crow's Nest Restaurant** (tel. 500-670).

Tom's Restaurant (Tom Jacksam, tel. 520-238) at the west entrance to Korotongo specializes in Chinese dishes, but there are four vegetarian items on the menu and six grilled choices such as steaks. They're open Monday to Saturday 1200-1500/1800-2200, Sunday 1800-2200, and to date all reviews have been good.

VATUKARASA

This small village between Korotongo and Korolevu is notable for its quaint appearance and the **Baravi Handicraft Boutique** (tel. 520-364), which carries a wide selection of Fijian handicrafts at fixed prices. They buy directly from the craftspeople themselves and add only a 20% markup, plus tax. It's a good place to get an idea of how much things should cost and is worth an outing by local bus if you're staying at one of the Coral Coast resorts.

KOROLEVU

Accommodations

At Korolevu, east of Korotongo, the accommodations cater to a more upscale crowd, and cooking facilities are not provided for guests. These places are mostly intended for people on package holidays who intend to spend most of their time unwinding on the beach. Distances between the resorts are great, so for sightseeing you'll be dependent on your hotel's tour desk.

The **Tambua Sands Beach Resort** (Box 77, Singatoka; tel. 500-399, fax 520-265), in an attractive location facing the sea about 10 km east of the Reef Resort, has 31 beach bungalows at F$81/104 single/double (plus F$35 pp for breakfast and dinner). Ask for a unit near the beach—they all cost the same. There's a very nice swimming pool, live music most evenings, and a *meke* on Tuesday and Friday nights. Thrifty Car Rental has a desk in this hotel. It's recommended as a good medium-priced choice for a couple of nights of relaxation.

The 56-room **Hideaway Resort** (Box 233, Singatoka; tel. 500-177, fax 520-025) at Korolevu, three km east of Tambua Sands and 20 km east of Singatoka, tries to cater to both ends of the market. Set on a palm-fringed beach before a verdant valley, the smaller fan-cooled *mbures* are F$110 single or double; larger units suitable for up to six people go for F$154. Where Hideaway differs from its neighbors is in the F$30-a-night dormitories—men and women are mixed here with 15 beds downstairs and nine upstairs. Cooking your own food is not possible and no grocery stores are to be found nearby, but three meals are included in the dorm rates (though not in the *mbure* rates). Hideaway provides free entertainment nightly, including a real *meke* on Tuesday and Friday, and an all-you-can-eat Fijian feast Sunday night (F$18). Valuables can be left in safety deposit boxes at the reception area for a refundable F$2 deposit. An afternoon excursion to a rainforest waterfall departs at 1330 on Tuesday and Saturday (F$15). Surfing is possible in the pass here (not for beginners), and you can scuba dive with Sea

two children near Hideaway Resort

DAVID STANLEY

Myriad snails crawl for the money at Hideaway's weekly mollusk marathon.

Sports Limited. Thrifty Car Rental is represented.

The **Naviti Beach Resort** (Box 29, Korolevu; tel. 530-444, fax 530-343), just west of Korolevu and 100 km from Nandi Airport, has 140 spacious a/c rooms in a series of two-story blocks beginning at F$182 single or double. There's a *lovo* (F$25) on Friday night, and nonguests may use the nine-hole golf course for F$10. Scuba diving is arranged by Sea Sports Limited. This resort has difficulty competing with other medium-priced properties such as the Tambua Sands, Hideaway, and Reef Resort, and a good

percentage of the rooms lie empty most of the time.

The **Warwick Fiji** (Box 100, Korolevu; tel. 530-555, fax 530-010), on the Queens Road just east of Korolevu, 107 km from Nandi Airport, is the second-largest hotel on the Coral Coast (after The Fijian). Erected in 1979 and part of the Hyatt Regency chain until 1991, it's now under the same ownership as the Naviti Beach; there's a shuttle bus between the two. The 246 a/c rooms in three-story wings running east and west from the lobby begin at F$191 single or double, F$215 triple, and rise to F$347 for a club suite. In 1995 the rooms were completely refurbished. There's live music in the Hibiscus Lounge nightly until 0100 and disco dancing on Sunday. This plush resort also offers a complete sports and fitness center, an excellent beach, and scuba diving with Sea Sports Limited. There's even a small offshore island connected to the main beach by a causeway. Avis Rent A Car has a desk in the Warwick.

The **Man Friday Resort** (Box 20, Korolevu; tel. 500-185, fax 520-666), right by the beach, six km off Queens Road at Namboutini, is the most secluded place to stay on the Coral Coast. The 30 thatched *mbures* are F$66 double, with cooking facilities F$10 extra. The footprint-shaped freshwater swimming pool alludes to Daniel Defoe's novel *Robinson Crusoe,* which gave Man Friday its name.

Coral Village Resort (Box 104, Korolevu; tel./fax 500-807), also known as Gaia Beach Resort, is on the side of Namanggumanggua village opposite Man Friday. This 12-bungalow property on a lovely beach functions as a health resort dedicated to "permaculture," a system dedicated to earth-friendly agriculture and energy use. Special programs to help guests lose weight and stop smoking are available.

NAVUA AND VICINITY

Southeastern Viti Levu from Deumba to Suva is wetter and greener than the Coral Coast, and the emphasis changes from beach life to cultural and natural attractions. Pacific Harbor satisfies both sporting types and culture vultures, while Fiji's best river trips begin at Navua. Here too scattered Fiji Indian dwellings join the Fijian villages which predominate farther west. All of the places listed below are easily accessible on the fairly frequent Ngaloa bus from Suva market.

Deumba

The **Coral Coast Christian Camp** (Box 36, Pacific Harbor; tel. 450-178), 13 km west of Navua near Pacific Harbor, offers four five-bed Kozy Korner dormitories with a good communal kitchen and cold showers at F$13/22/31 single/double/triple. The six adjoining motel units go for F$22/40/58, complete with private bath, kitchen, fridge, and fan. Camping costs F$7 pp. No dancing and no alcoholic beverages are permitted on the premises; on Sunday at 1930 you're invited to the Fellowship Meeting in the manager's flat. The Camp is just across the highway from long golden Loloma Beach, the closest public beach to Suva, but if you swim here, watch your valuables. You can technically camp free on this beach, but rampant theft has made this impractical. The Christian Camp is useful as a base from which to visit Pacific Harbor, and it's a good budget place to spend the night while arranging to get out to the surfers' camp on Yanutha Island, but avoid arriving on a weekend as it's often fully booked by church groups from Friday afternoon until Monday morning.

Right next door to the Christian Camp is the **Deumba Inn** (Box 132, Pacific Harbor; tel. 450-544, fax 361-337), which opened in 1994. They have 10 rooms with shared bath at F$17/27 single/double and five self-catering units at F$50 double. The Inn's main drawback is that you can't cook your own food in the cheaper rooms and meals at the restaurant are expensive. However, inexpensive snacks are available at the takeaway counter at lunchtime and the Inn is a useful backup if you happen to arrive on a day when the Camp is full.

The grocery stores nearest the above are by the bridge, one km toward Pacific Harbor. For fruit and vegetables you must go to Navua.

PACIFIC HARBOR

Pacific Harbor is a sprawling, misplaced Hawaiian condo development and instant culture village, 152 km east of Nandi Airport and 44 km west of Suva. In July 1988 the Japanese corporation South Pacific Development purchased Pacific Harbor, and many of the 180 individual villas are owned by Australian or Hong Kong investors.

Pacific Harbor's imposing **Cultural Center** (Box 74, Pacific Harbor; tel. 450-177, fax 450-083) offers the chance to experience some freeze-dried Fijian culture. This re-created Fijian village on a small "sacred island" is complete with a 20-meter-tall temple and natives attired in jungle garb. Visitors tour the island hourly, seated in a double-hulled *ndrua* with a tour guide "warrior" carrying a spear, and at various stops village occupations such as canoe making, weaving, tapa, and pottery are demonstrated

a model of a fortified village at the Pacific Harbor Cultural Center

for the canoe-bound guests. At 1500 there are one-hour performances by the Dance Theater of Fiji (Monday, Wednesday, Thursday, and Friday) and Fijian firewalking (Tuesday and Saturday), and if you want to see one of the shows it's best to arrive with the tour buses in the early afternoon. Admission is F$17 pp for the village tour (Monday to Saturday 0930-1330), then another F$17 to see the dancing or firewalking, or F$28 for village tour and show combined. Rosie The Travel Service runs full-day bus tours to the Cultural Center from Nandi at F$84 pp including the tour and show but not lunch. The Dance Theater has an international reputation, with several successful North American tours to their credit.

Entry to the Waikiki-style **Marketplace of Fiji** at the Cultural Center, made up of mock-colonial boutiques and assorted historical displays, is free of charge. If you arrive here after 1630, all of the tourist buses will have left, and you'll be able to see quite a bit of the Cultural Center for nothing. The main Pacific Harbor post office is next to the Cultural Center.

Pacific Harbor's other main claim to fame is its 18-hole, par-72 championship **Country Club Golf Course** (Box 144, Pacific Harbor; tel. 450-048, fax 450-262), designed by Robert Trent Jones, Jr. and said to be the South Pacific's finest. It's Fiji's only fully sprinklered and irrigated golf course. Course records are 69 by Bobby Clampett of the U.S. (amateur) and 64 by Greg Norman of Australia (professional). Green fees are F$22 for hotel guests, F$44 for others; the hire of clubs is F$16.50, an electric golf cart F$33. Take along an extra pair of socks in case you get a hole in one. You'll find a restaurant and bar in the clubhouse, about two km inland off Queens Road. Rosie The Travel Service runs full-day golfing tours from Nandi with time for nine holes at F$44 (lunch and green fees not included).

Although golfing is the resort's main sporting draw, **Beqa Divers** (tel. 450-323), a branch of Suva's Scubahire, is based at the Pacific Harbor International Hotel's marina and organizes diving on the nearby Mbengga Lagoon daily at 0900. Excursions cost F$127 with two tanks and a mediocre lunch.

Serious divers also have at their disposal the 18-meter live-aboard *Beqa Princess* operated by

Tropical Expeditions (Box 271, Deumba; tel. 450-188, fax 450-426) from their Pacific Harbor base. The *Princess* specializes in three-night scuba cruises to the islands south of Viti Levu and day-trips to the Mbengga Lagoon.

There are three expensive hotels at Pacific Harbor. The 84 a/c rooms at the three-story **Pacific Harbor International Hotel** (Box 144, Pacific Harbor; tel. 450-022, fax 450-262) are F$143/165/198 single/double/triple, breakfast included. This hotel is at the mouth of the Nggaraninggio River, between Queens Road and a long sandy beach. There's a *lovo* (F$28) with island entertainment here every Saturday night.

The advantage of the **Fiji Palms Beach Club Resort** (Box 6, Pacific Harbor; tel. 450-050, fax 450-025), right next to the Pacific Harbor International Hotel, is that the 14 two-bedroom apartments (F$150 single or double) have cooking facilities, which allows you to skip the many expensive restaurants in these parts. Many of the units have been sold as part of a time-share scheme.

Equally upmarket is the **Atholl Hotel** (Box 14, Pacific Harbor; tel. 450-100, fax 450-153), alongside the golf course, inland a couple of kilometers behind the Cultural Center, with 22 plush rooms at F$150 double.

Kumarans Restaurant (tel. 450-294), across the highway from the Pacific Harbor International Hotel, has some cheap curries at lunchtime, but the dinner menu is pricey. There are three small grocery stores beside Kumarans, and the self-service Trading Post Supermarket at the Marketplace of Fiji has a good selection.

Only charter flights from Nandi Airport land at Pacific Harbor's airstrip, but all of the Queens Road express buses stop here. If coming to Pacific Harbor from Suva by express bus, you'll be dropped at the Pacific Harbor International Hotel, one km from the Cultural Center. The slower Ngaloa buses will stop right in front of the Cultural Center itself.

NAVUA

This bustling river town 39 km west of Suva is the market center of the rice-growing delta area near the mouth of the Navua River and the headquarters of Serua and Namosi provinces. If

DR. NIELSEN

The tortuous Navua River drains much of central Viti Levu.

low-grade copper deposits totaling 1,000 million tonnes just inland at Namosi are ever developed, Navua will become a major mining port, passed by a huge drain pipe for copper tailings, ore conveyors, and four-lane highways. The present quiet road between Navua and Suva will bustle with new housing estates and heavy traffic, and the change from today will be total!

All of the express buses between Suva and Nandi stop at Navua. Village boats leave from the wharf beside Navua market for Mbengga Island south of Viti Levu daily except Sunday, but more depart on Saturday. Flat-bottomed punts to **Namuamua** village, 25 km up the Navua River, depart on Thursday, Friday, and Saturday afternoons, but almost anytime you can charter an outboard from Navua wharf to Namuamua at F$50 for the boat roundtrip. The hour-long ride takes you between high canyon walls and over boiling rapids with waterfalls on

each side. Above Namuamua is the fabulous **Navua Gorge,** accessible only to intrepid river-runners in rubber rafts who go in by helicopter. It's also possible to reach the river by road at Nambukelevu.

A great way to experience the picturesque lower Navua is with **Wilderness Adventures** (Box 1389, Suva; tel. 386-498, fax 300-584), which runs full-day canoe trips (F$59 pp) down the river. Their minibus collects participants at Suva hotels around 0900, then there's a two-hour scenic drive to the embarkation point on the upper river, where the canoes and a rubber raft will be waiting. A stop is made halfway down the river for swimming and a picnic lunch (included). The canoe trips are intended for those aged 15-45, although physically fit older folks may join by signing a liability disclaimer. Everyone is welcome on Wilderness Adventures' motorized boat trips (adults F$54, children F$33) 20 km up the river from Navua to Nukusere village, where lunch is taken and visitors get an introduction to Fijian culture. These are probably the best day tours available in Fiji for the adventurous traveler, and any travel agent in Suva can make the bookings. In Nandi, book through Rosie The Travel Service. (If saving money is a priority and you can get a small group together, it's much cheaper to go to Navua by public bus and hire a market boat there.)

The building of the former Farmers Club, by the river in the center of Navua, 200 meters from the bus stand, was the four-room Heartbreak Hotel until recently, when it closed due to financial difficulties. Check to see if they've reopened, and whether the large public bar downstairs is back in service.

Toward Suva

The **Ocean Pacific Club** (Box 3229, Lami; tel. 304-864, fax 361-577), near Nambukavesi village on a hillside between Navua and Suva, is an upmarket sportfishing camp with eight bungalows at F$85 single or double if you book direct. Their nine-meter cruiser goes out for wahoo, mahimahi, giant trevally, yellowfin tuna, marlin, and sailfish each morning at 0830 (F$110 pp). Scuba diving is also offered here.

ISLANDS OFF SOUTHERN VITI LEVU

VATULELE ISLAND

This small island, just south of Viti Levu, is famous for its tapa cloth. Vatulele reaches a height of only 34 meters on its north end; there are steep bluffs on the west coast and gentle slopes facing a wide lagoon on the east. Both passes into the lagoon are from its north end. Five different levels of erosion are visible on the cliffs from which the uplifted limestone was undercut. There are also rock paintings, but no one knows when they were executed.

Other unique features of Vatulele are the sacred **red prawns,** which are found in a tidal pool at Korolamalama Cave near the island's rocky north coast. These scarlet prawns with remarkably long antennae are called *ura mbuta,* or cooked prawns, for their color. The red color probably comes from iron oxide in the limestone of their abode. It's strictly *tambu* to eat them or remove them from the pools. If you do, it will bring ill luck or even shipwreck. The story goes that a princess of yesteryear rejected a gift of cooked prawns from a suitor and threw them in the pools, where the boiled-red creatures were restored to life. Villagers can call the prawns by repeating a chant.

Village boats leave for the villages on the east side of Vatulele from Paradise Point near Korolevu Post Office on Tuesday, Thursday, and Saturday if the weather is good. Sunflower Airlines flies to Vatulele from Nandi four times a week (F$62 one-way). The island's small private airstrip is near the villages, six km from the resort described below, to which tourists are transferred by bus.

In 1990 Vatulele got its own luxury resort, the **Vatulele Island Resort** (Box 9936, Nandi Airport; tel. 520-300, fax 520-062) on Vatulele's west side. The 12 futuristic villas in a hybrid Fijian/New Mexico style sit about 50 meters apart on a magnificent white sand beach facing a protected lagoon. The emphasis is on luxurious exclusivity: villas cost F$1000 double per day, including all meals. The minimum stay is five nights, and children are only accepted at certain times of the year. To preserve the natural environment, motorized water sports are not offered, but there's lots to do, including sailing, snorkeling, windsurfing, paddling, tennis, and hiking, with guides and gear provided at no additional cost. The only thing you'll be charged extra for is scuba diving. This world-class resort is a creation of Australian TV producer Henry Crawford and local promoter Martin Livingston, a former manager of Turtle Island Resort in the Yasawas.

YANUTHA ISLAND

In 1994 a new surfers' camp opened on a splendid beach on Yanutha Island, to the west of Mbengga (not to be confused with the Yanutha Island on which The Fijian Resort Hotel is found). **Frigate Surfriders** (Ratu Penaia Drekeni, Box 39, Pacific Harbor; tel. 450-472) offers cots in a 10-bed dorm at F$55 pp for surfers, F$25 pp for nonsurfers, plus tax. Included are accommodation and all meals, windsurfing, surfing, and sportfishing. The lefthander in Frigate Passage has been called the most underrated wave in Fiji: "fast, hollow, consistent, and deserted." For information ask for Inoke at the video rental shop in the Marketplace of Fiji at Pacific Harbor's Cultural Center. Boat transfers are F$20 pp roundtrip. Village boats to the one Fijian village on Yanutha depart on Tuesday and Saturday afternoons from the bridge near the Pacific Harbor International Hotel.

MBENGGA ISLAND

Mbengga is the home of the famous Fijian firewalkers; Rukua, Natheva, and Ndakuimbengga are firewalking villages. Nowadays, however, they perform only at the hotels on Viti Levu. At low tide you can walk the 27 km around the island: the road only goes from Waisomo to Ndakuni. There are caves with ancient burials near Suliyanga, which can be reached on foot from Mbengga at low tide, but to visit you'll need permission from the village chief. Have your *sevusevu* ready. Malumu Bay, between the two

MBENGGA

WAISOMO

KOROLEVU
(439 m)

RAVIRAVI

SULIYANGA

MARLIN BAY
RESORT

MBENGGA
ISLAND

RUKUA

VANGA BAY

MOTURIKI

NDAKUNI

NATHEVA

NDAKUIMBENGGA

LAWAKI
BEACH

– N –

© DAVID STANLEY

0   5 km

branches of the island, is thought to be a drowned crater. Climb Korolevu (439 meters), the highest peak, from Waisomo or Lalati.

Frigate Passage on the west side of the barrier reef is one of the best dive sites near Suva. There's a vigorous tidal flow in and out of the passage, which attracts large schools of fish,

and there are large coral heads. **Sulfur Passage** on the east side of Mbengga is equally good. Kandavu Island is visible to the south of Mbengga.

The **Marlin Bay Resort** (Box 112, Deumba; tel. 304-042, fax 304-028) opened in 1991 on a golden beach between Raviravi and Rukua villages on the west side of Mbengga. The 12 luxurious *mbures* (no cooking facilities) go for F$178/220/260 single/double/triple. The meal plan is F$78 pp a day, and boat transfers from Pacific Harbor cost F$70 return. The area is a favorite of scuba divers (F$100 a dive) and horseback riding is also available. Boat pickups for the Marlin Bay Resort take place at The Pub Restaurant, Pacific Harbor.

The best beach is Lawaki, to the west of Natheva. Present the village chief of Natheva with a nice bundle of *waka* if you want to camp. It's quite possible to stay in any of the Fijian villages on Mbengga by following the procedure outlined in "Staying in Villages" under "Accommodations" in the On the Road chapter. Ask around the wharf at Navua around noon any day except Sunday and you'll soon find someone happy to take you. Alcohol is not allowed in the villages on Mbengga, so if you're asked to buy a case of beer, politely decline and offer to buy other groceries instead.

Golden cowry pendant. *The golden cowry (Cypraea aurantium), which the Fijians call* mbuli kula, *is one of the rarest of all seashells. On important ceremonial occasions, high chiefs would wear the shell around the neck as a symbol of the highest authority.*

SALVATORE CASA

SUVA

The pulsing heart of the South Pacific, Suva is the largest and most cosmopolitan city in Oceania. The port is always jammed with ships bringing goods and passengers from far and wide, and busloads of commuters and enthusiastic visitors constantly stream into the busy market bus station. In the business center are Indian women in saris, large sturdy chocolate-skinned Fijians, Australians and New Zealanders in shorts and knee socks, and wavy-haired Polynesians from Rotuma and Tonga.

Suva squats on a hilly peninsula between Lauthala Bay and Suva Harbor in the southeast corner of Viti Levu. The verdant mountains north and west catch the southeast trades, producing damp conditions year-round. Visitors sporting a sunburn from Fiji's western sunbelt resorts may appreciate Suva's warm tropical rains (most of which fall at night). In 1870 the Polynesia Company sent Australian settlers to camp along mosquito-infested Numbukalou Creek on land obtained from High Chief Cakobau. When efforts to grow sugarcane here failed, the company convinced the British to move their headquarters here, and since 1882 Suva has been the capital of Fiji.

Today this exciting multiracial city of 175,000—a fifth of Fiji's population—is also about the only place in Fiji where you'll see a building taller than a palm tree. High-rise office buildings and hotels overlook the compact downtown area. The British left behind imposing colonial buildings, wide avenues, and manicured parks as evidence of their rule. The Fiji School of Medicine, the University of the South Pacific, the Fiji Institute of Technology, the Pacific Theological College, and the headquarters of many regional organizations have been established here. In addition, the city offers some of the best nightlife between Kings Cross (Sydney) and North Beach (San Francisco), plus shopping, sightseeing, and many good-value places to stay and eat.

Keep in mind that on Sunday all shops will be closed, restaurants keep reduced hours, and far fewer taxis or buses will be operating. In short, the city will be dead. An excellent plan is to catch the Saturday bus/boat service to Levuka and spend the rest of the weekend there (book your ticket a day or two in advance). However, if you do find yourself in Suva, the fantastic choral singing makes dressing up and at-

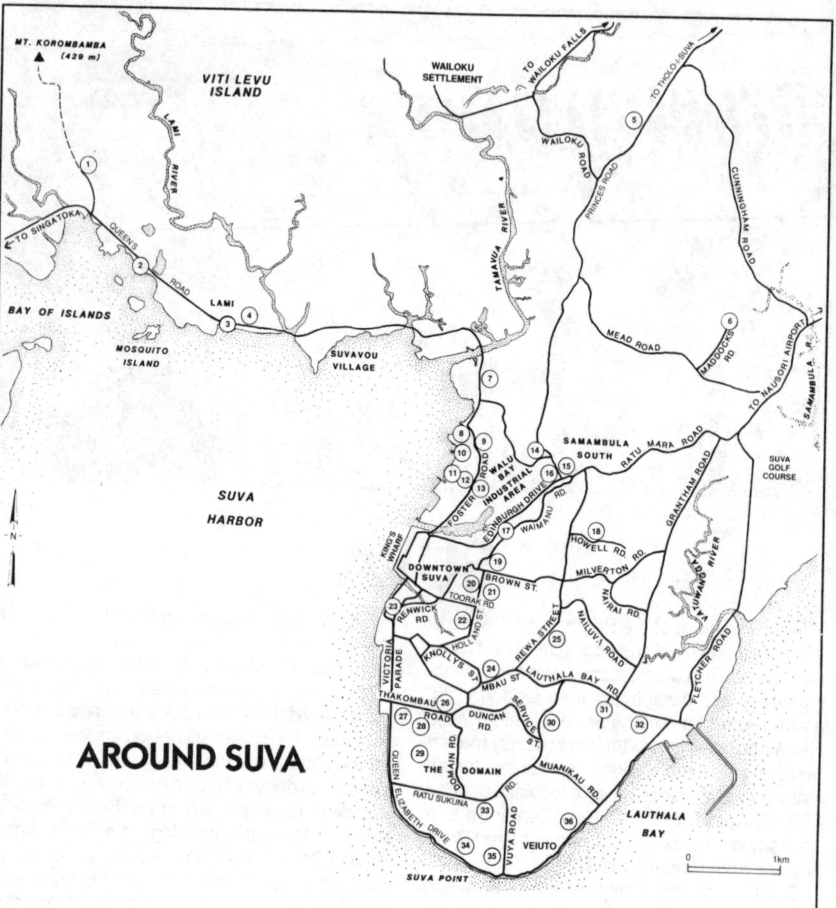

AROUND SUVA

1. cement factory
2. Raffles Tradewinds Hotel
3. Scubahire
4. Castle Restaurant
5. Fiji School of Medicine
6. Queen Elizabeth Barracks
7. Suva Cemetery
8. Royal Suva Yacht Club
9. Suva Prison
10. Carpenters Shipping
11. Muaiwalu Jetty
12. Dive Center Ltd.
13. Carlton Brewery

14. Australian Embassy
15. Fiji Institute of Technology
16. Tanoa House Private Hotel
17. Outrigger Hotel
18. Sangam Temple
19. C.W.M. Hospital
20. Pacific Concerns Resource Center
21. Amy Apartment Hotel
22. Jame Mosque
23. General Post Office
24. Suva Apartments
25. Flagstaff Boarding House

26. South Seas Private Hotel
27. Thurston Botanical Gardens
28. Fiji Museum
29. Government House
30. Forum Secretariat
31. University of the South Pacific
32. National Stadium
33. Parliament
34. Divisional Surveyor
35. Pacific Theological College
36. Pacific Regional Seminary

© DAVID STANLEY

tending church worthwhile. Most churches have services in English, but none compare with the 1000 Fijian service at Centenary Methodist Church on Stewart Street.

The lovely *Isa Lei,* a Fijian song of farewell, tells of a youth whose love sails off and leaves him alone in Suva, smitten with longing.

SIGHTS

Central Suva

Suva's wonderful, colorful **municipal market,** the largest retail produce market in the Pacific, is a good place to dabble. If you're a yachtie or backpacker, you'll be happy to know that the market overflows with fresh produce of every kind. It's worth some time looking around, and consider having kava at the *yanggona* dens at the back of the market for about F$2 a bowl (share the excess with those present). Fijian women sell fresh pineapple and guava juice from glass "fish tank" containers.

From the market, walk south on Scott Street, past the colorful old Metropole Hotel, to the **Fiji Visitors Bureau** in a former customs house (1912) opposite Suva's General Post Office. At the corner of Thomson and Pier streets opposite the Visitors Bureau is the onetime **Garrick Hotel** (1914) with a Sichuan Chinese restaurant behind the wrought-iron balconies upstairs. Go east on Thomson to Morris Hedstrom Supermarket and a picturesque colonial-style arcade (1919) along **Numbukalou Creek,** a campsite of Suva's first European settlers. You'll get good photos from the little park just across the bridge.

Cumming Street, Suva's main duty-free shopping area, runs east from the park on the site of Suva's original vegetable market before it moved to its present location just prior to WW II. During the war the street became a market of a different sort as Allied troops flocked here in search of evening entertainment. When import duties were slashed in the early 1960s to cater to an emerging tourist market, Cumming assumed its present form. To continue our walk, turn right on Renwick Road and head back into the center of town.

At the junction of Thomson Street, Renwick Road, and Victoria Parade is a small park known as **The Triangle** with five concrete benches

and a white obelisk bearing four inscriptions: "Cross and Cargill first missionaries arrived 14th October 1835; Fiji British Crown Colony 10th October 1874; Public Land Sales on this spot 1880; Suva proclaimed capital 1882." Inland a block on Pratt Street is the **Catholic Cathedral** (1902), one of Suva's finest buildings. Between The Triangle and the cathedral is the towering **Reserve Bank of Fiji** (1984), which is worth entering to see the currency exhibition.

Return to Suva's main avenue, Victoria Parade, and walk south past **Sukuna Park,** site of public protests in 1990 against Fiji's gerrymandered constitution; the colonial-style **Fintel Building** (1926), nerve center of Fiji's international telecommunications links; the picturesque **Queen Victoria Memorial Hall** (1904), later Suva Town Hall and now the Ming Palace restaurant; and the **City Library** (1909), which opened in 1909 thanks to a grant from American philanthropist Andrew Carnegie. All these sights are on your right.

South Suva

Continue south on Victoria Parade past the somber headquarters of the **Native Land Trust Board** which administers much of Fiji's land on behalf of indigenous landowners. Just beyond and across the street from the Travelodge Hotel is Suva's largest edifice, the imposing **Government Buildings** (1939), once the headquarters of the British colonial establishment in the South Pacific. Here on 14 May 1987 Col. Sitiveni Rabuka carried out his assault on parliament and for the next five years Fiji had no representative government. The statue of Chief Cakobau faces the door where the legislators were led out. The building's clock tower is a symbol of Suva.

The main facade of the Government Buildings faces **Albert Park,** where aviator Charles Kingsford Smith landed his trimotor Fokker VII-3M on 6 June 1928 after arriving from Hawaii on the first-ever flight from California to Australia. (The first commercial flight to Fiji was a Pan Am flying boat, which landed in Suva Harbor in October 1941.) Facing the west side of the park is the elegant, Edwardian-style **Grand Pacific Hotel,** built by the Union Steamship Company in 1914 to accommodate their transpacific passengers. The 75 rooms were designed to appear

Suva Bowling Club

DAVID STANLEY

as shipboard staterooms, with upstairs passageways surveying the harbor, like the promenade deck of a ship. For decades the Grand Pacific was the social center of the city, but it has been closed since 1992. The building's owners, the phosphate-rich Republic of Nauru, have announced that the building is soon to be fully renovated and expanded into a five-star luxury hotel managed by the French Accor chain, though that remains to be seen.

South of Albert Park are the pleasing **Thurston Botanical Gardens,** opened in 1913, where tropical flowers such as cannas and plumbagos blossom. The original Fijian village of Suva once stood on this site. On the grounds of the gardens is a clock tower dating from 1918 and the **Fiji Museum** (tel. 315-944, fax 305-143), founded in 1904 and the oldest in the South Pacific. Small but full, this museum is renowned for its maritime displays: canoes, outriggers, the rudder from HMS *Bounty,* and *ndrua* steering oars that were manned by four Fijians. The collection of Fijian war clubs is outstanding and the history section is being expanded as artifacts in overseas collections are returned to Fiji. The museum is open daily except Sunday, 0830-1630, admission F$3.30. (While you're there, pick up a copy of *Life in Feejee—Five Years Among the Cannibals* at the museum shop—one of the most fascinating books about the South Seas you'll ever read.)

South of the gardens is **Government House,** formerly the palace of the British governors of Fiji and now the residence of the president. The original building, erected after 1882, burned after being hit by lightning in 1921, and the present edifice, which dates from 1928, is a replica of the former British governor's residence in Colombo, Sri Lanka. The grounds cannot be visited. The sentry on ceremonial guard duty wears a belted red tunic and an immaculate white *sulu* (kilt). Military officers on duty here do not care to be photographed, though the sentry won't mind having his picture taken. The changing of the guard takes place daily at noon with an especially elaborate ceremony the first Friday of every month to the accompaniment of the military band.

From the seawall south of Government House you get a good view across Suva Harbor to Mbengga Island (to the left) and the dark, green mountains of eastern Viti Levu punctuated by Joske's Thumb, a high volcanic plug (to the right). Follow the seawall south past a few old colonial buildings, and turn left onto Ratu Sukuna Road, the first street after the Police Academy. About 500 meters up this road is the new **Parliament of Fiji** (1992), an impressive, traditional-style building with an orange pyramid-shaped roof. From here it's a good idea to catch a taxi to the University of the South Pacific (a description of which follows). The Nasese bus does a scenic loop through the beautiful garden suburbs of South Suva: just flag it down if you need a ride back to the market.

University of the South Pacific

A frequent bus from in front of Zenon Bookstore, next to the National Bank of Fiji on Victoria Parade opposite Sukuna Park, will bring you direct to the University of the South Pacific (USP). Founded in 1968, this beautiful 72.8-hectare campus on a hilltop overlooking Lauthala Bay is jointly owned by 12 Pacific countries. Although over 70% of the almost 2,000 full-time and more than 600 part-time students are from Fiji, the rest are on scholarships from every corner of the Pacific.

The site of the Lauthala Campus was a Royal New Zealand Air Force seaplane base before the land was turned over to USP. As you enter from Lauthala Bay Road you'll pass the Botanical Garden (1988) and an information office on the right, then the British-built Administration Building on the left. Next comes the $3.5-million university library (1988), erected with Australian aid. The design of the Student Union Building (1975), just across a wooden bridge from the library, was influenced by traditional Pacific building motifs of interlocking circles. Look for the pleasant canteen in the Student Union (open Monday to Saturday 0800-2030 during the school year). It's interesting to observe the mixed batch of students and the ways they cope with the inconvenience of tiny chairs. There's a choice of Indian or island food.

Several buildings south of this is the **Institute of Pacific Studies** (Box 1168, Suva; tel. 314-306), housed in the former RNZAF officers' mess. Every available space on the walls of the IPS building has been covered with murals by Pacific painters. This Institute is a leading publisher of insightful books written by Pacific islanders, which may be purchased at their bookroom without the markup charged by commercial bookstores in town. Don't confuse this bookroom with the regular USP bookstore nearby.

Students from outside the Pacific islands pay about F$9500 a year tuition to study at USP. Room and board are available at around F$3360

THE FIJI TIMES

Fiji's emerald green banded iguana is the most striking reptile of the Pacific.

and books will run another F$400. There are academic minimum-entry requirements and applications must be in by 31 December for the following term. The two semesters are late February to the end of June, and late July until the end of November. Many courses in the social sciences have a high level of content pertaining to Pacific culture, and postgraduate studies in a growing number of areas are available. To obtain a calendar, application for admission, and other materials send US$20 to: The Registrar, University of the South Pacific, Box 1168, Suva, Fiji Islands (tel. 313-900, fax 302-556).

The USP is always in need of qualified staff, so if you're from a university milieu and looking for a chance to live in the South Seas, this could be it. The maximum contract is six years (you need seven years of residency to apply for Fijian citizenship). If your credentials are impeccable you should write to the registrar from home. On the spot it's better to talk to a department head about his/her needs before going to see the registrar. All USP staff, both local and expatriate, must leave the university if they run for political office or become officers of political parties.

Recently, the university's image as an agent of regional cooperation and integration has been tarnished by an increase in racial tension on the Suva campus, where ugly brawls between Fijian, Samoan, ni-Vanuatu, and Solomon Island students have often led to serious injuries and the expulsion of those involved. The university administration has attempted to sweep this situation under the carpet and the exploration of racial subjects in the classroom is unofficially taboo. Student associations and sporting teams on campus are organized along racial lines, greatly contributing to the problem.

Northwest of Suva

The part of Suva north of Walu Bay accommodates much of Suva's shipping and industry. Carlton Brewery on Foster Road cannot be visited. About 600 meters beyond the brewery is the vintage **Suva Prison** (1913), a fascinating colonial structure with high walls and barbwire. Opposite is the **Royal Suva Yacht Club,** where you can sign in and buy a drink, meet some yachties, and maybe find a boat to crew on.

Their T-shirts (F$12-18) are hot items. In the picturesque **Suva Cemetery,** just to the north, the Fijian graves are wrapped in colorful *sulus* and tapa cloth, and make good subjects for photographers.

Catch one of the frequent Shore, Lami, or Ngaloa buses west on Queens Road, past **Suvavou** village, home of the Suva area's original Fijian inhabitants (and most contemporary "sword sellers"), and past Lami town to the **Raffles Tradewinds Hotel,** seven km from the market. Many cruising yachts tie up here, and the view of the Bay of Islands from the hotel is good.

Orchid Island

Seven km northwest of Suva is the **Orchid Island Cultural Center** (Box 1018, Suva; tel. 361-128, fax 361-064). In the past it offered a good synopsis of Fijian customs through demonstrations, dancing, and historical exhibits, affording a glimpse into traditions such as the kava ceremony, tapa and pottery making, etc. At the miniature zoo you could see and photograph Fiji's rare banded and crested iguanas up close. Replicas of a Fijian war canoe and thatched temple *(mbure kalou)* were on the grounds. We've used the past tense here because Orchid Island has gone downhill and now looks abandoned, although some readers report being admitted and shown around the empty, decaying buildings by residual staff who were only too happy to pocket their F$10 pp admission fee. You might check Orchid Island's current status at the Fiji Visitors Bureau (and don't bother going on a Sunday). The Shore and Ngaloa buses pass this way.

Tholo-i-Suva Forest Park

This lovely park, at an altitude of 150-200 meters, offers 3.6 km of trails through the beautiful mahogany forest flanking the upper drainage area of Waisila Creek. Enter from the Forestry Station along the Falls Trail. A half-km nature trail begins near the Upper Pools, and aside from waterfalls and natural swimming pools there are thatched pavilions with tables at which to picnic. With the lovely green forests behind Suva in full view, this is one of the most breathtaking places in all of Fiji and you may spot a few

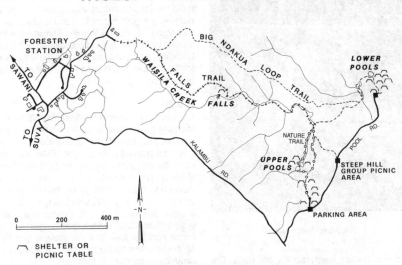

THOLO - I - SUVA FOREST PARK

FORESTRY STATION

TO SAWANI

TO SUVA

BIG NDAKUA LOOP TRAIL

WAISILA CREEK

FALLS TRAIL

FALLS

LOWER POOLS

NATURE TRAIL

KALAMBU RD.

POOL RD.

UPPER POOLS

STEEP HILL GROUP PICNIC AREA

PARKING AREA

0   200   400 m

-N-

⌒ SHELTER OR PICNIC TABLE

A good cross section of Fiji's tropical flora can be seen in Tholo-i-Suva Forest National Park near Suva.

DAVID STANLEY

Wailoku Falls, Suva

native butterflies, birds, reptiles, and frogs. The park is so unspoiled it's hard to imagine you're only 11 km from Suva.

When the park first opened in 1973, camping was allowed near the upper and lower pools. Then in the mid-1980s the rangers were forced to prohibit camping due to thefts from both campers and swimmers. Recently security patrols have been stepped up and camping is once again allowed, but someone must still keep watch at the campsite at all times, especially on weekends. You must also keep an eye on your gear if you go swimming. There's been talk of imposing a F$5 pp entry fee to cover park maintenance and management, but even with such a fee Tholo-i-Suva would still be worth visiting. Get there on the Sawani or Serea bus (55 cents), which leave from Lane No. 3 at Suva Bus Station every hour, but come on a dry day as it's even rainier than Suva and the creeks are prone to flooding.

On your way back to Suva from Tholo-i-Suva ask the bus driver to drop you at Wailoku Road, just past the Fiji School of Medicine in Tamavua Heights. Every half hour the Wailoku bus runs down the hill: stay on till the bus stops and turns

around, then continue down the road a few hundred meters to a bridge. Take the trail on the left just across the bridge and hike about five minutes upstream to **Wailoku Falls,** where you can swim in a deep pool of cold, clear water amid the idyllic verdant vegetation. This nice picnic spot is government land and no admission is charged. The nearby Wailoku Settlement is inhabited by descendants of blackbirded Solomon Islanders. If you only want to visit the falls, look for the Wailoku bus in Lane No. 2 at the market bus station.

Hiking

For a bird's-eye view of Suva and the entire surrounding area, spend a morning climbing to the volcanic plug atop **Mt. Korombamba** (429 meters), the highest peak around. Take a Shore bus to the cement factory beyond the Tradewinds Hotel at Lami, then follow the dirt road past the factory up into the foothills. After about 45 minutes on the main track, you'll come to a fork just after a sharp descent. Keep left and cross a small stream. Soon after, the track divides again. Go up on the right and look for a trail straight up to the right where the tracks rejoin. It's a 10-minute scramble to the summit from here.

There's a far more challenging climb to the top of **Joske's Thumb,** a volcanic plug 15 km west of Suva. Take a bus to Naikorokoro Road, then walk inland 30 minutes to where the road turns sharply right and crosses a bridge. Follow the track straight ahead and continue up the river till you reach a small village. Request permission of the villagers to proceed. From the village to the Thumb will take just under three hours, and a guide might be advisable. The last bit is extremely steep, and ropes may be necessary.

Sports and Recreation

At the 18-hole, par-72 **Suva Golf Club** (tel. 382-872), 15 Rifle Range Rd., Vatuwangga, the course record is 65. Green fees are F$6/12 for 9/18 holes, plus F$12 for club and trolley hire. Visitors are welcome, though Tuesday and Saturday afternoons are reserved for club competitions (General Rabuka and Ratu Mara are regulars).

Scubahire (G.P.O. Box 777, Suva; tel. 361-088, fax 361-047), 75 Marine Dr., opposite the Lami Shopping Center, is the country's oldest dive shop (established 1970) and one of only two PADI five-star dive centers in Fiji. Also known as "Beqa Divers," they arrange full-day diving trips to the Mbengga Lagoon from their Pacific Harbor base for F$127, including two tanks, weight belt, backpack, and lunch. Other equipment can be rented. Scubahire will also take snorkelers out on their full-day dive trips for F$66 pp, snorkeling gear and lunch included. The 65 km of barrier reef around the Mbengga Lagoon features multicolored soft corals and fabulous sea fans at Side Streets, and an exciting wall and big fish at Cutter Passage. Scubahire's four-day PADI certification course (F$450) involves six boat dives, an excellent way to learn while getting in some great diving. An introductory dive is F$138. Fiji's only purpose-built diver training pool is on their Lami premises. You'll need to show a medical certificate proving you're fit for diving.

Dive Center Ltd. (Box 3066, Lami; tel. 300-599, fax 302-639), 4 Matua St., Walu Bay (opposite Carlton Brewery), rents and sells scuba gear at daily and weekly rates, and fills tanks.

Surfers should call Matthew Light (tel. 361-560), who runs a shuttle out to Sandspit Lighthouse where there's good surfing at high tide. He'll pick you up at the Raffles Tradewinds Hotel in Lami for F$15 pp roundtrip.

The Suva **Olympic Swimming Pool,** 224 Victoria Parade, charges F$1.10 admission. It's open Monday to Friday 1000-1800, Saturday 0800-1800 (April to September), or Monday to Friday 0900-1900, Saturday 0600-1900 (October to March). Lockers are available.

The Fijians are a very muscular, keenly athletic people who send champion teams far and wide in the Pacific. You can see rugby (April to September) and soccer (March to October) on Saturday afternoons at 1500 at the **National Stadium** near the University of the South Pacific. Rugby and soccer are also played at Albert Park Saturday, and you could also see a cricket game here (mid-October to Easter).

ACCOMMODATIONS

There's a wide variety of places to stay and the low-budget accommodations can be divided into two groups. The places on the south side of the downtown area near Albert Park are mostly decent and provide communal cooking facil-
ities to bona fide travelers. However, many of those northeast of downtown are dicey and cater mostly to "short-time" guests; few of these bother to provide cooking facilities. Many of the medium-priced hotels and self-catering apartments are along Gordon Street and its continuation, MacGregor Road. In this book we include every known hotel, regardless of its category or lack thereof. If you want to spend some time in Suva to take advantage of the city's good facilities and varied activities, look for something with cooking facilities and weekly rates. Many apartments are available on a short-term basis.

Budget Accommodations around Albert Park

Women are accommodated at the big, modern **Y.W.C.A.** (Box 534, Suva; tel. 304-829, fax 303-004) on Sukuna Park—a good place to meet Fijian women. There are only two singles and one double available for foreign visitors (F$10 pp).

Suva's original backpacker's oasis is the **Coconut Inn** (Box 12539, Suva; tel. 312-904, fax 701-169), 8 Kimberly St., which charges F$8.50 per bunk in the stuffy four-bed dormitories. The four double rooms are F$22, and there's a small flat upstairs for up to six persons at F$38 double. The Inn offers cooking facilities and luggage storage, though it's sometimes a little dirty and disorganized (take care with your gear here). It's far less crowded now than it was back in the days when it was the only cheap place to stay.

The 42-room **South Seas Private Hotel** (Box 2086, Government Buildings, Suva; tel. 312-296, fax 340-236), 6 Williamson Rd., one block east of Albert Park, has clean singles/doubles with fan and shared bath at F$11/18, or F$8 pp in the five-bed dorms. A room with private bath is F$26 double—good value. This quiet hotel has a pleasant veranda and a large communal kitchen which may be used 0700-2000 only. For a refundable F$10 deposit, you may borrow a plate, mug, knife, fork, and spoon, but there's a long-standing shortage of pots and pans (blankets in the rooms and toilet paper in the toilets are two other things in short supply here). They have a solar hot water system, so you'll probably have hot water in evening but not in the morning. It's possible to leave excess luggage at the South

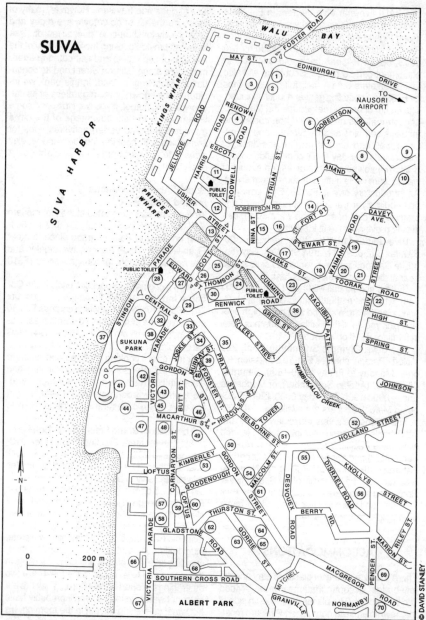

SUVA

WALU BAY

FOSTER ROAD

MAY ST.

EDINBURGH DRIVE

TO NAUSORI AIRPORT

SUVA HARBOR

KINGS WHARF

JELLICOE ROAD

PRINCES WHARF

USHER STREET

HARRIS ROAD

RENOWN ROAD

ESCOTT ROAD

RODWELL ROAD

PUBLIC TOILET

PARADE

EDWARD

SCOTT ST.

THOMSON ST.

ST.

PUBLIC TOILET

CENTRAL ST.

STINSON

SUKUNA PARK

PARADE

VICTORIA

GORDON

BUTT ST.

MACARTHUR ST.

JOSKE ST.

MURRAY ST.

FORSTER ST.

PRATT ST.

HERCULES ST.

SELBORNE ST.

TOWER ST.

HOLLAND STREET

RENWICK ROAD

ELLERY STREET

GREIG ST.

CUMMING

RAQIBHAI PATEL ST.

NUBUKALOU CREEK

MARKS ST.

STEWART ST.

WAIMANU ROAD

TOORAK ROAD

SUVA STREET

HIGH ST.

SPRING ST.

DAVEY AVE.

ROBERTSON RD.

ANAND ST.

STRUAN ST.

NINA ST.

FORT ST.

ROBERTSON RD.

JOHNSON

LOFTUS

CARNARVON ST.

KIMBERLEY

GOODENOUGH

GORDON STREET

MALCOLM ST.

DESVOEUX ROAD

BERRY RD.

DISRAELI ROAD

KNOLLYS STREET

RILEY ST.

MARION ST.

PENDER ST.

THURSTON ST.

GORRIE ST.

GLADSTONE ROAD

MITCHELL

MACGREGOR ROAD

GRANVILLE

NORMANBY

VICTORIA PARADE

SOUTHERN CROSS ROAD

ALBERT PARK

0   200 m

-N-

© DAVID STANLEY

SUVA

1. Bali Hai Nightspot
2. Phoenix Cinema
3. Pacific Forum Line
4. Health Office
5. buses to Lautoka
6. Motel Capital
7. Tropic Towers Apartment Motel
8. Motel Crossroad
9. New Haven Motel
10. Suva Oceanview Hotel
11. bus station
12. market
13. Metropole Hotel
14. Capricorn Apartment Hotel
15. Patterson Brothers Shipping
16. Centenary Methodist Church
17. Century Cinema
18. Kings Suva Hotel
19. Karishma Cinema
20. New Lilac Cinema
21. Bouganvillia Motel
22. Immigration office
23. Chequer's Nightspot
24. Morris Hedstrom Supermarket

25. Harbor Center/Dominion Arcade
26. Fiji Visitors Bureau
27. General Post Office
28. Curio and Handicraft Market
29. The Triangle
30. Sunflower Airlines
31. Y.W.C.A.
32. Air Pacific
33. Hare Krishna Vegetarian Restaurant
34. Central Police Station
35. Catholic Cathedral
36. Travelworld Services
37. Tiko's Floating Restaurant
38. Regal Cinema
39. Town House Apartment Hotel
40. Sunset Apartment Motel
41. Suva Civic Auditorium
42. Fiji International Telecommunications office
43. Air Fiji
44. Suva Olympic Pool
45. Lucky Eddie's
46. Emosi Ferry Service
47. Suva City Library

48. Air Nauru/Government Handicraft Center
49. Anglican Cathedral
50. Southern Cross Hotel
51. The Playhouse
52. Laxmi Narayan Temple
53. Coconut Inn
54. Elixir Motel Apartments
55. Coconut Frond Bookstore
56. Victoria Tennis Courts
57. Golden Dragon
58. Native Land Trust Board
59. Old Mill Cottage Cafe60. U.S. Embassy/Tourism Council
61. Berjaya Hotel
62. Pacific Conference of Churches
63. Tuvalu Embassy
64. Gordon St. Medical Center
65. Travel Inn
66. Suva Travelodge
67. Grand Pacific Hotel
68. Government Buildings
69. Pender Court
70. Suva Peninsula Hotel

Seas while you're off visiting other islands, but lock your bag securely with a padlock that can't be picked. Traveler's checks are changed at bank rates. Since this hotel received rave reviews in the Australian guidebooks (which they also sell) it has always been crowded with travelers (not all of them friendly), and you may arrive to find it full. Catch a taxi here from the market the first time (F$2). The staff can arrange minibus transfers to Nandi at F$10.

Travel Inn (Box 2086, Government Buildings, Suva; tel. 304-254, fax 340-236), formerly known as Loloma Lodge and Pacific Grand Holiday Apartments, an older two-story building at 19 Gorrie St., is owned by the same company as the South Seas Private Hotel. There are 16 fan-cooled rooms with shared bath at F$17/22 single/double, all with access to communal cooking facilities, and four self-contained apartments for F$40 triple daily (weekly rates available). Again, the solar heating means no hot water unless

the sun shines but there are plenty of blankets and good locks on the doors. Visitors from other Pacific islands often stay here, as this is one of Suva's best buys. For a longer stay check **Nukurua Apartments** (tel. 312-343) nearby at 25 Gorrie Street.

Budget Accommodations
Northeast of Downtown
The **Metropole Hotel** (Box 404, Suva; tel. 304-112), on Scott Street opposite the market, is an old-fashioned British pub gone native. There are four rooms with shared bath at F$17/25 single/double. The bars next to and below the hotel section are extremely noisy, but they usually close at 2100 (ask).

The **Kings Suva Hotel** (Box 5141, Raiwangga; tel. 304-411, fax 304-384) on Waimanu Road is rougher, and the four noisy bars make it more appealing to hookers than travelers. The 24 rooms are F$17/20 single/double without bath, F$25/30 with bath, but have a look beforehand as quality varies. In short, this place is a dive.

The 42-room **Oceanview Private Hotel** (Box 16037, Suva; tel. 312-129), 270 Waimanu Rd., charges F$14/20 single/double, F$30 for a four-person family room, or F$8 in the dorm. It has a pleasant hillside location, but avoid the noisy rooms over the reception area and bar. The new management has tried to clean the place up, but because of its former reputation, the Oceanview isn't listed in any other travel guidebook to Fiji, so here's your chance to escape the backpack brigade without going upmarket.

Just up the hill at 587 Waimanu Rd. is the 14-room **New Haven Motel** (G.P.O. Box 992, Suva; tel. 315-220), which is cheap (F$17 single or double downstairs, F$20 upstairs) but rather dirty, and it hosts a lot of couples for *very* short stays. The **Motel Crossroad** (tel. 300-089), 124 Robertson Rd. (F$15 single or double), and the 22-room **Motel Capital** (tel. 313-246), 91 Robertson Rd. (F$18 single or double with bath), are similar. Only consider these three if your main interest is Suva's seedier side.

The 23 units at **Amy Apartments Motel** (Box 3985, Samambula; tel. 315-113), at 98 Amy St. several blocks east of Waimanu Road, are F$20/25 single/double on the first floor, F$30/33 on the second and third floors. A larger "family unit" is F$66. Many of the people staying here seem to have more on their minds than sleep, and it can be rather noisy with shouts and laughter echoing through the halls.

Another place to avoid is the **Flagstaff Boarding House** (Box 1328, Suva; tel. 313-873), 62 Rewa St., which is also well frequented by "short time" guests.

The **Tanoa House Private Hotel** (Box 704, Suva; tel. 381-575), 5 Princes Rd. in Samambula South, is a totally respectable guesthouse run by an ex-colonial from the Gilberts. The place has a garden with a view, and you meet genuine island characters. The 10 rooms with shared bath are F$15/25/30 single/double/triple; breakfast is F$5 extra, and other meals are available. It's situated across from the Fiji Institute of Technology near the end of Waimanu Road, too far to walk from downtown, but you can get there easily on the Samambula bus.

Apartment Hotels

Two apartment hotels behind the Central Police Station are worth a try. The congenial **Town House Apartment Hotel** (G.P.O. Box 485, Suva; tel. 300-055, fax 303-446), 3 Forster St., is a five-story building with panoramic views from the bar on the roof. The 28 a/c units with cooking facilities are good value at F$44/55 single/double and up.

Nearby and under the same management is the **Sunset Apartment Motel** (G.P.O. Box 485, Suva; tel. 301-799, fax 303-446), corner of Gordon and Murray streets. The 15 self-catering apartments in this normal four-story suburban apartment block begin at F$40/49 single/double. Some of the singles lack cooking facilities, are noisy, and have uncomfortably soft beds.

Four-story **Elixir Motel Apartments** (Box 2347, Government Buildings, Suva; tel. 303-288, fax 303-383), on the corner of Gordon and Malcolm streets, has 14 two-bedroom apartments with cooking facilities and private bath at F$55 without a/c, F$66 with a/c for up to three people. Weekly and monthly rates are also available, so check it out for a long stay (on a daily basis you can do better elsewhere).

Also consider the apartments with fan at **Pender Court** (31 Pender St., Suva; tel. 313-973, fax 300-381). The 13 studios with kitchenettes begin around F$35 single or double (10% reduction by the week), and there are also six one-bedroom apartments with kitchens for F$45. It's sometimes a little noisy, so don't make it your first choice.

Eleven better self-catering units owned by the National Olympic Committee are available at **Suva Apartments** (Box 12488, Suva; tel. 304-280, fax 303-446), 17 Mbau St., a block or two east of Pender Court. They're F$28/33/43 single/double/triple daily, with 10% off on weekly rentals. Be prepared for some traffic noise.

Up in the Waimanu Road area, the **Capricorn Apartment Hotel** (G.P.O. Box 1261, Suva; tel. 303-732, fax 303-069), 7 St. Fort St., has 25 spacious a/c units with cooking facilities beginning at F$75 single or double, F$85 triple. It's very clean, comfortable, and good value. The three- and four-story apartment blocks edge the swimming pool, and there are good views of the harbor from the individual balconies.

Tropic Towers Apartment Motel (G.P.O. Box 1347, Suva; tel. 304-470, fax 304-169), 86 Robertson Rd., has 34 a/c apartments with cooking facilities in a four-story building at F$50/61/72 single/double/triple. Ask about the 13 "budget" units without a/c in the annex, which are about F$15 cheaper. Washing machines (F$5) and a swimming pool are available for guests; screened windows or mosquito nets are not. This and the Capricorn are good choices for families.

Medium-Priced Hotels

The **Bougainvillea Motel** (Box 15030, Suva; tel. 303-690, fax 303-289), 55 Toorak Rd., tries to cater to businesspeople. The 13 spacious self-contained rooms with balcony, phone, TV, and coffee-making facilities are F$39 double with fan, F$50 with a/c.

Up the hill beyond the hospital is the two-story **Outrigger Hotel** (Box 750, Suva; tel. 314-944, fax 302-944), 349 Waimanu Road. The 20 a/c rooms with bath are F$43/50 single/double; a four-person suite is F$66. Most of the rooms have an excellent view of Suva Harbor and there's a swimming pool. **Papa La Pizza** on the premises is said to serve the best pizza in Suva. Get there on the frequent Hospital bus from the bus station.

The **Suva Peninsula Hotel** (Box 888, Suva; tel. 313-711, fax 300-804), at the corner of Macgregor Road and Pender Street, is a stylish four-floor building with swimming pool. The 32 a/c rooms begin at F$55/65 single/double, while the eight suites with kitchenettes run F$77.

Upmarket Hotels

Suva's largest and most expensive hotel is the **Suva Travelodge** (Box 1357, Suva; tel. 301-600, fax 300-251), on the waterfront opposite the Government Buildings. It's a big American-style place with 132 a/c rooms beginning at F$176 single or double. The swimming pool behind the two-story buildings compensates for the lack of a beach. Special events here include "island night" (F$25) on Wednesday with a *meke* at 2000, and the Sunday poolside barbecue lunch (F$11). This is the only Suva hotel where reservations are often necessary.

The **Southern Cross Hotel** (G.P.O. Box 1076, Suva; tel. 314-233, fax 302-901) is a high-rise concrete building at 63 Gordon Street. At F$83/96/116 single/double/triple, the price of

the 34 a/c rooms has increased sharply in recent years. Beware of rooms on the lower floors which are blasted by band music six nights a week. The hotel restaurant on the 6th floor serves delicious Fijian and Korean dishes.

The eight-story **Berjaya Inn** (G.P.O. Box 112, Suva; tel. 312-300, fax 301-300), formerly the Suva Courtesy Inn, at the corner of Malcolm and Gordon streets, is the tallest hotel in Fiji. The 56 a/c rooms all face the harbor, but at F$134 single or double they're overpriced. Ask for the F$99 "local rate." This Malaysian-owned hotel hosts Suva's only Malaysian restaurant.

The 110-room **Raffles Tradewinds Hotel** (Box 3377, Lami; tel. 362-450, fax 361-464), at Lami on the Bay of Islands just west of Suva, re-opened in August 1992 after a US$4-million renovation, complete with a convention center and floating seafood restaurant. Rates are F$130/150/170 single/double/triple with private bath and a/c. Many cruising yachts anchor here. Though bus service into Suva is good, the location is inconvenient for those without a car.

Camping

There's camping on Nukulau, a tiny reef island southeast of Suva. For many years Nukulau was the government quarantine station where most indentured laborers spent their first two weeks in Fiji. Now it's a public park. Get free three-day camping permits from the Divisional Surveyor, Central/Eastern Office, Lands and Surveys Department, Suva Point (Nasese bus) during office hours. The island has toilets and drinking water, and the swimming is good. Problem is, the only access is the F$52 tourist boat (includes lunch) departing Suva at 0930 when there are at least eight passengers. Contact **Coral See Cruises** (Box 852, Suva; tel. 321-570) for information. You're allowed to return to Suva a couple of days later at no extra charge, provided there's a trip.

FOOD

Budget Eateries

Choy's Cafeteria (tel. 315-127) at 151 Victoria Parade opposite Fintel has good breakfast specials, and **Judes** (tel. 315-461), in the arcade opposite Sukuna Park, has good sandwiches at lunchtime. A good inexpensive snack bar with concrete outdoor picnic tables is at the back side of the Handicraft Market facing the harbor.

If you just want a snack, check out **Donald's Kitchen** (tel. 315-587), 103 Cumming Street. One block over on Marks Street are cheaper Chinese restaurants, such as **Kim's Cafe** (tel. 313-252), 128 Marks St., where you can get a toasted egg sandwich and coffee for just over a dollar. There are scores more cheap milk bars around Suva and you'll find them for yourself as you stroll around town.

Fijian Restaurants

The **Y.W.C.A. cafeteria** (tel. 311-617, Monday to Saturday 0800-1700) on Sukuna Park is the place to try native Fijian food, such as *wathi poki* (palusami) or *kuita* (octopus) in *lolo* (coconut cream). You have to come early to get the best dishes.

Another excellent place to sample Fijian food is the **Old Mill Cottage Cafe** (tel. 312-134; closed Sunday and evenings), 49 Carnarvon St.—the street behind the Golden Dragon nightclub. Government employees from nearby offices descend on this place at lunchtime for the inexpensive curried freshwater mussels, curried chicken livers, fresh seaweed in coconut milk, taro leaves creamed in coconut milk, and fish cooked in coconut milk. It's great, but don't come here for coffee as it's cold and overpriced.

Indian Restaurants

The **Hare Krishna Restaurant** (tel. 314-154; closed Sunday), at the corner of Pratt and Joske streets, serves ice cream (12 flavors), sweets, and snacks downstairs, main meals upstairs. If you want the all-you-can-eat vegetarian thali (F$6.50), just sit down and they'll bring it to you. But if you're not that starved, go up to the self-service counter and pick up a couple of vegetable dishes which you can have with one or two rotis. This will cost about half as much as the full meal, though ordering individual dishes can be unexpectedly expensive, so unless you want the full meal it's better to look elsewhere. No smoking or alcohol are allowed.

Another excellent Indian place is the **Curry House** (tel. 313-000), in the old town hall on Victoria Parade next to the Ming Palace, with vegetarian curries for F$3 and meat curries from F$5.

Chinese Restaurants

Suva has many excellent, inexpensive Chinese restaurants. The **Diamond Restaurant,** upstairs at 30 Cumming St., in the heart of the duty-free shopping area, serves generous portions, and the staff and surroundings are pleasant. **Geralyne's Restaurant** (tel. 311-037; closed Sunday), 160 Renwick Rd., is similar.

The **Sichuan Pavilion** Restaurant (tel. 315-194), upstairs in the old Garrick Hotel building at 6 Thomson St., is perhaps Suva's finest Asian restaurant. Employees of the Chinese Consulate frequent it for the spicy-hot Chinese dishes (though not as hot as Sichuan food elsewhere). Weekdays they have a lunchtime buffet that allows you to sample six dishes. Weather permitting, sit outside on the balcony and watch all Suva go by.

Also try the good-value **Lantern Palace Restaurant** (tel. 314-633) at 10 Pratt St. near Hare Krishna. The **Phoenix Restaurant** (tel. 311-889), 165 Victoria Parade, has inexpensive Chinese food and cheap beer. Their takeaways are good. The upmarket **New Peking Restaurant** (tel. 312-714), 195 Victoria Parade, has a weekday lunchtime smorgasbord worth checking out.

Suva's most imposing Chinese restaurant is the **Ming Palace** (tel. 315-111; closed Sunday) in the Old Town Hall next to the public library on Victoria Parade.

The best place to eat Chinese style near the Raffles Tradewinds Hotel yacht anchorage is the **Castle Restaurant** (tel. 361-223) in the Lami Shopping Center.

Expensive Restaurants

Leonardo's Restaurant (tel. 312-884; closed Sunday), 215 Victoria Parade, is Suva's upmarket Italian specialist. If it fails to please, you can always fall back on **Pizza Hut** (tel. 311-825; Monday to Saturday 1100-2230, Sunday 1900-2200), nearby at 207 Victoria Parade. In the past we've been critical about this place, but several readers disagreed and said they thought it was fine (no connection with the Pizza Hut chain).

For German or French cuisine it's the **Swiss Tavern** (tel. 303-233; closed Sunday), 16 Kimberly St. at Gordon (say hello to Hans).

Tiko's Floating Restaurant (tel. 313-626) is housed in the MV *Lycianda,* an ex-Blue Lagoon cruise ship launched at Suva in 1970 and now anchored off Stinson Parade behind Sukuna Park. Their steaks and seafood (dinner only) are good for a splurge.

ENTERTAINMENT AND EVENTS

Movie houses are plentiful downtown, charging F$2 for a hard seat, F$3 for a soft seat. The selection of films is fairly good, and they change every three days, which makes Suva a paradise for movie lovers. Regal Cinema near Sukuna Park is very comfortable, but rats run freely beneath the seats as soon as the lights go out at Century Cinema on Marks Street.

The **Fiji Indian Cultural Center,** 271 Toorak Rd., offers classes in Indian music, dancing, and art. It's well worth dropping in to find out if any public performances are scheduled during your visit.

The best time to be in Suva is around the end of August or early September, when the **Hibiscus Festival** fills Albert Park with stalls, games, and carnival revelers.

Nightclubs

There are many nightclubs, all of which have cover charges of around F$4 and require neat dress, but nothing much happens until after 2200 and women shouldn't enter alone.

Gays will feel comfortable at **Lucky Eddie's** (tel. 312-884; daily except Sunday after 2000), 217 Victoria Parade, but it's not really a gay bar, as the Fijian women present try to prove. The Lucky Eddie's cover charge is also valid for the more sedate **Urban Jungle Night Club** (Thursday to Saturday after 2100) in the same building.

Signals Night Club, also on Victoria Parade, is a new place. **Traps** (tel. 312-922), at 305 Victoria Parade next to the Shell service station, has loud live jazz and pitchers of beer from 2130 on Monday, Wednesday, and Saturday (free admission but reasonable dress required). Sometimes it's a groupie Suva social scene. One reader recommended a new spot on Carnarvon Street, the **Birdland Jazz Club,** which has live music on weekends and recorded jazz other nights.

A shade rougher but also very popular is the **Golden Dragon** (tel. 311-018; open Monday to Saturday 1930-0100), 379 Victoria Parade.

The most interracial of the clubs is **Chequers Nightspot** (tel. 313-563), 127 Waimanu Rd., which has live music Tuesday to Saturday after 2100. Hang onto your wallet here.

For real earthy atmosphere try the **Bali Hai** (tel. 315-868) on Rodwell Road, the roughest club in Suva. Friday and Saturday nights the place is packed with Fijians (no Indians) and tourists are rare, so beware. If you're looking for action, you'll be able to pick a partner within minutes, but take care with aggressive males. The dance hall on the top floor is the swingingest, with body-to-body jive—the Bali Hai will rock you.

Bars

O'Reilly's Pub (tel. 312-968), 5 MacArthur St., just around the corner from Lucky Eddie's, has a happy hour with local beer at F$1 a mug weekdays 1700-1945, Saturday 1800-1945. It's a nice relaxed way to kick off a night on the town.

Unescorted female travelers and those in search of more subdued drinking should try the bar at Tiko's Floating Restaurant or the lounge at the Southern Cross Hotel. The piano bar at the Travelodge is even more upmarket.

SHOPPING

The **Government Handicraft Center** behind Ratu Sukuna House, MacArthur and Carnarvon streets, is a low-pressure place to familiarize yourself with what is authentic, though prices have jumped sharply here in recent years, making it better to do your buying elsewhere. The large **Curio and Handicraft Market** (Monday to Saturday 0800-1700) on the waterfront behind the post office is a good place to haggle over crafts, so long as you know what is really Fijian (avoid masks and "tikis").

For clothing see the fashionable hand-printed shirts and dresses at **Tiki Togs** (tel. 304-381), 38 Thomson St. across from the post office, or at their second location at 199 Victoria Parade next to the Pizza Hut. You could come out looking like a real South Seas character at a very reasonable price. Also check **Sogo Fiji** (tel. 313-941), 189 Victoria Parade.

Cumming Street (site of the main Suva produce market until the 1940s) is Suva's duty-free shopping area. The wide selection of goods in the large number of shops makes this about the best place in Fiji to shop for electrical and other imported goods. Expect to receive a 10-40% discount by bargaining, but *shop around* before you buy. Be wary when purchasing gold jewelry, as it might be fake. And watch out for hustlers who will try to take you around to the shops and get you a "good price." Dealers with a sticker from the Fiji National Duty Free Merchants Association in the window tend to be more reliable. Never buy anything on the day when a cruise ship is in port—prices shoot up.

Some of the most offbeat buys in Suva are in the pawn shops, most of which are off Marks or Cummings streets. Ask for the behind-the-counter selection.

J.R. White & Co. (tel. 302-325), in the mall behind Air New Zealand, has all kinds of sporting equipment (but not camping gear or backpacks). They can repair worn-out zippers.

The **Philatelic Bureau** (G.P.O. Box 100, Suva; tel. 312-928) at the General Post Office sells the stamps of Tuvalu, Western Samoa, Pitcairn, Solomon Islands, and Vanuatu, as well as those of Fiji.

Beware of the seemingly friendly men (usually with a small package or canvas bag in their hands) who will greet you on the street with a hearty *"Mbula!"* These are "sword sellers" who will ask your name, quickly carve it on a sword, and then demand F$15 for a set that you could buy at a Nandi curio shop for F$5. Try to avoid people like this, as they can become suddenly aggressive. Their swords and masks themselves have nothing to do with Fiji.

SERVICES

Money
The **Westpac Bank** (tel. 300-666), 1 Thomson St., usually gives the best rate on exchanges. **Thomas Cook Travel** (tel. 301-603), 21 Thomson St. next to the post office, will change foreign currency weekdays 0830-1700, Saturday 0830-1200, at a comparable rate. On Sunday you may be able to change money at the Travelodge for a rate about three percent lower than the bank's.

Telecommunications
Fintel, the **Fiji International Telecommunications** office (tel. 312-933), 158 Victoria Parade, is open Monday to Saturday 0800-2200 for trunk calls and telegrams. The basic charge for three minutes is F$5.28 to Australia or New Zealand, F$8.91 to North America and Europe (no minimum when using card phones). The card phones at Fintel require a different type of magnetic card than the public telephones on the street, such as those outside the post office.

Immigration and Consulates
The **Immigration Office** for extensions of stay, etc., is at the corner of Toorak Road and Suva Street (tel. 312-622; open Monday to Friday 0830-1200/1400-1530). Bring along your ticket to leave Fiji and traveler's checks/credit cards.

Cruising yachts wishing to visit the outer islands must first obtain a permit at the **Ministry of Fijian Affairs** (Box 2100, Government Buildings, Suva; tel. 304-200), 61 Carnarvon Street. They'll want to see the customs papers for the boat and all passports. (Yachties anchoring off a Fijian village should present a *sevusevu* of kava to the chief.)

The following countries have **diplomatic missions** in Suva: Britain (tel. 311-033), Canada (tel. 300-589), China (tel. 300-215), the Federated States of Micronesia (tel. 304-566), France (tel. 312-233), Israel (tel. 303-420), Japan (tel. 304-633), Korea (tel. 300-977), Malaysia (tel. 312-166), Marshall Islands (tel. 387-899), Nauru (tel. 313-566), Netherlands (tel. 301-499), New Zealand (tel. 311-422), Papua New Guinea (tel. 304-244), Taiwan (tel. 315-922), Tuvalu (tel. 301-355), and the U.S.A. (tel. 314-466).

Everyone other than New Zealanders requires a visa to visit Australia, and these are readily available free of charge at the Australian Embassy, 10 Reservoir Rd., off Princes Road, Samambula (Box 214, Suva; tel. 382-219; weekdays 0830-1200). It's probably easier to take a taxi there and return to town on the Samambula bus.

Public Conveniences
Free public toilets are just outside the Handicraft Market on the side of the building facing the harbor; beside Numbukalou Creek off Renwick Road; and between the market and the bus station.

Yachting Facilities
The Royal Suva Yacht Club (G.P.O. Box 335, Suva; tel. 312-921, fax 304-433) on Foster Road between Suva and Lami offers visiting yachts

such amenities as mooring privileges, warm showers, laundry facilities, cheap drinks, Sunday barbecues, and the full use of facilities by the whole crew for F$25 a week. There have been reports of thefts from boats anchored here, so watch out. Many yachts anchor off the Raffles Tradewinds Hotel in Lami.

INFORMATION

The **Fiji Visitors Bureau** (tel. 302-433) is on Thomson Street across from the General Post Office, open Monday to Friday 0800-1630, Saturday 0800-1200.

The **Tourism Council of the South Pacific** (tel. 304-177, fax 301-995), 35 Loftus St. next to the U.S. Embassy, provides general brochures on the entire South Pacific.

The Publications Division of the **Ministry of Information** (tel. 211-305), Ground Floor, Government Buildings, hands out a few official brochures on the country. Nearby in the same building is the **Maps and Plans Room** (tel. 211-395) of the Lands and Survey Department, which sells excellent maps of Fiji (Monday to Thursday 0900-1300/1400-1530, Friday 0900-1300/1400-1500).

Carpenters Shipping (tel. 312-244), Neptune House, 4th Floor, Tofua Street, Walu Bay, sells navigational charts (F$43 each). Nearby is the **Fiji Hydrographic Office,** Top Floor, Freeston Road, Walu Bay (tel. 315-457; weekdays 0830-1300/1400-1600), with local navigational charts.

Bookstores

Suva's best bookstore by far is the **USP Book Center** (Monday to Thursday 0830-1615, Friday 0830-1545) at the Lauthala Bay university campus. While you're in the area visit the Book Display Room in the Institute of Pacific Studies building, not far from the Book Center. They sell interesting books by local authors published by the IPS itself.

The **Desai Bookshop** (tel. 314-088), on Thomson Street opposite the post office, and the **Zenon Bookshop** (tel. 312-477), on Victoria Parade opposite Sukuna Park, also have books on Fiji. The **Fiji Museum** shop sells a number of excellent books at reasonable prices.

You can purchase the hard-to-find *Pacific Islands Yearbook* at the **Fiji Times Limited Circulation Office** (tel. 304-111), 177 Victoria Parade. Several other good books on the Pacific are sold here.

Lotu Pasifika Productions (Box 208, Suva; tel. 301-314, fax 301-183), in the Pacific Conference of Churches building, 4 Thurston St., publishes a number of excellent books on regional social issues and carries Nuclear-Free Pacific posters. If you are at all interested in contemporary religion, pick up a copy of Manfred Ernst's *Winds of Change* here.

The **Government Bookshop,** shop No. 38 in the arcade at 68 Rodwell Rd. opposite the bus station (tel. 311-711; Monday to Thursday 0830-1630, Friday 0800-1600, Saturday 0800-1500), sells Fijian school textbooks, a Fijian dictionary, and official reports at very reasonable prices.

The **Pacific Concerns Resource Center** (Private Mail Bag, Suva, Fiji Islands; tel. 304-649, fax 304-755), 83 Amy St. off Toorak Road (enter from the rear of the building), sells a number of issue-related books and booklets on social and political problems in the South Pacific. The Center is the directing body of the Nuclear-Free and Independent Pacific (NFIP) movement, one of the few regional grass roots coalitions in the struggle against militarism and colonialism.

The **Coconut Frond** (tel. 311-963), 8 Disraeli Rd., looks like a fast-food place, but in a room in back they run the largest secondhand book exchange in Suva, though most of the books here are adventure or romance. Better titles are obtained at the **Missions to Seamen** on the main wharf (inside—go through the security gate) which trades paperback books, one for one (tel. 300-911; open weekdays 0900-1300/1330-1600).

Libraries

The **Suva City Library** on Victoria Parade is worth a look (tel. 313-433; Monday, Tuesday, Thursday, Friday 0930-1800, Wednesday 1200-1800, Saturday 0900-1300). Visitors can take out books upon payment of a F$11 fee, plus a F$10 refundable deposit (there's no charge to sit and read inside the library itself).

If you understand French, the **Alliance Française** (tel. 313-802), 77 Thakombau Rd., has an excellent selection of French books, magazines, and newspapers in their reading room which you're welcome to peruse weekdays from 0830-1200/1300-1700. Ask about their video and film evenings.

Travel Agents

Hunts Travel (Box 686, Suva; tel. 315-288), in the Dominion Building arcade behind the Fiji Visitors Bureau, is the place to pick up air tickets. They often know more about Air Pacific flights than the Air Pacific employees themselves!

Also compare **Travelworld Services** (tel. 315-870), 18 Waimanu Rd., which gives five percent discounts on plane tickets to other Pacific countries.

For domestic tickets on **Vanua Air** go to **Macquarie Tours & Travel** (Box 1170, Suva; tel. 315-855, fax 303-856), 12 Pier St. (opposite Sunflower Airlines).

Airline Offices

Reconfirm your onward flight at your airlines' Suva office: **Air Calédonie International** (tel. 302-133), 64 Renwick Rd. (in the arcade), **Air Fiji** (tel. 314-666), 185 Victoria Parade (also represents Air Vanuatu and Solomon Airlines), **Air Marshall Islands** (tel. 303-888), 30 Thomson St., **Air Nauru** (tel. 312-377), Ratu Sukuna House, 249 Victoria Parade, **Air New Zealand** (tel. 313-100), Queensland Insurance Centre, Victoria Parade, **Air Pacific** (tel. 384-955), CML Building, Victoria Parade, **Qantas Airways** (tel. 313-888), CMLA Building, Victoria Parade, and **Sunflower Airlines** (tel. 315-755), corner of Renwick Road and Pier Street (also represents Royal Tongan Airlines). While you're there, check your seat assignment.

HEALTH

You'll receive good attention at the **Gordon St. Medical Center** (tel. 313-355, fax 302-423), Gordon and Thurston streets (consultations F$17). There's a female doctor there. Fiji's only recompression chamber (tel. 305-154) is adjacent to this clinic (donated by the Cousteau Society in 1992).

The **J.P. Bayly Clinic** (tel. 315-888), 190 Rodwell Rd. opposite the Phoenix Cinema, is a church-operated low-income clinic.

The poorly marked **Health Office** (tel. 314-988; open weekdays 0800-1630), beside the bus stand on Rodwell Road, gives tetanus, polio, cholera, typhoid, and yellow fever vaccinations. They're F$6 each, except yellow fever which is F$16.

Two recommended dentists are Dr. Abdul S. Haroon (tel. 313-870), Suite 12, Epworth House off Nina Street (just down the hall from Patterson Shipping); and Dr. (Mrs.) S. Khan (tel. 302-289), Jannif Building, Victoria Parade.

TRANSPORTATION

Although nearly all international flights to Fiji arrive at Nandi, Suva is still the most important transportation center in the country. Interisland shipping crowds the waterfront, and if you can't find a ship going precisely your way at the time you want to travel, Air Fiji and Sunflower Airlines fly to all the major Fiji islands, while Air Pacific serves New Zealand, Tonga, and Samoa—all from Nausori Airport. Make the rounds of the shipping offices listed below, then head over to Walu Bay to check the information. Compare the price of a cabin and deck passage, and ask if meals are included. Start checking early, as many domestic services within Fiji are only once a week and trips to other countries are far less frequent.

A solid block of buses await your patronage at the market bus station near the harbor, with continuous local service, and frequent long-distance departures to Nandi and Lautoka. Many of the points of interest around Suva are accessible on foot, but if you wander too far, jump on any bus headed in the right direction and you'll end up back in the market. Taxis are also easy to find and relatively cheap (F$2 in the city center, F$3 to the suburbs).

Suva's bus station can be a little confusing as there are many different companies, and timetables are not posted. Most drivers know where a certain bus will park, so just ask. For information on bus services on Viti Levu and domestic flights from Nausori Airport, see "Getting Around" in the main Introduction chapter. Shipping services from Suva are covered below.

Ships to Other Countries

The Wednesday issue of the *Fiji Times* carries a special section on international shipping, though most are container ships which don't accept passengers. Most shipping is headed for Tonga and Samoa—there's not much going westward and actually getting on any of the ships mentioned below requires considerable persistence.

It's often easier to sign on as crew on a yacht. Try both yacht anchorages in Suva: put up a notice, ask around, etc.

Carpenters Shipping (tel. 312-244, fax 301-572), Neptune House, 4th Floor, Tofua Street, Walu Bay, is an agent for the *Moana III* and *Moana IV,* which sail occasionally from Suva to Wallis and Futuna, then on to Nouméa. They can't sell the ticket but will tell you when the ship is expected in, and you can book with the captain. This is a beautiful trip, not at all crowded between Fiji and Wallis. Book a cabin, however, if you're going right through to Nouméa.

Carpenters is also an agent for the monthly **Banks Line** service to Lautoka, Nouméa, Port Vila, Honiara, Port Moresby, and on to Great Britain. They cannot sell you a passenger ticket and will only tell you when the ship is due in and where it's headed. It's up to you to make arrangements personally with the captain, and the fare won't be cheap.

The **Tuvalu Embassy** (Box 14449, Suva; tel. 301-355, fax 301-023), 16 Gorrie St., runs the *Nivaga II* to Funafuti about four times a year, but the dates are variable. Tickets are sold by the **Pacific Forum Line** (tel. 315-444, fax 302-754), 187 Rodwell Rd., at F$124 without meals or F$200 with meals second class, F$139 without meals or F$215 with meals first class, F$70 deck. They only know about a week beforehand approximately when the ship may sail. After reaching Funafuti, the ship cruises the Tuvalu Group.

The Pacific Forum Line also knows about ships from Suva to Apia, Pago Pago, and Nuku'alofa, such as the Samoan government-owned *Forum Samoa* (every three weeks) and the Tongan government-owned *Fua Kavenga* (monthly service). They don't sell passenger tickets, so just ask when these ships will be in port, then go and talk to the captain, who is the only one who can decide if you'll be able to go.

Shipping Services Limited (G.P.O. Box 12671, Suva; tel. 313-354, fax 301-615), corner of Robertson and Rodwell roads (behind Suva Supermarket), also knows the departure dates of container ships to Tonga and Samoa. Again, they don't sell passenger tickets and you must see the captain in person to arrange passage.

When they need hands, **Sofrana Unilines** ships sometimes accept work-a-passage crew for New Zealand, Australia, or other ports. You must arrange this with the captain. Their Suva office (tel. 304-528, fax 300-951) is in the same building as Carpenters Shipping.

Ships to Other Fijian Islands

Quite a few ships leave Suva on Saturday, but none depart on Sunday. **Patterson Brothers** (G.P.O. Box 1041, Suva; tel. 315-644, fax 301-652), Suite 1, 1st Floor, Epworth Arcade off Nina Street, takes obligatory reservations for the Suva-Natovi-Nambouwalu-Lambasa bus/ferry/bus combination, which departs Suva's Western Bus Stand Tuesday to Saturday at 0400. Fares from Suva are F$30 to Nambouwalu or F$38 right through to Lambasa, an excellent 10-hour trip.

Patterson's *Princess Ashika* or *Ovalau II* links Suva to Ngau (five hours, F$29), Koro (10 hours, F$31), Savusavu (14.5 hours, F$31), and Taveuni (22 hours, F$36) weekly, departing Muaiwalu Jetty, Walu Bay, at midnight Monday. Thursday at 2200 one of these ships departs Suva for Kandavu (six hours, F$34). Forthcoming departures are listed on a blackboard in their Suva office and the schedule varies slightly each week. Patterson Brothers also has offices in Lambasa, Lautoka, Levuka, Savusavu, and Taveuni.

Consort Shipping Line (G.P.O. Box 152, Suva; tel. 302-877, fax 303-389), in the Dominion House arcade on Thomson Street, operates the MV *Spirit of Free Enterprise* (popularly known as the "Sofe"), a 450-passenger car ferry which formerly shuttled between the north and south islands of New Zealand. The *Sofe* leaves Suva on Wednesday at 0500 and Saturday at 1800 for Savusavu (13 hours, F$30 one-way) and Taveuni (23 hours, F$35). The ship also calls at Koro. The northbound Saturday voyage spends all day Sunday tied up at Savusavu and Taveuni passengers can get off and walk around. The two-berth cabins of the *Sofe* are quite comfortable and excellent value at F$55 pp to Savusavu or F$66 pp to Taveuni. For a refundable F$20 deposit the purser will give you the key to your cabin, allowing you to wander around the ship without worrying about your luggage. Another advantage of taking a cabin is that you're able to order meals in the pleasant first-class restaurant. Only cabin passengers may do this and the meals are excellent value at F$3.

Beachcomber Cruises offers a bus/ferry connection from Suva to Savusavu via Natovi every morning except Sunday (F$60). Their high-speed catamaran *Ndrondrolangi* takes only two hours for the crossing from Natovi to Vanua Levu. The Fiji Visitors Bureau will have the address of their booking office.

Ask on the smaller vessels tied up at Muaiwalu Jetty, Walu Bay, for passage to Nairai, Ngau, Kandavu, etc. Don't believe the first person who tells you there's no boat going where you want—*ask around*. **Walu Shipping** (tel. 312-668) at the Ports Authority Building, Rona Street, Walu Bay, has regular services to the Lau Group on the MV *Katika,* costing F$65 deck (no cabins) to any island in Lau. Food is included in the price and on the outward journey it will probably be okay, but on the return don't expect much more than rice and tea.

The **Marine Department** (tel. 315-266) at Walu Bay handles government barges to all of the Fiji Islands, but tourists are not usually accepted on those boats. If you're planning a long voyage by interisland ship, a big bundle of kava roots to captain and crew as a token of appreciation for their hospitality works wonders.

Keep in mind that all of the ferry departure times mentioned above and elsewhere in this book are only indications of what was true in the past. It's essential to check with the company office for current departure times during the week you wish to travel.

To Ovalau Island

Air Fiji flies from Suva to Levuka (F$33) two or three times a day, but the most popular trips are the bus/launch/bus combinations via Natovi or Mbau Landing. Two different companies operate these trips, which take four or five hours

right through. Reservations are recommended on Saturday and public holidays.

The **Patterson Brothers** service (book at their office mentioned above) leaves from the Western Bus Stand in Suva Monday to Saturday at 1400 (F$19). This express bus goes from Suva to Natovi, where it drives onto a ferry to Mburesala on Ovalau, then continues on to Levuka, where it arrives around 1730. For the return journey you leave the Patterson Brothers office in Levuka Monday to Saturday at 0500, arriving in Suva at 0830. Tickets must be purchased in advance at the office—no exceptions.

A second choice is the *Emosi Express,* departing Suva Monday, Wednesday, Friday, and Saturday at 1200 for Mbau Landing, where you board a speedboat powered by two 40-horsepower Yamaha engines to Leleuvia Island and Levuka (four hours, F$18 one-way). A free stopover on Leleuvia is possible. To book this, go to Rosie Tours, 46 Gordon St. (tel. 313-366). For variety and the most convenient timings, we recommend traveling with Patterson northbound and Emosi southbound. It's a beautiful circle trip not to be missed (sit up on the boat's roof if it's nice weather).

Tours

For information on the exciting day-trips from Suva offered by **Wilderness Adventures** (Box 1389, Suva; tel. 386-498, fax 300-584), turn to "Navua and Vicinity" in the Southwest Viti Levu chapter and to "Nausori and Vicinity" in this chapter. Wilderness also runs excellent two-hour city sightseeing tours three times a day (adults F$25, children under 12 years F$15). These trips can be booked through any travel agency in Suva. Another company called **Livai Tours** (tel. 394-251) offers almost identical trips.

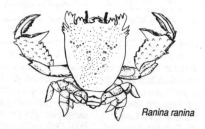

Ranina ranina

(preceding page) the reef off Ovalau (Don Pitcher);
(this page top) Beachcomber Island; (this page bottom) the tourist boat *Tui Tai*
(photos this page courtesy Islands in the Sun)

NAUSORI AND VICINITY

NAUSORI

In 1881 the Rewa River town of Nausori, 19 km northeast of Suva, was chosen as the site of Fiji's first large sugar mill, which operated until 1959. In those early days it was incorrectly believed that sugarcane grew better on the wetter eastern side of the island. Today cane is grown only on the drier, sunnier western sides of Viti Levu and Vanua Levu. The old sugar mill is now a rice mill and storage depot, as the Rewa Valley has become a major rice-producing area.

Nausori is Fiji's fifth-largest city (population 15,000) and the headquarters of Central Division, plus Rewa and Tailevu provinces. The nine-span bridge across the river here was built in 1937. The town is best known for its large international airport three km southeast, built as a fighter strip to defend Fiji's capital during WW II. There are several banks in Nausori.

Accommodations and Food
The **Kings Nausori Hotel** (Box 67, Nausori; tel. 478-833), 99 Kings Rd., beside the rice mill, has three grubby rooms with private bath and hot water at F$25 single or double. The dingy rooms are attached to the noisy bar and are rented mostly for "short times"—only of interest to people on the make. Due to licensing restrictions, women are not admitted to the hotel bar.

A far nicer drinking place is the **Whistling Duck Pub,** a block from the bus station in the center of town (ask directions). Upstairs in the adjacent building is a good, inexpensive restaurant where you can get cold beer with your curries (Monday to Wednesday 1200-1430, Thursday to Saturday 1200-1430/1800-2100).

From Nausori
Local buses to the airport (35 cents) and Suva (80 cents) are fairly frequent, but the last bus to Suva is at 2100. You can also catch Sunbeam Transport express buses to Lautoka from Nausori at 0715, 1400, and 1745 (5.5 hours).

AROUND NAUSORI

Rewa Delta
Take a bus from Nausori to Nakelo Landing to explore the heavily populated Rewa River Delta. Many outboards leave from Nakelo to take villagers to their riverside homes and passenger fares are under a dollar for short trips. Larger boats leave sporadically from Nakelo for Levuka, Ngau, and Koro, but finding one would be pure chance. Some also depart from nearby Wainimbokasi Landing.

Wilderness Adventures (Box 1389, Suva; tel. 386-498) runs half-day boat tours of the Rewa Delta, with stops at Nailili Catholic Mission to visit St. Joseph's Church (1901), and at Nambua village, where Fijian pottery is still made. The tour leaves twice daily at 0930 and 1300, and the F$35 pp price includes minibus transfers from Suva hotels (it only operates if at least four people sign up). A full-day delta trip with lunch at Nasilai village is F$49 (F$25 for children). This is a refreshing change of pace.

Mbau Island
Mbau, a tiny, eight-hectare island just east of Viti Levu, has a special place in Fiji's history as this was the seat of High Chief Cakobau, who used European cannons and muskets to subdue most of western Fiji in the 1850s. At its pinnacle Mbau had a population of 3,000, hundreds of war canoes to guard its waters, and over 20 temples on the island's central plain. After the Battle of Verata on Viti Levu in 1839, Cakobau and his father, Tanoa, presented 260 bodies of men, women, and children to their closest friends and allied chiefs for gastronomical purposes. Fifteen years after this slaughter, Cakobau converted to Christianity and prohibited cannibalism on Mbau. In 1867 he became a sovereign, crowned by European traders and planters desiring a stable government in Fiji to protect their interests.

For a lively account of Mbau in the mid-19th century read *Life in Feejee—Five Years Among the Cannibals* by Mary Wallis (available at the Fiji Museum in Suva).

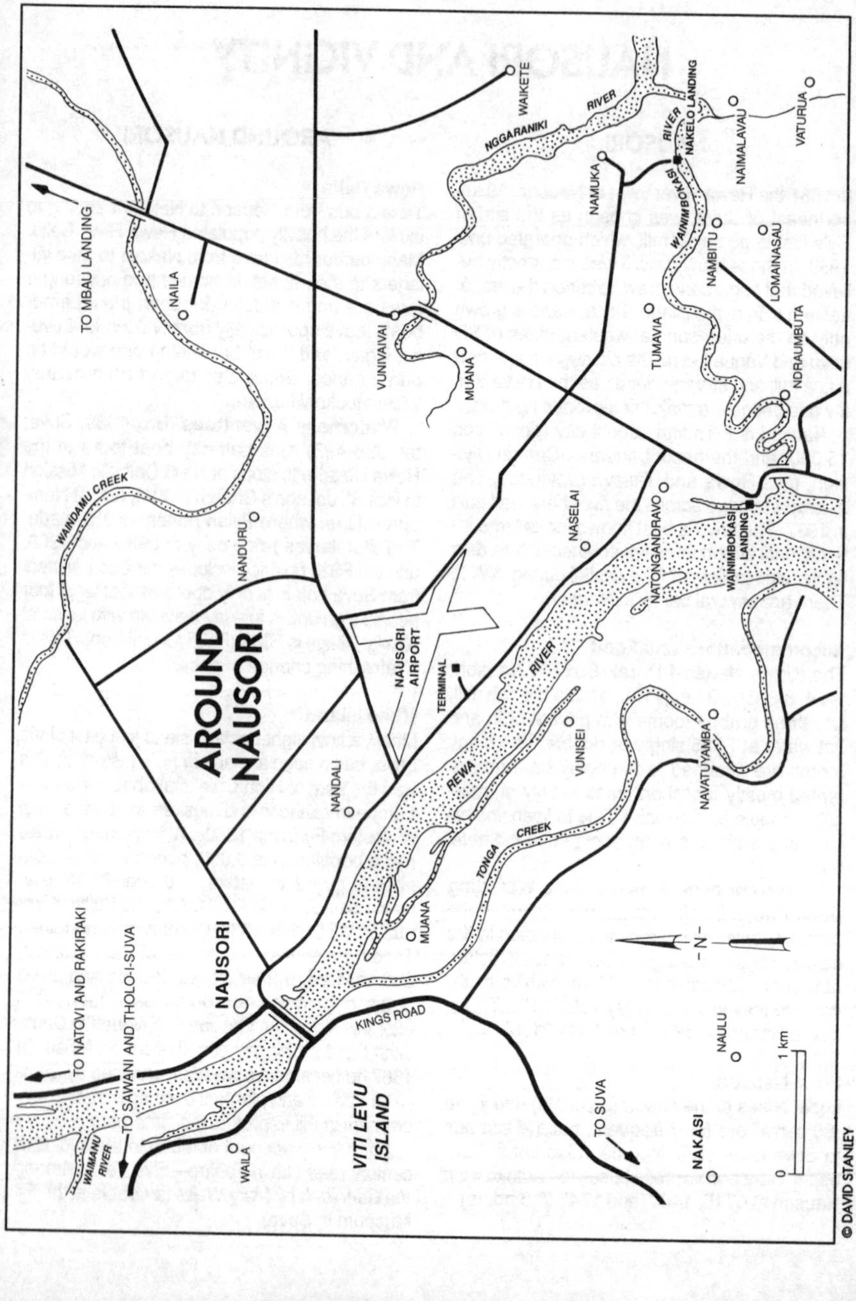

AROUND NAUSORI

TO MBAU LANDING

WAIKETE

NGGARANIKI RIVER

RIVER

NAILA

NAMUKA

WAINIMBOKASI RIVER

NAKELO LANDING

NAIMALAVAU

VATURUA

VUNIVAIVAI

MUANA

TUMAVIA

NAMBITU

LOMAINASAU

NDRAUMBUTA

WAINDAMU CREEK

NANDURU

NASELAI

AITONGANDRAVO

WAINIMBOKASI LANDING

NANDALI

Nausori Airport

TERMINAL

REWA RIVER

VUNISEI

TONGA CREEK

NAVATUVAMBA

MUANA

TO NATOVI AND RAKIRAKI

TO SAWANI AND THOLO-I-SUVA

NAUSORI

KINGS ROAD

VITI LEVU ISLAND

TO SUVA

NAKASI

NAULU

WAIMANU RIVER

WAILA

-N-

1 km

0

© DAVID STANLEY

Sights of Mbau

The great stone slabs that form docks and sea-walls around much of the island once accommodated Mbau's fleet of war canoes. The graves of the Cakobau family and many of the old chiefs lie on the hilltop behind the school. The large,

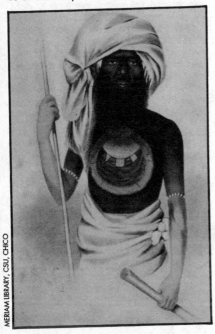

MERIAM LIBRARY, CSU, CHICO

Tanoa, the cannibal king of Mbau. Tanoa was about 65 years of age in 1840 when the United States Exploring Expedition, under Lt. Charles Wilkes, toured Fiji. His rise to power threw the island into several years of strife, as Tanoa had to do away with virtually every minor chief who challenged his right to rule. With long colorful pennants playing from the mast and thousands of Cypraea ovula shells decorating the hull, his 30-meter outrigger canoe was the fastest in the region. One of Tanoa's favorite sports was overtaking and ramming smaller canoes at sea. The survivors were then fair game for whoever could catch and keep them. At feasts where most nobles were expected to provide a pig, Tanoa always furnished a human body. Wilkes included this sketch of Tanoa in volume three of the Expedition's monumental Narrative, published in 1845.

sturdy stone church located near the provincial offices was the first Christian church in Fiji. Inside its nearly one-meter-thick walls, just in front of the altar, is the old sacrificial stone once used for human sacrifices, today the baptismal font. Now painted white, this font was once known as King Cakobau's "skull crusher." It's said a thousand brains were splattered against it. Across from the church are huge ancient trees and the thatched Council House on the site of the onetime temple of the war god Cagawalu. The family of the late Sir George Cakobau, governor-general of Fiji 1973-82, has a large traditional-style home on the island. You can see everything on the island in an hour or so.

Getting There

Take the Mbau bus (five daily, 50 cents) from Nausori to Mbau Landing where there are outboards to cross over to the island. Be aware that Mbau is not considered a tourist attraction, and from time to time visitors are prevented from going to the island. It's important to get someone to invite you across, which they'll do willingly if you show a genuine interest in Fijian history. Like most Fijians, the inhabitants of Mbau are very friendly people. Bring a big bundle of *waka* for the *turanga-ni-koro,* and ask permission very politely to be shown around. There could be some confusion about who's to receive the *sevusevu,* however, as everyone on Mbau's a chief! The more respectable your dress and demeanor, the better your chances of success. If you're told to contact the Ministry of Fijian Affairs in Suva, just depart gracefully as that's only their way of saying no. After all, it's up to them. Alternatively, you get a good close look at Mbau from the *Emosi Express* ferry service to/from Levuka via Leleuvia.

Viwa Island

Before Cakobau adopted Christianity in 1854, Methodist missionaries working for this effect resided on Viwa Island, just across the water from Mbau. Here the first Fijian New Testament was printed in 1847; Rev. John Hunt, who did the translation, lies buried in the graveyard beside the church that bears his name.

Viwa is a good alternative if you aren't invited to visit Mbau itself. To reach the island, hire an outboard at Mbau Landing. If you're lucky, you'll be able to join some locals who are going. A single Fijian village stands on the island.

Tomberua Island

Tomberua Island Resort (Michael Dennis, Box 567, Suva; tel. 479-177, fax 302-215), on a tiny reef island off the east tip of Viti Levu, caters to upmarket honeymooners, families, and professionals. Built in 1968, this was one of Fiji's first outer-island resorts. The 14 thatched *mbures* are designed in the purest Fijian style, yet it's all very luxurious and the small size means peace and quiet. The tariff is F$319/352/404 single/double/triple, plus F$81 pp for three gourmet meals, F$68 pp for two meals; baby-sitters are F$13 a day. Two children under 16 sharing with adults are accommodated free and they're fed for half price or less. Tomberua is out of eastern Viti Levu's wet belt, so it doesn't

get a lot of rain like nearby Suva, and weather permitting, all meals are served outdoors. Friday nights there's a *lovo* and *meke*.

Don't expect tennis courts or a golf course at Tomberua, though believe it or not, there's tropical golfing on the reef at low tide! (Nine holes from 90-180 meters, course par 27, clubs and balls provided free.) Deep-sea fishing is F$44 an hour and scuba diving F$60 a dive. All other activities are free, including snorkeling, sailing, windsurfing, and boat trips to a bird sanctuary or mangrove forest. The launch transfer from Nakelo landing to Tomberua is F$24 pp each way; a Turtle Airways seaplane from Nandi will be F$330 pp one-way (minimum of three persons).

SALVATORE CASA

NORTHERN VITI LEVU

NORTHWEST OF NAUSORI

Vunindawa

If you have a few days to spare, consider exploring the river country northwest of Nausori. The main center of Naitasiri Province is Vunindawa on the Wainimala River, a big village with four stores, a hospital, a post office, a police station, two schools, and a provincial office. There are five buses a day except Sunday from Suva to Vunindawa, but no bus connection to Korovou or Monasavu.

Go for a swim in the river or borrow a horse to ride around the countryside. Stroll two km down the road to Waindawara, where there's a free hourly punt near the point where the Wainimbuka and Wainimala rivers unite to form the mighty Rewa River. Take a whole day to hike up to Nairukuruku and Navuniyasi and back.

River-Running

There's an exciting bamboo raft (mbilimbili) trip through the Waingga Gorge between Naitauvoli and Naivuthini, two villages on the Cross-Island Highway west of Vunindawa. Two men with long poles guide each raft through the froth-ing rapids as the seated visitor views towering boulders enveloped in jungle. Reservations for the two-hour ride must be made in advance because an individual mbilimbili will have to be constructed for you. (There's no way to get a used mbilimbili back up to Naitauvoli.)

Write Turangi-ni-koro, Naitauvoli village, Wainimala, Naitasiri, P.A. Naikasanga, Fiji Islands, at least two weeks ahead, giving the exact date of your arrival in the village and the number in your party. Mr. Ilai Naibose (tel. 361-940) in Suva may be able to help you arrange this trip (and if not, ask at the Fiji Visitors Bureau). No trips are made on Sunday. If you plan to spend the night at Naitauvoli, specify whether you require imported European-style food or will be satisfied with local village produce. If you stay overnight, a sevusevu and monetary contribution to your hosts are expected in addition to the fee for the raft trip. One bus a day (except Sunday) departs Suva for Naivuthini at 1455; once there you'd have to look for a carrier on to Naitauvoli. There's no bus service on the Cross-Island Highway to Monasavu beyond Naivuthini.

THE TRANS-VITI LEVU TREK

For experienced hikers there's a rugged two-day trek from the Cross-Island Highway to Waini-makutu, up and down jungle river valleys through the rainforest. It will take a strong, fast hiker about three hours from Mbalea on the highway to Nasa-va, then another four over the ridge to Waini-makutu. The Trans-Viti Levu Trek passes through several large Fijian villages and gives you a good cross section of village life.

On this traditional route, you'll meet people going down the track on horseback or on foot. Since you must cross the rivers innumerable times, the trek is probably impossible for visitors during the rainy season (December to April), although the locals still manage to do it. If it's been raining, sections of the trail become a quagmire, stirred up by horses' hooves. Hiking boots aren't much use here; you'd be better off with shorts and an old pair of running shoes in which to wade across the rivers. There are many refreshing places to swim along the way. Some of the villages have small trade stores, but you're better off carrying your own food. Pack some *yanggona* as well. You can always give it away if someone invites you in.

But remember, you are not the first to undertake this walk; the villagers have played host to trekkers many times and some previous hikers have not shown much consideration to local residents along the track. Unless you have been specifically invited, do not presume automatic hospitality. If a villager provides food or a service, be prepared to offer adequate payment. This applies equally to the Singatoka River Trek. Camping is a good alternative, so take your tent if you have one.

The Route

Bus service on the Cross-Island Highway from Suva to Nandarivatu was interrupted in 1993 by Hurricane Keno, which destroyed the bridge at Lutu just beyond **Mbalea,** the Trans-Viti Levu trailhead. Buses from Suva now go only as far as Naivuthini, so instead look for a carrier bound for Lutu, which could drop you at Mbalea. In Suva, the Lutu carriers park near Santa Ram Supermarket, corner of Robertson Road and Struan Street near the market, and most depart around midday.

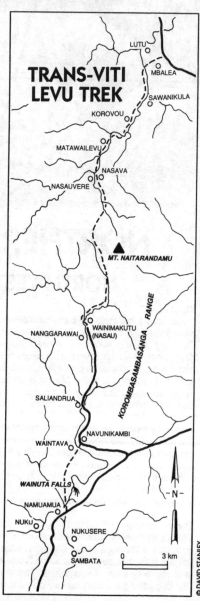

TRANS-VITI LEVU TREK

© DAVID STANLEY

From Mbalea walk down to the Wainimala River, which must be crossed three times before you reach the bank opposite Sawanikula. These crossings can be dangerous and well-nigh impossible in the rainy season, in which case it's better to stop and wait for some local people who might help you across. From Sawanikula it's not far to **Korovou**, a fairly large village with a clinic and two stores. Between Korovou and **Nasava** you cross the Wainimala River 14 times, but it's easier because you're farther upstream. Try to reach Nasava on the first day. If you sleep at Korovou you'll need an early start and a brisk pace to get to the first village south of the divide before nightfall on the second day.

From Nasava, follow the course of the Waisomo Creek up through a small gorge and past a waterfall. You zigzag back and forth across the creek all the way up almost to the divide. After a steep incline you cross to the south coast watershed. There's a clearing among the bamboo groves on top where you could camp, but there's no water. Before **Wainimakutu** (Nasau) the scenery gets better as you enter a wide valley with Mt. Naitarandamu (1,152 meters) behind you and the jagged outline of the unscaled Korombasambasanga Range to your left. Wainimakutu is a large village with two stores and bus service to Suva twice a day, at 0600 and 1300 Monday to Friday only. This fact makes it wise to begin your trek early in the week in order not to get stuck here on a weekend.

Namosi

The bus from Wainimakutu to Suva goes via **Namosi**, spectacularly situated below massive Mt. Voma (927 meters), with sheer stone cliffs on all sides. You can climb Mt. Voma in a day from Namosi for a sweeping view of much of Viti Levu. It's steep but not too difficult. Allow at least four hours up and down (guides can be hired at Namosi village). Visit the old Catholic church at Namosi.

There are low-grade copper deposits estimated at one-half million tonnes at the foot of the Korombasambasanga Range, which Rupert Brooke called the "Gateway to Hell," 14 km north of Namosi by road. No mining has begun due to depressed world prices and high production costs, though feasibility studies continue. A 1979 study indicated that an investment of F$1 billion would be required.

NORTHERN VITI LEVU

Northern Viti Levu has far more spectacular landscapes than the southern side of the island, and if you can only travel one way by road between Suva and Nandi, you're better off taking the northern route. Kings Road is now paved from Suva north to Korovou, then again from Ellington Wharf to Lautoka. Roadwork continues between Korovou and Ellington, but even now the smooth gravel road is good. Since Kings Road follows the Wainimbuka River from Wailotua village almost all the way to Viti Levu Bay, you get a good glimpse of the island's interior, and the north coast west of Rakiraki is breathtaking. Many visitors stop for a few days at Nananu-i-Ra Island off Rakiraki, and intrepid hikers can trek south down the Singatoka River from the hill station of Nandarivatu.

Korovou to Natovi and Beyond

A good paved highway runs 31 km north from Nausori to **Korovou**, a small town on the east side of Viti Levu at the junction of Kings Road and the road to **Natovi**, terminus of the Ovalau and Vanua Levu ferries. Its crossroads position in the heart of Tailevu Province makes Korovou an important stop for buses plying the northern route around the island. Sunbeam Transport express buses leave Korovou for Lautoka at 0800, 1500, and 1830 (five hours). (Be aware that because "korovou" means "new village," there are many places called that in Fiji—don't mix them up.)

The **Tailevu Hotel** (Box 189, Korovou; tel. 430-028), on a hill overlooking the river just across a bridge from Korovou, has 14 rooms at F$22/30 single/double, and four cottages with cooking facilities at F$40 for up to four persons. Camping is F$8 a night. This colonial-style hotel features a large bar and restaurant, and it makes a good base for visiting the surrounding area.

For a sweeping view of the entire Tailevu area, climb **Mt. Tova** (647 meters) in a day from

Silana village, eight km northwest of Nang-gatawa.

The large dairy farms along the highway just west of Korovou were set up after WW I. At Wailotua No. 1, 20 km west of Korovou, is a large **cave** (admission F$5) right beside the village and easily accessible from the road. One stalactite in the cave is shaped like a six-headed snake.

Ra Province

The old Catholic Church of St. Francis Xavier at **Naiserelangi**, on a hilltop above Navunimbitu Catholic School, on Kings Road about 25 km southeast of Rakiraki, was beautifully decorated with frescoes by Jean Charlot in 1962-63. Typical Fijian motifs such as the *tambua, tanoa,* and *yanggona* blend in the powerful composition behind the altar. Father Pierre Chanel, who was martyred on Futuna Island in 1841, appears on the left holding the weapon that killed him, a war club. Christ and the Madonna are portrayed in black. The church is worth stopping to see, and provided it's not too late in the day, you'll find an onward bus. At Nanukuloa village just north of here is the headquarters of Ra Province.

This part of northern Viti Levu is known as **Rakiraki** but the main town is called **Vaileka.** The Penang Sugar Mill was erected here in 1881 and the mill is connected by an 11-km cane railway to Ellington Wharf, where the sugar is loaded aboard ships. The sugar mill is about a kilometer from the main business section of Vaileka, and the Fiji Sugar Corporation owns the golf course here. There are three banks and a large produce market in the town, but most visitors pass through on their way to Nananu-i-Ra Island. A taxi from Vaileka to Ellington Wharf will run F$7. Otherwise take a local bus east on Kings Road to the turnoff and walk two km down to the wharf. The express buses don't stop at the turnoff, but all buses from Lautoka (F$4) and Suva (F$7) stop in Vaileka.

The **Rakiraki Hotel** (Box 31, Rakiraki; tel. 694-101, fax 694-545) on Kings Road has 36 a/c rooms with fridge and private bath at F$100 single or double, and 10 fan-cooled rooms at F$33/38/44 single/double/triple. When several people request it, one of the fan-cooled rooms becomes "dormitory accommodation" with everyone contributing to make up the regular room rate. If you arrive alone, however, they'll probably insist that you pay the single rate, in which case bargaining over the price sometimes works. There are no communal cooking facilities. The reception area and restaurant occupy the core of the original hotel dating back to 1945; the two-story accommodations blocks were added much later. Extensive gardens surround the hotel. The Rakiraki's outdoor bowling green draws middle-aged lawn bowling enthusiasts from Australia and New Zealand, the sort that like old-fashioned "colonial" touches like the typed daily menu featuring British-Indian curry dishes, and gin and tonic in the afternoon. This hotel is a couple of km north of Vaileka and only the local or "stage" buses will drop you off on Kings Road right in front of the hotel (the express buses will drop you in Vaileka).

Wananavu Beach Resort (General Delivery, Rakiraki; tel. 694-433, fax 694-499), on Volivoli Road facing Nananu-i-Ra Island, four km off Kings Road, opened in 1994. There are 14 self-contained rooms at F$85 for up to three people, and two eight-bedded dormitories at F$16 pp, breakfast included. No cooking facilities are provided, but each regular room does have a fridge. Ra Divers offers scuba diving from the resort, and a variety of other water sports are available.

Right beside Kings Road, just a hundred meters west of the turnoff to Vaileka, is the grave of **Ratu Udre Udre,** the cannibal king of this region who is alleged to have consumed 99 corpses. **Navatu Rock,** a few kilometers west of Vaileka, was the jumping-off point for the disembodied spirits of the ancient Fijians. A fortified village once stood on its summit. Navatu's triangular shape is duplicated by a small island just offshore.

The **Nakauvandra Range,** towering south of Rakiraki, is the traditional home of the Fijian serpent-god Degei, who is said to dwell in a cave on the summit of Mt. Uluda (866 meters). This "cave" is little more than a cleft in the rock. To climb the Nakauvandra Range, which the local Fijians look upon as their primeval homeland, permission must be obtained from the chief of Vatukathevatheva village who will provide guides. A *sevusevu* should be presented.

NANANU-I-RA ISLAND

This small 355-hectare island, three km off the northernmost tip of Viti Levu, is a good place to spend some time amid perfect tranquility and beauty without the commercialization of the resorts off Nandi. Here too the climate is dry and sunny, and there are great beaches, reefs, snorkeling, walks, sunsets, and moonrises over the water—only roads are missing. Seven or eight separate white sandy beaches lie scattered around the island. The island is large enough that you won't ever feel confined. In the early 19th century Nananu-i-Ra's original Fijian inhabitants were wiped out by disease and tribal warfare, and an heir sold the island to the Europeans whose descendants now operate small resorts and a 219-hectare plantation on the island.

The northern two-thirds of Nananu-i-Ra Island, including all of the land around Kontiki Island Lodge, is owned by Mrs. Louise Harper of southern California, who bought it for a mere US$200,000 in 1966 (she also owns a sizable chunk of Proctor & Gamble back in the States). Today some 22 head of Harper cattle graze beneath coconuts on the Harper Plantation, and the plantation management actively discourages trespassing by tourists. The plantation manager lives in a house adjoining Kontiki, and it's common courtesy to ask his permission before climbing the hill behind the lodge.

To hike right around Nananu-i-Ra on the beach takes about four hours of steady going, or all day if you stop for picnicking and snorkeling. The thickest section of mangroves is between Kontiki and Mokusingas Island Resort, on the back side of the island, and this stretch is best covered at low tide. However you do it, at some point you'll probably have to take off your shoes and wade through water just over your ankles, but it's still a very nice walk. The entire coastline is public, but only as far as two meters above the high tide line. Avoid becoming stranded by high tide and forced to cut across Harper land.

An American couple, Edward and Betty Morris, have lived next to Nananu Beach Cottages since 1970. Ed is a former president of the International Brotherhood of Magicians and he doesn't mind sharing his magic with visitors, when he feels like it.

Ra Divers (Box 417, Rakiraki; tel. 694-511) offers scuba diving at F$40 for one tank, F$75 for two tanks. Snorkelers can go along for F$7, if space is available. Ra Diver's resort course costs F$75, full certification F$300. Add 10% tax to all rates. They pick up clients regularly from Betham's, Charley's, and Kontiki.

Accommodations

The number of beds on Nananu-i-Ra is limited, and with the island's growing popularity, it's strongly recommended that you call ahead to one of the resorts and arrange to be picked up at Ellington Wharf. Of course, none of the innkeepers bother coming over in search of guests when

NANANU - I - RA

ONE BAY

KONTIKI ISLAND LODGE ● ● PLANTATION OFFICE

THE HARPER PLANTATION

NAWAWA BAY

NANANU - I - RA ISLAND

WAINIMOLOVO BAY

MOKUSINGAS ISLAND RESORT

NANANU BEACH COTTAGES

BETHAM'S BUNGALOWS

CHARLEY'S PLACE

RA DIVERS ■

LOMANISUE BAY

- N -

YANUTHA ISLAND

0   1km

© DAVID STANLEY

they're fully booked. There's no public telephone at Ellington Wharf.

If you want an individual room or *mbure* make 100% sure one is available, otherwise you could end up spending quite a few nights in the dormitory waiting for one to become free. All the budget places have cooking facilities, but it's necessary to take most of your own supplies, as shopping possibilities on the island are very limited. There's a large market and several supermarkets in Vaileka where you can buy all the supplies you need. If you run out, groceries can be ordered from Vaileka for a small service charge and Betham's Bungalows runs a small grocery store with a few things (including beer). Also bring enough cash, as only the Mokusingas Island Resort accepts credit cards. Add 10% tax to all prices quoted below.

Of all the budget places on Nananu-i-Ra, **Kontiki Island Lodge** (Box 87, Rakiraki; tel. 694-290) has more of the feeling of a genuine resort, with ample opportunity for group activities. Because they cater mostly to backpackers, the dormitory guests are treated the same as everyone else, and the atmosphere is friendly and congenial. It's also ideal if you want to do your own thing, as the long deserted beach facing One Bay is just a 20-minute walk away. Kontiki is at the unspoiled north end of the island, with no other resorts or houses (except the Harper caretaker) nearby. It's quite popular and on Saturday night they're full (reservations essential).

Kontiki offers three modern self-catering bungalows, each with two double rooms and three dorm beds. If you want privacy ask for one of the four rooms in the two thatched duplex *mbures*. Either way, dormitory beds are F$12 pp and double rooms F$26. Camping is not allowed. It's basic but well maintained. All guests have access to fridges and cooking facilities, and a few very basic supplies are sold, as well as cold beer. The staff will serve you a generous breakfast (F$2.50) and dinner (F$5) upon request. In the evening everyone gets together and swaps stories around the kava bowl. The generator runs until 2200. Enjoy the beach, snorkel, and rest—four nights is the average stay, though some people stay four weeks. If you get the right room, this could be one of the nicest low-budget places you'll encounter on your South Pacific trip.

At the other end of Nananu-i-Ra, a one-hour walk along the beach at low tide, are three other inexpensive places to stay, all offering cooking facilities, but no camping. They experience more speedboat noise than Kontiki but are less crowded and perhaps preferable for a restful holiday. They almost always have a few free beds in the dorms.

Nananu Beach Cottages (Box 140, Rakiraki; tel. 694-633), also known as "MacDonald's" and "Dive Lodge," offers three individual houses at F$50 single or double, plus F$6 pp for additional persons, and two five-bed dormitory rooms at F$13 pp. The dorms feature bunk beds and the cooking facilities are in the same room. It's peaceful and attractive with a private wharf and pontoon off their beach. The scuba diving operation based here is not always functioning, so check when booking if it makes a difference.

Right next to MacDonald's is **Betham's Bungalows** (Box 5, Rakiraki; tel. 694-132) with four cement-block duplex houses at F$44 single or double, F$53 triple, plus two dormitories, one with 10 beds and another with eight beds, at F$13 pp.

Sharing the same high sandy beach with MacDonald's and Betham's is **Charley's Place** (Charley and Louise Anthony, Box 407, Rakiraki; tel. 694-676) run by a delightful, friendly family. The dormitory building has six beds (F$12 each) in the same room as the cooking facilities, plus one double room (F$30). The adjacent bungalow can sleep up to six people at F$50 for two, plus F$5 for each additional person. Both buildings are on a hill and you can watch the sunrise on one side and the sunset on the other. Charley's also rents two other houses further down the beach, one at F$40 double, another at F$50 double.

In August 1991 **Mokusingas Island Resort** (Box 268, Rakiraki; tel. 694-449, fax 694-404) opened on Nananu-i-Ra. The 20 comfortable bungalows with fridge are F$175 for up to three persons, but cooking facilities are not provided and meals at the restaurant/bar are extra (F$74 pp meal plan). The resort's dive shop offers scuba diving at F$55 from a boat or F$26 from shore. A five-day PADI certification course costs F$400. To create a diving attraction, the 43-

meter *Papuan Explorer* was scuttled in 25 meters of water, 60 meters off the 189-meter Mokusingas jetty, which curves out into the sheltered lagoon. The snorkeling off the wharf is good, especially at low tide, with lots of coral and fish. Don't be disappointed by the skimpy little beach facing a mudflat you first see when you arrive at the jetty: the mile-long picture-postcard beach in their brochure is a few minutes away over the hill on the other side of the island. All the resort facilities, including the restaurant, bar, and dive shop, are strictly for house guests only.

Getting There
Boat transfers from Ellington Wharf to Nananu-i-Ra are F$14-18 pp return (20 minutes), though the resorts may levy a surcharge if you're alone. Check prices when you call to make your accommodation booking. A taxi to Ellington Wharf from the express bus stop next to the market in Vaileka is F$7 for the car. Several budget hotels in Nandi (including Sunny Holiday Motel, the Nandi Town Motel, and Kontiki Nandi) arrange minibus rides from Nandi direct to Ellington Wharf at F$26 pp, though it's cheaper to take an express bus from Lautoka to Vaileka, then a taxi to the landing.

As you return to Ellington Wharf from Nananu-i-Ra, taxis will be waiting to whisk you to Vaileka where you'll connect with the express buses (share the F$7 taxi fare with other travelers to cut costs). You could also hike two km out to the main highway and try to flag down a bus, but only local buses will stop at this junction.

Patterson Brothers operates a car ferry service between Ellington Wharf and Nambouwalu on Tuesday, Thursday, and Saturday, a great shortcut to/from Vanua Levu (F$26.40 one-way). The ferry leaves Ellington Wharf at the difficult hour of 0600, so it's more useful as a way of coming here from Vanua Levu since it departs Nambouwalu at 1130. There's a connecting bus to/from Lambasa. Sometimes you can arrange to spend the night on the boat at Ellington (ask at the Patterson Brothers office in Lautoka).

NORTHWESTERN VITI LEVU

TAVUA

West of Rakiraki, Kings Road gets much better, and you pass the Yanggara Cattle Ranch where Fijian cowboys keep 5,500 head of cattle and 200 horses on a 7,000-hectare spread enclosed by an 80-km fence. At Tavua, an important junction on the north coast, buses on the north coast highways meet the daily service to Nandarivatu. Catching a bus from Tavua to Vaileka, Vatukoula, or Lautoka is no problem, but the bus to Nandarivatu only leaves at 1500. There are two banks in Tavua.

The two-story **Tavua Hotel** (Box 81, Tavua; tel. 680-522, fax 680-390), an old wooden building on a hill, a five-minute walk from the bus stop, has 11 rooms with bath at F$33/44 single/double. The **Golden Eagle Restaurant** (tel. 680-635) on Kings Road in Tavua serves standard Indian curries.

VATUKOULA

In 1932 gold was discovered at Vatukoula, eight km south of Tavua, by an old Australian prospector named Bill Borthwick. Two years later Borthwick and his partner, Peter Costello, sold their stake to an Australian company, and in 1935 the **Emperor Gold Mine** opened. In 1977 there was a major strike at the mine and the government had to step in to prevent it from closing. In 1983 the Western Mining Corporation of Australia bought a 20% interest in the mine and took over management. Western modernized the facilities and greatly increased production, but after another bitter strike in 1991 they sold out and the mine is now operated by the Emperor Gold Mining Company once again. At last report, the 700 miners who walked out in 1991 were still on strike and the Emperor was refusing to recognize their union.

The ore comes up from the underground area through the Smith Shaft near "Top Gate." It's

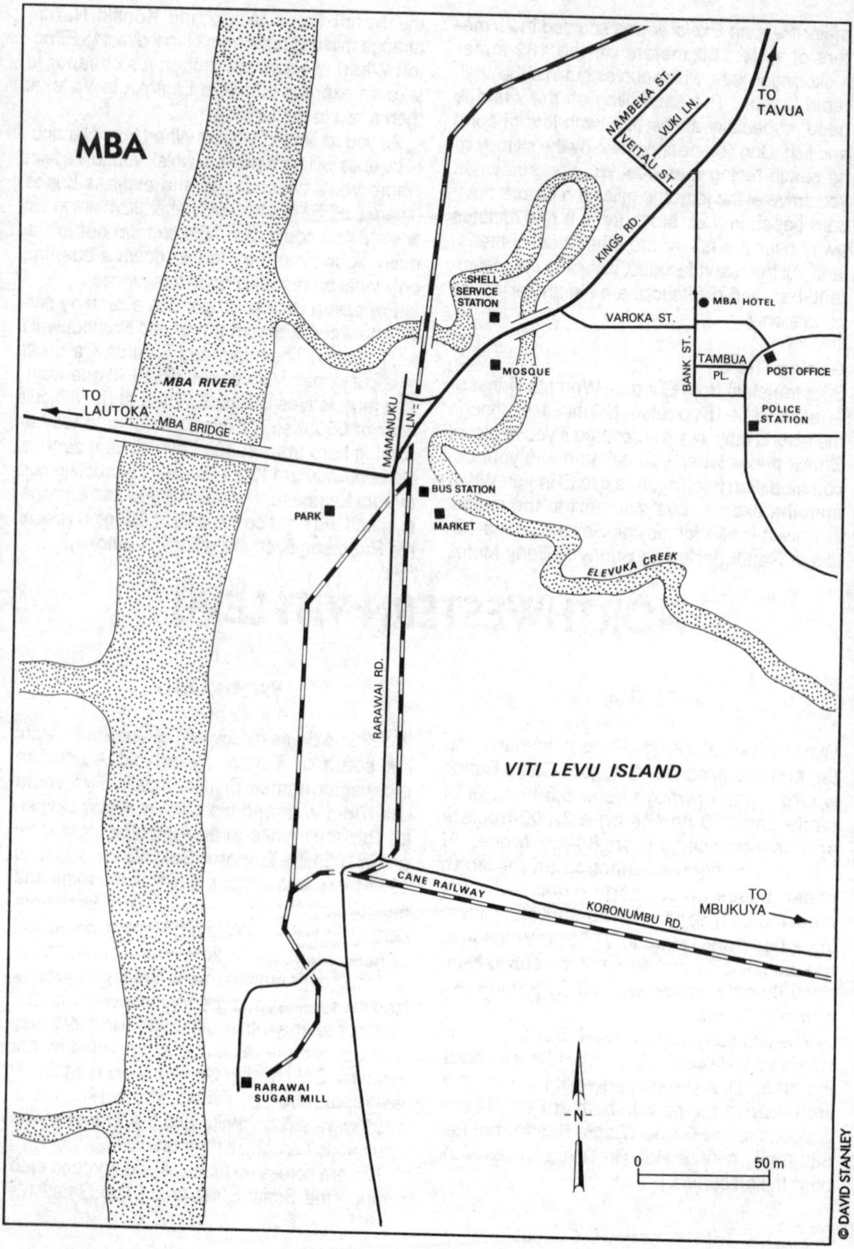

MBA

MBA RIVER

TO LAUTOKA, MBA BRIDGE

TO TAVUA

NAMBEKA ST.

VEITAU ST.

VUKI LN.

KINGS RD.

SHELL SERVICE STATION

VAROKA ST.

MBA HOTEL

BANK ST.

TAMBUA PL.

POST OFFICE

POLICE STATION

MOSQUE

MAMANUKU LN.

PARK

BUS STATION

MARKET

ELEVUKA CREEK

RARAWAI RD.

VITI LEVU ISLAND

CANE RAILWAY

KORONUMBU RD.

TO MBUKUYA

RARAWAI SUGAR MILL

-N-

0   50 m

© DAVID STANLEY

washed, crushed, and roasted, then fed into a flotation process and the foundry where gold and silver are separated from the ore. Counting both underground operations and an open pit, the mine presently extracts 135,000 ounces of gold annually from 600,000 tonnes of ore. A tonne of silver is also produced each year and waste rock is crushed into gravel and sold. Proven recoverable ore reserves at Vatukoula are sufficient for another decade of mining, and in 1985 additional deposits were discovered at nearby Nasomo, where extraction began in 1988.

Vatukoula is a typical company town, with education and social services under the jurisdiction of the Emperor. Company housing consists in part of WW II-style Quonset huts. The 2,000 miners employed here, most of them indigenous Fijians, live in racially segregated ghettos and are paid low wages. In contrast, tradespeople and supervisors, most of them Rotumans and part-Fijians, enjoy much better living conditions, and senior staff and management live in colonial-style comfort. Sensitive to profitability, the Emperor has tenaciously resisted the unionization of its work force.

To arrange a guided tour of the mine you must contact the Public Relations Officer, Emperor Gold Mining Co. Ltd. (tel. 680-477, fax 680-772), at least one week in advance. It's not possible to just show up and be admitted. There's bus service from Tavua to Vatukoula every half hour, and even if you don't get off, it's well worth making the round trip to "Bottom Gate" to see the varying classes of company housing, to catch a glimpse of the golf course and open pit, and to enjoy the lovely scenery. Rosie Tours in Nandi runs gold mine tours (F$39 without lunch), but these do not enter the mine itself and you can see almost as much from the regular bus at a fraction the cost.

MBA

The large Indian town of Mba (population 11,000) on the Mba River is seldom visited by tourists. As the attractive mosque in the center of town indicates, nearly half of Fiji's Muslims live in Mba Province. Small fishing boats depart from behind the Shell service station opposite the mosque, and it's fairly easy to arrange to go along on all-night trips. A wide belt of mangroves covers much of the river's delta. Mba is better known for the large Rarawai Sugar Mill, opened by the Colonial Sugar Refining Co. in 1886.

The **Mba Hotel** (Box 29, Mba; tel. 674-000, fax 670-139), 110 Bank St., is the only organized accommodations. The 14 a/c rooms with bath are F$40/52 single/double—very pleasant with a swimming pool, bar, and restaurant. Many inexpensive restaurants serving Indian and Chinese meals are found along Kings Road.

If you're spending the night here check out Venus Cinema beside the Mba Hotel, and the Metro and Civic cinemas on opposite sides of Tambua Park near the post office. The Central Club is also in Tambua Park. Four banks have branches in Mba.

Three buses a day (except Sunday) run from Mba to Mbukuya in Viti Levu's high interior. If you'd like to stay in a village, you'll be welcome at **Navala** on the road to Mbukuya. Take along a *sevusevu* for the *turanga-ni-koro* and be prepared to pay your way (just don't arrive on a Sunday). Navala's thatched *mbures* stand picturesquely against the surrounding hills. When water levels are right, whitewater rafters shoot the rapids through the Mba River Gorge near here.

Important express buses leaving Mba daily are the Pacific Transport bus to Suva via Singatoka at 0615 (six hours, F$9), and the Sunbeam Transport buses to Suva via Tavua at 0715, 1300, and 1715 (five hours).

INTO THE INTERIOR

Nandarivatu

An important forestry station is at Nandarivatu, a small settlement above Tavua. Its 900-meter altitude means a cool climate and a fantastic panorama of the north coast from the ridge. Beside the road right in front of the Forestry Training Center is **The Stone Bowl,** official source of the Singatoka River, and a five-minute walk from the Center is the **Governor General's Swimming Pool** where a small creek has been dammed. Go up the creek a short distance to the main pool, though it's dry much of the year and the area has not been maintained. The trail to the fire tower atop **Mt. Lomalangi** (Mt. Heaven) begins nearby, a one-hour hike each way. The tower itself has collapsed and is no longer climbable, but the forest is lovely and you may see and hear many native birds. Pine forests cover the land.

In its heyday Nandarivatu was a summer retreat for expatriates from the nearby Vatukoula gold mine and during the 1980s their large bungalow served as a Forestry Rest House. This ended after a small kitchen fire in 1989, and although the building is still there, it's in a dilapidated state and remains officially closed. Hopefully some local entrepreneur will recognize the possibilities for mountain tourism in this area, lease the building from the government, and carry out much-needed repairs. Meanwhile visitors with tents are allowed to camp at the Forestry Training Center. Ask permission at the Ministry of Forests office as soon as you arrive. Some canned foods are available at the canteen opposite the former Rest House, but bring food from Suva or Lautoka. Cabin crackers are handy.

There's only one bus a day (excluding Sunday) between Tavua and Nandarivatu, leaving Tavua at 1500, Nandarivatu at 0700—a spectacular one-and-a-half-hour bus ride. Arrive at the stop in Tavua at least 30 minutes ahead, as this bus does fill up. This bus originates/terminates in Nandrau. It's also quite easy to hitch.

Mount Victoria

The two great rivers of Fiji, the Rewa and the Singatoka, originate on the slopes of Mt. Victoria (Tomanivi), highest mountain in the country (1,323 meters). The climb begins near the bridge at Navai, 10 km southeast of Nandarivatu. Turn right up the hillside a few hundred meters down the jeep track, then climb up through native bush on the main path all the way to the top. Beware of misleading signboards. There are three small streams to cross; no water after the third. On your way down, stop for a swim in the largest stream. There's a flat area on top where you could camp—if you're willing to take your chances with Mbuli, the devil king of the mountain. Local guides are available, but allow about six hours for the roundtrip. Bright red epiphytic orchids *(Dendrobium mohlianum)* are sometimes in full bloom. Mount Victoria is on the divide between the wet and dry sides of Viti Levu, and from the summit you should be able to distinguish the contrasting vegetation in these zones.

Monasavu Hydroelectric Project

The largest development project ever undertaken in Fiji, this massive F$234 million scheme at Monasavu, on the Nandrau Plateau near the center of Viti Levu, took 1,500 men and six years to complete. An earthen dam, 82 meters high, was built across the Nanuka River to supply water to the four 20-megawatt generating turbines at the Wailoa Power Station on the Wailoa River, 625 meters below. The dam forms a lake 17 km long, and the water drops through a 5.4-km tunnel at a 45-degree angle, one of the steepest engineered dips in the world. Overhead transmission lines carry power from Wailoa to Suva and Lautoka. Monasavu is capable of filling Viti Levu's needs well into the 1990s, representing huge savings on imported diesel oil.

The Cross-Island Highway which passes the site was built to serve the dam project. Bus service ended when the project was completed and the construction camps closed in 1985. Traffic of all kinds was halted in 1993 when a hurricane took out the bridge at Lutu, although 4WD vehicles can still ford the river when water levels are low. At the present time there are only buses from Tavua to Nandrau and from Suva to Naivuthini, although occasional carriers go further.

THE SINGATOKA RIVER TREK

One of the most rewarding trips you can make on Viti Levu is the three-day hike south across the center of the island from Nandarivatu to Korolevu on the Singatoka River. There are many superb campsites along the trail, and luckily this trek is not included in the Australian guidebooks, so the area isn't overrun by tourists. Even so, villages like Numbutautau, Namoli, and Korolevu have hosted overnight visitors far too often for it to be pure Fijian hospitality anymore: a monetary *sevusevu* spiced with a generous bundle of *waka* are in order. (Kava for presentations on subsequent days can be purchased at villages along the way.) Set out from Nandarivatu early in the week, so you won't suffer the embarrassment of arriving in a village on Sunday. Excellent topographical maps of the entire route can be purchased at the Maps and Plans Room of the Lands and Survey Department in Suva.

Follow the dirt road south from Nandarivatu to **Nangatangata** where you should fill your canteen as the trail ahead is rigorous and there's no water to be found. From Nangatangata walk south about one hour. When you reach the electric high-power line, where the road turns right and begins to descend toward Koro, look for the well-worn footpath ahead. The trail winds along the ridge, and you can see as far as Mba. The primeval forests which once covered this part of Fiji were destroyed long ago by the slash-and-burn agricultural techniques of the Fijians.

When you reach the pine trees the path divides, with Nanoko to the right and Numbutautau down to the left. During the rainy season it's best to turn right and head to Nanoko, where you may be able to find a carrier to Mbukuya or all the way to Nandi. There's bus service between Mbukuya and Mba three times a day. If you do decide to make for Nanoko, beware of a very roundabout loop road on the left. Another option is to skip all of the above by staying in the bus from Tavua right to the end of the line at Nandrau, from whence your hike would then begin.

Reverend Thomas Baker, the last missionary to be clubbed and devoured in Fiji (in 1867), met his fate at **Numbutautau.** Jack London

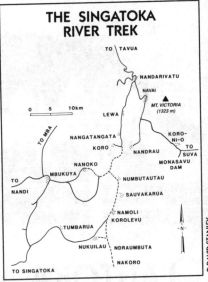

THE SINGATOKA RIVER TREK

wrote a story, "The Whale Tooth," about the death of the missionary, and the axe which brought about Reverend Baker's demise is still kept in the village. You should be able to stay in the community center in Numbutautau. The Numbutautau-Korolevu section of the trek involves 22 crossings of the Singatoka River, which is easy enough in the dry season (cut a bamboo staff for balance), but almost impossible in the wet (December to April). Hiking boots will be useless in the river, so wear a pair of old running shoes.

It's a fantastic trip down the river to **Korolevu** if you can make it. The Korolevu villagers can call large eels up from a nearby pool with a certain chant, and a few hours' walk away are the **pottery villages,** Ndraumbuta and Nakoro, where traditional, long Fijian pots are still made. From Korolevu you can take a carrier to Tumbarua, where there are two buses a day to Singatoka (F$2). A carrier leaves Korolevu direct to Singatoka every morning except Sunday, departing Singatoka for the return around 1400 (if you want to do this trip in reverse). Reader Bruce French of Edgewood, Kentucky, wrote that "this trek was a big highlight of my South Pacific experience."

SALVATORE CASA

LAUTOKA AND VICINITY
LAUTOKA

Fiji's second-largest city, Lautoka (population 50,000) is the focus of the country's sugar and timber industries, a major port, and the Western Division and Mba Province headquarters. It's an amiable place with a row of towering royal palms along the main street. Though Lautoka grew up around the Fijian village of Namoli, it's a predominantly Indian town today, with temples and mosques prominent in the center of town. Shuttle boats to Beachcomber and Treasure islands depart from Lautoka, and this is the gateway to the Yasawa Islands with everything from Blue Lagoon cruises to village boats. Yet because Lautoka doesn't depend only on tourism, you get a truer picture of ordinary life, and the town has a rambunctious nightlife. There's some duty-free shopping, but mainly this is just a nice place to wander around. Unless you're hooked on tourist-oriented activities, Lautoka is a good alternative to Nandi for a stay.

SIGHTS OF LAUTOKA AND VICINITY

South of the Center

Begin next to the bus station at Lautoka's big, colorful **market,** which is busiest on Saturday (open weekdays 0700-1730, Saturday 0530-1600). From here, walk south on Yasawa Street to the photogenic **Jame Mosque.** Five times a day local male Muslims direct prayers toward a small niche known as a *mihrab,* where they fuse and fly to the *Kabba* in Mecca, thence to Allah. During the crushing season (June to November) narrow-gauge trains rattle past the mosque along a line parallel to Vitongo Parade, bringing cane to Lautoka's large sugar mill.

Follow the line east a bit to the **Sikh Temple,** rebuilt after a smaller temple was burned by Methodist youths in October 1989. To enter you must wash your hands and cover your head (kerchiefs are provided at the door), and ciga-

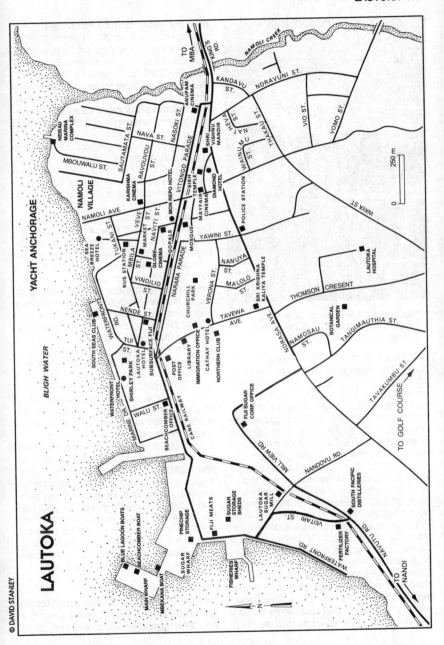

LAUTOKA

© DAVID STANLEY

DAVID STANLEY

The Sunday afternoon festival and feast at Lautoka's Hare Krishna Temple, fifth largest in the South Pacific, is worth attending.

rettes and liquor are forbidden inside the compound. The teachings of the 10 Sikh gurus are contained in the Granth, a holy book prominently displayed in the temple. Sikhism began in the Punjab region of northwest India in the 16th century as a reformed branch of Hinduism much influenced by Islam: for example, Sikhs reject the caste system and idolatry. The Sikhs are easily recognized by their beards and turbans.

Follow your map west along Ndrasa Avenue to the **Sri Krishna Kaliya Temple** on Tavewa Avenue, the most prominent Krishna temple in the South Pacific (open daily until 2030). The images inside are Radha and Krishna on the right, while the central figure is Krishna dancing on the snake Kaliya to show his mastery over the reptile. The story goes that Krishna chastised Kaliya and exiled him to the island of Ramanik Deep, which Fiji Indians believe to be Fiji. (Curiously, the indigenous Fijian people have also long believed in a serpent-god, named Degei, who lived in a cave in the Nakauvandra Range.) The two figures on the left are incarnations of Kr-

ishna and Balarama. At the front of the temple is a representation of His Divine Grace A.C. Bhaktivedanta Swami Prabhupada, founder of the International Society for Krishna Consciousness (ISKCON). On Sunday, 15 October 1989, members of a Methodist youth group carried out a firebomb attack on this and three other Indian places of worship in Lautoka. The damage has since been repaired but a security guard is now posted at the gate.

Nearby off Thomson Crescent is the entrance to Lautoka's **Botanical Garden** (closed Sunday). It will be a few more years before the plants in the garden reach maturity, but the landscaping here is attractive.

Sugar and Spirits

Continue up Ndrasa Avenue a block from the garden and turn right on Mill View Road. The large Private Property sign at the beginning of the road is intended mostly to keep out heavy vehicles, and tourists are allowed to walk through this picturesque neighborhood, past the colonial-era residences of sugar industry executives and century-old banyan trees. Just beyond the Fiji Sugar Corporation offices is the **Lautoka Sugar Mill,** one of the largest in the Southern Hemisphere. The mill was founded in 1903, and until the 1987 military coups it was possible to visit. Although the security situation in Fiji is now about back to normal, the mill tours remain suspended, though you can see quite a lot of the operation (busiest from June to November) as you walk down Mill View Road toward the main gate.

Continue straight ahead on Navutu Road (the dirt road beside the railway line) to **South Pacific Distilleries** (Box 1128, Lautoka; tel. 662-088, fax 664-361), where free plant tours can be arranged on the spot weekdays during business hours. This government-owned plant bottles rum, whisky, vodka, and gin under a variety of labels, and, of course, molasses from the sugar mill is the distillery's main raw material. The **fertilizer factory** across the highway uses mill mud from the sugar-making process.

The Waterfront

Backtrack to the sugar mill and turn left toward **Fisheries Wharf,** from which you'll have a fine view of the huge sugar storage sheds next to the mill and many colorful fishing boats. If you were thinking of taking a village boat to the Yasawa Islands, this is where you'll board.

To the north, just beyond the conveyor belts used to load raw sugar onto the ships, is a veritable mountain of **pine chips** ready for export to Japan where they are used to make paper. Forestry is becoming more important as Fiji attempts to diversify its economy away from sugar. The **Main Wharf** behind the chips is the departure point for the famous Blue Lagoon Cruises to the Yasawa Islands, plus the 39-meter Beachcomber Island shuttle boat *Tui Tai.* If you have time, take the **Mbekana Island** shuttle boat from just inside the main gate over to the small resort here (see "Mbekana Island" under "Accommodations") on the only beach right at Lautoka—it only costs F$1 each way. As you return to central Lautoka, turn left onto **Marine Drive** for its view of the harbor, especially enchanting at sunset.

North of Lautoka
One of the largest reforestation projects yet undertaken in the South Pacific is the **Lololo Pine Scheme,** eight km off Kings Road between Lautoka and Mba. The logs are sawn into timber if straight or ground into chip if twisted and then exported from Lautoka. There's a shady picnic area along a dammed creek at the forestry station where you could swim, but even if you don't stop, it's worthwhile taking the one-and-a-half-hour roundtrip bus ride from Lautoka to see this beautiful area and to learn how it's being used. The buses follow a circular route, returning by a different road.

East of Lautoka
Ambatha village east of Lautoka is the perfect base for hiking into the **Mount Evans Range** behind Lautoka. Guides are available. For permission to hike around this area, take a *sevusevu* of *yanggona* roots for the *turanga-ni-koro* and make a monetary contribution. Four waterfalls are near the village, and **Table Mountain,** with sweeping views of the coast and Yasawas, is only an hour away. More ambitious hikes to higher peaks are possible. The landscape of wide green valleys set against steep slopes is superb.

You can get there by taking the Tavakumba bus as far as Ambatha junction, then hiking another 10 km to the village. A better idea is to hire a carrier direct to Ambatha from Lautoka Bus Station for about F$15. Fiji-style accommodations and food are provided in the village at fixed rates. It's all part of a local income-generating project, so you'll be well received. Avoid arriving in Ambatha on Sunday, the traditional day of worship and rest.

South of Lautoka
A popular legend invented in 1893 holds that **Viseisei village,** between Lautoka and Nandi, is

near Lautoka, Fiji

M.E. DE VOS

the guns of Lomolomo on a hilltop between Lautoka and Nandi

DAVID STANLEY

the oldest settlement in Fiji. It's told how the first Fijians, led by Chiefs Lutunasobasoba and Degei, came from the west, landing their great canoe, the *Kaunitoni,* at Vunda Point, where the oil tanks are now. A Centennial Memorial (1835-1935) in front of the church commemorates the arrival of the first Methodist missionaries in Fiji, and opposite the memorial is a traditional Fijian *mbure*—the residence of the present Tui Vunda.

Near the back of the church is another monument topped by a giant war club, the burial place of the village's chiefly family. The late Dr. Timoci Bavadra, the former prime minister of Fiji who was deposed by the Rabuka coup in 1987, hailed from Viseisei and is interred here in an unmarked grave. Dr. Bavadra's traditional-style home faces the main road near the church. His son presently lives there, and with his permission you'll be allowed to enter to see the photos hanging from the walls.

All this is only a few minutes' walk from the bus stop (frequent service), but you're expected to have someone accompany you through the village. Ask permission of anyone you meet at the bus stop and they will send a child with you. As you part, you could give the child a pack of chewing gum (give something else if your escort is an adult). Nearby is a **Memorial Cultural Center,** where souvenirs are sold to cruise ship passengers. There's a fine view of Nandi Bay from the Center.

A couple of kilometers from the village on the airport side of Viseisei, just above Lomolomo

Public School, are two **British six-inch guns** set up here during WW II to defend the north side of Nandi Bay. It's a fairly easy climb from the main highway, and you get an excellent view from the top.

Sports and Recreation

Subsurface Fiji (Box 5202, Lautoka; tel. 664-422, fax 664-496), at the corner of Nende and Naviti streets near the Lautoka Hotel, arranges scuba diving at F$65 for one tank, F$115 for two tanks. Trips to Waya Island in the Yasawas are offered for scuba divers and snorkelers on Thursday, Friday, and Saturday. Divers should call for free pickup at Nandi/Lautoka hotels. Tank air fills at offshore islands can also be arranged.

You can rent tanks and have them filled at **Dive Center Ltd.** (Box 5015, Lautoka; tel. 663-797, fax 662-211), 11 Walu Street.

Saturday you can catch an exciting rugby or soccer game at the stadium in Churchill Park. Admission is reasonable—check locally for the times of league games.

ACCOMMODATIONS

In Town

A good choice is the clean, quiet, three-story **Sea Breeze Hotel** (Box 152, Lautoka; tel. 660-717), at 5 Mbekana Lane on the waterfront near the bus station. They have 26 rooms with private bath from F$25/30 single/double (rooms with a/c cost F$4 more). A larger family room accommodating four adults is F$50. At first they'll try to give you an a/c room; then if you convince them to let you have a fan-cooled room, they may want to stick you in a noisy room near the reception, even when the top floor is completely empty. Ask to see the room before signing the register. For reasons unknown, they'll occasionally claim they're fully booked even when the place is almost empty. There's a very pleasant lounge and swimming pool overlooking the lagoon.

To be closer to the action, stay at the 38-room **Lautoka Hotel** (Box 51, Lautoka; tel. 660-388, fax 660-201), 2 Naviti St., which has a good restaurant and nightclub on the premises. There's also a swimming pool. Room prices vary from F$17/22 single/double for a fan-cooled room with shared bath to F$44 single or double for a/c and private bath, F$66 for a/c, private bath, fridge, and waterbed, or F$9 pp in the dorm.

Also recommended are the 40 rooms at the friendly **Cathay Hotel** (Box 239, Lautoka; tel. 660-566, fax 340-236) on Tavewa Avenue, which features a small swimming pool, TV room, and bar. The charge is F$25/33 single/double with fan and private bath, F$33/41 with a/c. There are several dormitories of varying size, cleanliness, and facilities at F$10 pp. They offer free luggage storage for guests.

The 18-room **Diamond Hotel** (Box 736, Lautoka; tel. 661-920) on Nathula Street charges F$8 pp in the dorm (three beds), or F$19/25 single/double for a room with fan. Though plain and basic, it's okay for one night if everything else is full.

Another step down is the **Mon Repo Hotel** (Box 857, Lautoka; tel. 661-595), 75 Vitongo Parade, at F$14/22 single/double with shared bath. This building is a former police station and the cells (guest rooms) are still frequented by prostitutes.

Lautoka's most expensive hotel is the **Waterfront Hotel** (Box 4653, Lautoka; tel. 664-777, fax 665-870), a two-story building erected in 1987 on Marine Drive. The 41 waterbed-equipped a/c rooms are F$100 single or double, F$120 triple (children under 16 are free if no extra bed is required). There's a swimming pool, and members of tour groups departing Lautoka booked on Blue Lagoon cruises often stay here.

South of Lautoka
Saweni Beach Apartments (Box 239, Lautoka; tel. 661-777, fax 340-236), a km off the main highway south of Lautoka, offers a row of 12 self-catering apartments with fan at F$38/44 single/double, plus a F$11 pp dorm. You can pitch your own tent here at F$5 pp (provided the communal toilets are working). Fishermen on the beach sell fresh fish every morning, and cruising yachts often anchor off Saweni Beach. Saweni is quieter than the Anchorage mentioned below, and the so-so beach only comes alive on weekends when local picnickers arrive. A bus runs right to the hotel from Lautoka three times a day. Otherwise any of the local Nandi buses will drop you off a 10-minute walk away.

The **Anchorage Beach Resort** (Box 9472, Nandi Airport; tel. 662-099, fax 665-571), between Viseisei and Vunda Point, a few km south of the Saweni Beach, has 10 rooms at F$70/75 single/double, and a F$17 pp dorm with cooking facilities. A swimming pool, washing machine, and panoramic views are among the other attractions. Stay at the Anchorage if you like meeting people, at the Saweni if you want to regenerate. It's about a 15-minute walk from the highway to Anchorage Resort.

Mediterranean Villas (Box 5240, Lautoka; tel. 664-011, fax 661-773), on Vunda Hill overlooking Viseisei village, has six attractive villas beginning at F$77/88 single/double. Cooking facilities are not provided, but a licensed Italian seafood restaurant is on the premises. The beach is far from here.

For information on Beachcomber Island and Treasure Island resorts, both accessible from Lautoka, turn to "The Mamanutha Group" in the Southwest Viti Levu chapter.

Mbekana Island
The most easily accessible island resort in Fiji is **Mbekana Island Resort** (Tracy and Robert Walker, Box 4091, Lautoka; tel. 665-222, fax 665-409), formerly known as "Paradise Island," just offshore from Lautoka. They offer 12 thatched fan-cooled *mbures* with private bath and fridge (but no cooking facilities) at F$115 for up to four persons. A six-bed dormitory lodge is F$38 pp including breakfast and dinner. Water taxi transfers from Lautoka's main wharf are F$1 pp each way. Mbekana's biggest draw is its

easy access to Lautoka, allowing you to combine beach life with organized shopping and sightseeing, and a night here can be memorable if you don't mind spending more than you would at the city hotels. It's peaceful and the view of the Lautoka skyline backed by the Mount Evans Range is unsurpassed. Mbekana itself is an uninteresting flat island with nothing to see beyond the boundaries of the resort (although it's fascinating to kayak through the nearby mangroves). Water sports such as windsurfing, kayaking, and sailing are freely available to guests, and the clean swimming pool makes up for the lack of snorkeling possibilities around here. Even if you aren't staying, their F$10 Sunday barbecue at 1230 is a good way to put in a Sunday afternoon.

FOOD

Several inexpensive local restaurants are opposite the bus station. The **Pacific Restaurant** (open Monday to Saturday 0700-1900, Sunday 1000-1600), on Yasawa Street near the Singatoka Bookshop, has some of the hottest (spiciest) food you'll find anywhere in the Pacific—excellent if that's to your taste. This is also a good place to get a coffee or breakfast.

For the best vegetarian food and ice cream in town, it's **Gopal's** (tel. 662-990; closed Sunday). It's on the corner of Naviti and Yasawa streets near the market, with a second location at 117 Vitongo Parade (tel. 660-938) opposite Churchill Park. This is the Lautoka equivalent of Suva's Hare Krishna Restaurant.

Rennee's Restaurant (tel. 662-473; also open Sunday night), 62 Naviti St., has the standard curry- and chop suey-type stuff, but tasty big portions and reasonable prices (add 10% tax to what it says on the menu). Cold beer is available with the meal. The **Hot Snax Shop,** 56 Naviti St., is also good for Indian dishes.

Enjoy ample servings of Cantonese food at the a/c **Sea Coast Restaurant** (tel. 660-675; closed Sunday) on Naviti Street near the Lautoka Hotel. (Conversely, avoid the nearby Great Wall of China Restaurant, which is notable for its poor service, miserly portions, and erratic pricing.)

Eat Italian at the **Pizza Inn** (tel. 660-388) in the Lautoka Hotel, 2 Naviti Street.

On Sunday the best thing to do is attend a barbecue, and the **Mbekana Island Resort** (tel. 665-222) puts one on at 1230 (F$10, plus F$2 pp for boat transfers from the main wharf). The **Neisau Marina** (tel. 664-858) has another barbecue at 1800 (also F$10).

ENTERTAINMENT

There are four movie houses with several showings daily except Sunday.

The disco scene in Lautoka centers on the **Hunter's Inn** at the Lautoka Hotel (tel. 660-388; open Friday and Saturday 2100-0100 only; F$4 cover). There's also **Coco's** (tel. 667-900) at 91 Naviti St., above the Great Wall of China Restaurant, but you won't be admitted if you're wearing a T-shirt, jeans, shorts, running shoes, or flip-flops.

The roughest place in town is **Kings Nite Club** (tel. 665-822), above Gopal's in the center of town. It's open Monday to Saturday 1800-0100, but nothing much happens at Kings before 2200. The cover charge on Thursday, Friday, and Saturday is F$3, and flip-flops aren't allowed.

Lautoka's old colonial club is the **Northern Club** (tel. 662-469) on Tavewa Avenue opposite the Cathay Hotel. The sign outside says Members Only, but the club secretary is usually happy to sign in foreign visitors. Lunch and dinner are available here from Monday to Saturday; there's tennis and a swimming pool. Happy hour is Tuesday 1800-1900.

The **Lautoka Club** (tel. 660-637), at 17 Tukani St. next to the Sea Breeze Hotel, is another good drinking place with a sea view.

Day cruises to Beachcomber Island (F$58 pp including lunch, reductions for children) depart Lautoka daily at 1000—a great way to spend a day. Any travel agency can book them.

Sunday *Puja*

The big event of the week is the Sunday evening *puja* (prayer) at the **Sri Krishna Kaliya Temple** on Tavewa Avenue from 1630-2030, followed by a vegetarian feast. Visitors may join in the singing and dancing, if they wish. Take off your shoes and sit on the white marble floor, men on one side, women on the other. The female devotees are especially stunning in their beautiful *saris.* Bells ring, drums are beaten, conch shells blown, and stories from the Vedas, Srimad Bhagavatam, and Ramayana are acted out as everyone chants, *"Hare Krsna, Hare Krsna, Krsna Krsna, Hare Hare, Hare Rama, Hare Rama, Rama, Rama, Hare, Hare."* It's a real celebration of joy and a most moving experience. At one point children will circulate with small trays covered with burning candles, on which it is customary to place a modest donation; you may also drop a dollar or two in the yellow box in the center of the temple. You'll be readily invited to join the vegetarian feast later, and no more money will be asked of you.

SERVICES AND INFORMATION

The ANZ Bank, National Bank, and Westpac Bank are all on Naviti Street near the market. The receptionist at the Cathay Hotel will change traveler's checks anytime at the regular bank rate without commission.

The **Immigration Department** (tel. 662-283) is in the Housing Authority building near the Cathay Hotel.

Public toilets are on the back side of the bus station facing the market.

The **Book Exchange,** 19 Yasawa St., trades and sells used books. The **Western Regional Library** (tel. 660-091) on Tavewa Avenue is open weekdays 1000-1700, Saturday 0900-1200.

Yachting Facilities

The **Neisau Marina Complex** (Box 3831, Lautoka; tel. 664-858, fax 663-807), at the end of Mbouwalu Street, provides complete haul-out facilities for yachts in need of repair. There's also an authentic token-operated laundromat here (F$3 to wash, F$3 to dry), and Spencer's Bar, which puts on a barbecue Sunday at 1800 (F$10). The bar's terrace is a great place to enjoy a beer while your clothes are washing.

Health

There's an outpatient service and dental clinic at the **Lautoka Hospital** (tel. 660-399; Monday to Friday 0800-1600, Saturday 0800-1100), off Thomson Crescent south of the center. A consultation with a private doctor is more convenient.

Vaccinations for international travelers are available at the **Health Office** (tel. 663-542) on Naviti Street opposite the Lautoka Hotel on Tuesday and Friday 0800-1200.

TRANSPORTATION

Sunflower Airlines (tel. 664-753) is at 27 Vindilo Street.

Anyone headed toward Vanua Levu should check with **Beachcomber Cruises** (tel. 661-500) which runs the high-speed catamaran *Ndrondrolangi* from Lautoka to Savusavu daily except Sunday at 0600 (three hours, F$55).

Patterson Brothers (tel. 661-173), on Tukani Street opposite the bus station, runs a bus/ferry/bus service between Lautoka, Ellington Wharf, Nambouwalu, and Lambasa (F$34), departing Lautoka on Tuesday, Thursday, and Saturday around 0400.

Buses, carriers, taxis—everything leaves from the bus stand beside the market. **Pacific Transport** (tel. 660-499) has express buses to Suva daily at 0630, 0700, 1210, and 1730 (five hours, F$7.80) via Singatoka (Queens Road). Four other "stage" buses also operate daily along this route (six hours). **Sunbeam Transport** (tel. 662-822) has expresses to Suva at 0630, 1215, and 1630 (six hours) via Tavua (Kings Road), plus two local buses on the same route (nine hours). The northern route is more scenic than the southern. Local buses to Nandi (F$1.15) and Mba (F$1.25) depart every half hour or so.

SALVATORE CASA

THE YASAWA ISLANDS

The Yasawas are a chain of 16 main volcanic islands and dozens of smaller ones, stretching 80 km in a north-northeast direction, roughly 35 km off the west coast of Viti Levu. In the lee of Viti Levu, the Yasawas are dry and sunny, with beautiful, isolated beaches, cliffs, bays, and reefs. The waters are crystal clear and almost totally shark-free. The group was romanticized in two movies titled *The Blue Lagoon:* a 1949 original starring Jean Simmons, and the 1980 remake with Brooke Shields. It was from the north end of the Yasawas that two canoe-loads of cannibals sallied forth in 1789 and gave chase to Capt. William Bligh and his 18 companions less than a week after the famous mutiny.

Two centuries later, increasing numbers of mini-cruise ships ply the chain. Though an abundance of luxury resorts dot the Mamanutha Islands off Nandi and a couple have appeared in the Yasawas, there aren't many regular, inexpensive places to stay. The backpackers' usual routine is to take a village boat to Tavewa or Waya (see below). If you'll be going off on your own trekking or kayaking, you should take along a good supply of *yanggona* (which doesn't grow in the Yasawas) for use as a *sevusevu* to village chiefs. All access to the Yasawas is via Lautoka. In the local dialect, *thola* is "hello" and *vina du riki* is "thank you."

WAYA ISLAND

Just 60 km northwest of Lautoka is Waya, the closest of the larger Yasawas to Viti Levu and also the highest island (579 meters). A sheer mass of rock rises above Yalombi village. Yalombi has a beautiful beach and the offshore reef features cabbage coral, whip coral, and giant fan corals in warm, clear waters teeming with fish. At low tide you can wade from Waya across to neighboring Wayasewa Island: there's good snorkeling there and a remarkable 354-meter-high volcanic thumb that overlooks the south coast. Also from Yalombi, it's a 30-minute hike across the ridge to Natawa village on the east side of Waya. There's a deserted beach another 20 minutes north of Natawa. In a long day you can hike right around Waya, passing two villages and many friendly people along the way.

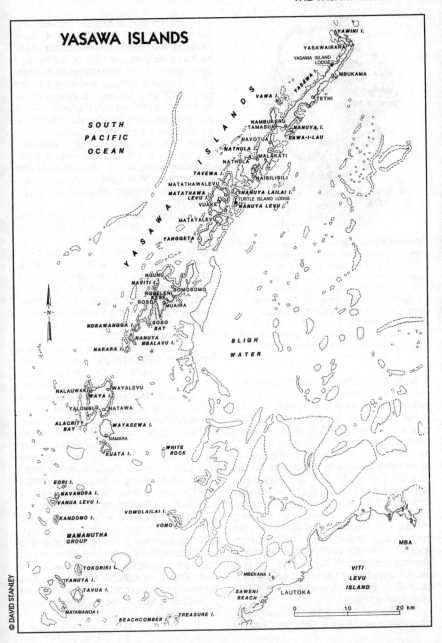

YASAWA ISLANDS

SOUTH
PACIFIC
OCEAN

YAWINI I.

YASAWAIRARA

YASAWA ISLAND
LODGE

MBUKAMA

VAWA I.

YASAWA

TETHI

NAMBUKERU

TAMASUA

NANUYA I.

NAVOTUA

SAWA-I-LAU

NATHULA I.

MALAKATI

NATHULA

HAISILISILI

TAVEWA I.

MATATHAWALEVU

NANUYA LAILAI I.

MATATHAWA
LEVU I.

TURTLE ISLAND LODGE

VUAKE

NANUYA LEVU

MATAYALEVU

YANGGETA

Y A S A W A   I S L A N D S

NGUNU

NAVITI I.

SOMOSOMO

NGGELENI
ESE

SOSO

MUAIRA

NDRAWANGGA I.

SOSO
BAY

NANUYA
MBALAVU I.

BLIGH

NARARA I.

WATER

NALAUWAKI

WAYALEVU

WAYA I.

YALOMBI

NATAWA

ALACRITY
BAY

WAYASEWA I.

NAMARA

WHITE
ROCK

KUATA I.

EORI I.

NAVANDRA I.

VANUA LEVU I.

KANDOMO I.

VOMOLAILAI I.

MAMANUTHA
GROUP

VOMO

MBA

TOKORIKI I.

YANUYA I.

TAVUA I.

MBEKANA I.

VITI
LEVU
ISLAND

SAWENI
BEACH

LAUTOKA

MATAMANOA I.

BEACHCOMBER I.

TREASURE I.

0   10   20 km

© DAVID STANLEY

Captain William Bligh. In 1789, after being cast adrift by the mutineers on his HMS Bounty, Captain Bligh and 18 others in a seven-meter longboat were chased by two Fijian war canoes through what is now called Bligh Water. His men pulled the oars desperately, heading for open sea, and managed to escape the cannibals. They later arrived in Timor, finishing the most celebrated open-boat journey of all time. Captain Bligh did some incredible charting of Fijian waters along the way.

Andi Sayaba's Place (Box 1163, Lautoka) at Yalombi on the south side of Waya consists of a former schoolhouse partitioned into 10 "rooms" at F$8 pp in a five- to 10-bed dorm, or F$20 double. Campers pay F$6 pp, and three decent meals are an additional F$10 pp, but bring your own drinks. The rooms are usually used by scuba divers sent over by **Subsurface Fiji Ltd.** (Box 502, Lautoka; tel. 664-422) near the Lautoka Hotel, and you can get full information about Andi's Place from Harry in Subsurface Fiji's Lautoka office on the corner of Nende and Naviti streets. Subsurface provides speedboat transportation to Waya from Lautoka's Fisheries Wharf at 1000 on Thursday, Friday, and Saturday (two hours, F$66 pp return). This local resort makes a good base for observing traditional Fijian life and enjoying nature, while retaining some privacy.

On a lovely white-sand beach in Likuliku Bay on northwestern Waya is **Octopus Club Fiji** (Box 1861, Lautoka; tel. 666-337, fax 666-210), run by Ingrid and Wolfgang Denk. They have three thatched *mbures* with private bath at F$49 pp double occupancy, or F$29 pp in a four-bed dorm, breakfast and dinner included. They organize a *meke* every Tuesday evening (F$15 for guests, F$25 for nonguests). Fishing trips and island visits are F$17 pp including lunch. Hike to Waya's highest point for a splendid view. Yachts are welcome to anchor offshore and use the facilities. Transfers depart Lautoka's Neisau Marina Monday at 1400 and Thursday at 1000, departing Waya for the return Monday and Wednesday at 0800 (F$66 roundtrip). Information should be available at the Cathay Hotel reception in Lautoka.

Dive Trek Nature Lodge (Semi Koroilavesau, Box 23, Nandi; tel. 720-977, fax 720-978), adjacent to old Namara village on the south side of neighboring Wayasewa Island, opened in June 1994. The former village school building on a hill overlooking the beach has been partitioned into 14 tiny double rooms costing F$30 pp, including ample Fijian meals. Toilets, showers, and the eating area are in separate buildings nearby, and lighting is by hurricane lamp. In addition there are 10 traditional guest *mbures* with private bath and a small porch at F$100 double, meals included. Add 10% tax to all rates. Beer and soft drinks are sold, kava is served three evenings a week, and on Sunday afternoon a *lovo* is prepared. Informal musical entertainment occurs nightly. Three different guided hikes into the nearby hills are arranged; the extra charge for this service is worth it. Good snorkeling is available right off their beach—giant clams—and daily boat trips to nearby Kuata Island are organized. Scuba diving is also offered (F$65/100/130 one/two/three tanks, equipment included), as is a PADI scuba certification course (F$330). Boat transfers from Nandi depart Tuesday, Thursday, and Saturday at 1330 (F$35 pp each way including bus transfers to Nandi/Lautoka hotels). At Nandi Airport inquire about the lodge at Fiji Holiday Connections in Suite 8 in the international arrivals area. This sensitively planned ecotourism resort operated in partnership with the local villagers is highly recommended.

NAVITI ISLAND

Naviti, at 33 square km, is the largest of the Ya-sawas. Its king, one of the group's highest chiefs, resides at Soso, and the church there houses fine woodcarvings. Every Wednesday at noon the people of Soso gather to sell shells to a button factory. On the hillside above Soso are two caves containing the bones of ancestors. Yawesa, the secondary boarding school on Naviti, is

a village in itself. There's no wharf on Naviti, so you must wade ashore from the boat.

TAVEWA ISLAND

Tavewa is much smaller than Waya and twice as far from Lautoka, yet it's also strikingly beautiful with excellent bathing in the warm waters off a picture-postcard beach on the southeast side, and a good fringing reef with super snorkeling.

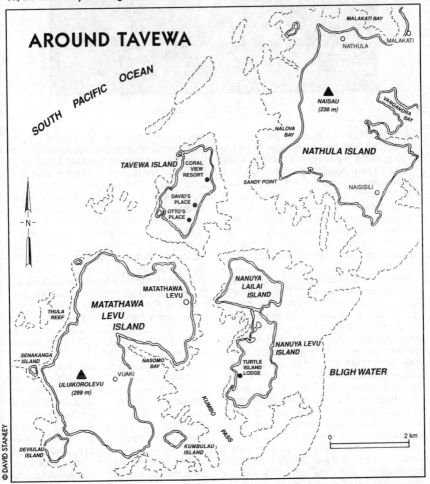

village house, Nathula, Yasawa Island

Tall grass covers the hilly interior (splendid sunsets from the hill). It's a small island about two km long, with a population of around 50 souls. There's no chief here, as this is freehold land. The people are friendly and welcoming; in fact, accommodating visitors is their main source of income. Most of their guests are backpackers who usually stay six nights, and most are sorry to leave. It's idyllic if you don't mind a non-Fijian atmosphere and a lack of privacy. Bring along mosquito coils, toilet paper, a flashlight (torch), and a *sulu* to cover up.

There's a reasonable choice of places to stay. **David and Kara Doughty's Place** (tel. 663-939), in a coconut grove near the small church, has several quite acceptable *mbures* for travelers at F$40 double, or F$18 pp in the dorm, three huge meals included. Camping is F$8 pp with your own tent, or F$13 pp to sleep in one of their tents, meals included (occasional extra charge for special barbecues). There's no electricity in the *mbures,* but David runs a generator in the house and his small store sells cold beer, drinks, and cigarettes. Since they started cutting the grass the mosquito problem has declined, but the communal toilets could use a cleaning. David and Kara will invite you to join in family activities, and the results of David's fishing trips often appear at dinner. He'll take you to a scenic cave or drop you off on an isolated beach, and in

the evening men can sit around playing backgammon and drinking kava with David, or women might help Kara weave a mat. Often someone sings a couple of songs. In short, it's a good escape from civilization, and you'll be made most welcome. Their boat leaves Lautoka Tuesday and Saturday at 0700, returning Monday and Friday (F$30 pp each way). Bookings can be made at the reception of the Lautoka Hotel (though we've heard the system is erratic, with people who didn't book ahead occasionally given priority).

The other main accommodation on Tavewa is **Coral View Resort** (Box 3764, Lautoka), also known as "Uncle Robert de Bruce's Place." Prices here are similar at F$49 double, F$22 in the dorm, or F$16 pp to camp, including all meals and one organized activity a day. It's a bit more primitive than David's and the food isn't quite as good, but it's still quite okay and mosquito nets are supplied. Their Thursday morning village excursion with lunch and "folkloric entertainment" (F$12 pp) is better than David's, and there are also boat trips to the Sawa-i-Lau cave (F$20 pp). A German reader who stayed at Robert's liked Meca's meals of fresh fish seasoned with garlic and ginger, and enjoyed Robert's evening tales of 10-headed snakes and buried treasure. Their boat leaves Lautoka Tuesday and Saturday at 0800, and Wednesday at 1400, departing Tavewa for the return on Monday, Wednesday, and Friday mornings (F$66 pp roundtrip). Bookings are handled by the reception at the Cathay Hotel in Lautoka.

Village boats such as the *Calm Sea, Babale,* and *Nukunindreke* leave from Lautoka's Fisheries Wharf near Fiji Meats very early Tuesday and Saturday mornings, returning to Lautoka on Monday and Friday (F$30 one-way). This schedule means you can spend either two, three, six, or more nights in the Yasawas. Any boat headed for Nathula village on Nathula Island will drop you off on Tavewa and there are always Yasawans around Lautoka market on Fridays. The boat ride from Lautoka can take anywhere from three to six hours (or more) depending on weather conditions, and it's a scenic trip across Bligh Water through the Yasawa Group to Tavewa. Just don't expect luxuries such as toilets on these boats, so limit how much you drink before boarding. Also limit what you eat, or take seasickness pills if you're a poor sailor. The boats can become very crowded, and if it's a nice day you ought to sit on the roof (bring sunscreen). Be prepared to wade ashore with your pack over your head at Tavewa.

NANUYA LEVU ISLAND

In 1972 an eccentric American millionaire named Richard Evanson bought 200-hectare Nanuya Levu Island in the middle of the Yasawa Group for US$300,000. He still lives there, and his **Turtle Island Lodge** (Box 9317, Nandi Airport; tel. 722-921, fax 720-007) has gained a reputation as one of the South Pacific's ultimate hideaways. Only 14 fan-cooled, two-room *mbures* grace Turtle, and Evanson swears there'll never be more.

Turtle is Tavewa at 25 times the price. The 28 guests (English-speaking mixed couples only, please) pay around F$1000 per couple per night, but that includes all meals, drinks, and activities. You'll find the fridge in your cottage well stocked with beer, wine, soft drinks, and champagne, refilled daily, with no extra bill to pay when you leave. Sports such as sailing, snorkeling, scuba diving, canoeing, windsurfing, glass-bottom boating, deep-sea fishing, catamaraning, horseback riding, guided hiking, and moonlight cruising are all included in the tariff.

Lodge staff will even do your laundry at no charge.

If you want to spend the day on any of the dozen secluded beaches, just ask and you'll be dropped off. Later someone will be back with lunch and a cooler of wine or champagne (or anything else you'd care to order over the walkie-talkie). Otherwise use the beach a few steps from your door. Meals are served at remote and romantic dine-out locations, or taken at the community table; every evening Richard hosts a small dinner party. He's turned down many offers to develop the island with hundreds more units or to sell out for a multimillion-dollar price. That's not Richard's style, and he's quite specific about who he *doesn't* want to come: "Trendies, jetsetters, obnoxious imbibers, and plastic people won't get much out of my place. Also, opinionated, loud, critical grouches and anti-socials should give us a miss."

Of course, all this luxury and romance has a price. Aside from the per diem, it's another F$750 per couple for roundtrip seaplane transportation to the island from Nandi. There's also a seven-night minimum stay, but as nearly half the guests are repeaters that doesn't seem to be an impediment. (Turtle Island is off-limits to anyone other than hotel guests.) Turtle's success may be measured by its many imitators, including the Vatulele Island Resort, the Wakaya Club, Lauthala Island, Kaimbu Island, and the Yasawa Island Lodge.

Turtle Island has also set the standard for environmentally conscious resort development. Aside from planting thousands of trees and providing a safe haven for birds, Evanson has preserved the island's mangroves, cleverly erecting a boardwalk to turn what others may have considered an eyesore into a major attraction. The beach on neighboring **Nanuya Lailai Island** is used by passengers on Blue Lagoon cruises.

SAWA-I-LAU ISLAND

On Sawa-i-Lau is a large limestone cave illuminated by a crevice at the top. There's a clear, deep pool in the cave where you can swim, and an underwater opening leads back into a smaller, darker cave (bring a light). A Fijian legend tells how a young chief once hid his love in this cave when her family wished to marry her off to another. Each day he brought her food until both could escape to safety on another island. All the cruise ships stop at this cave. If you get there on your own, present a *sevusevu* to the chief of Nambukeru village, just west of the cave, to visit.

YASAWA ISLAND

The Tui Yasawa, highest chief of the group, resides at Yasawairara village at the north end of Yasawa, northernmost island of the Yasawa group.

For many years the Fiji government had a policy that the Yasawas were "closed" to land-based tourism development, and it was only after the 1987 coups that construction of **Yasawa Island Lodge** (Box 10128, Nandi Airport; tel. 663-364, fax 665-044) was approved. This $8.5-million Australian-owned resort opened in 1991 on a creamy white beach on Yasawa's upper west side. Most of the resort's employees come from Mbukama village, which owns the land.

The 16 thatched a/c *mbures* with private baths consist of four duplexes at F$798 double, 10 deluxes at F$886, a two-bedroom unit at F$1025, and a honeymoon unit also at F$1025. All meals are included, but unlike at most other resorts in this category, alcoholic drinks are *not*. Scuba diving and game fishing also cost extra. Guests arrive on a chartered flight (F$165 pp each way), which lands on the resort's private airstrip. Here they're met by a thatched six-wheel-drive truck called the "*mbula* bus" that seats them on padded wooden benches in back and carries them to the resort. Children under 14 are only admitted during school holiday periods four times a year.

Fijian war clubs

KANDAVU

This big, 50-by-13-km island 100 km south of Suva is the fourth largest in Fiji. A mountainous, varied island with waterfalls plummeting from the rounded hilltops, Kandavu is outstanding for its vistas, beaches, and reefs. The three hilly sections of Kandavu are joined by two low isthmuses, with the sea biting so deeply into the island that on a map its shape resembles that of a wasp. Just northeast of the main island is smaller Ono Island and the fabulous Astrolabe Reef, stretching halfway to Suva. The famous red-and-green Kandavu parrots may be seen and heard.

In the 1870s steamers bound for New Zealand and Australia would call at the onetime whaling station at Ngaloa Harbor to pick up passengers and goods, and Kandavu was considered as a possible site for a new capital of Fiji. Instead Suva was chosen and Kandavu was left to lead its sleepy village life; only today is the outside world making a comeback with the arrival of roads, planes, and a handful of visitors. Some 8,000 indigenous Fijians live in 60 remote villages scattered around the island.

SIGHTS

The airstrip and wharf are each a 10-minute walk, in different directions, from the post office and hospital in the tiny government station of **Vunisea,** the largest of Kandavu's 60 Fijian villages and headquarters of Kandavu Province. Vunisea is strategically located on a narrow, hilly isthmus where Ngaloa Harbor and Namalata Bay almost cut Kandavu in two.

The longest sandy beach on the island is at **Ndrue,** an hour's walk north from Vunisea. Another good beach is at **Muani** village, eight km south of Vunisea by road. Just two km south of the airstrip by road and a 10-minute hike inland is **Waikana Falls.** Cool spring water flows over a 10-meter-high rocky cliff between two deep pools, the perfect place for a refreshing swim on a hot day. A second falls six km east of Vunisea is even better.

The women of **Namuana** village just west of the airstrip can summon **giant turtles** up

KANDAVU

© DAVID STANLEY

from the sea by singing traditional chants to the *vu* (ancestral spirits) Raunindalithe and Tinandi Thambonga. On a bluff 60 meters above the sea, the garlanded women begin their song, and in 15 minutes a large turtle will appear. This turtle, and sometimes its mates, will swim up and down slowly offshore just below the overhanging rocks. For various reasons, the calling of turtles is performed very rarely these days.

A Hiking Tour

Hike over the mountains from Namuana to **Tavuki** village, seat of the Tui Tavuki, paramount chief of Kandavu. A couple of hours beyond is the **Yawe** District, where large pine tracts have been established. In the villages of Nalotu,

Yakita, and Nanggalotu at Yawe, traditional Fijian **pottery** is still made. Without potter's wheel or kiln, the women shape the pots with a paddle and fire them in an open fire. Sap from the mangroves provides a glaze.

Carry on from Yawe to **Lomati** village, from where you begin the ascent of **Nambukelevu** (838 meters). There's no trail—you'll need a guide to help you hack a way. The abrupt extinct cone of Nambukelevu (Mt. Washington) dominates the west end of Kandavu and renders hiking around the cape too arduous. Petrels nest in holes on the north side of the mountain.

There's **surfing** off Nambukelevuira village at the island's west point, but you'll need a boat. It's strongly suggested that you present a *sevusevu* to the village chief before engaging in this ac-

(top) female green iguana, Orchid Island, near Suva (Doug Hankin);
(bottom left) boy at Tholo-i-Suva Forest Park, near Suva (David Bowden);
(bottom right) Lovoni hike, Ovalau (Don Pitcher)

(top) village on the Trans-Viti Levu trek (David Stanley);
(bottom left) vendors, Singatoka market, Viti Levu (David Stanley);
(bottom right) guard at Government House, Suva (David Bowden)

tivity. Unfortunately, the villagers have become rather hostile to stray tourists who turn up unannounced and pay no heed to local customs.

Cut south from Lomati to **Ndavinggele** village, where another trail leads east along the coast to **Mburelevu,** end of the road from the airstrip. This whole loop can be done in three days without difficulty, but take food and be prepared to sleep rough.

The Great Astrolabe Reef

The Great Astrolabe Reef stretches unbroken for 30 km along the east side of the small islands north of Kandavu. One km wide, the reef is unbelievably rich in coral and marinelife, and because it's so far from shore, it still hasn't been fished out. The reef surrounds a lagoon containing 10 islands, the largest of which is Ono. The reef was named by French explorer Dumont d'Urville, who almost lost his ship, the *Astrolabe,* here in 1827.

There are frequent openings on the west side of the reef and the lagoon is never over 10 fathoms deep, which makes it a favorite of scuba divers and yachties. The Astrolabe also features a vertical drop-off of 10 meters on the inside and 1,800 meters on the outside, with visibility of about 75 meters. The underwater caves and walls here must be seen to be believed.

ACCOMMODATIONS

Near Vunisea

Reece's Place (Bill and Sarah Reece, Box 6, Vunisea, Kandavu; tel. 315-703), on tiny Ngaloa Island just off the northwest corner of Kandavu, was the first to accommodate visitors to Kandavu, and it's still the only inexpensive place to stay at Vunisea station. Conditions are said to have improved since a new management took over in 1994. It's a 15-minute walk from the airstrip to the dock, then a short launch ride to Ngaloa itself (F$6 pp return). There are eight beds (F$12 pp) in four Fijian *mbures,* and a F$9 dormitory; or pitch your tent for F$4 pp. Three good meals cost F$24 pp, and unless you have a camp stove, cooking your own food is not possible. They use an electric generator in the evening. The view of Ngaloa Harbor from Reece's Place is excellent, and there's a long,

dark beach a 10-minute walk away, but the snorkeling in the murky water is only fair. For F$8 pp (minimum of four), you can ride to the Ngaloa Barrier Reef, where the snorkeling is vastly superior. Scuba diving (F$50/75 one/two tanks) and even PADI certification courses (F$295) are offered. If you're there on Sunday, consider attending the service in the village church to hear the wonderful singing.

A more upscale operation is **Matana Resort** (Box 8, Vunisea, Kandavu; tel. 311-780, fax 303-860) at Ndrue, six km north of Vunisea. The four "budget rooms" with shared bath in the beachfront *mbure* are F$55/78/110 single/double/triple, or F$40 pp in a shared three-bed dormitory. An attractive thatched *mbure* with private bath will run F$110 double on the hillside, or F$140/172/203 double/triple/quad for the two larger units on the beach (the only accommodations in which children are accepted). Add F$63 pp a day for the meal plan, as no cooking facilities are available. Sunsets over Mt. Washington from the bar's open terrace can be spectacular. Matana caters mostly to scuba divers who've booked from abroad to dive with **Dive Kandavu,** and diving is available Monday to Saturday at 0930 and 1430 (F$55 per boat dive). Their open-water certification course is F$400. Windsurfers and paddle-boards are free. The snorkeling off Matana's white-sand beach is good and the fantastic Namalata Reef is straight out from the resort. Airport transfers by boat are F$16 pp.

Malawai Resort (Box 1277, Suva; tel. 361-159, fax 361-536) offers colonial-style cottages on a 140-hectare plantation owned by the McLauchlan family, on the north side of Kandavu 15 km east of Vunisea and accessible only by boat. The package price is F$297/390 single/double including meals and airport transfers (three-night minimum stay). Aside from quiet country life, the main attractions here are scuba diving (F$110 for two tanks) and deep-sea fishing (F$500 for four hours). If you don't mind paying top dollar for the ultimate in comfort, convenience, and elegance, Malawai is for you.

Accommodations on North Kandavu

Albert's Place (Albert O'Connor, c/o P.O. Naletha, Kandavu; tel. 302-896), at Langalevu at

Shoppers from outlying villages headed for Kandavu's market land on this beach near Vunisea. The hiking trails of Kandavu vie with untouched beaches such as this one in "downtown" Vunisea.

the east end of Kandavu, is similar to Reece's Place but more remote, more laid-back, and less crowded. Each of the 10 *mbures* has a double and a single bed, coconut mats on the floor, and a kerosene lamp for light. Accommodations are F$15 pp (share twin); camping is F$6 pp. The units share rustic flush toilets and cold showers with plenty of running water (except during droughts), and everything is kept fairly clean. Mosquito nets and coils are supplied.

Meals cost another F$29 pp for all three, but Ruth O'Connor and her daughter Ramona serve huge portions, so breakfast and dinner (F$19) should suffice. Their meals are exceptional, consisting of fresh fish, lobster, chicken curry, or seafood soup, and they bake their own bread daily. Campers who wish to do their own cooking should bring their own food and cooking equipment, as little is available in Michel and Jesse's small store on the premises. There are several lovely waterfalls nearby where you can swim, and in the evening everybody sits around the kava bowl and swaps stories. As there are never more than 20 guests here at a time, it gets very chummy. The snorkeling right off Albert's beach is excellent, and scuba with **Naiqoro Divers** (run by Albert's sons Bruce and Julian) is F$50/88 for a one/two tank boat dive, shore dives F$25. The equipment is new, the prices as good as you'll find anywhere, and these guys know their waters.

The easiest way to get there is on Whippy's twice-weekly boat from Suva (F$38 one-way), which will bring you directly to Albert's Place. The larger and more comfortable Patterson Brothers ferry *Princess Ashika* should leave Suva for Kavala Bay (a good hour west of Albert's on foot) Thursday at midnight every other week (weekly to Vunisea). Albert will pick you up at Vunisea Airport for F$55 each way for two persons, F$25 pp for three or more for the two-hour boat ride (these prices are fixed, so don't bother bargaining). Be sure to let him know you're coming. It's best to allow plenty of time coming and going, so plan a stay at Albert's Place early on during your visit to Fiji so you don't have to be in a big rush to leave. People rave about this property, and we have no hesitation in recommending it as one of the South Pacific's top resorts—just don't expect luxuries like electricity at those prices!

The **Nukumbalavu Resort** (Box 228, Suva; tel. 520-089, fax 303-160) faces a two-km stretch of white sandy beach on the north side of Kandavu, between Albert's and Kavala Bay. Originally a backpackers' camp, the resort has recently been upgraded, and the estate subdivided into 31 lots and sold to American and Australian investors. Two-week dive vacationers are now the target market. With electricity, hot water, and private baths installed, rates for the beachfront *mbures* have quadrupled to

F$55/86/110 single/double/triple, F$32 dorm beds, or F$8 pp for camping. The three-meal package is another F$43. Scuba diving costs F$63/118 one/two tanks for boat dives, F$39 for beach dives, or F$78 for night dives, and a wide range of PADI certification courses are offered at prices that are high for Fiji. The gorgeous Great Astrolabe Reef is only a five-minute boat ride away, and Nukumbalavu claims to have purchased the exclusive right to dive on 50 different sites there! It's still cheaper than Dive Kandavu, though they don't have the same kind of boats available. Every Wednesday there are three-night trekking expeditions at F$255 pp including village accommodations and guides. The Nukumbalavu launch can pick you up at Vunisea airport (F$35 pp each way), or come on Whippy's boat (see "Getting There," below), which will drop you directly at the resort. (Incidentally, there's intense rivalry between Nukumbalavu and Albert's Place, so take whatever you hear from one side or the other with a grain of salt.)

Accommodations on Ono

Jona's Paradise Resort (Box 15447, Suva; tel. 315-889, fax 315-992), formerly known as "Kenia Paradise," at Vambea on the south side of Ono Island, offers accommodation in traditional *mbures* at F$40 pp or camping at F$25 pp. All prices include three hearty meals a day. It's a small, family-style resort with a fine white-sand beach, good snorkeling, and scuba diving. Boat trips are F$65/100 per half/full day and you can also go hiking in the hills. Husband Jona is the best fisherman around (expect fresh fish and lobster every day), wife Ledua is a super cook, young son Veita is an expert guide, and grandfather Villame is a master builder. One reader called this place "the image of paradise." Whippy's boat drops passengers here twice a week, or you can arrange to be collected at Vunisea airport (F$25 pp).

OTHER PRACTICALITIES

There are no restaurants at Vunisea, but a coffee shop at the airstrip opens mornings, and two general stores sell canned goods. A woman at the market serves tea and scones when the market is open, Tuesday through Saturday. Buy *waka* at the co-op store for formal presentations to village hosts.

Occasional carriers ply the roads of Kandavu, but no buses. No banks are to be found on Kandavu either, so change enough money before coming.

GETTING THERE

The easy way to come is on **Air Fiji** from Suva (F$52) four times a week (air pass accepted). **Sunflower Airlines** (tel. 42-010, ext. 42) flies Nandi-Kandavu four times a week (F$66 one-way). The agent at Kandavu watches closely for overweight baggage and sometimes sells more seats than there are in the plane, in which case the locals get priority. Be sure to reconfirm your return flight immediately upon arrival. Only Reece's Place meets all flights—pickups by the resorts on north Kandavu and Ono must be prearranged.

Boats arrive at Vunisea from Suva about twice a week, calling at villages along the north coast. The **Patterson Brothers** ferry *Princess Ashika* departs Suva's Muaiwalu Wharf at Walu Bay every Thursday night at midnight (F$34), returning to Suva on Friday morning. This ship gets crowded so arrive early. The MV *Gurawa* of **Whippy's Shipping Co.** (G.P.O. Box 9, Suva; tel./fax 340-015) leaves Suva for Ono and northern Kandavu Tuesday and Friday at 0600 (F$38 pp), returning to Suva on Wednesday and Saturday. Ask if lunch is included in the fare. Also ask about the new *Kandavu Ferry* which leaves Suva for Kavala Bay on Monday and Wednesday, a comfortable three-and-a-half-hour trip.

THE LOMAIVITI GROUP

The Lomaiviti ("Central Fiji") Group lies in the Koro Sea near the heart of the archipelago, east of Viti Levu and south of Vanua Levu. Of its nine main volcanic islands, Ngau, Koro, and Ovalau are among the largest in Fiji. Lomaiviti's climate is moderate, neither as wet and humid as Suva, nor as dry and hot as Nandi. The population is mostly Fijian, engaged in subsistence agriculture and copra making.

The old capital island, Ovalau, is by far the best known and most visited island of the group, and several small islands south of Ovalau on the way to Suva bear popular backpackers' resorts. Naingani also has a tourist resort of its own, but Koro and Ngau are seldom visited, due to a lack of facilities for visitors. Ferries ply the Koro Sea to Ovalau, while onward ferries run to Vanua Levu a couple of times a week.

OVALAU ISLAND

Ovalau, a large volcanic island just east of Viti Levu, is the main island of the Lomaiviti Group. Almost encircled by high peaks, the Lovoni Valley in the center of Ovalau is actually the island's volcanic crater and about the only flat land. The crater's rim is pierced by the Mbureta River, which escapes through a gap to the southeast. The highest peak is 626-meter Nandelaiovalau (meaning, "the top of Ovalau"), behind Levuka. Luckily Ovalau lacks the magnificent beaches found elsewhere in Fiji, which has kept the package-tour crowd away, and it's still one of the most peaceful, pleasant, and picturesque places to visit in Fiji.

LEVUKA

The town of Levuka on Ovalau's east side was Fiji's capital until the shift to Suva in 1882. Founded as a whaling settlement in 1830, Levuka became the main center for European traders in Fiji, and a British consul was appointed in 1857. The cotton boom of the 1860s brought new settlers and Levuka quickly grew into a boisterous town with over 50 hotels and taverns along Beach Street. Escaped convicts and debtors fleeing creditors in Australia swelled the throng, until it was said that a ship could find the reef passage into Levuka by following the empty gin bottles floating out on the tide. The honest traders felt the need for a stable government, so in 1871 Levuka became capital of Cakobau's Kingdom of Fiji. The disorders continued, with extremist elements forming a "Ku Klux Klan," defiant of any form of Fijian authority.

On 10 October 1874, a semblance of decorum came as Fiji was annexed by Great Britain and a municipal council was formed in 1877. Ovalau's central location seemed ideal for trade, and sailing boats could easily reach the port from Lau or Vanua Levu. Yet the lush green hills that rise behind the town were its downfall, as colonial planners saw that there was no room for the expansion of their capital, and in August 1882 Gov. Sir Arthur Gordon moved his staff to Suva. After a hurricane in 1886, Levuka's devastated buildings were not replaced.

Levuka remained the collection center for the copra trade right up until 1957, but the town seemed doomed when that industry, too, moved to a new mill in Suva. With the establishment of a fishing industry in 1964 things picked up, and today Levuka is a minor educational center, the headquarters of Lomaiviti Province, and a low-impact tourist center. The false-fronted buildings and covered sidewalks along Beach Street give this somnolent town of 3,000 inhabitants a 19th-century, Wild West flavor. It's a perfect base for excursions into the mountains, along the winding coast, or out to the barrier reef a km offshore.

It's customary to say "Good morning," "Mbula," or simply "Hello" to people you meet while strolling around Levuka, especially on the back streets, and the locals have been rather put off by tourists who failed to do so. This is one of the little adverse effects of tourism, and a very unnecessary one at that.

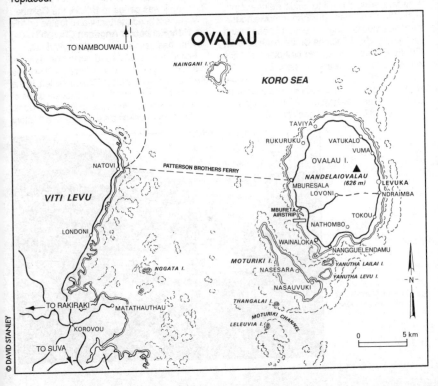

© DAVID STANLEY

SIGHTS

Near Queen's Wharf is the old Morris Hedstrom Ltd. store, erected by Percy Morris and Maynard Hedstrom in 1878, great-granddaddy of today's Pacific-wide Morris Hedstrom chain. In 1980 the building was restored and converted into the **Levuka Community Center** with a museum and library (closed Sunday), where cannibal forks vie with war clubs and clay pots for your attention. Ask at the Community Center next to the museum about guided walking tours of historic Levuka and hikes to Lovoni. The YWCA here sells handicrafts with most of the money going to the craftspeople themselves.

Stroll along Levuka's sleepy waterfront. The **Church of the Sacred Heart,** with its square stone clock tower, was erected by French Marist priests who arrived in 1858. The green neon cross on the tower lines up with another green light farther up the hill to guide mariners into port. When you reach the former movie house, turn left onto Hennings Street and head inland on the left side of Totonga Creek to the **Levuka Public School** (1879), the birthplace of Fiji's present public educational system. Before WW I the only Fijians allowed to attend this school were the sons of chiefs. Other Levuka firsts include Fiji's first newspaper (1869), first Masonic Lodge (1875), and first bank (1876).

Continue straight up Garner Jones Road for about 10 minutes, past the lovely colonial-era houses, and you'll eventually reach the source of the town's water supply, from which there's a good view. The path to **The Peak** branches off to the left between the steel water tank and the gate at the end of the main trail. It takes about an hour to scale The Peak, preferably with the guidance of some of the local kids.

As you come back down the hill, turn left across a small bridge to the **Ovalau Club** (see "Entertainment" below), adjoining the old **Town Hall** (1898) and **Masonic Lodge.** A few blocks north of the Club, past the Royal Hotel, are the 199 steps up **Mission Hill** to an old Methodist school with a fine view.

North of Levuka

On a low hill farther north along the waterfront is the **European War Memorial,** which recalls British residents of Levuka who died in WW I. Before Fiji was ceded to Britain, the Cakobau government headquarters was situated on this hill. **Holy Redeemer Anglican Church** (1904) beyond has period stained-glass windows.

Follow the coastal road north from Levuka to a second yellow bridge, where you'll see the **old Methodist church** (1869) on the left. In the small cemetery behind the church is the grave of the first U.S. consul to Fiji, John Brown Williams. For the story of Williams's activities, see "History

view of Levuka, as
seen from Gun Rock

DAVID STANLEY

The Provincial Council meeting place at Levuka is built like a traditional Fijian chief's mbure.

and Government" in the Introduction chapter. Across the bridge and beneath a large *ndilo* tree is the tomb of an old king of Levuka. The large house in front of the tree is the residence of the present Tui Levuka.

Directly above is **Gun Rock,** which was used as a target in 1849 to show Cakobau the efficacy of a ship's cannon so he might be more considerate to resident Europeans. The early Fijians had a fort atop the Rock to defend themselves against the Lovoni hill tribes. Ask permission of the Tui Levuka (the "Roko") or a member of his household to climb Gun Rock for a splendid view of Levuka. If a small boy leads you up and down, it wouldn't be out of place to give him something for his trouble. From the summit, let your eyes follow the horizon from right to left to view the islands of Ngau, Mbatiki, Nairai, Wakaya, Koro, Makongai, and Vanua Levu, respectively.

Continue north on the road, round a bend, pass the ruin of a large concrete building, and you'll reach a cluster of government housing on the site of a cricket field where the Duke of York (later King George V) played in 1878.

There's a beautiful deep pool and waterfall behind **Waitovu** village, about two km north of Levuka. You may swim here, but please don't skinny-dip; this is offensive to the local people and has led to serious incidents in the past. Since they're good enough to let you use this idyllic spot (which they own), it's common courtesy to respect their wishes.

South of Levuka

The **Pacific Fishing Company** tuna cannery (Box 41, Levuka; tel. 440-005, fax 440-400) is south of Queen's Wharf. A Japanese cold-storage facility opened here in 1964, the cannery in 1975. After sustaining losses for four years, the Japanese company involved in the joint venture pulled out in 1986, turning the facility over to the government, which now owns the cannery. In 1989 a F$2 million state-of-the-art can-making factory opened alongside the cannery, and major improvements to the wharf, freezer, storage, and other facilities were completed in 1992. The plant is supplied with albacore tuna caught in Kiribati and Solomons waters by Taiwanese longline fishing boats, and with skipjack and yellowfin by pole-and-line ships of the government-owned Ika Corporation. For both environmental and quality-control reasons, fish caught with nets are not accepted here. Most of the F$50 million worth of canned tuna produced each year is marketed in Britain by Sainsbury and John West, and in Canada by B.C. Packers. A thousand residents of Ovalau have jobs directly related to tuna canning, and a rumored privatization and shift of the whole operation to Suva would have devastating consequences for Levuka.

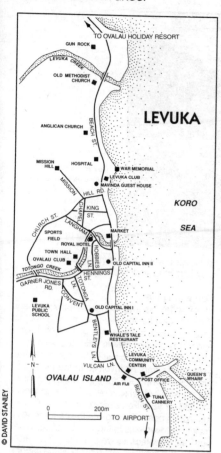

LEVUKA

KORO

SEA

OVALAU ISLAND

0   200m

© DAVID STANLEY

A little farther along is the **Cession Monument**, where the Deed of Cession, which made Fiji a British colony, was signed by Chief Cakobau in 1874. A traditional *mbure* used for Provincial Council meetings is on the other side of the road.

One of Fiji's best hikes begins at Ndraimba village, one km south of the Cession Monument. A road to the right, just before four single-story rows of apartments, marks the start of the four-and-a-half-hour hike through enchanting forests and across clear streams to **Lovoni** village. Go straight back on the road, pass a metal scrapyard, cut up the hill, and follow the beaten path ahead. The trail is no longer used by the locals and requires attentiveness to follow, so consider hiring a guide at the Community Center next to the museum if you're not an experienced hiker. Be sure to reach Lovoni before 1500 to be able to catch the last bus back to Levuka. It's also possible to hike to Lovoni from Rukuruku. In 1855 the fierce Lovoni tribe, the Ovalau, burned Levuka, and they continued to threaten the town right up until 1871 when they were finally captured during a truce and sold to European planters as laborers. In 1875 the British government allowed the survivors to return to their valley, where their descendants live today.

If you forgo this hike and continue on the main road, you'll come to an old **cemetery** a little south of Ndraimba. A few kilometers farther is the **Devil's Thumb,** a dramatic volcanic plug towering above **Tokou** village, one of the scenic highlights of Fiji. Catholic missionaries set up a printing press at Tokou in 1889 to produce gospel lessons in Fijian. In the center of the village is a sculpture of a lion made by one of the early priests. It's five km back to Levuka.

Wainaloka village on the southwest side of Ovalau is inhabited by descendants of Solomon Islanders from the Lau Lagoon region who were blackbirded in Fiji over a century ago.

ACCOMMODATIONS

There's a good choice of inexpensive places to stay around Levuka. The **Old Capital Inn I** (Box 50, Levuka; tel. 440-057) on Convent Road is one of the cheapest, with six double rooms above the restaurant at F$9/16 single/double, and dorm beds at F$8 pp, a cooked breakfast included (if you want to skip the breakfast you'll save a dollar). There's no hot water.

The low-budget traveler's best bet is the Inn's annex, the **Old Capital Inn II** (tel. 440-013) on Beach Street. The 15 fan-cooled rooms cost the same as rooms at Inn I (where guests at both places take their breakfast). A separate cottage with cooking facilities is F$13/24/29 single/double/triple—good value. It's quieter than Inn I, but the quality of the beds in the dorm section here is poor. A cool breeze blowing in from the east keeps the mosquitoes away.

Mavinda Guesthouse (Box 4, Levuka; tel. 440-477) on Beach Street, which has been functioning since 1869, is Fiji's oldest guesthouse. This old-fashioned English bed and breakfast owned by Patterson Brothers Shipping occupies a spacious colonial house on the waterfront near the Levuka Club. The 12 rooms are F$12/24 single/double, or F$8 in the dormitory, cooked breakfast included. You can order an excellent dinner here for F$5. It's worth asking to see the room beforehand as all are different, and they're sometimes reluctant to give out their best rooms for some reason. Ask for a mosquito net. If you do get a good room, it's excellent, otherwise you'll do better elsewhere. Backpackers are accepted here, but if you quibble over the rates they'll suggest you try the Old Capital Inn.

For the full Somerset Maugham flavor, stay at the 15-room **Royal Hotel** (Box 47, Levuka; tel. 440-024). Built in 1852 and renovated in the 1890s, this is Fiji's oldest regular hotel, now run by the Ashley family. In the lounge, ceiling fans revolve above the rattan sofas and potted plants, and the fan-cooled rooms upstairs with private bath are pleasant, with much-needed mosquito nets provided. At F$16/23/27 single/double/triple, the colonial atmosphere and impeccable service make it about the best value in Fiji. There's also a F$7 dorm, and they have one two-bedroom cottage with cooking facilities at F$55. Checkout time is 1000, but you can arrange to stay until 1500 by paying another 50% of the daily rate. Hotel staff will do your laundry for about F$5. Everybody loves this place, but don't order dinner (F$8) here as the food isn't highly rated. The bar, beer garden, snooker tables, and videos are strictly for guests only.

Beach Resorts

A good choice for families is the **Ovalau Holiday Resort** (Stephen and Rosemary Diston, Box 113, Levuka; tel. 440-329) on a rocky beach at Vuma, four km north of Levuka (taxi F$5). *Mbures* are F$22/35/45 single/double/triple, or F$8 pp in the dorm. Camping is F$5 pp, with the use of the dorm facilities. Cooking facilities and hot showers are provided, and there's the Mbula Beach Bar in a converted whaler's cottage. The restaurant does some fine home cooking, and the snorkeling here is good. The swimming pool is the only one on Ovalau. The resort has a six-passenger boat for rent for full-day excursions to Makongai (F$100) or fishing trips (F$25 for three hours).

On the northwest side of Ovalau is quiet, lovely **Rukuruku Resort** (Box 112, Levuka; no phone), 20 km from Levuka. There's a large campground (F$6 pp), complete with toilets, showers, barbecue, and kitchen. Dormitory-style accommodations (F$8 pp including breakfast) are also available, or stay in a four-person *mbure* for F$15 pp a day. The restaurant/bar is somewhat overpriced, but basic groceries may be purchased in the adjacent Fijian village, though there are no cooking facilities. The black-sand beach is only so-so, but the snorkeling out on the reef is good, and there's a natural freshwater swimming pool in the river adjacent to the resort. A vanilla plantation and beautiful verdant mountains cradle Rukuruku on the island side. Rukuruku bookings can be made at the Whale's Tale Restaurant in Levuka, but be aware, poor management has allowed it to become run-down and the service is lackadaisical.

FOOD

Few of the guesthouses in Levuka provide cooking facilities, but the recent influx of backpackers has caused a half dozen small restaurants to blossom where there was formerly nowhere to eat out. All of these places are patronized mostly by foreigners, and prices are higher that what you may have paid in Suva or Lautoka, but with luck you'll enjoy some superior meals.

An inexpensive place for lunch is the little **takeaway stand** in Patterson Gardens, between the Levuka Community Center and the power plant. It serves fish and curry plates and tasty homemade desserts, which you can consume seated at one of the picnic tables overlooking the sea. It's closed on Sunday.

Cafe Levuka (tel. 440-095), on Beach Street adjacent to the Community Center, serves a three-course dinner (F$7) daily until 2000. When this place opened in 1990, it quickly became the town's premier eatery. Since then it has been rather eclipsed by newer places, although it's still a good place to find out what's happening around town over coffee and cakes. Their fruit pancakes are great for breakfast. This place recently changed ownership and things could be different.

Kim's Restaurant (Monday to Saturday 0800-1400/1800-2000), on Beach Street diagonally opposite the Community Center, is slightly cheaper than some of the other tourist-oriented restaurants, but the food is excellent with each dish individually prepared. Peruse their extensive menu posted over the counter—recommended.

The Chinese restaurant at **Old Capital Inn I** (tel. 440-057; daily 0700-2100) on Convent Road is famous for its all-you-can-eat dinner Sunday at 1800 (F$7), a long-running local institution. There's a good selection of items in their buffet, and cold beer is available.

The **Whale's Tale Restaurant** (tel. 440-235; daily 1130-2100) on Beach Street is the current favorite for its real home cooking at medium prices (delicious mahimahi and salad for F$7). They're fully licensed so you can get a beer with your meal, but it's also a nice place to stop for a coffee. They sell bags of kava and genuine Fijian handicrafts (no bizarre devil masks).

The **Shipwreck Restaurant,** another component of the Old Capital Inn empire, on Beach Street next to the Church of the Sacred Heart, posts its menu in the window. Their prices are just a bit above Kim's, and the food is also good.

Deepak's Restaurant (tel. 440-314), on Beach Street just north of the Church of the Sacred Heart, is cheap but basic and not very inviting.

ENTERTAINMENT

Despite the Members Only sign, you're welcome to enter the **Ovalau Club** (tel. 440-102), said to be the oldest membership club in the South Pacific. You'll meet genuine South Seas characters here, and the place is brimming with atmosphere. Ask the bartender to show you the framed letter from Count Felix von Luckner, the WW I German sea wolf. Von Luckner left the letter and some money at the unoccupied residence of a trader on Katafanga Island in the Lau Group, from which he took some provisions. In the letter, Count von Luckner identifies himself as Max Pemberton, an English writer on a sporting cruise through the Pacific.

A good place for sunsets is the **Levuka Club** (tel. 440-272) on Beach Street, which has a nice backyard with picnic tables for a drink by the waterside. It's less visited by tourists and a better choice than the Ovalau Club if you only want a quick beer.

SERVICES AND INFORMATION

The **Westpac Bank** (tel. 440-346) and the **National Bank** on Beach Street change traveler's checks; the Westpac gives a slightly better rate. Cafe Levuka will change traveler's checks anytime at the bank rate less a three percent commission.

Cafe Levuka will wash, dry, and fold your laundry within three hours for F$7.

Public toilets are available behind the Levuka Community Center (ask directions).

Lisa at the Whale's Tale Restaurant (tel. 440-235) will be happy to give you her frank opinion of the offshore resorts—invaluable when planning a trip. Cafe Levuka (tel. 440-095) maintains a "Visitors' Information Book" containing current information about almost every aspect of travel around Ovalau. The restaurant staffs are the people most likely to give you a straight answer to any question you may have about Levuka. Cafe Levuka also runs a one-for-one book exchange.

TRANSPORTATION

Air Fiji (tel. 440-139), across the street from the museum, has two or three flights a day from Mbureta Airport to Suva (F$33). The Ovalau Tours minibus from Levuka to the airstrip is F$3 pp (a taxi will run F$17).

Inquire at **Patterson Brothers** (tel. 440-125) beside the market on Beach Street about the direct ferry from Ovalau to Nambouwalu, Vanua Levu, via Natovi. The connecting bus departs Levuka at about 0500 Monday to Saturday. At Nambouwalu, there's an onward bus to Lambasa, but bookings must be made in advance (F$35 straight through).

The bus/ferry/bus service between Suva and Levuka was discussed previously under "Transportation" in the Suva chapter. Two competing services are available, each taking around five hours right through and costing around F$19.

The Patterson Brothers combination involves an express bus from Levuka to Mburesala daily except Sunday at 0500, a 45-minute ferry ride from Mburesala to Natovi, then the same bus on to Suva (change at Korovou for Lautoka). The other choice is the *Emosi Express* leaving Queen's Wharf, Levuka, at 0900 on Monday, Wednesday, Friday, and Saturday to Mbau Landing, then a minibus to Suva (arriving at 1400). Southbound you can get off in Nausori and connect with the Sunbeam Transport bus to Lautoka at 1400. Inquire at the Old Capital Inn. From Levuka, Emosi's boat is more conveniently timed and there's a brief stop at Leleuvia Island, where free stopovers are possible. Advance bookings are required on the Patterson Brothers ferry/bus service but not on Emosi's boat. Use a different service each way for a scenic circle trip from Suva.

Both taxis and carriers park across the street from the Church of the Sacred Heart in Levuka. Due to steep hills on the northwest side of Ovalau, there isn't a bus right around the island. Carriers leave from Levuka at 0715 or 1200 for Rukuruku village (F$1.30) along a beautiful, hilly road. There are also occasional buses and carriers to Lovoni (F$1). There's no service on Sunday or late in the afternoon.

The YWCA next to Cafe Levuka rents mountain bikes at F$12 a day, but most are in bad shape.

Tours

Ratu Niumaia Turaganicolo at the Levuka Community Center (Box 124, Levuka; tel. 440-356) on Beach Street offers 15 different guided tours around Levuka and Ovalau. His guided hike from Levuka or Rukuruku to Lovoni is F$16 pp including lunch. The bus tour to Lovoni is also F$16, or pay F$21 for a trip right around Ovalau, both including lunch. The reef tours (F$10 pp including lunch) are great for swimming and snorkeling, and you'll be shown sharks if you ask. Four people are required for any of these tours. If you'd like to climb the peak that towers behind Levuka, a guide can be arranged. Ratu Niumaia welcomes visitors who want to drop into his office Monday to Saturday around 1700 for a chat about the history of Ovalau. There's no charge for this; it's just a way of drumming up business for his trips. Soft drinks are sold at normal Fijian prices. A guided walk around Levuka with Ratu Niumaia is F$5 pp.

ISLANDS OFF OVALAU

Yanutha Lailai Island

It was on tiny Yanutha Lailai Island, just off the south end of Ovalau, that the first 463 indentured Indian laborers to arrive in Fiji landed from the ship *Leonidas* on 14 May 1879. To avoid the introduction of cholera or smallpox into Fiji, the immigrants spent two months in quarantine on Yanutha Lailai. Later Nukulau Island off Suva became Fiji's main quarantine station.

It's possible to stay on Yanutha Lailai at **Lost Island Resort**. Dorm beds cost F$7 pp, *mbures* F$9 pp, camping F$6 pp, and three meals a day are another F$8 (F$5 for the *lovo* special). Reef tours from Lost Island are F$5 pp, and transfers from Levuka F$11 pp each way. It's also possible to visit on a day-trip from Levuka at F$25 pp, lunch included. For information contact Levi at the Levuka Community Center.

Moturiki Island

Small outboards to Moturiki Island depart Nangguelendamu Landing most afternoons. The best beaches are on the east side of Moturiki. Camping is officially discouraged, but possible.

Thangalai Island

Thangalai is owned by the Methodist Church of Fiji, which runs a small backpackers' resort on this palm-fringed island. The 12 *mbures* are F$12 pp (triple occupancy), otherwise pay F$7 pp in the dormitory without meals, or camp for F$7 pp. Three meals are another F$10 pp. It's primitive but adequate, and the island and people are great. Dress up for Sunday service in the village church. Information should be available at Cafe Levuka (boat from Levuka daily at 1000, F$10 pp). Reader Philip R. Marshall of Playa del Rey, California, sent us this:

Thangalai is not for every tourist. It's very small, taking about 10 minutes to walk around, and has simple unhygienic facilities. The one outhouse-style toilet must be flushed with buckets of seawater. Bathing is accomplished in a small shed with brackish water handpumped into buckets. Electricity is generated only during dinner hours, if the generator works (it did briefly on only one of my three nights there). On the positive side, the people are wonderfully friendly hosts, with music and kava in the evenings, but there is little to do. The snorkeling is fairly good in the vicinity (bring your own gear). I think Thangalai might appeal to people who have not spent much time on islands, who would enjoy a rough Gilligan's Island experience.

Leleuvia Island

Emosi Yee Show of Levuka's Old Capitol Inn runs a small backpackers' resort (tel. 301-584) on Leleuvia, a lovely isolated reef island with nothing but coconut trees, sandy beaches, and a ramshackle assortment of tourist huts scattered across the island. Accommodations run F$19 pp in the dorm, F$22 pp in a thatched hut, F$28 pp in a wooden bungalow, or F$17 pp if you camp. Included are three basic meals (rationed, not buffet) served punctually at 0800, 1200, and 1800. You get lots of fried food and repeats of the same dishes, but vegetarian food is possible. Water is in short supply on Leleuvia, and bathing is with a bucket of brackish water. The small shop sells candy, cake, and drinks. The owners' boat drops off as many people as possible, and it can get *very* crowded (pick Thangalai instead if you'd rather do your own thing).

Leleuvia is popular among backpackers who like to drink beer and party a lot (live music in the evening), so don't come expecting a rest. Actually, it sort of depends on who is on the island at the time. Sometimes it's great fun with lots of neat people, but other times the scene is dominated by "groupies" and newcomers are excluded. One reader called it "a Boy Scout holiday camp." Peace returns around 2230 when the generator switches off.

Plenty of activities are laid on, especially reef trips by boat (F$5 pp) and scuba diving (F$44/66 one/two tanks on the same day), and on Sunday they'll even take you to church! For a nominal amount they'll drop you off on one-tree "Honeymoon Island." Leleuvia is the only Lomaiviti resort offering scuba diving, and resident instructors Nobi and Andrea have taught diving to quite a few guests. This isn't surprising because at F$298, it's about the cheapest PADI open-water certification course available in Fiji (this price only applies if several people are taking lessons at the same time). If you just want a taste of diving their resort course is F$44 from shore, or F$77 from boat and shore. The snorkeling is also excellent though the sea is sometimes cold.

Getting there is easy on the *Emosi Express* from Levuka at 0800 daily except Sunday. From Suva, you can catch the bus at 46 Gordon St. Monday, Wednesday, Friday, and Saturday at 1200 and arrive via Mbau Landing (F$18 roundtrip). Leleuvia is a free stopover on all of Emosi's regular trips between Levuka and Suva. Day-trips to Leleuvia from Levuka with lunch are also possible. All bookings should be made through the Old Capital Inn in Levuka, or at Rosie Tours (tel. 313-366), 46 Gordon St., Suva.

Naingani

Naingani, 11 km off Viti Levu, is a lush tropical island near Ovalau at the west end of the Lomaiviti Group, with pristine beaches and only one Fijian village in the southwest corner. It's just the right size for exploring on foot, and there's a medium-priced place to stay.

Naingani Island Resort (Box 12539, Suva; tel. 300-925, fax 300-539), also known as Mystery Island Resort, offers 12 comfortable fan-cooled bungalows sleeping up to six persons at F$180. Children under 12 get a 50% discount, so this is a good place for families, and lower off-season rates sometimes apply from mid-September to March (excepting Christmas)—ask. Unfortunately the cooking facilities have been removed from the units and you're now required to take the F$35 pp meal plan. Some nonmotorized water sports are free. The minibus/launch connection from Suva daily at 1000 is F$55 roundtrip, and bookings can be made at their Suva office at 22 Cumming St., 2nd Floor. From Levuka, call them up and arrange to be collected by the speedboat at Taviya village on the northwest side of Ovalau (accessible on the Rukuruku truck) at F$12 pp each way.

OTHER ISLANDS OF THE LOMAIVITI GROUP

Makongai

Makongai shares a figure-eight-shaped barrier reef with neighboring Wakaya. The anchorage is in Dalithe Bay on the northwest side of the island. From 1911 to 1969 this was a leper colony staffed by Catholic nuns; the colony also received patients from various other Pacific island groups. Many of the old hospital buildings still stand. Today Makongai is owned by the Department of Agriculture, which runs an experimental sheep farm here, with some 2,000 animals. A new breed obtained by crossing British and Caribbean sheep bears little wool and is intended as a source of mutton.

Wakaya

A high cliff on the west coast of Wakaya is known as Chieftain's Leap, for a young chief who threw himself over the edge to avoid capture by his foes. Chief Cakobau sold Wakaya to Europeans in 1840, and it has since had many owners. In 1862 David Whippy set up Fiji's first sugar mill on Wakaya. Red deer imported from New Caledonia run wild across the island.

In 1976 Canadian industrialist David Harrison Gilmour bought the island for US$3 million, and in 1990 he opened **The Wakaya Club** (Box 15424, Suva; tel. 440-128, fax 440-406), with eight spacious cottages at F$1050/1375 single/double, all-inclusive (three-night minimum stay). Children under 16 are not accommodated. There's a nine-hole golf course open to guests, scuba diving, and an airstrip for charter flights (F$1200 roundtrip per couple from Nandi). As you might expect at these prices (Fiji's highest!), it's all very tasteful and luxurious. The rest of Wakaya has been subdivided into 150 parcels, which are being sold to foreigners as homesites at US$385,000 and up (contact René Boehm in Hamburg, Germany, at fax 040-340-568).

The German raider, Count Felix von Luckner, was captured on Wakaya during WW I. His ship, the *Seeadler,* had foundered on a reef at Maupihaa in the Society Islands on 2 August 1917.

The 105 survivors (prisoners included) camped on Maupihaa while on 23 August von Luckner and five men set out in an open boat to capture a schooner and continue the war. On 21 September 1917 they found a suitable ship at Wakaya. Their plan was to go aboard pretending to be passengers and capture it, but a British officer and four Indian soldiers happened upon the scene. Not wishing to go against the rules of chivalry and fight in civilian clothes, the count gave himself up and was interned at Auckland as a prisoner of war. He later wrote a book, *The Sea Devil,* about his experiences.

Mbatiki

Mbatiki has a large interior lagoon of brackish water surrounded by mudflats. Four Fijian villages are on Mbatiki, but due to hazardous reefs there's no safe anchorage for ships. Fine baskets are made here.

Nairai

Seven Fijian villages are found on this 336-meter-high island between Koro and Ngau. The inhabitants are known for their woven handicrafts. Hazardous reefs stretch out in three directions, and in 1808 the brigantine *Eliza* was wrecked here. Among the survivors was Charles Savage, who served as a mercenary for the chiefs of Mbau for five years until falling into the clutches of Vanua Levu cannibals.

Koro

Koro is an eight-by-16-km island shaped like a shark's tooth. A ridge traverses the island from northeast to southwest, reaching 561 meters near the center. High jungle-clad hillsides drop sharply to the coast. The best beach is along the south coast between Mundu and the lighthouse at Muanivanua Point. Among Koro's 14 large Fijian villages is **Nasau,** the government center with post office, hospital, and schools.

The road to **Vatulele** village on the north coast climbs from Nasau to the high plateau at the center of the island. The coconut trees and mangoes of the coast are replaced by great tree ferns and thick rainforest. Mr. Amena Tave, chief of Vatulele, can arrange accommodations in the village or give you a place to camp.

At **Nathamaki** village, in the northeast corner of Koro, turtle calling is still practiced. The caller stands on Tuinaikasi, a high cliff about a kilometer west of the village, and repeats the prescribed words to bring the animals to the surface. The ritual does work, although the turtles are becoming scarce and only one or two may appear. If anyone present points a finger or camera at a turtle, they quickly submerge. Actually, it's not possible to photograph the turtles, as magic is involved—the photos wouldn't show any turtles. Anyway, you're so high above the water you'd need the most powerful telephoto lens just to pick them out. (One reader wrote in to report that no turtles have appeared since 1987, due to the killing of a shark by a local villager.)

KORO

The track south between Nathamaki and Tua Tua runs along a golden palm-fringed beach. There's a cooperative store at **Nangaindamu** where you can buy *yanggona* and supplies. Koro kava is Fiji's best. A 30-minute hike up a steep trail from the co-op brings you to a waterfall and idyllic swimming hole. Keep left if you're on your own (taking a guide would be preferable).

Koro has an unusual inclined **airstrip** on the east side of the island near Namathu village. You land uphill, take off downhill. Sunflower Airlines can bring you here from Suva three times a week (F$60), and several carriers meet the flights.

The weekly Patterson Brothers and Consort Shipping Line ships from Suva tie up to the wharf near Muanivanua Point. All the ferries plying between Suva and Savusavu/Taveuni call here. Consort's *Spirit of Free Enterprise* calls northbound on Wednesday afternoon and early Sunday morning; the southbound trips often pass Koro without stopping. The Patterson Brothers ferry *Princess Ashika* leaves Suva for Koro at midnight Monday (F$31), departs Koro for Savusavu at 1100 Tuesday, then leaves Savusavu again for Koro at 1700 Wednesday, departing Koro for Suva at 2030. This vessel can also be used to travel between Koro and Ngau.

There are no hotels on Koro or Ngau, so you'll have to stay with locals or ask permission to camp. On both islands your best bet is to wait till you meet someone from there, then ask them to write you a letter of introduction to their relatives back home on the island. It's always best to know someone before you arrive. Make it clear you're willing to pay your own way, then don't neglect to do so.

Ngau

Ngau is the fifth-largest island in Fiji, with 16 villages and 13 settlements. There's a barrier reef on the west coast, but only a fringing reef on the east. A hot-spring swimming pool is close to the P.W.D. depot at **Waikama**. From Waikama, hike along the beach and over the hills to **Somosomo** village. If you lose the way, look for the creek at the head of the bay and work your way up it until you encounter the trail. There's a bathing pool in Somosomo with emerald green water.

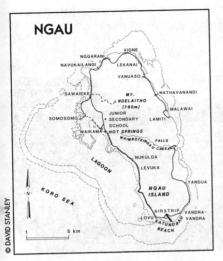

A road runs from Somosomo to **Sawaieke** village, where the Takalaingau, high chief of Ngau, resides. The remnants of one of the only surviving pagan temples *(mbure kalou)* in Fiji is beside the road at the junction in Sawaieke. The high stone mound is still impressive.

It's possible to climb **Mt. Ndelaitho** (760 meters), highest on the island, from Sawaieke in three or four hours. The first hour is the hardest. From the summit there is a sweeping view. MacGillivray's Fiji petrel, a rare seabird of the albatross family, lays its eggs underground on Ngau's jungle-clad peaks. Only two specimens have ever been taken: one by the survey ship *Herald* in 1855, and a second by local writer Dick Watling in 1984.

The co-op and government station (hospital, post office, etc.) are at **Nggarani** at the north end of Ngau. Two ships a week arrive here from Suva on an irregular schedule, but there is no wharf so they anchor offshore. The wharf at **Waikama** is used only for government boats.

There are a number of waterfalls on the east coast, the best known behind **Lekanai** and up Waimboteingau Creek, both an hour's walk off the main road. The "weather stone" is on the beach, a five-minute walk south of **Yandua** village. Bad weather is certain if you step on it or hit it with another stone.

There are no guesthouses on Ngau, but the driver of the carrier serving the airstrip may be willing to arrange village accommodations. Have your *sevusevu* ready and also contribute F$10 pp a day, at least. The airstrip is on Katundrau Beach at the south end of Ngau. Flights to/from Suva on Sunflower Airlines are F$42 each way.

The Patterson Brothers ferry *Princess Ashika* departs Suva for Ngau Monday at midnight, leaving Ngau for Savusavu Tuesday at 0600. Southbound, the same ship departs Savusavu for Ngau Wednesday at 1700, leaving Ngau for Suva Thursday at 0700 (F$29). The same vessel also calls at Koro and Taveuni.

Fijian mbure

SALVATORE CASA

VANUA LEVU

Though only half as big as Viti Levu, 5,556-square-km Vanua Levu ("Great Land") has much to offer. The transport is good, the scenery varied, the people warm and hospitable, and far fewer visitors reach this part of Fiji than heavily promoted Nandi/Singatoka/Suva. Fijian villages are numerous all the way around the island—here you'll be able to experience real Fijian life, so it's well worth making the effort to visit Fiji's second largest island.

The drier northwest side of Vanua Levu features sugarcane fields and pine forests, while on the damper southeast side copra plantations predominate, with a little cocoa around Natewa Bay. Toward the southeast the scenery is the more bucolic beauty of coconut groves dipping down toward the sea. Majestic bays cut into the island's south side, and one of the world's longest barrier reefs flanks the north coast. There are some superb locations here just waiting to be discovered, both above and below the waterline.

Fiji Indians live in the large market town of Lambasa and the surrounding cane-growing area; most of the rest of Vanua Levu is Fijian. Together Vanua Levu, Taveuni, and adjacent islands form Fiji's Northern Division (often called simply "the north"), which is subdivided into three provinces: the west end of Vanua Levu is Mbua Province; most of the north side of Vanua Levu is Mathuata Province; and the southeast side of Vanua Levu and Taveuni comprise Thakaundrove Province. You won't regret touring this area.

Nambouwalu

The ferry from Viti Levu ties up to the wharf at this friendly little government station (the headquarters of Mbua Province), near the southern tip of Vanua Levu. The view from the wharf is picturesque, with Seseleka (421 meters) and, in good weather, Yandua Island visible to the northwest. From here it's 137 km by bus to Lambasa, or 141 km to Savusavu.

There are no hotels at Nambouwalu, but the lovely **Government Rest House,** up on the hillside above Nambouwalu, has two rooms with shared cooking facilities at F$5.50 pp. Try to make advance reservations with the district officer, Mbua, in Nambouwalu (tel. 84-010, ext. 60). Upon arrival, you could inquire at the Administrative Offices next to the post office, up on

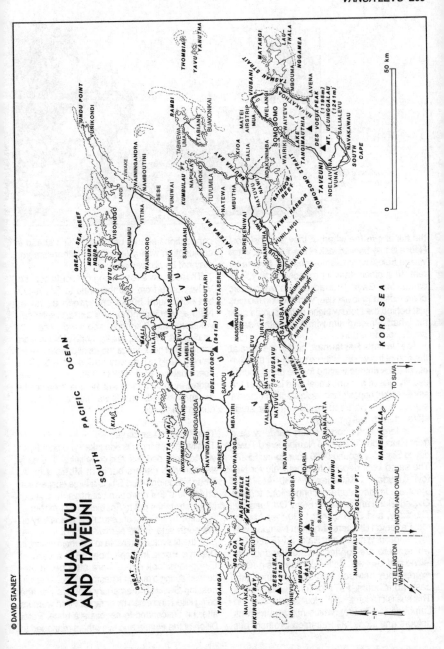

Dillon's fight
with the Fijians

M. G. L. DOMENY DE RIENZI

the hill above the wharf. If they say the Rest House is fully booked, ask at the **Y.W.C.A.** in the village below which sometimes has a room for rent. In a pinch, they'll probably allow you to camp. **Mr. Gaya Prasad** runs a very basic *dharamshala* (guesthouse) with cooking facilities just behind the store with the petrol pumps near the wharf. Present him with a monetary *sevu-sevu* upon departure.

The **Seaside Restaurant,** next to the store at the end of the wharf, is there mostly for the benefit of truck drivers waiting for the ferry, and it's usually closed at night. Local food is sold at the small market opposite this restaurant and there's sometimes a barbecue outside. Four small stores nearby sell groceries.

The large Patterson Brothers car ferry sails from Natovi on Viti Levu to Nambouwalu Tuesday to Saturday around 0600 (four hours, F$27). The same boat departs Nambouwalu for Natovi Tuesday to Saturday at 1030. At Natovi there are immediate ferry connections to/from Ovalau Island and buses to Suva. On Tuesday, Thursday, and Saturday at 1130 there's a direct Patterson Brothers ferry from Nambouwalu to Ellington Wharf near Rakiraki (F$26.40), where there are connections to Nananu-i-Ra Island and Lautoka. Patterson Brothers runs an express bus between Nambouwalu and Lambasa (four hours, F$7) for ferry passengers. This bus is quicker than the four regular buses to Lambasa (six hours), which make numerous detours and stops. All Patterson Brothers bus connections should be booked well ahead in conjunction with a ferry ticket, otherwise you may not be allowed aboard.

There's now a road along the south coast of Vanua Levu from Nambouwalu to Savusavu, but eastbound buses only reach as far as Ndaria, westbound buses as far as Nandi-vakarua. The 20-km gap is covered by carriers (trucks). At Thongea, five km north of Ndaria, are some small hot springs the local people use for bathing. Gold mining was carried out at Mt. Kasi near Ndawara from 1932 to 1943, and a study is underway to determine whether the mine can be recommissioned. Bauxite was mined in this area during the 1970s.

The Road to Lambasa

This twisting, tiring bus ride takes you past Fijian villages, rice paddies, and cane fields. The early sandalwood traders put in at **Mbua Bay.** At Mbua village on Mbua Bay is a large suspension bridge and the dry open countryside west of Mbua stretches out to Seseleka (421 meters).

About 13 km west of Lekutu, at Ngaloa Bay on the north side of the narrow neck of land that joins the Naivaka Peninsula to the main island, is **Dillon's Rock.** In September 1813 a party of Europeans took refuge here after being ambushed during a raid on a nearby village. After witnessing Swedish mercenary Charles Savage being killed and eaten by enraged Fijian warriors after he descended to negotiate a truce, Peter Dillon of the *Hunter* and two others managed to escape to their boat by holding muskets to the head of an important chief and walking between the assembled cannibals. (In 1826 Dillon earned his place in Pacific history by discovering relics from the La Pérouse expedition on Vanikoro Island in the Solomons, finally solving the mystery of the disappearance in 1788 of that famous French contemporary of Captain Cook.)

About five km north of Lekutu Secondary School, one km off the main road (bus drivers know the place), is Fiji's most accessible yet least known waterfall, the **Naselesele Falls.** This is a perfect place to picnic between bus rides, with a nice grassy area where you could camp. The falls are most impressive during the rainy season, but the greater flow means muddy water, so swimming is best in the dry season. There's a large basalt pool below the falls, and since nobody lives in the immediate vicinity you'll probably have the place to yourself. Much of this part of the island has been reforested with pine.

Farther east the road passes a major rice-growing area and runs along the **Ndreketi River,** Vanua Levu's largest. A rice mill at Ndreketi and citrus project at Mbatiri are features of this area. The pavement begins near the junction with the road from Savusavu. In the Seanggangga settlement area between Mbatiri and Lambasa, about 60 square km of native land were cleared and planted with sugarcane and pine during the 1970s.

LAMBASA

Lambasa is a busy Indian market town, which services Vanua Levu's major cane-growing area. It's Fiji's third-largest city, with 18,000 inhabitants, four banks, and the Northern Division and Mathuata Province headquarters. Lambasa was built on a delta where the shallow Lambasa and Oawa rivers enter the sea; maritime transport is limited to small boats. Large ships must anchor off Malau, 11 km north. Lambasa's lack of an adequate port has hindered development.

Other than providing a good base from which to explore the surrounding countryside and a place to spend the night, Lambasa has little to interest the average tourist. That's its main attraction: since few visitors come, there's adventure in the air, good food in the restaurants, and fun places to drink (for males—women might find them rowdy). It's not beautiful but it is real, and the bus ride that brings you here is great.

SIGHTS

Lambasa has an attractive riverside setting with one long main street lined with shops and restaurants. The park along the riverside near the Lambasa Club is quite pleasant.

The **Lambasa Sugar Mill,** on the Oawa River two km east of town, opened in 1894. At the height of the crushing season from May to December there's usually a long line of trucks, tractors, and trains waiting to unload cane at the mill—a most picturesque sight. From the road here you get a view of **Three Sisters Hill** to the right.

Anyone with an interest in archaeology should take the two-km ride on the Nakoroutari bus to **Wasavula** on the southern outskirts of Lambasa. Parallel stone platforms bearing one large monolith and several smaller ones are found among the coconut trees to the east of the road. This site (Fiji's first "national monument") is not well known, so just take the bus to Wasavula, get off, and ask.

Around Lambasa
Other curiosities easily accessible by local bus include the suspension footbridge at **Mbulileka,** six km east (take the yellow and blue bus); the Firewalkers Temple at **Vunivau,** five km northeast, where Indian firewalking takes place twice a year between June and October; the Fiji Forests plant at **Malau,** 11 km north, where Lambasa's sugar harvest is loaded; the Snake Temple (Naag Mandir) at **Nangingi,** 12 km northeast, which contains a rock which Hindu devotees swear is growing; and the **Wainggele hot springs** (no bathing), 10 km southwest beyond the airport. Farther afield is the Floating Island at **Kurukuru,** between Nakelikoso and Numbu, 44 km northeast of Lambasa.

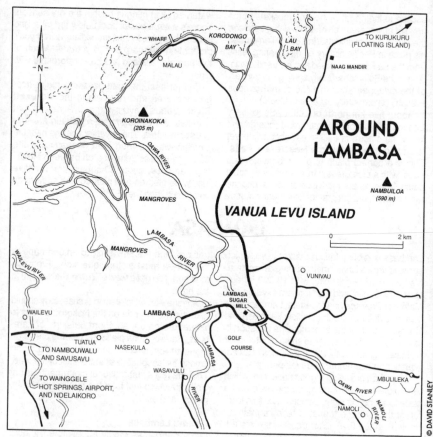

AROUND LAMBASA

VANUA LEVU ISLAND

© DAVID STANLEY

You can get a view of much of Vanua Levu from the telecommunications tower atop **Ndelaikoro** (941 meters), 25 km south of Lambasa, farther down the same road past the airport. Only a 4WD vehicle can make it to the top.

If you're a surfer, ask about hiring a boat out to the **Great Sea Reef** north of Kia Island, 40 km northwest of Lambasa.

PRACTICALITIES

Accommodations

The budget traveler's first choice should be the **Lambasa Guest House** (Box 259, Lambasa; tel. 812-155) on Nanuku Street which has 10 rooms at F$10/11 single/double. Communal cooking facilities are provided but the Hindu hosts don't allow guests to cook beef on the premises, and previous visitors seem to have walked off with all the cutlery.

The seven-room **Riverview Private Hotel** (Box 129, Lambasa; tel. 811-367), on Namara Street beyond the police station, charges F$17/22 single/double for a room with shared bath in a quiet two-story concrete building. No cooking is allowed but the terrace overlooking the river is nice. The Riverview is a good second choice if the Lambasa Guest House is full.

The two-story **Grand Eastern Hotel** (Box 641, Lambasa; tel. 811-022, fax 814-011) on Gibson Street, just a few minutes' walk from the bus station, is a grand old colonial hotel overlooking the river. The 26 rooms in the rather run-down main building are F$14/20 single/double with shared bath, F$6 extra with bath, F$12 extra for a/c. The new wing by the river is much more expensive at F$53/60 single/double with a/c. Unfortunately the rooms in the old section are grubby and overpriced, and unless you're planning on going upmarket in the new wing, you'll do better elsewhere. No communal cooking facilities are provided but the meals in the atmospheric dining room are good.

The **Lambasa Club** (tel. 811-304) on Nanuku Street beside the river has two dark and dingy rooms at F$11/15 single/double. Also try the **Farmers Club** (tel. 811-633) on the main street with three rooms at F$10 single or double. You must arrive during regular business hours to get one (the same applies at the Lambasa Club).

Lambasa's most upmarket place to stay is the **Takia Hotel** (Box 7, Lambasa; tel. 811-655, fax 813-527), at 10 Nasekula Rd. above the shopping area right in the middle of town. The 32 rooms are F$55/65 single/double with fan,

F$70/80 with a/c. If you have a business card, try asking for the commercial rate.

Offshore Resort

In 1992 the upmarket **Nukumbati Island Resort** (Box 1928, Lambasa; tel. 813-901, fax 813-914) opened on remote Nukumbati Island, 40 km west of Lambasa. The four spacious bungalows are F$660 double including meals (emphasis on seafood) and activities, with a seven-night minimum stay. Children are not allowed, and alcoholic drinks are extra. It's F$550 a day to hire the resort's game-fishing boat; land safaris are F$300. Access is by speedboat or 4WD vehicle from Lambasa (free for guests), or by chartered seaplane direct from Nandi (F$600).

Food

Simple Fijian, Chinese, and Indian meals are available for under F$3 at many places along Nasekula Road, including the **Moon Restaurant** (tel. 813-215), next to Elite Cinema, and the **Wun Wuh Cafe** (tel. 811-653), across from the bus station. For Indian food try the **Isalei**

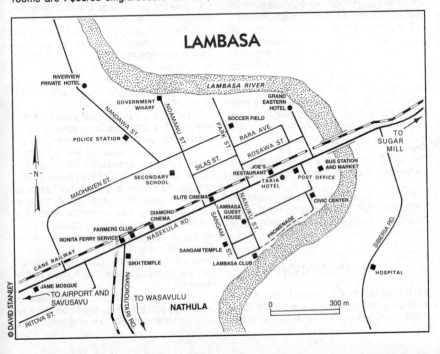

Restaurant (tel. 811-490) on Sangam Avenue, or the **Hare Krishna Restaurant** next to Sunflower Airlines on Nasekula Road.

Joe's Restaurant (tel. 811-766), upstairs in a building on Nasekula Road in the center of town, has an inexpensive fast-food area with Formica tables, and an upmarket "wine and dine" section that wouldn't be out of place in Las Vegas. Despite the jarring decor, both are very popular, and the Chinese food served here puts Lambasa's ubiquitous chow mein houses to shame. Ask about the linen-tablecloth, low-light back room reserved for couples.

Entertainment

There are two movie houses in Lambasa. **Elite Cinema** has films in English and there's an evening show, while the **Diamond Cinema** is closed at night. Occasionally Diamond is the venue of live cultural programs, so check.

Calypso Nite Club (tel. 811-220), on Rara Avenue near the Grand Eastern Hotel, has music and dancing Friday and Saturday around 2200 (cover charge). You can dance, but it's sometimes a little rough. This is a predominantly Indian town so most of the nightlife is male oriented.

The **Lambasa Club** and the **Farmers Club** both serve cheap beer in a congenial male-oriented atmosphere. Couples will feel more comfortable at the Lambasa Club than at the Farmers, and the Lambasa has a nice terrace out back facing the river. The pub upstairs in the **Takia Hotel** is a safe, fun place to drink even though the bartenders are enclosed in a cage! There's also a disco at the Takia.

Services

The ANZ Bank is opposite the bus station, and the Westpac Bank is farther west on Nasekula Road.

There's a **public library** (weekdays 0900-1300/1400-1700, Saturday 0900-1200) in the Civic Center near Lambasa Bus Station. Public toilets are adjacent to the library.

TRANSPORTATION

Air Fiji (tel. 811-188) has service three or four times a day from Lambasa to Suva (F$73). **Sunflower Airlines** (tel. 811-454) flies direct to Nandi (F$96) and Suva (F$72) twice daily, and to Taveuni (F$45) three times a week. **Vanua Air** (tel. 814-400) also arrives twice daily from Suva (F$66). To get to the airport, 10 km southwest of Lambasa, take the green and yellow Wainggele bus.

Patterson Brothers (tel. 812-444, fax 813-460) has an office in the arcade beside the Takia Hotel where you can book your bus/ferry/bus ticket through to Suva via Nambouwalu and Natovi (11.5 hours, F$38). This bus leaves Lambasa at 0530 daily except Sunday and Monday, and passengers arrive in Suva at 1700. There's also a direct bus/boat/bus connection from Lambasa to Lautoka via Ellington Wharf (near Nananu-i-Ra Island), and another service straight through to Levuka. Ask about through bus/boat services from Lambasa to Taveuni, departing Lambasa Wednesday to Saturday at 0630 (six hours, F$22).

Ronita Ferry Services (Box 361, Lambasa; tel. 811-361), opposite the Mobil service station on Nasekula Road, sells tickets for a combined bus/boat service from Lambasa to Taveuni, departing Lambasa on Monday, Wednesday, and Friday at 0730.

To be dropped off on Kia Island, negotiate with the fishing boats tied up near the Lambasa Club. Village boats from Kia sometimes unload at the Government Wharf at the north end of Damanu Street on the other side of town. The **Consort Shipping Line** (tel. 811-144) has an office at the Government Wharf.

There are four regular buses a day (at 0630, 1030, 1315, and 1430) to Nambouwalu (F$6), a dusty, tiring six-hour trip. Another four buses a day run from Lambasa to Savusavu (2.5 hours, F$4), a very beautiful ride on an excellent paved highway over the Waisali Saddle between the Korotini and Valili mountains and along the palm-studded coast. The 0700 Lambasa-Savusavu bus connects with the bus/ferry service to Taveuni, making it possible to go straight through from Lambasa to Taveuni in a day. Other buses to Savusavu leave Lambasa at 0900, 1200, and 1500, but take the early bus before clouds obscure the views.

If your time is very limited but you want to see a lot, catch a morning flight from Suva or Nandi to Lambasa, then take an afternoon bus on to Savusavu, the best part of the trip. Otherwise stay in Savusavu and see Lambasa on a long day-trip.

Getting to outlying areas around Lambasa by bus can be confusing as there are several different bus companies and to get departure times you just have to keep asking. Otherwise, take

pot luck: when you see a bus headed for one of the places mentioned under "Around Lambasa" above, just jump on and go for the ride.

Rental cars are available from **Budget Rent A Car** (tel. 811-199) on Ndongo Road west of town. Obtaining gasoline outside the two main towns is difficult, so tank up.

SAVUSAVU

Savusavu is a picturesque small town opposite Nawi Island on Savusavu Bay. The view from here across to the mountains of southwestern Vanua Levu and down the coast towards Nambouwalu is superlatively lovely. In the 1860s Europeans arrived to establish coconut plantations. They mixed with the Fijians and, although business went bust in the 1930s, their descendants and Fijian villagers still supply copra to the small coconut oil mill, eight km west of Savusavu, giving this side of Vanua Levu a pleasant agricultural air.

Savusavu is Vanua Levu's main port, and cruising yachts often rock at anchor offshore. The surrounding mountains and reefs make Savusavu a well-protected hurricane refuge. The diving possibilities of this area have been recognized by the Cousteau Society, which began using Savusavu as the base for Jean-Michel Cousteau's Ocean Search Project in 1990. Savusavu is also the administrative center of Thakaundrove Province and has three banks. In the past few years tourism has taken off around Savusavu, with new resorts springing

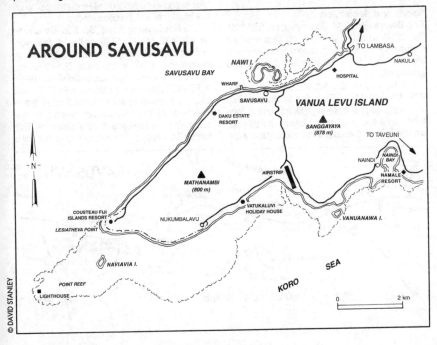

up all the time, though the town is far from being spoiled.

Sights

The one main street through Savusavu consists of a motley collection of Indian and Chinese shops, parked taxis, loitering locals, and the odd tourist. Visit the small **hot springs** boiling out among fractured coral below the Hot Springs Hotel. Residents use the springs to cook native vegetables; bathing is not possible. Hopefully these quaint springs will never be developed for tourists and spoiled.

For a good circle trip, take a taxi from Savusavu past the airport to **Nukumbalavu** village (six km, F$5), at the end of road along the south side of the peninsula. From here you can walk west along the beach to the Cousteau Fiji Islands Resort on **Lesiatheva Point** in about an hour at low tide. Try to avoid cutting through the resort at the end of the hike as the Cousteau management disapproves. From Lesiatheva it's six km by road back to Savusavu.

Sports and Recreation

Eco Divers (Box 264, Savusavu; tel. 850-122, fax 850-344) at the Copra Shed Marina offers scuba diving, snorkeling, dinghy hire, windsurfing, sailing, village visits, waterfall tours, and guided hiking.

Fiji by Kayak (Box 43, Savusavu; tel. 850-372, fax 850-344) offers trips to Natewa Bay with kayaking, snorkeling, hiking, and a *lovo* lunch on a secluded sandy beach at F$99 pp, transfers from Savusavu included. It's a wonderful introduction to ocean kayaking and a great day out. Bookings can be made through Sea Fiji Travel (tel. 850-345) at the Copra Shed Marina.

PRACTICALITIES

Accommodations in Savusavu Town

We've arranged this accommodation section beginning at Savusavu Bus Station and working west through town to Lesiatheva Point, then east along the coast.

Hari Chand's **Hidden Paradise Guest House** (Box 41, Savusavu; tel 850-106), behind Sun Sang Cafe just beyond Morris Hedstrom, has six fan-cooled rooms at F$11/17 single/double with shared bath, including a good breakfast. Cooking and washing facilities are provided, and it's clean and friendly—don't be put off by the plain exterior. The Indian restaurant here is very inexpensive, but pork, beef, and booze are banned. A member of the Chand family may offer to show you around the Hindu temple up on the hill, if you ask. Recommended.

The **Hot Springs Hotel** (Box 208, Savusavu; tel. 850-430, fax 300-500), on the hillside overlooking Savusavu Bay, is named for the nearby thermal springs and steam vents. The 48 rooms, all with balconies offering splendid views, begin at F$44/55 single/double with fan, F$50/68 with a/c. (Sometimes special reduced rates are in effect—ask.) There's no beach nearby, but the swimming pool terrace is very pleasant. This former Travelodge is slightly run-down but still a

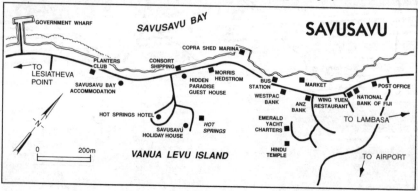

convenient, medium-priced choice, and the hotel bar is open daily including Sunday. Catch the sunset here at happy hour. The Saturday night buffet is worth the F$11, even if they do put corned beef in the *palusami*.

David Manohar Lal's six-room **Savusavu Holiday House** (Box 65, Savusavu; tel. 850-216), also known as "David's Place," is just below the Hot Springs Hotel. Bed and a Fijian breakfast are F$13/19/24 single/double/triple (shared bath), F$10 pp dorm, or F$6 per tent to camp. There's a well-equipped kitchen. David's a delightful character to meet and also a strict Seventh-Day Adventist, so no alcoholic beverages are allowed on the premises. A cacophony of dogs, roosters, and the neighbor's kids will bid you good morning.

Savusavu Bay Accommodation (Lal Chand and Suresh Chand, Box 290, Savusavu; tel. 850-100), above Sea Breeze Restaurant on the main street, has seven standard rooms at F$11/17 single/double, and four a/c rooms at F$22 single or double. Cooking facilities are provided, and on the roof is a terrace where travelers can wash and dry their clothes or just sit and relax. Many of the rooms are rented on a long-term basis, and the atmosphere is not as nice as in the places previously mentioned. Beware of a misleading sign outside reading The Hidden Paradise, which is intended to cause confusion with a competitor just down the street. Such are the petty politics of small town life.

The Anglican Diocese of Polynesia operates the **Daku Estate Resort** (Box 18, Savusavu; tel 850-046), one km west of the ferry landing. The six *mbures* with fan and fridge go for F$83/149/215/275 single/double/triple/quad. These prices include all meals, served in a large *mbure* next to the swimming pool. Three villas with fully equipped kitchens rent for F$66 single or double, F$104 triple, without meals. Profits from the resort are used to send gifted children from remote areas to boarding school, so you'll be contributing to a worthy cause. Daku faces a beach with some snorkeling possibilities.

Accommodations around Savusavu

On Lesiatheva Point six km southwest of Savusavu is the **Cousteau Fiji Islands Resort** (Private Bag, Savusavu; tel. 850-188, fax 850-340), which opened in mid-1987. In 1994 the resort was purchased by world-renowned oceanographer Jean-Michel Cousteau, and millions of dollars went into renovations prior to the reopening in April 1995. The original name Na Koro means "The Village," and that's what it re-creates, with 20 authentic thatched Fijian *mbures* (from F$374/442 double/triple including breakfast). The rooms have fans but no a/c, telephones, or cooking facilities. The restaurant is built like a towering pagan temple and executive chef Kathy Hoare can tell you anything you want to know about Fiji (as well as prepare healthy meals). Free activities include sailing, kayaking, fishing, and snorkeling. In addition, scuba diving, scuba instruction, underwater photography courses, and yacht charters with diving are offered by Gary Alford's on-site dive operation, "L'Aventure Cousteau." Also on the staff is marine biologist Jennifer Caselle, who arranges all kinds of cultural and environmental trips. There's good snorkeling off the beach, though the resort's large Private Property signs warn nonguests to keep out. A taxi from Savusavu will run F$5. Bring insect repellent.

The **Vatukaluvi Holiday House** (Box 262, Savusavu; tel. 850-561), on the south side of the peninsula, one km west of Savusavu airport, accommodates six people at F$45 single or double. Cooking facilities are provided, and there's good snorkeling off the beach. Ask for Geoff Taylor's place. A taxi to Vatukaluvi will cost F$2 from the airport, F$5 from Savusavu.

The most upmarket place around Savusavu is **Namale Resort** (Box 244, Savusavu; tel. 850-435, fax 850-400), a working copra plantation founded in 1874, on a white-sand beach nine km east of Savusavu. The superb food and homey atmosphere amid exotic landscapes and refreshing white beaches make this one of Fiji's most exclusive resorts. The nine thatched *mbures* are F$575 double a night including gourmet meals and drinks (no cooking facilities and no singles). The mosquito nets over the beds, ceiling fans, and louvered windows give the units a rustic charm. Airport transfers and all activities other than scuba diving are free. Namale caters only to in-house guests—there's no provision for sightseers who'd like to stop in for lunch.

Kontiki Resort (Private Mail Bag, Savusavu; tel. 850-262, fax 850-355), also known as "Matani Kavika," on the Hibiscus Highway 15

Fijian schoolgirls smile for the camera at Savusavu, Vanua Levu.

km east of Savusavu, has 16 small thatched bungalows from F$105/165/180 single/double/triple, including airport transfers. The restaurant offers a good selection of international, Fijian, and Indian dishes, with main courses averaging F$15. No groceries are sold in the resort shop, only souvenirs and suncream. Set in a well-kept coconut grove, Matani Kavika has nearby many interesting caves, pools, trails, falls, ponds, and lakes to explore. Matani Kavika means "land of the wild plum tree," and such trees still exist on the grounds. Scuba diving (F$80 for two tanks) is available and a dive site known as Dream House is right at Kontiki's front door. The snorkeling is fine as well. There's also a swimming pool, 9-hole golf course, tennis courts, a marina, and many other activities, but the nearest beach is a km away.

A more affordable choice would be **Mumu Resort** (Box 240, Savusavu; tel. 850-416), also east of Savusavu, about three km beyond Kontiki. The site is the spiritual home of Radini Mumu, a legendary queen of Fiji. In 1970 owner Gordon Edris, an ex-world traveler, did what many of us dream of doing: he retired to the South Seas and, together with his wife Rosie, slowly created a small retreat from their own resources without making the fatal mistake of taking a bank loan. Today the couple obviously enjoy sharing their wonderful little

world with 15 fortunate guests. Rooms are F$25/35 single/double, the five-person "dream house" F$50 double, and there's also a F$12 dorm (often full). Campers are always most welcome (F$4/7 single/double). Communal cooking facilities are available, and Mumu's kitchen serves tasty Fijian and European dishes at budget prices. Mumu is surrounded by the Koro Sea on three sides, and two small uninhabited islands nearby are easily accessible. The snorkeling and scenery are good, the staff friendly, and there's scuba diving nearby at Kontiki. Paths wind endlessly through the property to clifftop lookouts with benches, through natural rock arches, and through tunnels right along the water's edge. A natural swimming hole is surrounded by a concrete terrace. A taxi here from Savusavu should be around F$12, a bus around F$1. Gordon and Rosie promise you'll get the most for your money at Mumu, but unless you've got a tent, call ahead to make sure there's a room for you. This unique place merits our highest recommendation in the low-budget category.

Offshore Island

Moody's Namenalala Island Resort (Private Mail Bag, Savusavu; tel. 813-764, fax 812-366), on a narrow high island southwest of Savusavu in the Koro Sea, is one of Fiji's top hideaways.

Hosts Tom and Joan Moody ran a similar operation in Panama's San Blas Islands for 15 years until June 1981, when they were attacked by Cuna Indians who shot Tom in the leg and tried to burn the resort. The media reported at the time that the Indians had been scandalized by hotel guests who smoked marijuana and cavorted naked on the beach, but Joan claims it was all part of a ploy to evict foreigners from San Blas to cover up drug-running activities.

In 1984, after a long search for a replacement, the couple leased Namenalala from the Fiji government, which needed a caretaker to protect the uninhabited island from poachers. Their present resort occupies less than 10% of Namenalala's 45 hectares, leaving the rest as a nesting ground for great flocks of red-footed boobies, banded rails, and Polynesian starlings. Giant clams proliferate in the surrounding waters within the 24-km Namena Barrier Reef, and sea turtles from November to March haul themselves up onto the island's golden sands to lay their eggs.

Each of the Moody's five bamboo and wood hexagonal-shaped *mbures* are well tucked away in the lush vegetation to ensure maximum privacy. Illuminated by romantic gas lighting, each features a private hardwood terrace with 270° views. Alternative energy is used as much as possible to maintain the atmosphere (though there is a secret diesel generator used to do the laundry and recharge batteries).

The cost to stay here is F$214 single or double, plus F$80 pp extra for the meal plan. The food is excellent, thanks to Joan's firm hand in the kitchen and Tom's island-grown produce. The ice water on the tables and in the *mbures* is a nice touch, and they don't push liquor sales the way some other resorts do.

This resort is perfect for birdwatching, fishing, and snorkeling, and scuba diving is available at F$60 per tank. If you want a holiday that combines unspoiled nature with interesting characters and a certain elegance, you won't go wrong here. Daily except Sunday, Beachcomber Cruises' high-speed catamaran *Ndrondrolangi* can whisk you from Lautoka to Namenalala in three hours at a cost of F$105 pp, or from Savusavu in less than 40 minutes at F$84 pp. A chartered seaplane from Nandi will run F$975. Moody's closes from 1 March to 1 May every year.

Food and Entertainment
The **Captain's Table** (tel. 850-511; Monday to Thursday 0830-2030, Friday and Saturday 0830-2100, Sunday 1500-2100) at the Copra Shed Marina is a yachtie hangout claiming to offer "the best pizza on Vanua Levu," which isn't saying a lot when you think about it. Drop by even if you're not hungry to peruse the notice board, which bears photos of all the yachts that have called at Savasavu recently. Most of Savusavu's hip young locals show up here eventually and in the evening the outdoor seating on the wharf is nice.

Several simple places around town offer basic meals of varying quality. The surly-staffed **Wing Yuen Restaurant,** next to the National Bank, increases the prices of their plates in response to unusual requests, such as leaving the meat out. Beware of the F$2.50 charge for a tiny pot of tea here. In contrast, the **New Ping Ho Cafe** (tel. 850-300), opposite the municipal market, accommodates vegetarians and everyone else with substantial portions of good food at decent prices. All the local expats eat here—no wonder the Wing Yuen's owner is so sour.

The **Vika Vuai's Cafe,** behind the town council next to the market, prepares good Fijian food. The **A1 Restaurant** near the bus station also has Indian curries.

The cook at the **Sea Breeze Restaurant** (tel. 850-100) below Savusavu Bay Accommodation can prepare a special Saturday evening dinner, provided you let him know the day before. The regular menu contains mostly Chinese dishes, and the portions are large (open Sunday for lunch and dinner). It's slightly cheaper than the New Ping Ho Cafe, but not as pleasant.

Drinkers can repair to the **Planters Club** (tel. 850-233) toward the wharf—the place is never out of Fiji Bitter. The weekend dances at the club are local events. Despite the Members Only sign outside, visitors are welcome. It's a vintage colonial club even without the colonists.

Services and Information
The ANZ Bank, National Bank, and Westpac Bank all have branches at Savusavu.

The **Copra Shed Marina** (Box 3, Savusavu; tel. 850-518) near the bus station houses the **Savusavu Yacht Club,** and visiting yachts can moor alongside for F$44 a week; offshore hurricane moorings are F$165 a month. There's a handy public card phone in the marina, and you can have your laundry done at the Copra Shed for F$5.

The **Bula Bookshop** at the Copra Shed Marina sells nautical charts as well as books.

Sea Fiji Travel (tel. 850-345, fax 880-344), in the Copra Shed Marina, is a full-service travel agency specializing in scuba diving and yacht charters.

TRANSPORTATION

Air Fiji (tel. 850-538), next to the post office, flies into Savusavu twice daily from Suva (F$68) and three times a week from Taveuni. Ask Air Fiji about the flights from Savusavu to Levuka four times a week. **Sunflower Airlines** (tel. 850-141), around the corner from the ANZ Bank, has flights to Savusavu twice daily from Nandi (F$96) and daily from Taveuni (F$45). **Vanua Air** arrives twice daily from Suva (F$67) and Taveuni (F$44). The airstrip is beside the main highway, three km east of town, and you *will* pay for excess baggage here. Local buses to Savusavu pass the airport about once an hour, or take a taxi for F$2.

Beachcomber Cruises' high-speed catamaran *Ndrondrolangi* departs Savusavu for Natovi at 0945 (two hours, F$34) and Lautoka at 1400 (three hours, F$55) daily except Sunday. A bus connection to Suva (F$5) is available at Natovi.

The **Consort Shipping Line Ltd.** (tel. 850-279) runs the large car ferry *Spirit of Free Enterprise* from Suva to Savusavu (12 hours, F$30 deck, F$55 cabin). The ferry leaves Suva northbound Wednesday and Saturday, and leaves Savusavu southbound Monday and Thursday around 1700. Northbound the ship continues to Taveuni, and between Savusavu and Suva it calls at Koro.

Patterson Brothers Shipping (tel. 850-161) at the Copra Shed Marina operates the car ferries *Ovalau II* and *Princess Ashika*, which depart Suva for Savusavu Monday at midnight via Ngau and Koro (14.5 hours, F$31). The return journey departs Savusavu Wednesday at 1700. Ask Patterson Brothers about the bus/boat connection to Taveuni, which should depart Savusavu Wednesday to Saturday at 0915 (four hours, F$20). All of the above schedules change frequently, so check.

Four buses a day go from Savusavu to Lambasa (92 km, F$4). The 1030 bus from Savusavu to Napuka connects at Mbutha Bay with the daily ferry *Grace* to Taveuni (F$5), which departs Natuvu around 1300. It's a beautiful boat trip but it can be rough if the wind is up. The five-hour bus/boat connection goes straight through from Savusavu to Taveuni, so use a toilet before setting out (you won't find any along the way) and bring a snack. Westbound the connection is poor, involving a wait of several hours at Mbutha Bay. About nine local buses a day run to Lesiatheva Point (45 cents), a favorite snorkeling spot.

Numerous taxis congregate at Savusavu market; they're quite affordable for short trips in the vicinity.

Avis Rent A Car (tel. 850-184) has an office next to the Shell service station in Savusavu. **Budget Rent A Car** (tel. 850-700) is next to the post office, while **Thrifty Car Rental** (tel. 850-232) is near the Hot Bread Kitchen.

kalavi

MBUTHA BAY

ALONG THE HIBISCUS HIGHWAY

This lovely coastal highway runs 77 km east from Savusavu to Natuvu, then up the east side of Vanua Levu to the old Catholic mission station of **Napuka** at the end of the peninsula. Old frame mansions from the heyday of the 19th-century planters can be spotted among the palms. Mbutha Bay is a recognized "hurricane hole," where ships can find shelter during storms. Coupmaster Sitiveni Rabuka hails from **Ndrekeniwai** village on Natewa Bay, one of the largest bays in the South Pacific.

Large red prawns inhabit a saltwater crevice in the center of a tiny limestone island off **Naweni** village between Savusavu and Natuvu. The villagers believe the prawns are the spirit Urumbuta and call them up by singing,

Keitou onggo na marama ni vuna
keitou mai sara Urumbuta
I tumba i tumba e
I tumba i tumba e

The island is accessible on foot at low tide, but a *sevusevu* must first be presented to the chief of Naweni for permission to visit (no photos). Your local guides will also expect compensation. Ask to be shown the weather stone on the beach and, perhaps, a second pool of prawns on the other side of the village.

There are petroglyphs *(vatuvola)* on large stones in a creek near **Ndakunimba** village, 10 km south of Natuvu (no bus service). Look for a second group of rock carvings a couple of hundred meters farther up the slope. The figures resemble some undeciphered ancient script.

The **Mbutha Bay Resort and Yacht Club** (Natuvu, Mbutha Bay; tel. 880-370, fax 880-510), also known as Natuvu Plantation, next to the ferry wharf at Natuvu, has rooms with shared bath at F$39 double, with private bath F$50, and a five-room dorm at F$11 pp (campers F$6

pp). Managing director Sylvia Dobry hopes to eventually establish a writers' colony here and plans six medium-priced *mbures* for the coconut grove along the beach. The Reef Terrace Restaurant on the waterfront side of the plantation house serves meals upon request (check out the bakery items), and there are cooking facilities in the dorm. Yachties are welcome to anchor off the resort and use the facilities. Activities in this area include a hike to Tangithi Peak, birdwatching (the rare orange flame dove inhabits the upper forest), and the three-hour afternoon bus ride to Napuka and back (at 1300).

Buses to Savusavu leave Mbutha Bay at 0600, 0830, and 1600 (three hours, F$3). In the other direction, you can leave Savusavu for Mbutha at 1030, 1430, and 1630 except on Sunday.

KIOA

The Taveuni ferry passes between Vanua Levu and Kioa, home of some 300 Polynesians from Vaitupu Island, Tuvalu (the former Ellice Islands). In 1853 Captain Owen of the ship *Packet* obtained Kioa from the Tui Cakau, and it has since operated as a coconut plantation. In 1946 it was purchased by the Ellice islanders, who were facing overpopulation on their home island.

The people live at **Salia** on the southeast side of Kioa. The women make baskets for sale to tourists, while the men go fishing alone in small outrigger canoes. If you visit, try the coconut toddy *(kaleve)* or more potent fermented toddy *(kamanging)*. Kioa and nearby Rambi are the only islands in Fiji where the government allows trees to be cut for toddy.

RAMBI

In 1855, at the request of the Tui Cakau on Taveuni, a Tongan army conquered some Fijian rebels on Rambi. Upon the Tongans' departure a few years later, a local chief sold Rambi to

Europeans to cover outstanding debts. Before WW II the Australian firm Lever Brothers ran a coconut plantation here. In 1940 the British government began searching for an island to purchase as a resettlement area for the Micronesian Banabans of Ocean Island (Banaba) in the Gilbert Islands (present Kiribati), whose home island was being ravaged by phosphate mining. At first Wakaya Island in the Lomaiviti Group was considered, but the outbreak of war and the occupation of Ocean Island by the Japanese intervened. Back in Fiji, British officials decided Rambi Island would be a better homeland for the Banabans than Wakaya, and in March 1942 they purchased Rambi from Lever Brothers using £25,000 of phosphate royalties deposited in the Banaban Provident Fund.

Meanwhile the Japanese had deported the Banabans to serve as laborers on Kusaie (Kosrae) in the Caroline Islands, and it was not until December 1945 that the survivors could be brought to Rambi, where their 4,500 descendants live today. Contemporary Banabans are citizens of Fiji and live among Lever's former coconut plantations at the northwest corner of the island. The eight-member Rambi Island Council administers the island.

The island reaches a height of 472 meters and is well wooded. The former Lever headquarters is at Tabwewa, while the airstrip is near Tabiang. Rambi's other two villages are Uma and Buakonikai. At Nuku between Uma and Tabwewa is a post office, clinic, and four-room guesthouse. This colonial-style structure is the former Lever Brothers manager's residence and is little changed since the 1940s except for the extension now housing the dining area and lounge. One of the rooms is reserved for island officials; the rest are used mostly by contract workers. Other guests pay F$40 pp a night, which includes three meals. The facilities are shared (no hot water) and the electric generator operates 1800-2100 only—just enough time to watch a video. The former doctor's residence on Rambi is also rented out occasionally.

Considering the limited accommodations and the remoteness of Rambi, it's a good idea to contact the office of the **Rambi Council of Leaders** (Box 329, Suva; tel. 303-653, fax 300-543), 1st Floor, Ramson House, Pratt Street, Suva, before setting out. Hopefully this office will be able to make your guesthouse bookings and provide other information. You could also try phoning the Rambi Island Council at tel. 84-020, ext. 33. Remember that Rambi is not a tourist resort and it's very good form to obtain prior approval before visiting the community. Otherwise you could create unnecessary problems for yourself and others, and you could even be turned away.

Rambi lives according to a different set of rules than the rest of Fiji; in fact, about all they have in common are their monetary, postal, and educational systems, kava drinking (a Fijian implant), and Methodism. The local language is Gilbertese and the social order is that of the Gilbert Islands. Most people live in hurricane-proof concrete-block houses devoid of furniture, with personal possessions kept in suitcases and trunks. The cooking is done outside in thatched huts. If you happen to visit a family, your local contact will go in first to announce your arrival. Only after the house has been fixed up and other interested parties have arrived will you be eagerly welcomed into the home.

Alcoholic beverages other than traditional coconut toddy are not allowed on Rambi, so take something else as gifts. On Friday nights the local *maneaba* in Tabwewa village rocks to a disco beat and dancing alternates with sitting around the omnipresent kava bowl, but on Sunday virtually everything grinds to a halt. Another charming feature: adultery is a legally punishable offense on Rambi.

To get there catch the daily Napuka bus at 1030 from Savusavu to Karoko. Otherwise, a taxi from Savusavu Airport to Karoko will run F$80. A chartered speedboat from Karoko to the wharf at Tabwewa on the northwest side of Rambi costs F$45 each way, less if people off the Napuka bus are going over anyway. Patterson Brothers was considering instituting a direct ferry service from Natuvu and Taveuni to Rambi, so check. On Rambi itself, motorized transport consists of one 4WD vehicle, a truck, and a few school buses which ply the single 23-km road from Tabwewa to Buakonikai.

THE BANABANS

The Banaban people on Rambi are from Banaba, a tiny, six-square-km raised atoll 450 km southwest of Tarawa in the Gilbert Islands. Like Nauru, Banaba was once rich in phosphates, but from 1900 through 1979 the deposits were exploited by British, Australian, and New Zealand interests in what is perhaps the best example of a corporate/colonial rip-off in the history of the Pacific islands.

After the Sydney-based Pacific Islands Company discovered phosphates on Nauru and Banaba in 1899 a company official, Albert Ellis, was sent to Banaba in May 1900 to obtain control of the resource. In due course "King" Temate and the other chiefs signed an agreement granting Ellis's firm exclusive rights to exploit the phosphate deposits on Banaba for 999 years in exchange for £50 a year. Of course, the guileless Micronesian islanders had no idea what it was all about.

As Ellis rushed to have mining equipment and moorings put in place, a British naval vessel arrived on 28 September 1901 to raise the British flag, joining Banaba to the Gilbert and Ellice Islands Protectorate. The British government reduced the term of the lease to a more realistic 99 years and the Pacific Phosphate Company was formed in 1902.

Things ran smoothly until 1909, when the islanders refused to lease the company any additional land after 15% of Banaba had been stripped of both phosphates and food trees. The British government arranged a somewhat better deal in 1913, but in 1916 changed the protectorate to a colony so the Banabans could not withhold their land again. After WW I the company was renamed the British Phosphate Commission (BPC), and in 1928 the resident commissioner, Sir Arthur Grimble, signed an order expropriating the rest of the land against the Banabans' wishes. The islanders continued to receive their tiny royalty right up until WW II.

On 10 December 1941, with a Japanese invasion deemed imminent, the order was given to blow up the mining infrastructure on Banaba, and on 28 February 1942 a French destroyer evacuated company employees from the island.

In August some 500 Japanese troops and 50 laborers landed on Banaba and began erecting fortifications. The six Europeans they captured eventually perished as a result of ill treatment, and all but 150 of the 2,413 local mine laborers and their families were eventually deported to Tarawa, Nauru, and Kosrae. As a warning the Japanese beheaded three locals and used another three to test an electrified anti-invasion fence.

Meanwhile the BPC decided to take advantage of this situation to rid itself of the island's original inhabitants once and for all to avoid any future hindrance to mining operations. In March 1942 the commission purchased Rambi Island off Vanua Levu in Fiji for £25,000 as an alternative homeland for the Banabans. In late September 1945 the British returned to Banaba with Albert Ellis the first to step ashore. Only surrendering Japanese troops were found on Banaba; the local villages had been destroyed.

Two months later an emaciated and wild-eyed Gilbertese man named Kabunare emerged from three months in hiding and told his story to a military court:

We were assembled together and told that the war was over and the Japanese would soon be leaving. Our rifles were taken away. We were put in groups, our names taken, then marched to the edge of the cliffs where our hands were tied and we were blindfolded and told to squat. Then we were shot.

Kabunare either lost his balance or fainted, and fell over the cliff before he was hit. In the sea he came to the surface and kicked his way to some rocks, where he severed the string that tied his hands. He crawled into a cave and watched the Japanese pile up the bodies of his companions and toss them into the sea. He stayed in the cave two nights and, after he thought it was safe, made his way inland, where he survived on coconuts until he was sure the Japanese had left. Kabunare said he thought the Japanese had executed the others to destroy any evidence of their cruelties and atrocities on Banaba.

As peace returned the British implemented their plan to resettle all 2,000 surviving Banabans on Rambi, which seemed a better place for them than their mined-out homeland. The first group arrived on Rambi on 14 December 1945, and in time they adapted to their mountainous new home and traded much of their original Micronesian culture for that of the Fijians. There they and their descendants live today.

During the 1960s the Banabans saw the much better deal Nauru was getting from the BPC, mainly through the efforts of Hammer DeRoburt and the "Geelong Boys," who were trapped in Australia during the war and thus received an excellent education and understanding of the white people's ways. Thanks to this the Nauruan leadership was able to hold its own against colonial bullying, while the Banabans were simply forgotten on Rambi.

In 1966 Mr. Tebuke Rotan, a Banaban Methodist minister, journeyed to London on behalf of his people to demand reparations from the British for laying waste to their island, a case that would drag on for nearby 20 bitter years. After some 50 visits to the Foreign and Commonwealth offices, he was offered (and rejected) £80,000 compensation. In 1971 the Banabans sued for damages in the British High Court. After a lengthy litigation, the British government in 1977 offered the Banabans an *ex gratia* payment of A$10 million, in exchange for a pledge that there would be no further legal action.

In 1975 the Banabans asked that their island be separated from the rest of Kiribati and joined to Fiji, their present country of citizenship. Gilbertese politicians, anxious to protect their fisheries zone and wary of the dismemberment of the country, lobbied against this, and the British rejected the proposal. The free entry of Banabans to Banaba was guaranteed in the Kiribati constitution, however. In 1979 Kiribati obtained independence from Britain and mining on Banaba ended the same year. Finally, in 1981 the Banabans accepted the A$10 million compensation money, plus interest, from the British, though they refused to withdraw their claim to Banaba. The present Kiribati government rejects all further claims from the Banabans, asserting that it's something between them and the British. The British are trying to forget the whole thing.

For more information on Rambi and the Banabans see *On Fiji Islands,* by Ronald Wright.

triton shell

(top) Hindu temple, Navua (Peter McQuarrie)
(bottom) Parliament building, Suva, Viti Levu (David Stanley)

(top) cane fields near Lautoka (David Stanley)
(bottom) yacht anchorage, Malololailai Island (Robert Leger)

SALVATORE CASA

TAVEUNI

Long, green, coconut-covered Taveuni is Fiji's third-largest island. It's 42 km long, 15 km wide, and 470 square km in area. Only eight km across the Somosomo Strait from Vanua Levu's southeast tip, Taveuni is known as the Garden Island of Fiji because of the abundance of its flora. Around 60% of the land is under tropical rainforest. Its surrounding reefs and those off nearby Vanua Levu are one of the world's top dive sites. The strong tidal currents in the strait nurture the corals, but can make diving a tricky business for the unprepared. Because Taveuni is free of the mongoose, there are many wild chickens, *kula* parrots, silktails, ferntails, and orange-breasted doves, making this a special place for birders.

The island's 16-km-long, 1,000-meter-high volcanic spine causes the prevailing trade winds to dump colossal amounts of rainfall on the island's southeast side, and considerable quantities on the northwest side. At 1,241 meters, Uluinggalau in southern Taveuni is the second-highest peak in Fiji, and Des Voeux Peak (1,195 meters) in central Taveuni is the highest point in the country accessible by road. The European discoverer of Fiji, Abel Tasman, sighted this ridge on the night of 5 February 1643. The almost inaccessible southeast coast features plummeting waterfalls, soaring cliffs, and crashing surf. The 12,000 inhabitants live on the island's gently sloping northwest side.

The deep, rich volcanic soil nurtures indigenous floral species such as *Medinilla spectabilis,* which hang in clusters like red sleigh bells, and the rare *tangimauthia (Medinilla waterousei),* a climbing plant with red-and-white flower clusters 30 cm long. *Tangimauthia* grows only around Taveuni's 900-meter-high crater lake and on Vanua Levu. It cannot be transplanted and blossoms only from October to December. The story goes that a young woman was fleeing from her father, who wanted to force her to marry a crotchety old man. As she lay crying beside the lake, her tears turned to flowers. Her father took pity on her when he heard this and allowed her to marry her young lover.

In the past decade Taveuni has become very popular as a destination for scuba divers and those in search of a more natural vacation area than the overcrowded Nandi/Coral Coast strips. Even the producers of the film *Return to the Blue Lagoon* chose Taveuni for their 1990 re-

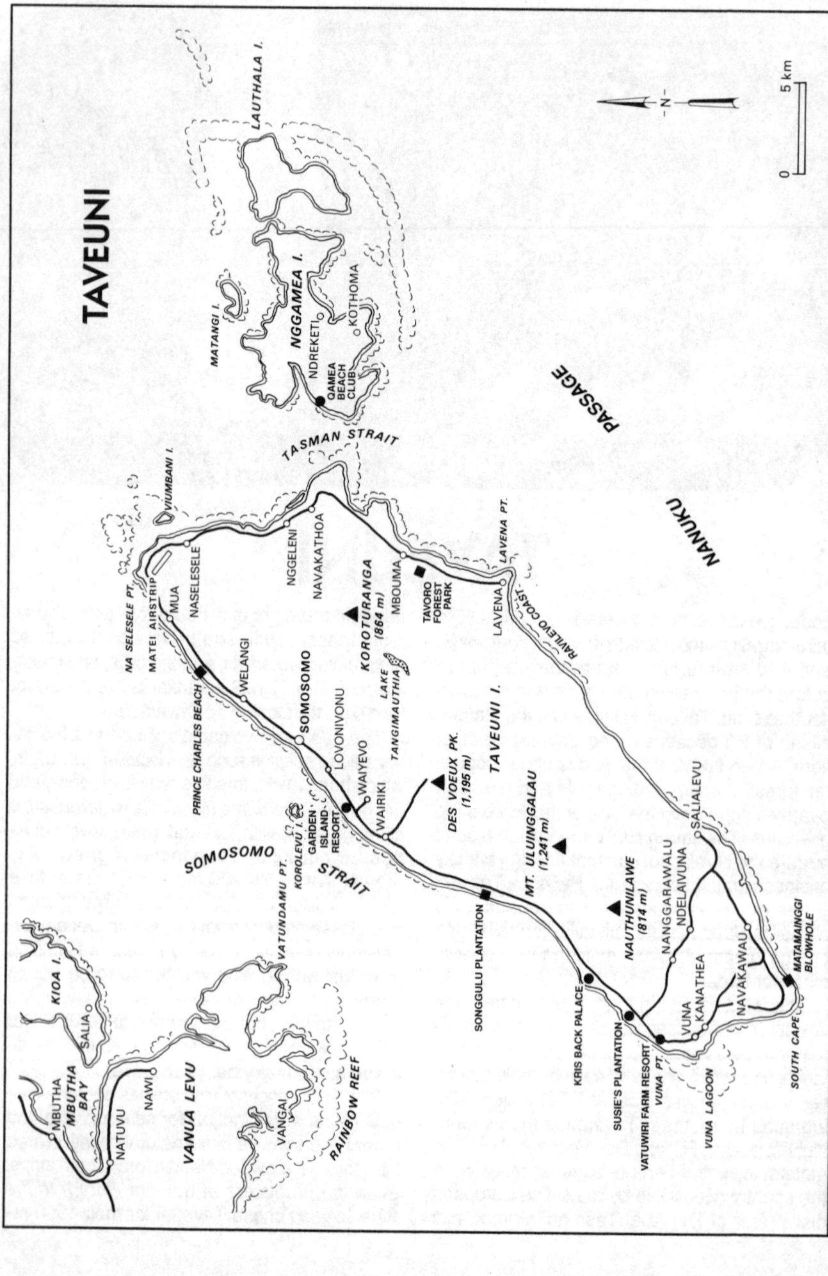
TAVEUNI
LAUTHALA I.
MATANGI I.
NGGAMEA I.
NDREKETI
KOTHOMA
QAMEA BEACH CLUB
TASMAN STRAIT
PASSAGE
NANUKU
VIUMBANI I.
NA SELESELE PT.
MATEI AIRSTRIP
MUA
NASELESELE
NGGELENI
NAVAKATHOA
KOROTURANGA (864 m)
MBOUMA
TAVORO FOREST PARK
LAVENA PT.
LAVENA
RAVILEVO COAST
PRINCE CHARLES BEACH
WELANGI
SOMOSOMO
LOVONIVONU
LAKE TANGIMAUTHIA
WAIYEVO
WAIRIKI
GARDEN ISLAND RESORT
DES VOEUX PK. (1,195 m)
TAVEUNI I.
MT. ULUINGGALAU (1,241 m)
SOMOSOMO
STRAIT
KOROLEVU I.
VATUNDAMU PT.
SONGGULU PLANTATION
NAUTHUNILAWE (814 m)
NANGGARAWALU
NDELAIVUNA
SALIALEVU
KRIS BACK PALACE
SUSIE'S PLANTATION
VATUWIRI FARM RESORT
VUNA PT.
VUNA
KANATHEA
NAVAKAWAU
MATAMAINGGI BLOWHOLE
SOUTH CAPE
VUNA LAGOON
KIOA I.
SALIA
MBUTHA
MBUTHA BAY
NATUVU
NAWI
VANUA LEVU
VANGAI
RAINBOW REEF
N
0
5 km
© DAVID STANLEY

make. Despite all this attention, Taveuni is still about the most beautiful, scenic, and friendly island in Fiji. It's a great place to hang out, so be sure to allow yourself enough time here.

SIGHTS

Central Taveuni

Taveuni's post office, police station, hospital, government offices, and Country Club are on a hilltop at **Waiyevo**, above the Garden Island Resort. On the coast below are the island's main banks and its biggest hotel.

To get to the **Waitavala Sliding Rocks,** walk north from the Garden Island Resort about four minutes on the main road, then turn right onto the signposted side road leading to Waitavala Estates. Take the first road to the right up the hill, and when you see a large metal building on top of a hill, turn left and go a short distance down a road through a coconut plantation to a clearing on the right. The trail up the river to the sliding rocks begins here. The water slide in the river is especially fast after heavy rains, yet the local kids go down standing up! Admission is free.

The **180th degree of longitude** passes through a point marked by a sign board a kilometer south of Waiyevo. One early Taveuni trader overcame the objections of missionaries to his doing business on Sunday by claiming the international date line ran through his property. According to him, if it was Sunday at the front door, it was already Monday around back. Similarly, European planters got their native laborers to work seven days a week by having Sunday at one end of the plantation, and Monday at the other. An 1879 ordinance ended this by placing all of Fiji west of the date line, so you're no longer able to stand here with one foot in the past and the other in the present.

At **Wairiki,** a kilometer south again, are a few stores and the picturesque Catholic mission, with a large stone church containing interesting sculptures and stained glass. There are no pews: the congregation sits on the floor Fijian style. From Wairiki Secondary School you can hike up a tractor track to the large **concrete cross** on a hill behind the mission in 30 minutes each way. You'll be rewarded with a sweeping view of much of western Taveuni and across

Somosomo Strait. A famous 19th-century naval battle occurred here when Taveuni warriors turned back a large Tongan invasion force, with much of the fighting done from canoes. The defeated Tongans ended up in Fijian ovens and the French priest who gave valuable counsel to the Fijian chief was repaid with laborers to build his mission.

A jeep road from Wairiki climbs to the telecommunications station on **Des Voeux Peak.** This is an all-day trip on foot with a view of Lake Tangimauthia as a reward (clouds permitting). To hire a jeep to the viewpoint would cost F$60-80. The lake itself is not accessible from here.

One of the only stretches of paved road on Taveuni is at Songgulu Plantation or "Taveuni Estates" (tel. 880-044), about eight km south of Waiyevo. This ill-fated condo development features an attractive golf course by the sea, tennis courts, and a bowling green, plus street signs pointing nowhere, empty roads, sewers, and 30 unfinished condominiums built by an undercapitalized real estate speculator who badly miscalculated Taveuni's potential for Hawaii-style residential development.

Southern Taveuni

Transportation to the south end of Taveuni is difficult with only two buses a day from Somosomo (at 1215 and 1645). Since the 1645 bus spends the night at Vuna and doesn't return to Somosomo until the next morning, the only way to really see southern Taveuni is to also spend the night down there. If this isn't possible, the roundtrip bus ride leaving Somosomo around noon is still well worth doing.

The bus from Somosomo runs south along the coast to Susie's Plantation, where it turns inland to Ndelaivuna. There it turns around and returns to the coast, which it follows southeast to Navakawau via South Cape. On the way back it cuts directly across some hills to Kanathea and continues up the coast without going to Ndelaivuna again. Southeast of Kanathea there is very little traffic.

A hike around southern Taveuni provides an interesting day out for anyone staying at Susie's Plantation or one of the other nearby resorts. From Susie's a road climbs east over the island to **Ndelaivuna,** where the bus turns around at a gate. The large Private Property sign here is mainly intended to ward off miscreants who create problems for the plantation owners by leaving open cattle gates. Visitors with sense enough to close the gates behind themselves may proceed.

You hike one hour down through the coconut plantation to a junction with two gates, just be-fore a small bridge over a (usually) dry stream. If you continue walking 30 minutes down the road straight ahead across the bridge you'll reach **Salialevu,** site of the Bilyard Sugar Mill (1874-96), one of Fiji's first. In the 1860s European planters tried growing cotton on Taveuni, turning to sugar when the cotton market collapsed. Later, copra was found to be more profitable. A tall chimney, boilers, and other equipment remain below the school at Salialevu.

After a look around, return to the two gates at the bridge and follow the other dirt road southwest for an hour through the coconut plantation to **Navakawau** village at the southeast end of the island. Some of Fiji's only Australian magpies (large black-and-white birds) inhabit this plantation.

Just east of South Cape as you come from Navakawau is the **Matamainggi Blowhole,** where trade wind-driven waves crash into the unprotected black volcanic rocks, sending geysers of sea spray soaring skyward, especially on a southern swell. The viewpoint is just off the main road.

At **Vuna** the lava flows have formed pools beside the ocean, which fill up with fresh water at low tide and are used for washing and bathing.

Northern Taveuni

Somosomo is the chiefly village of Thakaundrove and the seat of the Tui Cakau, Taveuni's "king"; the late Ratu Sir Penaia Ganilau, first president of Fiji, hailed from here. There are two distinct parts of the village, divided by a small stream where women wash their clothes. The southern portion is the island's commercial center with several large Indian stores and a couple of places to stay. Pacific Transport has its bus terminus here.

The northern part of Somosomo is the chiefly quarter with the personal residence of the Tui Cakau on the hill directly above the bridge (no entry). Beside the main road below is the large hall built for the 1986 meeting of the Great Council of Chiefs. Missionary William Cross, one of the creators of today's system of written Fijian, who died at Somosomo in 1843, is buried in the attractive new church next to the meeting hall. There's even electric street lighting in this part of town!

DAVID STANLEY

The ruins of the century-old Bilyard Sugar Mill at Salialevu, Taveuni, lie incongruously in the midst of today's coconut plantation. In the early days, planters believed sugar grew best in a wet, tropical environment such as that at southeastern Taveuni. Sugar fields in the Rewa Valley near Suva fed another mill at Nausori, which now processes rice. Today, all of Fiji's sugar is grown on the sunny, dry, northwestern sides of Viti Levu and Vanua Levu, with bustling sugar mills at Lambasa, Rakiraki, Mba, and Lautoka.

The challenging trail up to lovely **Lake Tangimauthia**, 823 meters high in the mountainous interior, begins behind the Mormon church at Somosomo. The first half is the hardest. You'll need a full day to do a roundtrip, and a guide (F$40) will be necessary as there are many trails to choose from. You must wade for half an hour through knee-deep mud in the crater to reach the lake's edge. Much of the lake's surface is covered with floating vegetation, and the water is only five meters deep.

Eastern Taveuni

There are three lovely waterfalls in **Tavoro Forest Park and Reserve** (admission F$5), just south of Mbouma on the northeast side of Taveuni. From the information kiosk on the main road it's an easy 10-minute walk up a broad path along the river's right bank to the lower falls, which plunge 20 meters into a deep pool. You can swim here, and change rooms, toilets, picnic tables, and a barbecue are provided. A well-constructed trail leads up to a second falls in about 30 minutes, passing a spectacular viewpoint overlooking Nggamea Island and Taveuni's northeast coast. You must cross the river once, but a rope is provided for balance. Anyone in good physical shape can reach this second falls with ease, and there's also a pool for swimming. The muddy, slippery trail up to the third and highest falls involves two river crossings with nothing to hold onto, and hiking it would be unpleasant in the rain. This trail does cut through the most beautiful portion of the rainforest, and these upper falls are perhaps the most impressive of the three, as the river plunges over a black basalt cliff, which you can climb and use as a diving platform into the deep pool. The water here is very sweet.

Tavoro Forest Park was developed with well-spent New Zealand aid money at the request of the villagers themselves, and all income goes to local community projects. In 1990 an agreement was signed putting the area in trust for 99 years and the forest park was established a year later. There are plans to eventually cut a trail from Tavoro right up to Lake Tangimauthia, but this awaits the creation of suitable overnight accommodations at Mbouma and additional outside funding. For the time being visitors are allowed to sleep on mats in the park information kiosk at F$5 per head; otherwise it might be possible to camp or stay with the locals.

Mbouma is easily accessible by public bus daily except Sunday. If you depart Waiyevo or Somosomo on the 0830 bus, you'll have about three and a half hours to see the falls and have a swim before catching the 1400 bus back to Waiyevo. This second bus does a roundtrip to Lavena, six km south (the 0830 bus finishes at Mbouma), and it's worth jumping on for the ride even if you don't intend to get off at Lavena.

At Lavena the New Zealand government has financed the **Lavena Coastal Walk,** which opened in May 1993. The information kiosk where you pay the F$5 admission fee is right at the end of the road at Lavena and, when space is available, it's possible to sleep on one of the four mattresses on the floor upstairs in the kiosk at F$5 pp. There's no store here but the villagers will prepare meals for you at F$3 each. Otherwise bring groceries and cook your own behind the kiosk—protect the food from mice. Lighting is by kerosene lamp, and mosquito coils are essential. Additional accommodation may be available by the time you get there, and this is urgently required as it's not possible to visit Lavena as a day-trip by public bus (taxis charge F$80 return to bring you here). Buses depart Lavena for Somosomo Monday to Saturday 0600 and 1400, Sunday at 0800. The beach at Lavena is one of Fiji's most spectacular beaches (be careful with the currents if you snorkel). The film *Return to the Blue Lagoon* was filmed here.

From the information kiosk at Lavena you can hike the five km down the Ravilevo Coast to stunning **Wainimbau Falls** in about an hour and a half. The last 30 minutes is a scramble up a creek bed, and during the rainy season you may have to wade or swim. There are two falls here which plunge into the same deep pool and diving off either is excellent fun (allow four hours there and back from Lavena with plenty of stops). It's also possible to visit the falls by motor boat, which can be arranged at the kiosk. A boat to Wainimbau Falls and Wainivakau Falls is F$50 for up to three persons, or F$15 pp for groups of four to six. If you also want to see **Savuleveyavonu Falls,** which plummets off a cliff directly into the sea, you must pay F$75 for up to three people or F$25 pp for up to six. Intrepid ocean kayakers sometimes paddle the 20 km down the back side of Taveuni, past countless cliffs and waterfalls. It's well worth spending a few days in this attractive area if you possibly can.

SPORTS AND RECREATION

Taveuni and surrounding waters have become known as one of Fiji's top diving areas. The fabulous 31-km Rainbow Reef off the south coast of eastern Vanua Levu abounds in turtles, fish, overhangs, crevices, and soft corals, all in 5-10 meters of water. Favorite dive sites here include White Sandy Gulley, Jack's Place, Cabbage Patch, Pot Luck, Blue Ribbon Eel Reef, the Ledge, Jerry's Jelly, Coral Garden, and especially the Great White Wall. Beware of strong currents in the Somosomo Strait.

Way back in 1976, Ric and Do Cammick of **Dive Taveuni** (Postal Agency Matei, Taveuni; tel. 880-441, fax 880-466) pioneered scuba diving in this area and they're still one of Fiji's most reliable operators. They charge F$105 for two tanks including lunch (hire gear not available), but their clients are mostly groups which have prebooked from abroad.

Walk-in divers are catered to by **Rainbow Reef Divers** (tel. 880-286) at the Garden Island Resort. The daily two-tank dives are F$99 (no one-tank dives), and PADI scuba certification costs F$440. You'll find cheaper dive shops but Rainbow's facilities are first rate.

Budget-minded divers should check out **The Dive Center** (Box 69, Taveuni; tel. 880-125, fax 880-202) at Susie's Plantation, which offers boat dives on the Rainbow Reef at F$44/77 for one/two tanks (plus F$15 extra for gear). Night diving is F$55; shore dives F$22. The Center's four-day NAUI scuba certification courses are F$415 if you're the only student, or F$363 pp for two or more students (group instruction usually begins on Monday). There's a five percent surcharge on credit card payments. Susie's makes a perfect base for these activities.

Offshore dive resorts such as Matangi Island and Qamea Beach Club receive mostly upscale divers who have booked from outside Fiji, and accommodations there are much more expensive than those on Taveuni.

The dive shop at the Garden Island Resort rents ocean kayaks at F$22 a half day, F$33 a full day.

Little Dolphin Sports (tel. 880-130), opposite the Matei Postal Agency Supermarket, near the east end of the airstrip, rents windsurfing boards (F$15 a day), mountain bikes (F$15 a day), paddle boats (F$15 a day), and snorkeling gear (F$5 a day). It's run by an Australian named Scott who is a mine of information.

For something special, consider a day cruise on the luxury yacht *Seax of Legra,* operating on Wednesday and Saturday (Warwick and Dianne Baine, tel./fax 880-141). You sail for two hours to one of the islands off northern Taveuni, spend three hours there swimming, snorkeling, and having lunch on board, then sail another two hours back. Reservations must be made by 1600 the day before (F$70 pp including a buffet lunch aboard, four-person minimum). In good weather it's sure to be an unforgettable experience.

ACCOMMODATIONS

Accommodations in Northern Taveuni

For convenience, the accommodations listings which follow are arranged from top to bottom down the west side of Taveuni. Expensive and budget properties are mixed, so scan the entire list before choosing your place to stay. **Tuvununu Paradise Garden Inn** (c/o Postal Agency, Matei, Taveuni; tel. 880-465), just east of Naselesele village, offers rooms in a large wooden building overlooking Viubani Island at F$39/61 single/double, or F$14 pp in the dorm. The tidal flat in front of the inn is beautiful but not ideal for swimming, and at last report the Tuvununu was closed.

Several residents of the airport area have built nice little bungalows next to their homes, or fixed up rooms in their personal residences which they rent to tourists. For instance, **Little Dolphin Sports** (tel. 880-130), less than a km east of the airport, has a bungalow at F$45 a night or F$300 a week. Audrey of **Audrey's Cafe** (tel. 880-039), a bit closer to the airport, has a cottage at F$55. An old steam tractor stands rusting under a coconut tree across the street. A couple of hundred meters west,

Mrs. Dolores Porter (tel. 880-299) of **Loma-langi Beachfront Home** has a four-bed apartment at F$65. Two houses west is the **Coconut Grove Cafe** (tel. 880-328, fax 880-050), where Ronna Goldstein rents a fan-cooled beachfront cottage for F$55/66 single/double. Cooking facilities are provided at all of these places (and a supermarket is nearby), but it's important to call ahead to check availability as the rooms are often full. Use the card phone at the airport for this purpose (Air Fiji sells phone cards).

Quiet, friendly **Niranjan's Budget Accommodation** (c/o Postal Agency, Matei, Taveuni; tel. 880-406), also known as Airport Motel, is just a five-minute walk east of the airport. The four clean rooms in the main building, each with two beds, fridge, fan, and cooking facilities, go for F$22/33/44 single/double/triple. These rooms are excellent value and Niranjan's also has an annex called "Airport Motel" two doors away, with four cheaper rooms with shared bath at F$22 double. The electric generator is on 1800-2200. The manager serves one of the best curry dinners you'll taste in these parts for F$10 pp. This is one of the best places to stay in this area—recommended.

Directly opposite the airport terminal is the absurdly expensive **Garden of Eden Villa** which costs F$1250 a night (minimum stay one week). If you can afford those bucks you can also afford to call the manager, Peter Madden (tel. 880-252), long distance from anywhere in the world and question him about what he's offering. Who knows, he may even throw in the yacht!

Bibi's Hideaway (Box 80, Waiyevo, Taveuni; tel. 880-443), about 500 meters south of the airport, has something of the gracious atmosphere of the neighboring resorts without the sky-high prices. One room in a two-room cottage is F$30 single or double, while a larger family unit is F$70/80 double/triple. The film crew from *Return to the Blue Lagoon* stayed here, and with the extra income the owners built a deluxe *mbure*, which is F$50 single or double. All three units have access to cooking facilities. Bibi's is located on lush, spacious grounds, and James, Victor, and Agnes Bibi will make you feel right at home. It's an excellent medium-priced choice if you don't mind being a bit away from the beach.

A hundred meters south are two of Taveuni's most exclusive properties. **Maravu Plantation Resort** (c/o Matei Postal Agency, Taveuni; tel. 880-555, fax 880-600) is a village-style resort in a real 20-hectare copra-making plantation, a kilometer south of the airport. It has 10 comfortable *mbures* with ceiling fans at F$167/198/227 single/double/triple. The meal plan at the resort restaurant is F$68 pp extra. There's also a bar and swimming pool on the landscaped grounds. Nonguests must make reservations to eat here (the food is good, but count on F$35 pp for dinner). Airport transfers are F$6.

Almost across the street from Maravu Plantation is the upmarket **Dive Taveuni Resort** (Ric and Do Cammick, Postal Agency, Matei, Taveuni; tel. 880-441, fax 880-466) which is patronized mostly by scuba divers who arrive on prepaid packages. This place doesn't really cater to people who stroll in unannounced looking for a place to stay (and they're closed in February and March). The eight very pleasant *mbures* accommodate 10 guests at F$178 pp, including three meals and transfers. The property is on a cliff overlooking the ocean, with great views from the open terrace dining area. No alcohol is sold, so bring your own.

Down the hill from these and just north of Prince Charles Beach, a little over a km south of the airport, are two of Taveuni's two best-established campgrounds. **Beverly Campground** (tel. 880-381), run by Bill Madden, is a shady place, nice if you value your privacy. It's F$5 pp in your own tent, F$6 pp in Bill's tent, or F$11 pp in a *mbure*. Cooking facilities (one-time charge of F$2 for gas) are available in a nearby *mbure*, but bring food. Bill can supply fresh fruit and vegetables, and he even serves a good dinner for F$7. It's right on the beach but the whole place could use a cleaning up and the snorkeling is poor.

A few hundred meters south is another good place just across the road from a white-sand beach. **Lisi's Campground** (Vathala Estate, Postal Agency Matei; tel. 880-194), in a small village one km southwest of Beverly, is F$5 pp to camp, or F$10 pp in a small *mbure*. If you don't have a tent, they may be able to rent you one. A separate shower/toilet block is reserved for guests. Cooking facilities are available in a *mbure* (fresh fruit provided every morning), and hosts Mary and Lote Tuisago serve excellent Fijian meals at reasonable prices. Horseback riding is possible, and you're welcome to help with the "work," collecting fruit or making copra, if you want. You get to meet local people here as everyone joins the afternoon volleyball game, and in the evening there's kava drinking, often with music.

British yachties Warwick and Dianne Baine (Box 89, Waiyevo, Taveuni; tel./fax 880-141) rent a self-catering apartment in their lovely two-story home adjacent to Lisi's Campground at F$105 for up to four persons (two single and one double bed).

Accommodations in Western Taveuni

The original budget hotel on Taveuni was **Kaba's Motel & Guest House** (Box 4, Taveuni; tel. 880-233, fax 880-202) at Somosomo, which charges F$15/25/35 single/double/triple in one of four double rooms with shared facilities in the guesthouse. The cooking facilities are very good. The newer motel section is F$30/38/48 for one of the six larger units with kitchenette, fridge, fan, phone, and private bath—good value. The water is solar-heated, so cold showers are de rigueur in overcast weather (ask for a discount if this is the case). Kaba's Supermarket up the street has a huge selection of videos you can rent to play on the guesthouse VCR.

A friendly Indian family runs **Kool's Accommodation** (Box 10, Waiyevo, Taveuni; tel. 880-395), just south of Kaba's at Somosomo. The six rooms in two long blocks facing the eating area are F$9/14 single/double, and cooking facilities are provided. As the price may suggest, it's more basic than Kaba's and only for those on the lowest of budgets.

Sunset Accommodation (Box 15, Taveuni; tel. 880-229), on a dusty corner near the wharf at Lovonivonu, has two basic rooms behind a small store at F$8/12 single/double. Again, this is only a low-budget place to crash.

The **Garden Island Resort** (Box 1, Waiyevo, Taveuni; tel. 880-286, fax 880-288), by the sea at Waiyevo, three km south of Somosomo, has 28 a/c rooms in an attractive two-story building at F$55/77/88 single/double/triple, or F$18 in the four-bed dorm. If your air-conditioner isn't operating, the ceiling fan should suffice. The buffet breakfast-and-dinner plan is F$32 pp,

and eating by the pool is fun. Formerly known as the Castaway, this was Taveuni's premier (and only) hotel when it was built by the Travelodge chain in the 1960s. Several changes of ownership later, the Garden Island has been eclipsed by the offshore resorts. There's no beach, but the Garden Island offers a restaurant, bar (happy hour 1700-1800), evening entertainment, swimming pool, excursions, and water sports. Snorkeling trips are offered three times a day to Korolevu Island (F$11). It's a nice medium-priced place in which to hang out if you like large hotels.

Accommodations in Southern Taveuni

Kris Back Palace (Box 22, Taveuni; tel. 880-246), between Songgulu Plantation and Susie's Plantation, is still being developed but their beautiful stretch of rocky coastline and crystal clear snorkeling waters have always existed. For now, you can only count on a good place to pitch your tent (F$8 pp), or perhaps a bed in a thatched two-bed *mbure* (F$12 pp). The friendly managers will allow you to pick fruit at no cost in their plantation, and scuba diving can be arranged.

Susie's Plantation (Box 69, Waiyevo, Taveuni; tel. 880-125, fax 880-202), just north of Vuna Point at the south end of Taveuni, offers peace and quiet amid picturesque rustic surroundings, at the right price. Rates begin at F$35 double for a room with shared bath in the plantation house, or F$45 double for a simple seaside *mbure*. The dorm costs F$12.50 pp; camping F$10 per tent (tolerated but not encouraged). You can cook your own food (a well-stocked grocery store is at Vatuwiri Farm, a 10-minute walk south). Otherwise pay F$30 pp extra for three meals in the restaurant, housed in the oldest missionary building on the island (nonguests welcome). Electricity only exists during dinner hours. This atmospheric resort right on the ocean has its own resident diving instructor, who leads daily trips to the Great White Wall and Rainbow Reef. The PADI scuba certification course offers a great opportunity to learn how to dive, but even if you're not a diver, you'll enjoy the superb snorkeling right off their rocky beach or at nearby Namoli Beach (best at low tide, as the current picks up appreciably when the tide comes in). Horseback riding can be arranged. Susie is a real character and some people stay here for months. Recommended.

The **Vatuwiri Farm Resort** (c/o Postal Agency, Vuna, Taveuni; tel. 880-316) at Vuna Point, one km south of Susie's, offers the possibility of staying on an authentic working farm established in 1871 by James Valentine Tarte. The Tartes now produce beef, vanilla, and copra, and rent several small cottages to tourists for F$70 a night. A long workers' dormitory block has been renovated, and beds in the six double rooms are F$20 each. Three good meals are F$35 pp extra. The rocky coast here is fine for snorkeling, and horseback riding is available. The Tarte family is congenial and this is perhaps your best chance to stay on a real working farm in Fiji.

Paul Masirewa owns land on lovely Namoli Beach, a 10-minute walk off the main road from Vuna village, a kilometer south of Vatuwiri Farm. He'll probably grant permission to camp if he likes you, and he's available as a guide for explorations of the surrounding area.

OTHER PRACTICALITIES

Food

Each of the three accommodation areas mentioned above has grocery shopping possibilities. Those staying on the northern part of the island will appreciate the well-stocked supermarket at the Matei Postal Agency between the airport and Naselesele village. Their generous ice cream cones are almost worth a special trip. The variety of goods available at Kaba's Supermarket in Somosomo is surprising and a cluster of other small shops is adjacent. Small grocery stores also exist at Wairiki and Waiyevo. The only well-stocked grocery store in southern Taveuni is at Vatuwiri Farm, one km south of Susie's Plantation.

The only nonhotel eatery on the island is the **Wathi-Po-Ee Restaurant** (open weekdays 0730-1700, Saturday 0730-1500) next to the Westpac Bank in Waiyevo. They serve reasonable Chinese and local meals, although prices are somewhat inflated by the nearby Garden Island Resort (which also has a restaurant).

Several of the one-unit accommodation places near the airport serve meals, including Ronna Goldstein's **Coconut Grove Cafe** (tel. 880-328). A bacon-and-cheese sandwich and coffee for lunch will run F$8, and at dinner you can get fresh fish of the day for F$13 or lobster for F$25, both with a choice of sauces, garlic bread, stir-fried vegetables, and rice. A F$8 "backpacker menu" is also available. Reservations are required for dinner but not at lunchtime. It's a bit of a splurge, but you dine on their veranda overlooking the sea, Mareta's cooking is excellent, and Ronna can tell you anything you want to know about Taveuni. A similar scene revolves around **Audrey's Cafe,** run by an American woman at Matei, a bit east of the airport. Audrey offers afternoon tea to guests who also enjoy the great view from her terrace, and she has various homemade goodies to take away.

Entertainment

The **180 Meridian Cinema** at Wairiki shows mainly violence and horror films.

There isn't any tourist-oriented nightlife on Taveuni beyond what's offered at the **Garden Island Resort,** which stages a *meke* and *lovo* Wednesday at 1830 (F$20 pp).

The **Taveuni Country Club** (tel. 880-133), next to the police station up the hill at Waiyevo, is a safe local drinking place. It's open Thursday to Saturday only.

Services

Traveler's checks can be changed at the Westpac Bank (tel. 880-035) and National Bank branches, both near the Garden City Resort at Waiyevo (Monday to Thursday 0930-1500, Friday 0930-1600).

A haircut from the barber next to Kaba's Motel in Somosomo is F$2/3 for men/women.

Getting There

Matei Airstrip at the north tip of Taveuni is serviced twice daily by **Air Fiji** (tel. 880-062) from Suva (F$87), and **Sunflower Airlines** (tel. 880-461) from Nandi (F$116) and Savusavu (F$45). Sunflower also arrives from Lambasa (F$45) three times a week. **Vanua Air** flies here twice daily from Suva (F$87) and Savusavu (F$44). Flights to/from Taveuni are often heavily booked. You get superb views of Taveuni from the plane: sit on the right side going up, the left side coming back. Krishna Brothers in Somosomo is the agent for Air Fiji; the agent of Vanua Air (tel. 880-291) is next to the Hot Bread Kitchen in Somosomo.

Patterson Brothers has the ferries *Princess Ashika* and *Ovalau II* from Suva to Taveuni via Ngau, Koro, and Savusavu (22 hours, F$36) every Monday at midnight, departing Taveuni for the return trip Wednesday at 1000. The Patterson agent is Lesuma Holdings (tel. 880-036) in the back of the store between the Westpac and National banks. **Consort Shipping** operates the weekly *Spirit of Free Enterprise* service from Suva to Taveuni via Koro and Savusavu (24 hours, F$34). This ferry departs Suva northbound Wednesday at 0500 and leaves Taveuni southbound Thursday at 1300. The Consort agent (tel. 880-261) is at the fish market opposite the Garden Island Resort.

Patterson Brothers also operates the barge *Yaumbula* between Taveuni and Natuvu at Mbutha Bay on Vanua Levu, leaving Taveuni Wednesday to Saturday at 0800 (two hours, F$10), leaving Natuvu at 1300. They also carry cars and vans for F$50. Through tickets are available to Savusavu (four hours, F$20) and Lambasa (six hours, F$22), but the bus connection at Natuvu doesn't work every day, so check.

The small passenger boat *Grace* (tel. 880-134), also known as the *Ronita,* departs Taveuni for Natuvu Monday to Friday at 0830 (two hours, F$5), with connections to Savusavu and Lambasa (F$22) on Monday, Wednesday, and Friday only. Ask about combined boat/bus tickets on both the *Yaumbula* and the *Grace,* and be aware that without such a prearranged connection, you might have to wait around at Mbutha Bay a couple of hours before the bus to Savusavu (F$3) shows up (there are only public buses from Natuvu to Savusavu in the early morning and at 1600). If no bus is around, you may be able to find a carrier, but expect a rough trip. Eastbound the bus/boat connection at Mbutha Bay is immediate.

If you arrive by boat at Taveuni, you could disembark at any one of three places. Some small boats from Vanua Levu transfer their passengers to the beach at Waiyevo by outboard. The *Spirit of Free Enterprise* and most of the other large ferries tie up at a wharf a km north of Waiyevo. There's a third wharf at Lovonivonu village, a km north again, midway between Waiyevo and Somosomo, and this is often used by the Vanua Levu boats and other smaller cargo boats.

Getting Around
Pacific Transport (tel. 880-278) buses leave Waiyevo and Somosomo northbound to Mbouma (F$2) at 0830, 1215, and 1645; southbound to Vuna (F$2) they leave at 1215 and 1645, Saturday at 0830, 1215, and 1645. The northbound 0830 bus turns around at Mbouma, but the 1215 and 1645 buses carry on to Lavena (F$2). Sunday service is very infrequent, although there are sometimes buses to Mbouma and Vuna at 1600. Check the current schedule carefully as soon as you arrive. The buses begin their journeys at the Pacific Transport garage at Somosomo, but they all head first south to Waiyevo hospital to pick up passengers.

One of Taveuni's biggest drawbacks is the extremely dusty road up the northwest coast, which makes it very unpleasant to walk anywhere between Wairiki and the airport when there's a lot of fast traffic passing. This combined with rather expensive taxi fares and sporadic buses can make getting around rather inconvenient. Taveuni's minibus taxis only operate on a charter basis and don't run along set routes picking up passengers at fixed rates. The taxi fare from the wharf to Somosomo is F$2; from the airport to Somosomo it will be F$10.

Kaba's Supermarket (tel. 880-058) in Somosomo rents cars at F$77 a day with unlimited mileage (minimum two days), or F$44 a day plus 30 cents per kilometer, insurance included. Fast-moving vehicles on the gravel roads throw up small stones which can smash your front window (and you'll have to pay the damages). As you pass approaching cars, hold your hand against the windshield just in case. It may be cheaper to hire a minibus taxi and driver for the day than to rent a car. Write out a list of everything you want to see, then negotiate a price with a driver. Otherwise, save money by using the buses for long rides and taxis for shorter hops.

ISLANDS OFF TAVEUNI

Nggamea Island
Nggamea (Qamea) Island, just three km east of Taveuni, is the 12th-largest island in Fiji. It's 10 km long with lots of lovely bays, lush green hills, and secluded white-sand beaches. Land crabs

(lairo) are gathered in abundance during their migration to the sea here in late November or early December. The birdlife is also rich, due to the absence of the mongoose. Outboards from villages on Nggamea land near Navakathoa village on the northeast side of Taveuni. Best time to try for a ride over is Thursday or Friday afternoons. Vatusongosongo village on Nggamea is inhabited by descendants of blackbirded Solomon islanders.

The **Qamea Beach Club Resort** (Postal Agency, Matei, Taveuni; tel. 880-220, fax 880-092) opened on the west side of Nggamea in 1984. The 11 thatched *mbures* with fans and fridges go for F$270/315/345 single/double/triple (no children under 12 allowed), and the meal plan is another F$75 pp a day (no cooking facilities). Meals are taken in a central dining room and lounge designed like a *mburekalau* (temple). The boat transfer from Taveuni airport is F$60 pp return. Activities such as windsurfing, snorkeling, sailing, outrigger canoeing, and hiking are included in the basic price, but scuba diving and fishing are extra. Some of the best dive sites in the world are close at hand and the snorkeling off the fine white-sand beach is superb

Matangi Island

Matangi is a tiny volcanic island just north of Nggamea, its sunken crater forming a lovely palm-fringed bay. The island is privately owned by the Douglas family, which has been producing copra on Matangi for five generations and still does. In 1988 they diversified into the hotel business.

Matangi Island Resort (Box 83, Waiyevo, Taveuni; tel. 880-260, fax 880-274), 10 km northeast of Taveuni, makes no bones about serving as a base for scuba divers. They also cater to families and couples looking for a quiet holiday, and the deluxe treehouse *mbure,* perched 10 meters up in an almond tree, is popular among honeymooners (F$310 pp). Other guests are accommodated in 10 neat thatched *mbures*

costing F$188/255/290 single/double/triple, well spaced among the coconut palms below Matangi's high jungly interior. To the above, add another F$86 pp for the compulsory meal package (no cooking facilities), and boat transfers from Taveuni are F$63 pp return (reduced rates available for children). Diving costs F$118 for two tanks, and the live-aboard dive boat MV *Matangi Princess II* is based here, costing from F$415 pp a day double occupancy including diving.

Lauthala Island

Lauthala Island, which shares a barrier reef with Nggamea, was depopulated and sold to Europeans in the mid-19th century by the chief of Taveuni, after the inhabitants sided with Tongan chief Enele Ma'afu in a local war. Today it's owned by the estate of the late multimillionaire businessman and New York publisher Malcolm Forbes, who is buried on the island. In 1972 Forbes bought 12-square-km Lauthala from the Australian company Morris Hedstrom for US$1 million. He then spent additional millions on an airstrip, wharf, and roads, and on replacing the thatched *mbures* of the 225 Fijian inhabitants with red-roofed cement-block boxes. Forbes's former private residence stands atop a hill overlooking the native village, the inhabitants of which make copra.

Prior to his death in 1990, Forbes opened his island to affluent tourists who now stay in seven *mbures,* each with living room, bar, and kitchen. The housekeeper prepares guests' breakfasts in their cottages; other meals can be served in the plantation house, in Forbes's house, at the beachside barbecue area, or as a picnic anywhere on the island. The price is F$425 pp per night (three-night minimum stay), including all meals, "a reasonable supply" of liquor, sports, scuba diving, and deep-sea fishing. The resident general manager of **Fiji Forbes Inc.** (Box 41, Waiyevo, Taveuni; tel. 880-077, fax 880-099) is the only chief on Lauthala.

SALVATORE CASA

THE LAU GROUP

Lau is by far the most remote part of Fiji, its 57 islands scattered over a vast area of ocean between Viti Levu and Tonga. Roughly half of them are inhabited. Though all are relatively small, they vary from volcanic islands to uplifted atolls, to some combination of the two. Tongan influence has always been strong in Lau, and due to Polynesian mixing the people have a somewhat lighter skin color than other Fijians. Historically the chiefs of Lau have always had a political influence on Fiji far out of proportion to their economic or geographical importance.

Vanua Mbalavu (52 square km) and Lakemba (54 square km) are the largest and most important islands of the group. These are also the only islands with organized accommodations, and Vanua Mbalavu is the more rewarding of the

two. Similarly, Moala is a large mountainous island with much to offer, while there is little for the average visitor on Thithia.

Once accessible only after a long sea voyage on infrequent copra-collecting ships, four islands in Lau—Lakemba, Vanua Mbalavu, Moala, and Thithia—now have regular air service from Suva. Occasional private ships also circulate through Lau, usually calling at five or six islands on a single trip, but they usually only offer deck passage (see "Transportation" in the Suva chapter for details). As none of these islands is prepared for tourism, the reception you may receive varies. Sometimes you'll be welcomed as a guest, other times they'll only want to know when you're leaving. No banks are to be found in Lau.

NORTHERN LAU

VANUA MBALAVU

The name means the "long land." The southern portion of this unusual, seahorse-shaped island is mostly volcanic, while the north is up-

lifted coral. An unspoiled environment of palm-fringed beaches backed by long grassy hillsides and sheer limestone cliffs, this is a wonderful area to explore. There are varied vistas and scenic views on all sides. To the east is a barrier reef enclosing a lagoon 37 by 16 km. The

Bay of Islands at the northwest end of Vanua Mbalavu is a recognized hurricane shelter. The villages of Vanua Mbalavu are impeccably clean, the grass cut and manicured. Large mats are made on the island and strips of pandanus can be seen drying before many of the houses.

In 1840 Commodore Wilkes of the U.S. Exploring Expedition named Vanua Mbalavu and its adjacent islands enclosed by the same barrier reef the Exploring Isles. In the days of sail, Lomaloma, the largest settlement, was an important Pacific port. The early trading company Hennings Brothers had its headquarters here. The great Tongan warlord Enele Ma'afu conquered northern Lau from the chiefs of Vanua Levu in 1855 and made Lomaloma the base for his bid to dominate Fiji. A small monument flanked by two cannons on the waterfront near the wharf recalls the event. Fiji's first public botanical garden was laid out here over a century ago, but nothing remains of it. History has passed Lomaloma by. Today it's only a big sleepy village with a hospital and a couple of general stores. Some 400 Tongans live in Sawana, the south portion of Lomaloma village, and many of the houses have the round ends characteristic of Lau.

Sights

Copra is the main export and there's a small coconut oil mill at **Lomaloma**. A road runs inland from Lomaloma up and across the island to **Ndakuilomaloma**. From the small communications station on a grassy hilltop midway there's an excellent view.

Follow the road south from Lomaloma three km to **Narothivo** village, then continue two km beyond to the narrow passage separating Vanua Mbalavu and Malata islands. At low tide you can easily wade across to **Namalata** village. Alternatively, work your way around to the west side of Vanua Mbalavu, where there are isolated tropical beaches. There's good snorkeling in this passage.

There are **hot springs** and **burial caves** among the high limestone outcrops between Narothivo and Namalata, but you'll need a guide to find them. This can be easily arranged at Nakama, the tiny collection of houses closest to the cliffs, upon payment of a nominal fee. Small bats inhabit some of the caves.

Rent a boat to take you over to the **Raviravi Lagoon** on Susui Island, the favorite picnic spot near Lomaloma for the locals. The beach and snorkeling are good, and there's even a cave if you're interested. **Munia Island** is a privately owned coconut plantation where paying guests are accommodated in two *mbures*.

Events

A most unusual event occurs annually at Masomo Bay, west of **Mavana** village, usually around Christmas. For a couple of days the Mavana villagers, clad only in skirts of *ndrauninggai* leaves, enter the waters and stir up the muddy bottom by swimming around clutching logs. No one understands exactly why, and magic is thought to be involved, but this activity stuns the *yawa* or mullet fish that inhabit the bay, rendering them easy prey for waiting spears. Peni, the *mbete* (priest) of Mavana, controls the ritual. No photos are allowed. A Fijian legend tells how the *yawa* were originally brought to Masomo by a Tongan princess.

Accommodations

Mr. Poasa Delailomaloma and his brother Laveti operate a charming traditional-style resthouse in

VANUA MBALAVU

0   4 km

© DAVID STANLEY

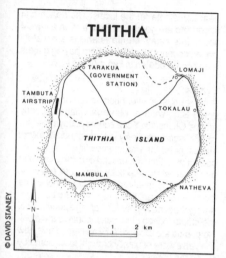

THITHIA

TARAKUA (GOVERNMENT STATION)

LOMAJI

TAMBUTA AIRSTRIP

TOKALAU

THITHIA ISLAND

MAMBULA

NATHEVA

-N-

0   1   2 km

© DAVID STANLEY

the middle of Lomaloma village. A bed and all meals cost F$25 pp. It makes a great base from which to see the island, and you get a feel for village life while retaining a degree of privacy. Recommended.

The **Lomaloma Resort** (Box 55, Lomaloma; tel. 880-446, fax 880-303), on Yanuyanu Island just off Lomaloma, is the creation of Ratu Sir Kamisese Mara, paramount chief of the Lau Group. Ratu Mara strongly opposed tourist development in Lau during his long tenure as Fiji's prime minister, so this is a rather ironic retirement project. He's also a part owner of Vanua Air. The seven round-ended *mbures* (or *fales*) furnished in the traditional style rent for F$275/450 single/double, including meals, drinks, nonmotorized activities, and airport transfers. Less expensive shared accommodation may be also available, and scuba diving is possible with Lomaloma Crystal Divers. Book direct or through Sun Tours Ltd. (Box 9403, Nandi Airport; tel. 722-666, fax 790-075).

Getting There

Vanua Air flies to Vanua Mbalavu twice a week from Suva (F$98 one-way) and Thithia (F$22). The flights are heavily booked, so reserve your return journey before leaving Suva. A bus runs from the airstrip to Lomaloma. After checking in at the airstrip for departure you'll probably

have time to scramble up the nearby hill for a good view of the island. Boat service from Suva is only every couple of weeks.

Several carriers a day run from Lomaloma north to Mualevu, and some carry on to Mavana.

OTHER ISLANDS OF NORTHERN LAU

After setting himself up at Lomaloma on Vanua Mbalavu in 1855, Chief Ma'afu encouraged the establishment of European copra and cotton plantations, and several islands are freehold land to this day. **Kanathea,** to the west of Vanua Mbalavu, was sold to a European by the Tui Cakau in 1863, and the Kanathea people now reside on Taveuni. **Mango Island,** a copra estate formerly owned by English planter Jim Barron, was purchased by the Tokyu Corporation of Japan in 1985 for F$6 million.

In 1983 **Naitamba Island** was purchased from TV star Raymond Burr by the California spiritual group Johannine Daist Communion for US$2.1 million. Johannine Daist (45 Lovoni Rd., Samambula, Suva; tel. 381-466, fax 370-196) holds four-to-eight-week meditation retreats on Naitamba for longtime members of the communion. The communion's founder and teacher, Baba Da Free John, the former Franklin Albert Jones (tel. 880-188), who attained enlightenment in Hollywood in 1970, resides on the island.

There's a single Fijian village and a gorgeous white-sand beach on **Yathata Island.** Right next to Yathata and sharing the same lagoon is 260-hectare **Kaimbu Island** which was owned by the Rosa family from 1872 to 1969, when it was purchased by fiberglass millionaires Margie and Jay Johnson. In 1987 the Johnsons opened **Kaimbu Island Resort** (Kaimbu Island Postal Agency; tel. 880-333, fax 880-334), which consists of only three spacious octagonal guest cottages renting at F$1550 per couple per day (minimum stay six nights—children not accommodated). The price includes gourmet meals, drinks, snorkeling, sailing, windsurfing, sport fishing, scuba diving, and just about anything else you desire, plus a chartered flight from Suva or Taveuni to Kaimbu's central airstrip. Bookings are handled by Kaimbu Island Associates (Box 10392, Newport Beach, CA 92658, U.S.A.; tel.

800/473-0332, fax 714/644-5773). At last report, a 50% interest in the resort was available for US$2.5 million (contact René Boehm in Hamburg, Germany, at fax 49-40/340-568).

Vatu Vara to the south, with its soaring interior plateau, golden beaches, and azure lagoon, is privately owned and unoccupied much of the time. The circular, 314-meter-high central limestone terrace, which makes the island look like a hat when viewed from the sea, gives it its other name, Hat Island. There is reputed to be buried treasure on Vatu Vara.

Katafanga to the southeast of Vanua Mbalavu was at one time owned by Harold Gatty, the famous Australian aviator who founded Fiji Airways (later Air Pacific) in 1951.

Thithia, between Northern and Southern Lau, receives Vanua Air flights from Suva (F$95) twice a week. Several Fijian villages are found on Thithia, and land is leased to European companies for copra planting. Fiji's only black-and-white Australian magpies have been introduced to Thithia and Taveuni.

Wailangi Lala, northernmost of the Lau Group, is a coral atoll bearing a lighthouse, which beckons to ships entering Nanuku Passage, the northwest gateway to Fiji.

SOUTHERN LAU

LAKEMBA

Lakemba is a rounded volcanic island reaching 215 meters. The fertile red soils of the rolling interior hills have been planted with pine, but the low coastal plain, with eight villages and all the people, is covered with coconuts. To the east is a wide lagoon enclosed by a barrier reef. In the olden days, the population lived on Delai Kendekende, an interior hilltop well suited for defense.

The original capital of Lakemba was Nasanggalau on the north coast, and the present inhabitants of Nasanggalau retain strong Tongan influence. When the Nayau clan conquered the island, their paramount chief, the Tui Nayau, became ruler of all of Southern Lau from his seat at Tumbou. During the 1970s and 1980s Ratu Sir Kamisese Mara, the present Tui Nayau, served as prime minister of Fiji.

Sights
A 29-km road runs all the way around Lakemba. From the Catholic church you get a good view of **Tumbou,** an attractive village and one of the largest in Fiji, with a hospital, wharf, several stores, and the Lau provincial headquarters. Tumbou was originally situated at Korovusa just inland, where the foundations of former houses can still be seen. Farther inland on the same road is the forestry station and a nursery.

The Tongan chief Enele Ma'afu (died 1881) is buried on a stepped platform behind the Provincial Office near Tumbou's wharf. In 1869 Ma'afu united the group into the Lau Confederation and took the title Tui Lau. Two years later he accepted the supremacy of Cakobau's Kingdom of Fiji, and in 1874 he signed the cession to Britain. Alongside Ma'afu is the grave of Ratu Sir Lala Sukuna (1888-1958), an important figure in the development of indigenous Fijian self-government. David Cargill and William Cross, the first Methodist missionaries to arrive in Fiji, landed on the beach just opposite the burial place on 12 October 1835. Here they invented the present system of written Fijian.

Coconut Factory
Four km west of Tumbou is the coir (husk fiber) and coconut oil factory of the **Lakemba Cooperative Association** at Wainiyambia. Truckloads of coconuts are brought in and dehusked by hand. The meat is then removed and sent to the copra driers. Coconut oil is pressed from the resulting copra and exported in drums. The dry pulp remaining after the extraction is bagged and sold locally as feed for pigs. The husks are flattened and soaked, then fed through machinery that separates the fiber. This is then made into twine, rope, brushes, and doormats, or it is bundled to be used as mattress fiber. Nothing is wasted. Behind the factory is Wainiyambia Beach, one of the most scenic on Lakemba.

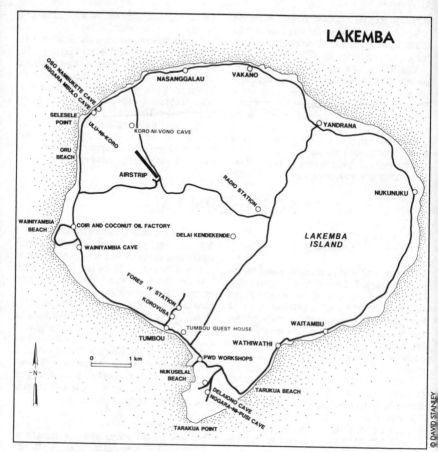

LAKEMBA

OSO NAMBUKETE CAVE
NGGARA MBULO CAVE
NASANGGALAU
VAKANO
SELESELE POINT
ULU-NI-KORO
KORO-NI-VONO CAVE
YANDRANA
ORU BEACH
AIRSTRIP
RADIO STATION
NUKUNUKU
WAINIYAMBIA BEACH
COIR AND COCONUT OIL FACTORY
DELAI KENDEKENDE
LAKEMBA ISLAND
WAINIYAMBIA CAVE
FORESTRY STATION
KOROVUSA
TUMBOU GUEST HOUSE
WAITAMBU
TUMBOU
WATHIWATHI
PWD WORKSHOPS
NUKUSELAL BEACH
DELAIONO CAVE
NGGARA-NI-PUSI CAVE
TARUKUA BEACH
TARAKUA POINT

0   1 km

-N-

© DAVID STANLEY

Nasanggalau and Vicinity

The best limestone caves on the island are near the coast on the northwest side of Lakemba, 2.5 km southwest of Nasanggalau. **Oso Nambukete** is the largest; the entrance is behind a raised limestone terrace. You walk through two chambers before reaching a small, circular opening about one meter in diameter, which leads into a third chamber. The story goes that women attempting to hide during pregnancy are unable to pass through this opening, thus giving the cave its name, the "Tight Fit to the Pregnant" Cave.

Nearby is a smaller cave, **Nggara Mbulo** ("Hidden Cave"), which one must crawl into. Warriors used it as a refuge and hiding place in former times. The old village of Nasanggalau was located on top of the high cliffs behind the caves at Ulu-ni-koro. The whole area is owned by the Nautonggumu clan of Nasanggalau, and they will arrange for a guide to show you around for a fee. Take a flashlight and some newspapers to spread over the openings to protect your clothing.

Each October or November the Nasanggalau people perform a shark-calling ritual. A month before the ritual, a priest *(mbete)* plants a post with a piece of tapa tied to it in the reef. He then keeps watch to ensure that no one comes near the area, while performing a daily kava ceremony. When the appointed day arrives, the caller wades out up to his neck and repeats a chant. Not long after, a large school of sharks led by a white shark arrives and circles the caller. He leads them to shallow water, where all but the white shark are formally killed and eaten.

East of Tumbou
Two less impressive caves can be found at Tarakua, southeast of Tumbou. **Nggara-ni-pusi** has a small entrance, but opens up once you get inside. **Delaiono Cave** is just below a huge banyan tree; this one is easier to enter and smaller inside.

The best beach near Tumbou is **Nukuselal,** which you can reach by walking east along the coastal road as far as the P.W.D. workshops. Turn right onto the track, which runs along the west side of the compound to Nukuselal Beach.

Into the Interior
Many forestry roads have been built throughout the interior of Lakemba. You can walk across the island from Tumbou to Yandrana in a couple of hours, enjoying excellent views along the way. A radio station operates on solar energy near the center of the island. **Aiwa Island,** which can be seen to the southeast, is owned by the Tui Nayau and is inhabited only by flocks of wild goats.

Accommodations
The **Tumbou Guest House** (Lau Provincial Office, Tumbou, Lakemba; tel. 42-090, ext. 35)

has four simple rooms with shared bath at F$16 pp bed/breakfast, plus F$3 each for lunch and dinner. It's a nice way to get off the beaten track, but be sure to call ahead for reservations as persons on official business have priority and there's nowhere else to stay. The locals at Tumbou concoct a potent homebrew *(umburu)* from cassava.

Getting There
Both **Air Fiji** and **Vanua Air** fly to Lakemba twice a week from Suva (F$98). Vanua Air also arrives twice weekly from Moala (F$39). A bus connects the airstrip to Tumbou, and buses run around the island four times weekdays, three times daily weekends.

OTHER ISLANDS OF SOUTHERN LAU

Aside from Lakemba, other islands of Central Lau include Nayau, Vanua Vatu, Aiwa, and Oneata. **Oneata** is famous for its mosquitoes and tapa cloth. In 1830 two Tahitian teachers from the London Missionary Society arrived on Oneata and were adopted by a local chief who had previously visited Tonga and Tahiti. The men spent the rest of their lives on the island, and there's a monument to them at Ndakuloa village.

In a pool on **Vanua Vatu** are red prawns similar to those of Vatulele and Vanua Levu. Here too the locals can summon the prawns with a certain chant.

The Tumbou Guest House (Lakemba) is typical of the simple yet comfortable accommodations available on the outer islands.

DAVID STANLEY

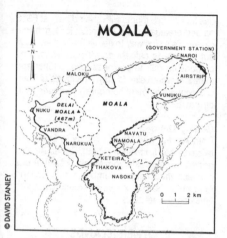

MOALA

(GOVERNMENT STATION)
NAROI
MALOKU
AIRSTRIP
VUNUKU
DELAI
NUKU   MOALA ▲   MOALA
(467m)
VANDRA
NAVATU
NARUKUA   NAMOALA
KETEIRA
THAKOVA
NASOKI

0   1   2 km

© DAVID STANLEY

Mothe is known for its tapa cloth, which is also made on Namuka, Vatoa, and Ono-i-Lau. **Komo** is known for its beautiful women and dances *(meke)*, which are performed whenever a ship arrives. Mothe, Komo, and Olorua are unique in that they are volcanic islands without uplifted limestone terraces.

The **Yangasa Cluster** is owned by the people of Mothe, who visit it occasionally to make copra. Fiji's best *tanoa* are carved from *vesi* (ironwood) at **Kambara**, the largest island in southern Lau. The surfing is also said to be good at Kambara, if you can get there.

Fulanga is known for its woodcarving; large outrigger canoes are still built on Fulanga, as well as on **Ongea**. Over 100 tiny islands in the Fulanga lagoon have been undercut into incredible mushroom shapes. The water around them is tinged with striking colors by the dissolved limestone, and there are numerous magnificent beaches. Yachts can enter this lagoon through a narrow pass.

Ono-i-Lau, far to the south, is closer to Tonga than to the main islands of Fiji. It consists of three small volcanic islands, remnants of a single crater, in an oval lagoon. A few tiny coral islets sit on the barrier reef. The people of Ono-i-Lau make the best *mangi mangi* (sennit rope) and *tambu kaisi* mats in the country. Only high chiefs may sit on these mats. Ono-i-Lau formerly had air service from Suva, but this has been suspended.

The Moala Group

Structurally, geographically, and historically, the high volcanic islands of Moala, Totoya, and Matuku have more to do with Viti Levu than with the rest of Lau. In the mid-19th century they were conquered by the Tongan warlord Enele Ma'afu, and today they're still administered as part of the Lau Group. All three islands have varied scenery, with dark green rainforests above grassy slopes, good anchorage, many villages, and abundant food. Their unexplored nature yet relative proximity to Suva by boat make them an ideal escape for adventurers. No tourist facilities of any kind exist in the Moala Group.

Triangular **Moala** is an intriguing 68-square-km island, the ninth largest in Fiji. Two small crater lakes on the summit of Delai Moala (467 meters) are covered with matted sedges, which will support a person's weight. Though the main island is volcanic, an extensive system of reefs flanks the shores. Ships call at the small government station of Naroi, also the site of an airstrip that receives Sunflower Airlines flights from Suva three times a week (F$77). **Vanua Air** lands on Moala twice a week from Suva (F$73) and Lakemba (F$39).

Totoya is a horseshoe-shaped high island enclosing a deep bay on the south. The bay, actually the island's sunken crater, can only be entered through a narrow channel known as the Gullet, and the southeast trades send high waves across the reefs at the mouth of the bay, making this a dangerous place. Better anchorage is found off the southwest arm of the island. Five Fijian villages are found on Totoya, while neighboring **Matuku** has seven. The anchorage in a submerged crater on the west side of Matuku is one of the best in Fiji.

ROTUMA

This isolated six-by-14-km volcanic island, 600 km north of Viti Levu, is surrounded on all sides by more than 322 km of open sea. There's a saying in Fiji that if you can find Rotuma on a map it's a fairly good map. The climate is damp.

In the beginning, Raho, the Samoan folk hero, dumped two basketfuls of earth here to create the twin islands, joined by the Motusa Isthmus, and installed Sauiftonga as king. Tongans from Niuafo'ou conquered Rotuma in the 17th century and ruled from Noa'tau until they were overthrown.

The first recorded European visit was by Captain Edwards of HMS *Pandora* in 1791, while he was searching for the *Bounty* mutineers. Christianity was introduced in 1842 by Tongan Wesleyan missionaries, followed in 1847 by Marist Roman Catholics. Their followers fought pitched battles in the religious wars of 1871 and 1878, with the Wesleyans emerging victorious. Escaped convicts and beachcombers also flooded in but mostly succeeded in killing each other off. Tiring of strife, the chiefs asked Britain to annex the island in 1881, and it has been part of Fiji ever since. European planters ran the copra trade from their settlement at Motusa until local cooperatives took over.

Rotuma is run like a colony of Fiji, with the administration in the hands of a district officer responsible to the district commissioner at Levuka. Decisions of the 15-member Rotuma island council are subject to veto by the national government. The island wasn't directly represented in the old house of representatives, being lumped into the Lau Group constituencies, although it did have an appointed senator. In early 1988 Rotuma attempted to secede from Fiji, citing human rights violations by the military-backed republican regime. The Fijian district officer on the island promptly demonstrated his disgust by blasting the flag of the new Republic of Rotuma with a shotgun. Soon after, a "peacekeeping force" of 13 Rotuman soldiers arrived.

Some 2,800 Rotumans presently inhabit the island, and another 4,600 of their number live in Suva. The light-skinned Polynesian Rotumans are easily distinguished from Fijians. The women weave fine white mats. Fiji's best oranges are grown here and Rotuma kava is noted for its strength.

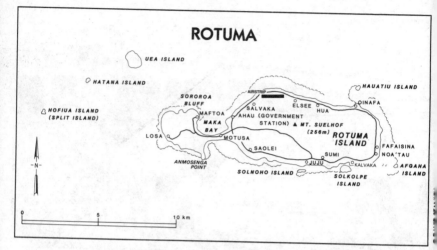

SIGHTS

Ships arrive at a wharf on the edge of the reef, connected to Oinafa Point by a 200-meter coral causeway, which acts as a breakwater. There's a lovely white beach at **Oinafa.** The airstrip is to the west, between Oinafa and Ahau, the government station. At **Noa'tau** southeast of Oinafa is a co-op store; nearby, at **Sililo,** visit a hill with large stone slabs and old cannons scattered about, marking the burial place of the kings of yore. Look for the fine stained-glass windows in the Catholic church at **Sumi** on the south coast. Inland near the center of the island is Mt. Suelhof (256 meters), the highest peak; climb it for the view.

Maftoa across the Motusa Isthmus has a cave with a freshwater pool. In the graveyard at Maftoa are huge stones brought here long ago. It's said four men could go into a trance and carry the stones with their fingers. **Sororoa Bluff** (218 meters) above Maftoa should also be climbed for the view. Deserted **Vovoe Beach** on the west side of Sororoa is one of the finest in the Pacific. A kilometer southwest of Sororoa is **Solmea Hill** (165 meters), with an inactive crater on its north slope. On the coast at the northwest corner of Rotuma is a natural **stone bridge** over the water.

Hatana, a tiny islet off the west end of Rotuma, is said to be the final resting place of Raho, the demigod who created Rotuma. A pair of volcanic rocks before a stone altar surrounded by a coral ring are said to be the King and Queen stones. Today Hatana is a refuge for seabirds. **Hofiua** or Split Island looks like it was cut in two with a knife; a circular boulder bridges the gap.

GETTING THERE

Both **Sunflower Airlines** and **Vanua Air** fly to Rotuma from Suva twice weekly (F$250). The monthly government boats carry mixed cargo out, copra back. Unless you really want to spend a month on Rotuma, book your return flight before leaving Suva.

As yet there are no organized accommodations on Rotuma. Many Rotumans live in Suva, however, and if you have a Rotuman friend, he/she may be willing to send word to his/her family to expect you. Ask your friend what you should take along as a gift. Tourism is discouraged, so flying into Rotuma without knowing anyone isn't a good idea; if you go by ship you'll probably have made some local friends by the time you get there. Although the National Bank of Fiji has a small branch at Ahau on Rotuma, to be safe you should change enough money before leaving Suva.

(top) car ferry, *Spirit of Free Enterprise,* at Taveuni
(bottom) unloading gear, Mbalea, central Viti Levu (photos by David Stanley)

(top) Matuku Island, Moala Group (Robert Kennington)
(bottom) Rewa River near Vunindawa, Viti Levu (David Stanley)

RESOURCES

GUIDEBOOKS

Douglas, Ngaire, and Norman Douglas. *Fiji Handbook: Business and Travel Guide.* Suva: Pacific Publications. Though the emphasis is on administrative structures, official statistics, and economic data, this encyclopedic overview is a useful background reference.

Hammick, Anne. *Ocean Cruising on a Budget.* Camden, ME: International Marine Publishing. Hammick shows how to sail your own yacht safely and enjoyably over the seas while cutting costs. Study it beforehand if you're thinking of working as crew on a yacht.

Health Information For International Travel. An excellent reference published annually by the Centers for Disease Control, U.S. Public Health Service. Available from the Superintendent of Documents, U.S. Government Printing Office, Washington, DC 20402, U.S.A.

Hinz, Earl R. *Landfalls of Paradise: The Guide to Pacific Islands.* Honolulu: University of Hawaii Press. With 97 maps and 40 tables, this is the only genuine cruising guide to all 32 island groups of Oceania.

Schroeder, Dirk. *Staying Healthy in Asia, Africa, and Latin America.* Chico: Moon Publications, 1993. Order a copy of this book if you'd like to acquire a degree of expertise in tropical medicine.

Schütz, Albert J. *Suva: A History and Guide.* Sydney: Pacific Publications, 1978. This slim volume is all you need to really get to know the city.

Stanley, David. *South Pacific Handbook.* Chico: Moon Publications. Covers the entire South Pacific in the same manner as the book you're reading. There's also a *Tahiti-Polynesia Handbook* by the same author.

DESCRIPTION AND TRAVEL

Theroux, Paul. *The Happy Isles of Oceania.* London: Hamish Hamilton, 1992. The author of classic accounts of railway journeys sets out with kayak and tent to tour the Pacific. Theroux has caught the mood of paradise in a way that makes his book really satisfying to read.

Siers, James. *Fiji Celebration.* New York: St. Martin's Press, 1985. Primarily a color-photo, coffee-table book, this also provides a good summary of the history of Fiji.

Wibberley, Leonard. *Fiji: Islands of The Dawn.* New York: Ives Washburn, Inc., 1964. A masterful mixture of history and travel.

Wright, Ronald. *On Fiji Islands.* New York: Penguin Books, 1986. Wright relates his travels to Fijian history and tradition in a most pleasing and informative way.

GEOGRAPHY

Derrick, R.A. *The Fiji Islands: Geographical Handbook.* Suva: Government Printing Office, 1965. Along with 140 maps and diagrams, this handbook contains a complete list of all of the islands of Fiji.

Donnelly, Quanchi, and Kerr. *Fiji in the Pacific: A History and Geography of Fiji.* Jacaranda Wiley Ltd., Box 1226, Milton, Queensland 4064, Australia (fax 61-7/3369-9155). This 4th edition was published in October 1994.

Oliver, Douglas L. *The Pacific Islands.* Honolulu: University of Hawaii Press, 1989. A new edition of the classic 1951 study of the history and economies of the entire Pacific area.

NATURAL SCIENCE

Lebot, Vincent, Lamont Lindstrom, and Mark Marlin. *Kava—the Pacific Drug*. Yale University Press, 1993. A thorough examination of kava and its many uses.

Martini, Frederic. *Exploring Tropical Isles and Seas*. Englewood Cliffs, N.J.: Prentice-Hall, 1984. A fine introduction to the natural environment of the islands.

Mitchell, Andrew W. *A Fragile Paradise: Man and Nature in the Pacific*. London: Fontana, 1990. Published in the U.S. by the University of Texas Press under the title *The Fragile South Pacific: An Ecological Odyssey*. Andrew Mitchell, an Earthwatch Europe deputy director, utters a heartfelt plea on behalf of all endangered Pacific wildlife in this brilliant book.

Watling, Dick. *Mai Veikau: Tales of Fijian Wildlife*. Suva: Fiji Times, 1986. A wealth of easily digested information on Fiji's flora and fauna. Copies are available in local bookstores.

Zug, George R. *The Lizards of Fiji*. Honolulu: Bishop Museum Press, 1991. A comprehensive survey of the 23 species of Fijian lizards.

HISTORY

Bain, Atu, and Tupeni Baba, eds. *Bavadra: Prime Minister, Statesman, Man of the People*. Nandi: Sunrise Press, 1990. A selection of Dr. Bavadra's speeches and writings, 1985-89.

Bellwood, Peter. *Man's Conquest of the Pacific*. New York: Oxford University Press, 1979. One of the most extensive studies of the prehistory of Southeast Asia and Oceania ever published.

Davis Wallis, Mary. *Life in Feejee: Five Years Among the Cannibals*. First published in 1851, this book is the memoir of a New England sea captain's wife in Fiji. It's a charming if rather gruesome firsthand account of early European contact with Fiji, and has some fascinating details of Fijian customs. You'll find ample mention of Cakobau, who hadn't yet converted to Christianity. Reprinted by the Fiji Museum, Suva, in 1983 and sold at the museum shop. A rare South Seas classic!

Dean, Eddie, and Stan Ritova. *Rabuka: No Other Way*. Sydney: Doubleday, 1988. An "as told to" biography of coupmaster Rabuka, in which he outlines his motives for overthrowing the elected government of Fiji.

Derrick, R.A. *A History of Fiji*. Suva: Government Press, 1950. This classic work by a former director of the Fiji Museum deals with the period up to 1874 only.

Ewins, Rory. *Color, Class and Custom: The Literature of the 1987 Fiji Coup*. Canberra: Discussion Paper Series, Department of Political and Social Change, Australian National University, 1992. A scholarly review of the various explanations for the first military coup as reflected in the literature to the end of 1990.

Gravelle, Kim. *Fiji's Times: A History of Fiji*. Suva: Fiji Times and Herald, 1979. An entertaining anthology of accounts originally published in the *Fiji Times*.

Howard, Michael C. *Fiji: Race and Politics in an Island State*. Vancouver: University of British Columbia Press, 1991. Perhaps the best scholarly study of the background and root causes of the Fiji coups.

Lal, Brij V. *Broken Waves: A History of the Fiji Islands in the 20th Century*. Honolulu: University of Hawaii Press, 1991. Lal is a penetrating writer who uses language accessible to the layperson.

Lal, Brij V. *Power and Prejudice: The Making of the Fiji Crisis*. Wellington: New Zealand Institute of International Affairs, 1988.

Lal, Victor. *Fiji: Coups in Paradise: Race, Politics, and Military Intervention*. London: Zed Books, 1990.

Lawson, Stephanie. *The Failure of Democratic Politics in Fiji*. Oxford: Clarendon Press, 1991.

Lawson claims that democracy failed in Fiji because the Fijian chiefs were unwilling to accept any changes that threatened their traditional privileges.

Robertson, Robert T., and Akosita Tamanisau. *Fiji—Shattered Coups*. Australia: Pluto Press, 1988. The first detailed analysis to emerge from Fiji of events which shook the South Pacific. Robertson, a history lecturer at the University of the South Pacific until expelled by Rabuka, and his wife Tamanisau, a reporter with the *Fiji Sun* until Rabuka closed down the paper, wrote the book secretly in Fiji and smuggled out the manuscript chapter by chapter. A military raid on their Suva home failed to uncover the book in preparation.

Scarr, Deryck. *Fiji: A Short History*. Honolulu: University of Hawaii Press, 1984. A balanced look at Fijian history from first settlement to 1982.

Sutherland, William. *Beyond the Politics of Race: An Alternative History of Fiji to 1992*. Canberra: Research School of Pacific Studies, 1992. William Sutherland was Dr. Bavadra's personal secretary.

PACIFIC ISSUES

Ernst, Manfred. *Winds of Change*. Suva: Pacific Conference of Churches, 1994. A timely examination of rapidly growing religious groups in the Pacific islands and unequaled source of information on contemporary religion in the South Pacific.

Robie, David. *Blood on their Banner*. London: Zed Books, 1989. Robie, a veteran New Zealand journalist specializing in the islands, examines political and social struggles in Fiji and other Pacific countries. In the U.S., it's available from Zed Books, 171 1st Ave., Atlantic Heights, NJ 07716; in Britain from Zed Books, 57 Caledonian Rd., London N1 9BU; in Australia from Pluto Press, Box 199, Leichhardt, NSW 2040. Highly recommended.

Robie, David, ed. *Tu Galala: Social Change in the Pacific*. Wellington: Bridget Williams Books, 1992. Distributed in Australia by Pluto Press. In this book, Robie has collected a series of essays examining the conflicting influences of tradition, democracy, and westernization, with special attention to environmental issues and human rights.

SOCIAL SCIENCE

Bigay, John, Mason Green, Dr. Freda Rajotte, and others. *Beqa: Island of Firewalkers*. Suva: Institute of Pacific Studies, 1981. Focuses on the interaction between the people and their environment, plus the transition from traditional to modern life.

Lifuka, Neli, edited and introduced by Klaus-Friedrich Koch. *Logs in the Current of the Sea: Neli Lifuka's Story of Kioa and the Vaitupu Colonists*. Canberra: Australian National University, 1978. The troubled story of the purchase in 1946 and subsequent settlement of Kioa Island off Vanua Levu by Polynesians from Tuvalu, as told by one of the participants.

Norton, Robert. *Race and Politics in Fiji*. St. Lucia, Queensland: University of Queensland Press, 1990. A revised edition of the 1977 classic. Norton emphasizes the flexibility of Fijian culture which was able to absorb the impact of two military coups without any loss of life.

Oliver, Douglas L. *Native Cultures of the Pacific Islands*. Honolulu: University of Hawaii Press, 1988. Intended primarily for college-level courses on precontact anthropology, history, economy, and politics of the entire region.

Prasad, Shiu. *Indian Indentured Workers in Fiji*. Suva: South Pacific Social Studies Association, 1974. Describes the life of laborers in the Lambasa area.

Roth, G. Kingsley. *Fijian Way of Life*. 2nd ed. Melbourne: Oxford University Press, 1973. A standard reference on Fijian culture.

Sahlins, Marshall D. *Moala: Culture and Nature on a Fijian Island*. Ann Arbor: University of Michigan Press, 1962. The results of a thorough study carried out in 1954 and 1955.

LANGUAGE AND LITERATURE

Capell, A. *A New Fijian Dictionary*. Suva: Government Printer, 1991. A Fijian-English dictionary invaluable for anyone interested in learning the language. Copies may be purchased at the Government Bookshop in the arcade opposite Suva Bus Station. The same bookshop sells C. Maxwell's *A New Fijian Grammar*.

Kikau, Eci. *The Wisdom of Fiji*. Suva: Institute of Pacific Studies, 1981. This extensive collection of Fijian proverbs opens a window to understanding Fijian society, culture, and philosophy.

Pillai, Raymond. *The Celebration*. Suva: South Pacific Creative Arts Society, 1980. A collection of short stories in which the heterogeneous nature of Fiji Indian society is presented by an accomplished narrator.

Schütz, Albert J. *Say It In Fijian*. Sydney: Pacific Publications, 1979. An entertaining introduction to the language. Another text by Schütz, *The Fijian Language,* is published by the University of Hawaii Press.

Subramani. *South Pacific Literature: From Myth to Fabulation*. Suva: Institute of Pacific Studies, 1992. Unlike most studies which give undue prominence to what outsiders have written about the islands, Subramani focuses on an emerging literature created by the islanders themselves. This refreshing approach makes his book *the* basic text for understanding the literature of the Pacific today, and the titles in his bibliography could keep the most enthusiastic reader busy for weeks.

REFERENCE BOOKS

Douglas, Ngaire, and Norman Douglas, eds. *Pacific Islands Yearbook*. Australia: Angus & Robertson Publishers. Despite the title, a new edition of this authoritative sourcebook has come out about every four years since 1932. Although a rather dry read, it's still the one indispensable reference work for students of the Pacific islands.

The Far East and Australasia. London: Europa Publications. An annual survey and directory of Asia and the Pacific. Provides abundant and factual political and economic data; an excellent reference source.

Fry, Gerald W., and Rufino Mauricio. *Pacific Basin and Oceania*. Oxford: Clio Press, 1987. A selective, indexed Pacific bibliography, which actually describes the contents of the books, instead of merely listing them.

Gorman, G.E., and J.J. Mills. *Fiji: World Bibliographical Series, Volume 173*. Oxford: Clio Press, 1994. Critical reviews of 673 of the most important books about Fiji.

Jackson, Miles M., ed. *Pacific Island Studies: A Survey of the Literature*. Westport: Greenwood Press, 1986. In addition to comprehensive listings, there are extensive essays that put the most important works in perspective.

Snow, Philip A., ed. *A Bibliography of Fiji, Tonga, and Rotuma*. Coral Gables, FL: University of Miami Press, 1969.

BOOKSELLERS AND PUBLISHERS

Some of the titles listed above are out of print and not available in regular bookstores. Major research libraries should have a few; otherwise write to the specialized antiquarian booksellers or regional publishers listed below for their printed lists of recycled or hard-to-find books on the Pacific.

Antipodean Books, Maps, and Prints. Antipodean Books, Box 189, Cold Spring, NY 10516, U.S.A. (tel. 914/424-3867, fax 914/424-3617). A complete catalog of out-of-print and rare items.

Australia and the Pacific. Peter Moore, Box 66, Cambridge, CB1 3PD, England. The European distributor of books from the Institute of Pacific Studies of the University of the South Pacific, Fiji. Moore's catalog also lists antiquarian and secondhand books.

Australia, the Pacific and South East Asia. Serendipity Books, Box 340, Nedlands, WA 6009, Australia (tel. 61-8/9382-2246, fax 61-8/9388-2728). The largest stocks of antiquarian, secondhand, and out-of-print books on the Pacific in Western Australia. Free catalogs are issued regularly.

Boating Books. International Marine Publishing Co., TAB Books, Blue Ridge Summit, PA 17294-0840, U.S.A. (tel. 800/822-8158, fax 717/794-5291). All the books you'll ever need to teach yourself how to sail.

Books from the Pacific Islands. Institute of Pacific Studies, University of the South Pacific, Box 1168, Suva, Fiji Islands (fax 679/301-594). Their specialty is books about the islands written by the Pacific islanders themselves.

Books, Maps & Prints of the Pacific Islands. Colin Hinchcliffe, 12 Queens Staith Mews, York, YO1 1HH, England (tel. 44-1904/610679, fax 44-1904/641664). An excellent source of antiquarian or out-of-print books, maps, and engravings.

Books on Oceania, Africa, Archaeology & Anthropology, & Asia. Michael Graves-Johnston, Bookseller, Box 532, London SW9 0DR, England (fax 44-171/738-3747).

Books Pasifika Catalogues. Box 68-446, Newton, Auckland 1, New Zealand (fax 64-9/377-9528). They carry the complete line of books published by the University of the South Pacific's Institute of Pacific Studies.

Books & Series in Print. Bishop Museum Press, Box 19000-A, Honolulu, HI 96817-0916, U.S.A. An indexed list of books on the Pacific available from Hawaii's Bishop Museum. A separate list of "The Occasional Papers" lists specialized works.

Defense Mapping Agency Catalog of Maps, Charts, and Related Products: Part 2—Hydrographic Products, Volume VIII, Oceania. National Ocean Service, Distribution Branch, N/CG33, 6501 Lafayette Ave., Riverdale, MD 20737, U.S.A. A complete index and order form for nautical charts of the Pacific. The National Ocean Service also distributes nautical charts put out by the National Oceanic and Atmospheric Administration (NOAA).

Hawaii and Pacific Islands. The Book Bin, 228 S.W. 3rd St., Corvallis, OR 97333, U.S.A. (tel./fax 503/752-0045). An indexed mail-order catalog of hundreds of rare books on the Pacific. If there's a particular book about the Pacific you can't find anywhere, this is the place to try. You can also order University of the South Pacific books through them.

Hawaii: New Books. University of Hawaii Press, 2840 Kolowalu St., Honolulu, HI 96822, U.S.A. This catalog is well worth requesting if you're trying to build a Pacific library.

Moon Handbooks. Moon Publications Inc., Box 3040, Chico, CA 95927, U.S.A. Write for a copy of this free catalog of Moon travel handbooks or, in you live in the U.S., dial 800/345-5473.

Pacificana. Messrs. Berkelouw, "Bendooley," Old Hume Highway, Berrima, NSW 2577, Australia (tel. 61-2/4877-1370, fax 61-2/4877-1102). A detailed listing of thousands of rare Pacific titles. Payment of an annual subscription of A$25 entitles one to 25 catalogs a year. They also have stores in Sydney (19 Oxford St., Paddington, NSW 2021, Australia; tel. 61-2/9360-3200) and Los Angeles (830 North Highland Ave., Los Angeles, CA 90038, U.S.A.; tel. 213/466-3321).

Pacificana. Books of Yesteryear, Box 257, Newport, NSW 2106, Australia (fax 61-2/9918-0545). Another source of old, fine, and rare books on the Pacific.

Pacific and Southeast Asia—Old Books, Prints, Maps. Catalog No. 39. Bibliophile, 24 Glenmore Rd., Paddington, NSW 2021, Australia (tel. 61-2/9331-1411, fax 61-2/9361-3371).

Publications List. Pacific Information Center, University of the South Pacific, Box 1168, Suva, Fiji Islands (fax 679/300-830). A useful list of bibliographical source material.

Technical Publications. South Pacific Regional

Environment Program, Box 240, Apia, Western Samoa (fax 685/20-231). A list of specialized publications on environmental concerns.

The 'Nesias & Down Under: Some Recent Books. The Cellar Book Shop, 18090 Wyoming, Detroit, MI 48221, U.S.A. (tel./fax 313/861-1776). A wide range of in-print and out-of-print books on the Pacific.

PERIODICALS

Asia & Pacific Viewpoint. Victoria University Press, Victoria University of Wellington, Box 600, Wellington, New Zealand. Twice a year; annual subscription NZ$60 worldwide. A scholarly journal encompassing a range of disciplines concerned with the systematic, regional, and theoretical aspects of economic growth and social change in the developed and developing countries.

Banaba/Ocean Island News. Stacey M. King, Box 536, Mudgeeraba, QLD 4213, Australia (tel./fax 61-7/5530-5298). This lively newsletter covers virtually everything relating to the Banabans of Fiji and Kiribati.

The Centre for South Pacific Studies Newsletter. Centre for South Pacific Studies, The University of New South Wales, Kensington, NSW 2033, Australia. A useful bimonthly publication which catalogs scholarly conferences, events, activities, news, employment opportunities, courses, scholarships, and publications across the region.

Commodores' Bulletin. Seven Seas Cruising Association, 1525 South Andrews Ave., Suite 217, Fort Lauderdale, FL 33316, U.S.A. (fax 305/463-7183; US$53 a year worldwide by airmail). This monthly bulletin is chock-full of useful information for anyone wishing to tour the Pacific by sailing boat. All Pacific yachties and friends should be Seven Seas members!

The Contemporary Pacific. University of Hawaii Press, 2840 Kolowalu St., Honolulu, HI 96822, U.S.A. (published twice a year, US$30 a year). Publishes a good mix of articles of interest to both scholars and general readers; the country-by-country "Political Review" in each number is a concise summary of events during the preceding year. The "Dialogue" section offers informed comment on the more controversial issues in the region, while recent publications on the islands are examined through book reviews. Those interested in current topics in Pacific island affairs should check recent volumes for background information. Recommended.

ENVIRONWatch. South Pacific Action Committee for Human Ecology and Environment, Box 1168, Suva, Fiji Islands (fax 679/302-548; US$10 a year). This quarterly newsletter from SPACHEE provides excellent background on environmental concerns in Fiji and throughout the region.

Europe-Pacific Solidarity Bulletin. Published monthly by the European Center for Studies Information and Education on Pacific Issues, Box 151, 3700 AD Zeist, The Netherlands (fax 31-3404/25614).

Globe Newsletter. The Globetrotters Club, BCM/Roving, London WC1N 3XX, England. This informative travel newsletter, published six times a year, provides lots of practical information on how to tour the world "on the cheap." Club membership (US$18 plus a US$5 joining fee) includes a subscription to *Globe,* a globetrotter's handbook, a list of other members, etc. This is *the* club for world travelers.

In Depth. Box 90215, Austin, TX 78709, U.S.A. (tel. 512/891-9812). A consumer protection-oriented newsletter for serious scuba divers. Unlike virtually every other diving publication, *In Depth* accepts no advertising, which allows them to tell it as it is.

Islands Business Pacific. Box 12718, Suva, Fiji Islands (annual airmailed subscription US$45 to North America, US$55 to Europe, A$35 to Australia, NZ$55 to New Zealand). A monthly newsmagazine with the emphasis on political, economic, and business trends in the Pacific.

Journal of Pacific History. Division of Pacific and Asian History, RSPAS, Australian National University, Canberra, ACT 0200, Australia. Since 1966 this publication has provided reliable scholarly information on the Pacific. Outstanding.

Journal of the Polynesian Society. Department of Maori Studies, University of Auckland, Private Bag 92019, Auckland, New Zealand. Established in 1892, this quarterly journal contains a wealth of material on Pacific cultures past and present written by scholars of Pacific anthropology, archaeology, language, and history.

Pacific Affairs. University of British Columbia, 2029 West Mall, Vancouver, B.C. V6T 1Z2, Canada (quarterly).

Pacific AIDS Alert. Published monthly by the South Pacific Commission, B.P. D5, Nouméa Cédex, New Caledonia. An informative news-oriented publication dedicated to limiting the spread of sexually transmitted diseases.

Pacific Islands Monthly. G.P.O. Box 1167, Suva, Fiji Islands (annual subscription A$42 to Australia, US$45 to North America, and A$63 to Europe; fax 679/303-809). Founded in Sydney by R.W. Robson in 1930, *PIM* is the granddaddy of regional magazines. In June, 1989, the magazine's editorial office moved from Sydney to Suva. Roman Grynberg's brilliant economic analyses and David North's political reports are alone worth the price of the magazine.

Pacific Journalism Review. South Pacific Center for Communication and Information in Development, University of PNG, Box 320, Uni P.O., NCD, Papua New Guinea (fax 675/267-187). Co-edited by noted Pacific writer David Robie, the *Review* tackles the controversial side of Pacific news coverage and is essential reading for anyone interested in the state of the media today in the Pacific.

Pacific Magazine. Box 25488, Honolulu, HI 96825, U.S.A. (every other month; US$15 annual subscription). This business-oriented newsmagazine, published in Hawaii since 1976, will keep you up-to-date on what's happening in the South Pacific. Recommended.

Pacific News Bulletin. Pacific Concerns Resource Center, Box 803, Glebe, NSW 2037, Australia (A$12 a year in Australia, A$25 a year elsewhere). A 16-page monthly newsletter with up-to-date information on nuclear, independence, environmental, and political questions.

Pacific Research. Research School of Pacific and Asian Studies, Coombs Building, Australian National University, Canberra, ACT 0200, Australia (fax 61-2/6249-0174; A$25 a year). This monthly periodical of the Peace Research Center publishes informative articles on regional conflicts.

The Review. G.P.O. Box 12095, Suva, Fiji Islands (fax 679/305-256; US$55 a year to Europe and North America). A monthly news magazine with excellent coverage of business and politics in Fiji.

South Sea Digest. G.P.O. Box 4245, Sydney, NSW 2001, Australia (A$150 a year in Australia, A$175 overseas). A private newsletter on political and economic matters, published every other week. It's a good way of keeping abreast of developments in commerce and industry.

Tok Blong Pasifik. South Pacific Peoples Foundation of Canada, 1921 Fernwood Rd., Victoria, BC V8T 2Y6, Canada (fax 604/388-5258; $25 a year). This quarterly of news and views focuses on regional environmental, development, human rights, and disarmament issues. Recommended.

Travel Matters. Moon Publications Inc., Box 3040, Chico, CA 95927, U.S.A. Residents of the U.S. can obtain a free subscription to this useful quarterly publication by calling 800/345-5473 or by writing. Others must send a credit card authorization for US$7 to cover postage.

AN IMPORTANT MESSAGE

Authors, editors, and publishers wishing to see their publications listed here should send review copies to:

David Stanley,
c/o Moon Publications Inc.,
P.O. Box 3040,
Chico, CA 95927, U.S.A.

GLOSSARY

AIDS—Acquired Immune Deficiency Syndrome

Andi—the female equivalent of Ratu

archipelago—a group of islands

atoll—a low-lying, ring-shaped coral reef enclosing a lagoon

bareboat charter—chartering a yacht without crew or provisions

bark cloth—*see tapa*

barrier reef—a coral reef separated from the adjacent shore by a lagoon

bêche-de-mer—sea cucumber; trepang; an edible sea slug

blackbirder—A 19th-century European recruiter of island labor, mostly ni-Vanuatu and Solomon Islanders taken to work on plantations in Queensland and Fiji

breadfruit—a large, round fruit with starchy flesh grown on an *uru* tree *(Artocarpus altilis)*

BYO—Bring Your Own (an Australian term used to refer to restaurants which allow you to bring your own alcoholic beverages)

cassava—manioc; the starchy edible root of the tapioca plant

chain—an archaic unit of length equivalent to 20 meters

ciguatera—a form of fish poisoning caused by microscopic algae

coir—coconut husk sennit used to make rope, etc.

confirmation—A confirmed reservation exists when a supplier acknowledges, either orally or in writing, that a booking has been accepted.

copra—dried coconut meat used in the manufacture of coconut oil, cosmetics, soap, and margarine

coral—a hard, calcareous substance of various shapes, comprised of the skeletons of tiny marine animals called polyps

coral bank—a coral formation over 150 meters long

coral head—a coral formation a few meters across

coral patch—a coral formation up to 150 meters long

cyclone—Also known as a hurricane (in the Caribbean) or typhoon (in Japan). A tropical storm which rotates around a center of low atmospheric pressure; it becomes a cyclone when its winds reach 64 knots. In the Northern Hemisphere, cyclones spin counterclockwise, while south of the equator they move clockwise. The winds of cyclonic storms are deflected toward a low-pressure area at the center, although the "eye" of the cyclone may be calm.

deck—Australian English for a terrace or porch

desiccated coconut—the shredded meat of dehydrated fresh coconut

direct flight—a through flight with one or more stops but no change of aircraft, as opposed to a nonstop flight

dugong—a large plant-eating marine mammal; called a manatee in the Caribbean

EEZ—Exclusive Economic Zone; a 200-nautical-mile offshore belt of an island nation or seacoast state that controls the mineral exploitation and fishing rights

endemic—native to a particular area and existing only there

ESCAP—Economic and Social Commission for Asia and the Pacific

expatriate—a person residing in a country other than his/her own; in the South Pacific such persons are also called "Europeans" if their skin is white, or simply "expats."

filaria—parasitic worms transmitted by biting insects to the blood or tissues of mammals. The obstruction of the lymphatic glands by the worms can cause an enlargement of the legs or other parts, a disease known as elephantiasis.

fissure—a narrow crack or chasm of some length and depth

FIT—foreign independent travel; a custom-designed, prepaid tour composed of many individualized arrangements

fringing reef—a reef along the shore of an island

GPS—Global Positioning System, the space-age successor of the sextant

guano—manure of seabirds, used as a fertilizer

guyot—a submerged atoll, the coral of which couldn't keep up with rising water levels

HIV—Human Immunodeficiency Virus, the cause of AIDS

ivi—the Polynesian chestnut tree (*Inocarpus edulis*)

jug—a cross between a ceramic kettle and a pitcher used to heat water for tea or coffee in Australian-style hotels

kai—freshwater mussel

kaisi—a commoner

kava—a Polynesian word for the drink known in the Fijian language as *yanggona*. This traditional beverage is made by squeezing a mixture of the grated root of the pepper shrub (*Piper methysticum*) and cold water through a strainer of hibiscus-bark fiber.

kokonda—chopped raw fish and sea urchins with onions and lemon

koro—village

kumala—sweet potato (*Ipomoea batatas*)

kumi—stenciled tapa cloth

lagoon—an expanse of water bounded by a reef

lali—a hollow log drum hit with a stick

Lapita pottery—pottery made by the ancient Polynesians from 1600 to 500 B.C.

leeward—downwind; the shore (or side) sheltered from the wind; as opposed to windward

liveaboard—a tour boat with cabin accommodation for scuba divers

LMS—London Missionary Society; a Protestant group that spread Christianity across the Pacific in the early 19th century

lolo—coconut cream

lovo—an underground, earthen oven (called an *umu* in the Polynesian languages); after A.D. 500 the Polynesians had lost the art of making pottery, so they were compelled to bake their food rather than boil it.

mahimahi—dorado, Pacific dolphin fish (no relation to the mammal)

mana—authority, prestige, virtue, "face," psychic power, a positive force

mangiti—feast

mangrove—a tropical shrub with branches that send down roots forming dense thickets along tidal shores

manioc—cassava, tapioca, a starchy root crop

masa kesa—freehand painted tapa

masi—see tapa

mata ni vanua—an orator who speaks for a high chief

matanggali—basic Fijian landowning group

matrilineal—a system of tracing descent through the mother's familial line

mbalawa—pandanus, screw pine

mbalolo—a reef worm (*Eunice viridis*)

mbete—a traditional priest

mbilimbili—a bamboo raft

mbilo—a kava cup

Mbose vaka-Turanga—Great Council of Chiefs

Mbose vaka-Yasana—Provincial Council

mbula shirt—a colorful Fijian aloha shirt

mbuli—Fijian administrative officer in charge of a *tikina;* subordinate of the Roko Tui

mbure—a village house

meke—traditional song and dance

Melanesia—the high island groups of the western Pacific (Fiji, New Caledonia, Vanuatu, Solomon Islands, Papua New Guinea)

Micronesia—chains of high and low islands mostly north of the Equator (Carolines, Gilberts, Marianas, Marshalls)

mynah—an Indian starlinglike bird (*Gracula*)

ndalo—see taro

Ndengei—the greatest of the pre-Christian Fijian gods

ndrua—an ancient Fijian double canoe

NGO—Non-government Organization

NFIP—Nuclear-Free and Independent Pacific movement

overbooking—the practice of confirming more seats, cabins, or rooms than are actually available to ensure against no-shows

Pacific Rim—the continental land masses and large countries fringing the Pacific

PADI—Professional Association of Dive Instructors

palusami—a Samoan specialty of coconut cream wrapped in taro leaves and baked

pandanus—screw pine with slender stem and prop roots. The sword-shaped leaves are used for plaiting mats and hats. In Tahitian, *fara*.

parasailing—a sport in which participants are carried aloft by a parachute pulled behind a speedboat

pass—a channel through a barrier reef, usually with an outward flow of water

passage—an inside passage between an island and a barrier reef

patrilineal—a system of tracing descent through the father's familial line

pawpaw—papaya

pelagic—relating to the open sea, away from land

Polynesia—divided into Western Polynesia (Tonga and Samoa) and Eastern Polynesia (Tahiti-Polynesia, Cook Islands, Hawaii, Easter Island, and New Zealand)

punt—a flat-bottomed boat

Quonset hut—a prefabricated, semicircular, metal shelter popular during WW II

rain shadow—the dry side of a mountain, sheltered from the windward side

rara—a grassy village square

Ratu—a title for Fijian chiefs, prefixed to their names

reef—a coral ridge near the ocean surface

Roko Tui—senior Fijian administrative officer

roti—a flat Indian bread

sailing—the fine art of getting wet and becoming ill while slowly going nowhere at great expense

salusalu—garland, lei

scuba—self-contained underwater breathing apparatus

SDA—Seventh-Day Adventist

self-contained—a room with private facilities (a toilet and shower not shared with other guests); as opposed to a "self-catering" unit with cooking facilities

sennit—braided coconut-fiber rope

sevusevu—a presentation of *yanggona*

shareboat charter—a yacht tour for individuals or couples who join a small group on a fixed itinerary

shifting cultivation—a method of farming involving the rotation of fields instead of crops

shoal—a shallow sandbar or mud bank

shoulder season—a travel period between high/peak and low/off-peak

SPARTECA—South Pacific Regional Trade and Economic Cooperation Agreement; an agreement that allows certain manufactured goods from Pacific countries duty-free entry to Australia and New Zealand

SPREP—South Pacific Regional Environment Program

subduction—the action of one tectonic plate wedging under another

subsidence—geological sinking or settling

sulu—a saronglike wraparound skirt, kilt, or loincloth

symbiosis—a mutually advantageous relationship between unlike organisms

takia—a small sailing canoe

tambu—taboo, forbidden, sacred, set apart, a negative force

tambua—a whale's tooth, a ceremonial object

tanoa—a special wide wooden bowl in which *yanggona* (kava) is mixed

tapa—a cloth made from the pounded bark of the paper mulberry tree *(Broussonetia papyrifera)*. It's soaked and beaten with a mallet to flatten and intertwine the fibers, then painted with geometric designs; tapa is called *masi* in Fijian.

taro—a starchy elephant-eared tuber *(Colocasia esculenta)*, a staple food of the Pacific islanders; called *ndalo* in Fijian

tavioka—tapioca, cassava, manioc, arrowroot

teitei—a garden

tikina—a group of Fijian villages administered by a *mbuli*

TNC—transnational corporation (also referred to as a multinational corporation)

trade wind—a steady wind blowing toward the equator from either northeast or southeast

trench—the section at the bottom of the ocean where one tectonic plate wedges under another

tridacna clam—eaten everywhere in the Pacific, it varies between 10 cm and one meter in size.

tropical storm—a cyclonic storm with winds of 35-64 knots tsunami—a fast-moving wave caused by an undersea earthquake

tui—king
turanga—chief
turanga-ni-koro—village herald or mayor

vakaviti—in the Fijian way
vigia—a mark on a nautical chart indicating a dangerous rock or shoal

windward—the point or side from which the wind blows, as opposed to leeward

yam—the starchy, tuberous root of a climbing plant
yanggona—see kava

zories—rubber shower sandals, thongs, flip-flops

CAPSULE FIJIAN VOCABULARY

Although most people in Fiji speak English fluently, mother tongues include Fijian, Hindi, and other Pacific languages. Knowledge of a few words of Fijian, especially slang words, will make your stay more exciting and enriching. Fijian has no pure *b, c,* or *d* sounds as they are known in English. When the first missionaries arrived, they invented a system of spelling, with one letter for each Fijian sound. To avoid confusion, all Fijian words and place-names in this book are rendered phonetically, but the reader should be aware that, locally, "mb" is written *b,* "nd" is *d,* "ng" is *g,* "ngg" is *q,* and "th" is *c.*

Au lako mai Kenada.—I come from Canada.
Au sa lako ki vei?—Where are you going?
au la o—Vanua Levu version of *mbarewa*
au lili—affirmative response to *au la o* (also *la o mai*)
Au ni lako mai vei?—Where do you come from?

dua tale—once more
dua oo—said by males when they meet a chief or enter a Fijian *mbure*

e rewa—a positive response to *mbarewa*

io—yes

kana—eat
kauta mai—bring
kauta tani—take away
kaivalangi—foreigner
koro—village
Kothei na yathamu?—What's your name?

lailai—small
lako mai—come
lako tani—go
levu—big, much
lima—five
loloma yani—please pass along my regards

maleka—delicious
mangiti—feast
marama—madam
matanggali—a clan lineage
mbarewa—a provocative greeting for the opposite sex
mbula—a Fijian greeting
mothe—goodbye

Na thava onggo?—What is this?
Ndaru lako!—Let's go!
ndua—one
ndua tale—one more
nggara—cave
Nice mbola.—You're looking good.
Ni sa mbula—Hello, how are you? (can also say *sa mbula* or *mbula vinaka;* the answer is an *sa mbula vinaka*)
ni sa mothe—good night
ni sa yandra—good morning

phufter—a gay male (a disrespectful term)
rewa sese—an affirmative response to *mbarewa*
rua—two

sa vinaka—it's okay
senga—no, none
senga na lengga—you're welcome

sota tale—see you again

talatala—reverend
tambu rewa—a negative response to *mbare-wa*
tolu—three
tulou—excuse me
turanga—sir, Mr.

va—four
vaka lailai—a little, small
vaka levu—a lot, great
vaka malua—slowly

vaka totolo—fast
vale—house
vale lailai—toilet
vanua—land, custom, people
vinaka—thank you
vinaka vaka levu—thank you very much
vu—an ancestral spirit

wai—water

yalo vinaka—please
yandra—good morning
yanggona—kava, grog

CAPSULE HINDI VOCABULARY

accha—good
bhaahut julum—very beautiful (slang)
dhanyabaad—thank you
hum jauo—I go (slang)
jalebi—an Indian sweet
kaise bhai?—how are you?
khana—food
kitna?—how much?

namaste—hello, goodbye
pani—water
rait—okay
ram ram—same as *namaste*
roti—a flat Indian bread
seedhe jauo—go straight
theek bhai—I'm fine

ALTERNATIVE PLACE-NAMES

Ba—Mba
Bau—Mbau
Beqa—Mbengga
Buca—Mbutha
Bukuya—Mbukuya
Cicia—Thithia
Colo-i-Suva—Tholo-i-Suva
Deuba—Deumba
Galoa—Ngaloa
Gau—Ngau
Kadavu—Kandavu
Korotogo—Korotongo
Labasa—Lambasa

Lakeba—Lakemba
Laucala—Lauthala
Mamanuca—Mamanutha
Nabouwalu—Nambouwalu
Nadarivatu—Nandarivatu
Nadi—Nandi
Natadola—Natandola
Qamea—Nggamea
Rabi—Rambi
Toberua—Tomberua
Sigatoka—Singatoka
Vanua Balavu—Vanua Mbalavu

INDEX

Page numbers in **boldface** indicate the primary reference. *Italicized* page numbers indicate information in maps, charts, or captions.

PLEASE HELP US

Well, you've heard what *we* have to say, now we want to hear what *you* have to say! How did the book work for you? Your experiences were unique, so please share them. Let us know which businesses deserve a better listing, what we should warn people about, and where we're spot on. It's only with the help of readers like yourself that we can make *Fiji Islands Handbook* a complete guide for *everyone*. Write:

David Stanley
c/o Moon Publications Inc.
P.O. Box 3040
Chico, CA 95927, U.S.A.

ABOUT THE AUTHOR

A quarter century ago, David Stanley's right thumb carried him out of Toronto, Canada, on a journey that has so far wound through 168 countries, including a three-year trip from Tokyo to Kabul. His travel guidebooks to the South Pacific, Micronesia, Alaska, and Eastern Europe opened those areas to budget travelers for the first time.

During the late 1960s, David got involved in Mexican culture by spending a year in several small towns near Guanajuato. Later he studied at the universities of Barcelona and Florence, before settling down to get an honors degree (with distinction) in Spanish literature from the University of Guelph, Canada.

In 1978 Stanley linked up with future publisher Bill Dalton, and together they wrote the first edition of *South Pacific Handbook*. Since then, Stanley has gone on to write additional definitive guides for Moon Publications, including *Micronesia Handbook*, *Fiji Islands Handbook*, *Tahiti-Polynesia Handbook*, and early editions of *Alaska-Yukon Handbook*. His books informed a generation of budget travelers.

Stanley makes frequent research trips to the areas covered in his guides, jammed between journeys to the 79 countries and territories worldwide he still hasn't visited. To maintain his independence, Stanley does not accept

subsidized travel arrangements or "freebies" from any source. In travel writing David Stanley has found a perfect outlet for his restless wanderlust.

MOON TRAVEL HANDBOOKS
THE IDEAL TRAVELING COMPANIONS

Moon Travel Handbooks provide focused, comprehensive coverage of distinct destinations all over the world. Our goal is to give travelers all the background and practical information they'll need for an extraordinary, unexpected travel experience.

Every Handbook begins with an in-depth essay about the land, the people, their history, art, politics, and social concerns—an entire bookcase of cultural insight and introductory information in one portable volume. We also provide accurate, up-to-date coverage of all the practicalities: language, currency, transportation, accommodations, food, and entertainment. And Moon's maps are legendary, covering not only cities and highways, but parks and trails that are often difficult to find in other sources.

Below are highlights of Moon's Asia and the Pacific Travel Handbook series. Our complete list of Handbooks covering North America and Hawaii, Mexico, Central America and the Caribbean, and Asia and the Pacific, are listed on the order form on the accompanying pages. To purchase Moon Travel Handbooks, please check your local bookstore or order by phone: (800) 345-5473 Monday-Friday 8 a.m.-5 p.m. PST.

MOON OVER ASIA
THE ASIA AND THE PACIFIC TRAVEL HANDBOOK SERIES

> "Moon guides are wittily written and warmly personal; what's more, they present a vivid, often raw vision of Asia without promotional overtones. They also touch on such topics as official corruption and racism, none of which rate a mention in the bone-dry, air-brushed, dry-cleaned version of Asia written up in the big U.S. guidebooks."
> —*Far Eastern Economic Review*

BALI HANDBOOK by Bill Dalton, 428 pages, **$12.95**
"This book is for the in-depth traveler, interested in history and art, willing to experiment with language and food and become immersed in the culture of Bali." — Great Expeditions

BANGKOK HANDBOOK by Michael Buckley, 222 pages, **$13.95**
"Helps make sense of this beguiling paradox of a city . . . very entertaining reading." —*The Vancouver Sun*

FIJI ISLANDS HANDBOOK by David Stanley, 275 pages, **$13.95**
"If you want to encounter Fiji and not just ride through it, this book is for you." —*Great Expeditions*

HONG KONG HANDBOOK by Kerry Moran, 300 pages, **$15.95**
Hong Kong has been called "the most cosmopolitan city on earth," yet it's also one of the few places where visitors can witness Chinese customs as they have been practiced for centuries. Award-winning author Kerry Moran explores this unusual juxtaposition of tradition and modern life in *Hong Kong Handbook*. Moran traces the history and cultural development of the British Colony, and anticipates the changes to come in 1997, when this fascinating city reverts to Chinese rule.

INDONESIA HANDBOOK by Bill Dalton, 1,300 pages, **$25.00**
"Looking for a fax machine in Palembang, a steak dinner on Ambon or the best place to photograph Bugis prahus in Sulawesi? Then buy this brick of a book, which contains a full kilogram of detailed directions and advice." —*Asia, Inc. Magazine*

"One of the world's great guides." —*All Asia Review of Books*

"The classic guidebook to the archipelago."
—*Condé Nast Traveler*

JAPAN HANDBOOK by J.D. Bisignani, 952 pages, **$22.50**
"The scope of this guide book is staggering, ranging from an introduction to Japanese history and culture through to the best spots for shopping for pottery in Mashie or silk pongee in Kagoshima." —*Golden Wing*

"More travel information on Japan than any other guidebook."
—*The Japan Times*

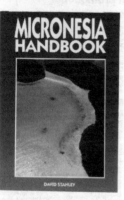

MICRONESIA HANDBOOK by David Stanley, 345 pages, **$11.95**
"Remarkably informative, fair-minded, sensible, and readable . . . Stanley's comments on the United States' 40-year administration are especially pungent and thought-provoking." —*The Journal of the Polynesian Society*

NEPAL HANDBOOK by Kerry Moran, 378 pages, **$12.95**
"This is an excellent guidebook, exploring every aspect of the country the visitor is likely to want to know about with both wit and authority." —*South China Morning Post*

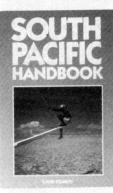

TIBET HANDBOOK   by Victor Chan, 1,100 pages, **$30.00**
"Not since the original three volume Murray's Handbook to India, published over a century ago, has such a memorial to the hot, and perhaps uncontrollable passions of travel been published. . . . This is the most impressive travel handbook published in the 20th century."   —*Small Press Magazine*

"Shimmers with a fine madness."   —*Escape Magazine*

VIETNAM, CAMBODIA & LAOS HANDBOOK
by Michael Buckley, 650 pages, **$18.95**
Available January 1996.
The new definitive guide to Southeast Asia's hottest travel destination from a travel writer who knows Asia like the back of his hand. Michael Buckley combines the most current practical travel information—much of it previously unavailable—with the perspective of a seasoned adventure traveler. Good maps to the region are rare, but this comprehensive guidebook includes 75 of them.

STAYING HEALTHY IN ASIA, AFRICA, AND LATIN AMERICA
by Dirk G. Schroeder, ScD, MPH, 200 pages, **$11.95**

"Your family doctor will not be able to supply you with this valuable information because he doesn't have it."

—*Whole Earth Catalog*

"Read this book if you want to stay healthy on any journeys or stays in Asia, Africa, and Latin America."

—*American Journal of Health Promotion*

PERIPLUS TRAVEL MAPS

Periplus Travel Maps are a necessity for traveling in Southeast Asia. Each map is designed for maximum clarity and utility, combining several views and insets of the area. Transportation information, street indexes, and descriptions of major sites are included in each map. The result is a single map with all the vital information needed to get where you're going. No other maps come close to providing the detail or comprehensive coverage of Asian travel destinations. All maps are updated yearly and produced with digital technology using the latest survey information. **$7.95**

Periplus Travel Maps are available to the following areas:

Bali
Bandung/W. Java
Bangkok/C. Thailand
Batam/Bintan
Cambodia
Hong Kong
Java

Ko Samui/
S. Thailand
Penang
Phuket/S. Thailand
Singapore
Vietnam
Yogyakarta/C. Java

MOONBELT

A new concept in moneybelts. Made of heavy-duty Cordura nylon, the Moonbelt offers maximum protection for your money and important papers. This pouch, designed for all-weather comfort, slips under your shirt or waistband, rendering it virtually undetectable and inaccessible to pickpockets. It features a one-inch high-test quick-release buckle so there's no more fumbling around for the strap or repeated adjustments. This handy plastic buckle opens and closes with a touch, but won't come undone until you want it to. Moonbelts accommodate traveler's checks, passports, cash, photos, etc. Size 5 x 9 inches. Available in black only. **$8.95**

TRAVEL MATTERS

Travel Matters is Moon Publications' free quarterly newsletter, loaded with specially commissioned travel articles and essays that tell it like it is. Recent issues have been devoted to Asia, Mexico, and North America, and every issue includes:

Feature Stories: Travel writing unlike what you'll find in your local newspaper. Andrew Coe on Mexican professional wrestling, Michael Buckley on the craze for wartime souvenirs in Vietnam, Kim Weir on the Nixon Museum in Yorba Linda.

Transportation: Tips on how to get around. Rick Steves on a new type of Eurail pass, Victor Chan on hiking in Tibet, Joe Cummings on how to be a Baja road warrior.

Health Matters: Articles on the most recent findings by Dr. Dirk Schroeder, author of *Staying Healthy in Asia, Africa, and Latin America.* Japanese encephalitis, malaria, the southwest U.S. "mystery disease" . . . forewarned is forearmed.

Book Reviews: Informed assessments of the latest travel titles and series. The Rough Guide to *World Music,* Let's Go vs. Berkeley, Dorling Kindersley vs. Knopf.

The Internet: News from the cutting edge. The Great Burma Debate in rec.travel.asia, hotlists of the best WWW sites, updates on Moon's massive "Road Trip USA" exhibit.

There are also booklists, Letters to the Editor, and anything else we can find to interest our readers, as well as Moon's latest titles and ordering information for other travel products, including Periplus Travel Maps to Southeast Asia.

To receive a free subscription to *Travel Matters,* call (800) 345-5473, write to Moon Publications, P.O. Box 3040, Chico, CA 95927-3040, or e-mail travel@moon.com.

Please note: subscribers who live outside the United States will be charged $7.00 per year for shipping and handling.

MOON TRAVEL HANDBOOKS

ASIA AND THE PACIFIC

Bali Handbook (3379) $12.95
Bangkok Handbook (0595) $13.95
Fiji Islands Handbook (0382) $13.95
Hong Kong Handbook (0560) $15.95
Indonesia Handbook (0625) $25.00
Japan Handbook (3700) $22.50
Micronesia Handbook (3808) $11.95
Nepal Handbook (3646) $12.95
New Zealand Handbook (3883) $18.95
Outback Australia Handbook (3794) $15.95
Philippines Handbook (0048) $17.95
Southeast Asia Handbook (0021) $21.95
South Pacific Handbook (3999) $19.95
Tahiti-Polynesia Handbook (0374) $13.95
Thailand Handbook (3824) $16.95
Tibet Handbook (3905) $30.00
*Vietnam, Cambodia & Laos Handbook (0293) $18.95

NORTH AMERICA AND HAWAII

Alaska-Yukon Handbook (0161) $14.95
Alberta and the Northwest Territories Handbook (0676) . . . $17.95
Arizona Traveler's Handbook (0536) $16.95
Atlantic Canada Handbook (0072) $17.95
Big Island of Hawaii Handbook (0064) $13.95
British Columbia Handbook (0145) $15.95
Catalina Island Handbook (3751) $10.95
Colorado Handbook (0137) $17.95
Georgia Handbook (0609) $16.95
Hawaii Handbook (0005) $19.95
Honolulu-Waikiki Handbook (0587) $14.95
Idaho Handbook (0617) $14.95
Kauai Handbook (0013) $13.95
Maui Handbook (0579) $14.95
Montana Handbook (0544) $15.95
Nevada Handbook (0641) $16.95
New Mexico Handbook (0153) $14.95
Northern California Handbook (3840) $19.95

Oregon Handbook (0102)............................... $16.95
Texas Handbook (0633)................................. $17.95
Utah Handbook (0684) $16.95
Washington Handbook (0552)........................... $15.95
Wyoming Handbook (3980) $14.95

MEXICO

Baja Handbook (0528)................................. $15.95
Cabo Handbook (0285) $14.95
Cancún Handbook (0501)............................... $13.95
Central Mexico Handbook (0234) $15.95
*Mexico Handbook (0315) $21.95
Northern Mexico Handbook (0226) $16.95
Pacific Mexico Handbook (0323) $16.95
Puerto Vallarta Handbook (0250) $14.95
Yucatán Peninsula Handbook (0242).................... $15.95

CENTRAL AMERICA AND THE CARIBBEAN

Belize Handbook (0370)............................... $15.95
Caribbean Handbook (0277)............................ $16.95
Costa Rica Handbook (0358)........................... $19.95
Jamaica Handbook (0129) $14.95

INTERNATIONAL

Egypt Handbook (3891)................................ $18.95
Moon Handbook (0668) $10.00
Moscow-St. Petersburg Handbook (3913)................ $13.95
Staying Healthy in Asia, Africa, and Latin America (0269) .. $11.95

* New title, please call for availability

PERIPLUS TRAVEL MAPS
All maps $7.95 each

Bali	Hong Kong	Singapore
Bandung/W. Java	Java	Vietnam
Bangkok/C. Thailand	Ko Samui/S. Thailand	Yogyakarta/C. Java
Batam/Bintan	Penang	
Cambodia	Phuket/S. Thailand	

WHERE TO BUY MOON TRAVEL HANDBOOKS

BOOKSTORES AND LIBRARIES: Moon Travel Handbooks are sold worldwide. Please write to our sales manager for a list of wholesalers and distributors in your area.

TRAVELERS: We would like to have Moon Travel Handbooks available throughout the world. Please ask your bookstore to write or call us for ordering information. If your bookstore will not order our guides for you, please contact us for a free title listing.

Moon Publications, Inc.
P.O. Box 3040
Chico, CA 95927-3040 U.S.A.
Tel: (800) 345-5473
Fax: (916) 345-6751
E-mail: travel@moon.com

IMPORTANT ORDERING INFORMATION

PRICES: All prices are subject to change. We always ship the most current edition. We will let you know if there is a price increase on the book you order.

SHIPPING AND HANDLING OPTIONS: Domestic UPS or USPS first class (allow 10 working days for delivery): $3.50 for the first item, 50 cents for each additional item.

EXCEPTIONS:

Tibet Handbook and *Indonesia Handbook* shipping $4.50; $1.00 for each additional *Tibet Handbook* or *Indonesia Handbook*.

Moonbelt shipping is $1.50 for one, 50 cents for each additional belt.

Add $2.00 for same-day handling.

UPS 2nd Day Air or Printed Airmail requires a special quote.

International Surface Bookrate 8-12 weeks delivery: $3.00 for the first item, $1.00 for each additional item. Note: Moon Publications cannot guarantee international surface bookrate shipping. Moon recommends sending international orders via air mail, which requires a special quote.

FOREIGN ORDERS: Orders that originate outside the U.S.A. must be paid for with either an international money order or a check in U.S. currency drawn on a major U.S. bank based in the U.S.A.

TELEPHONE ORDERS: We accept Visa or MasterCard payments. Minimum order is US$15.00. Call in your order: (800) 345-5473, 8 a.m.-5 p.m. Pacific Standard Time.

ORDER FORM

Be sure to call (800) 345-5473 for current prices and editions or for the name of the bookstore nearest you that carries Moon Travel Handbooks • 8 a.m.–5 p.m. PST.
(See important ordering information on preceding page.)

Name: _____ Date: _____

Street: _____

City: _____ Daytime Phone: _____

State or Country: _____ Zip Code: _____

QUANTITY	TITLE	PRICE

Taxable Total_____

Sales Tax (7.25%) for California Residents_____

Shipping & Handling_____

TOTAL_____

Ship: ☐ UPS (no P.O. Boxes) ☐ 1st class ☐ International surface mail

Ship to: ☐ address above ☐ other _____

_____

Make checks payable to: **MOON PUBLICATIONS, INC.** P.O. Box 3040, Chico, CA 95927-3040 U.S.A. We accept Visa and MasterCard. **To Order**: Call in your Visa or MasterCard number, or send a written order with your Visa or MasterCard number and expiration date clearly written.

Card Number: ☐ **Visa** ☐ **MasterCard**

☐ ☐ ☐ ☐ ☐ ☐ ☐ ☐ ☐ ☐ ☐ ☐ ☐ ☐ ☐ ☐

Exact Name on Card: _____

Expiration date: _____

Signature: _____

THE METRIC SYSTEM

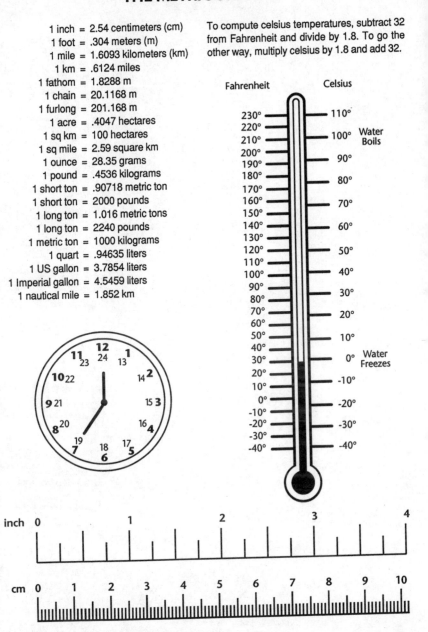

1 inch = 2.54 centimeters (cm)
1 foot = .304 meters (m)
1 mile = 1.6093 kilometers (km)
1 km = .6124 miles
1 fathom = 1.8288 m
1 chain = 20.1168 m
1 furlong = 201.168 m
1 acre = .4047 hectares
1 sq km = 100 hectares
1 sq mile = 2.59 square km
1 ounce = 28.35 grams
1 pound = .4536 kilograms
1 short ton = .90718 metric ton
1 short ton = 2000 pounds
1 long ton = 1.016 metric tons
1 long ton = 2240 pounds
1 metric ton = 1000 kilograms
1 quart = .94635 liters
1 US gallon = 3.7854 liters
1 Imperial gallon = 4.5459 liters
1 nautical mile = 1.852 km

To compute celsius temperatures, subtract 32 from Fahrenheit and divide by 1.8. To go the other way, multiply celsius by 1.8 and add 32.

Fahrenheit   Celsius

230°   110°
220°
210°   100°   Water
200°   Boils
190°   90°
180°   80°
170°
160°   70°
150°
140°   60°
130°
120°   50°
110°
100°   40°
90°
80°   30°
70°
60°   20°
50°
40°   10°
30°
20°   0°   Water
10°   Freezes
0°   -10°
-10°
-20°   -20°
-30°
-40°   -30°
                  -40°

inch 0   1   2   3   4

cm 0 1 2 3 4 5 6 7 8 9 10